Gleanings

from

Matthew's Gospel

Gleanings

from

Matthew's Gospel

LACHLAN MACKENZIE

MINISTER OF LOCHCARRON

REFORMATION PRESS

© 2025 by Reformation Press
11 Churchill Drive, Stornoway
Isle of Lewis, Scotland HS1 2NP

www.reformationpress.co.uk

Edited by: Dr Robert J Dickie
Cover photograph: Alamy/Ian Paterson
Cover design: Intermedia Services (Stornoway) Ltd.
Printed by Lulu: www.lulu.com

British Library Cataloguing-in-Publication Data
A catalogue record for this book is available from the British Library

ISBN numbers
Paperback 978-1-872556-65-9
Hardback 978-1-872556-66-6

Contents

Lectures

Contents

Contents

Contents

Preface

REFORMATION PRESS is delighted to present *Gleanings from Matthew's Gospel* to Christian readers in the twenty-first century. Lachlan Mackenzie was a much-loved Highland minister, whose spiritual legacy continues to nourish successive generations. This publication contains the full collection of Mackenzie's extant 'lectures' on the Gospel according to Matthew, together with valuable biographical and historical material.

The provenance of these sermons is a story of faithful stewardship and the diligence of men who wished to preserve edifying material for succeeding generations. Lachlan Mackenzie's manuscripts were carefully retained within his family circle, but over the years, many became tattered and torn. In the early twentieth century, these manuscripts were diligently sought out by Alexander Fraser of Inverness, who recognised their enduring spiritual value. The manuscripts were subsequently prepared for publication by James Campbell of Inverness. These were issued in two volumes: *Lectures, Sermons and Writings of Rev. Lachlan Mackenzie of Lochcarron* appeared in 1928, and *Additional Lectures, Sermons and Writings of Rev. Lachlan Mackenzie of Lochcarron* two years later in 1930. These books have long been out of print, but remain treasured on the second-hand market for their great spiritual worth.

In the Scottish church tradition, the term 'lectures' refers not to academic discourses, but to homiletic expositions delivered during public worship. Lectures comprised extended expositions of Scripture, intended to illuminate the text and apply its teaching to the lives of the congregation. Mackenzie's lectures on Matthew's Gospel exemplify this approach, combining careful explanation with warm, practical application.

Each of the two volumes issued by James Campbell contained a selection of Lachlan Mackenzie's lectures on the Gospel of Matthew. For the first time, *Gleanings from Matthew's Gospel* gathers together all the published lectures on the first Gospel into a single volume, following the order of the Scripture texts. Sadly, some lectures are not extant but nevertheless this book provides a valuable commentary on a large part of the Gospel.

To enrich the reader's understanding of the man and his times, this book reprints biographical sketches of Lachlan Mackenzie, together with a brief account of the spiritual and ecclesiastical context in which he ministered. This supplementary material is enhanced by a selection of Mackenzie's sayings and anecdotes, offering glimpses into both the character and the influence of the preacher: these were contributed by two renowned men from the Free Presbyterian Church of Scotland—the Rev. Neil Cameron of Glasgow and Finlay Beaton of Inverness.

The text presented here has been lightly edited with a view to modernising spelling and punctuation, while preserving the substance of Mackenzie's sermons. Typographical errors evident in the original volumes have been corrected. Special attention has been paid to quotations in Scottish Gaelic, which have been carefully examined and amended where necessary. Reformation Press gratefully acknowledges the work of Norman and Donella Campbell of Stornoway, whose expertise in the Gaelic language has been invaluable in verifying and correcting the Gaelic quotations. Their work has contributed greatly to the accuracy and authenticity of this edition.

It is the publisher's sincere hope that this new compilation will serve to deepen appreciation for Lachlan Mackenzie's ministry, and that his homely and straightforward Christ-centred expositions will continue to edify and encourage all who read them. May this volume be a means of spiritual blessing to a new generation of readers.

DR ROBERT J DICKIE
Stornoway, 2025

14

Foreword by Rev. Donald Beaton (1928)

'OF all the eminent ministers in the Highlands,' says Dr Kennedy, 'none is more famous than Mr Lachlan Mackenzie of Lochcarron.' Such is the verdict penned by the prince of Highland preachers on the famous minister of Lochcarron. The extraordinary hold Mr Lachlan had over his own people, who were privileged to hear his preaching and come under his saintly influence, can be easily explained, but when it is borne in mind that the sphere of his influence passed far beyond his own parish, until at last he occupied the pre-eminent position assigned to him in the above quoted sentence, it may be asked to what may this remarkable influence be due. Dr Kennedy attributes it to his genius, peculiar Christian experience, and his great acceptance as a preacher. None of the great Highland preachers—some of them very notable in their own different spheres—had the touch of genius that belonged to Mr Lachlan. His profound spiritual experiences appealed to the Lord's people in his own parish and throughout the Highlands, not only in his own day but also in ours. It is for this reason his writings are read and his sayings are treasured still by those who fear the Lord. Originality of thought, apt and striking illustrations, emphatic utterance, with an authority and unction in the delivery of his discourses, all combined to lift his sermons above the commonplace. Added to this, he fed the flock of God on the finest of the wheat, and they hung on his lips as those who were listening to a messenger of the Most High God.[1]

REV. DONALD BEATON
Wick, March 1928

---

[1] Foreword from *Lectures, Sermons and Writings of Rev. Lachlan Mackenzie of Lochcarron*, published in 1928.

Foreword by Rev. Ewen MacQueen (1930)

THE Christian Church must feel deeply indebted to the publisher for giving to the world these hitherto unpublished writings of the late Rev. Lachlan Mackenzie, of Lochcarron. 'Mr Lachlan', as he was and is still lovingly called, was no ordinary man among the ministers of his day and generation. He grew up, like Timothy, knowing the Scriptures from his childhood, and he was wont to be called to pray at meetings before he reached his teens. A great scholar and a great divine, he loved the Word of God and made it his counsellor in all things. Although often tempted of the devil, and hated by graceless sinners, he was a faithful feeder of the flock of Christ in his day, and of him it can truly be said that although dead, he yet speaketh. May many hear the voice of the Son of God through him in this as in the former volume, and may it have a ready sale and prove a great blessing![2]

REV. EWEN MACQUEEN
Inverness, July 1930

---

[2] Foreword from *Additional Lectures, Sermons and Writings of Rev. Lachlan Mackenzie of Lochcarron*, published in 1930.

A brief memoir of
the Rev. Lachlan Mackenzie

DURING the greater part of last century, the spiritual condition of the West Highlands of Ross-shire, though now much improved, was bordering upon complete moral death. With the exception of a few evangelical ministers, worldliness and indifference to religion characterised the generality of the clergy. When unconcerned preachers held forth a brief hour in the pulpit during the Sabbath Day, many of the parishioners often diverted themselves in the churchyard or collected in the public houses. Such was the state of Wester Ross previous to the labours of the author of the following discourses. It was his happy lot to be a principal instrument in promoting the cause of God, and greatly improving the spiritual condition of the people.

The Rev. Lachlan Mackenzie was born in 1754 in Kilmuir Wester, a parish of Ross-shire. His father, Mr Donald Mackenzie, a respectable and intelligent man, and of a very exemplary character, at that time occupied a farm on the property of Kilcoy, in that part of the country, and was connected with some of the first families in the district. His mother, Elizabeth Clark, was a native of the parish of Petty, and was of respectable descent. She was considered a remarkably clever and well-educated woman, and endeared herself exceedingly to the people among whom she resided, by her benevolence and substantial acts of kindness, as well as her medical skill, which were often exercised in relieving the indigent and the sick.

Mr Lachlan (the distinctive name by which he is known in the Highlands) received the elements of his education in the parish school of Petty, which was taught at that time by an excellent classical scholar. Mr Lachlan was only eight years of age when he was first brought under the power of the truth, and from that time forward, his life and conversation continued to shine brighter and brighter unto the perfect day. He was known to have been prevailed upon to engage in the duty of prayer at a meeting in the district before he was thirteen years of age, and even then appeared to have so much solemnity and unction that aged men regretted that, from his youthful modesty, they could not prevail upon him to come forward in public so much as they wished. He was observed to have the appearance of a solemn sense of the All-seeing Eye upon his spirit all along, in school and at college, as well as in after life.

He was kept very humble in early life by the mental and spiritual conflicts he endured, being deeply exercised with a sense of the corruption and wickedness of the heart, the suggestions of unbelief, and the wiles of Satan. Thus he was sent early and late in the day and in the night to his knees before a throne of grace. Few or none in his generation, at least in the part of the country in which he lived, were known to be so earnest or so often engaged in the duty of prayer as Mr Lachlan. And as the Psalmist would not engage in battle without first consulting the Lord, so was Mr Lachlan in the habit of seeking and receiving direction in regard even to the most minute actions of life.

We are not certain as to his precise age when he first entered the College of Aberdeen, but we are quite sure that he made a creditable appearance during his whole course at that university, and that his knowledge of the languages, especially, was more than ordinary. He was so conversant with his Hebrew Bible that he could use it at family worship.

Mr Lachlan taught the parish school of Lochcarron before receiving licence, and here his piety began to shine forth in life and conversation. His character and sentiments were now beginning to be appreciated by the pious people, not only in the immediate neighbourhood, but also in the surrounding parishes; far and near, they flocked to his prayer meetings, and highly esteemed his conversation and company.

'What communion hath light with darkness?' asks the apostle; so, when this light began to appear in the great moral waste, the rulers of darkness not only opposed, but attempted to extinguish it. These trials came upon Mr Lachlan from a quarter whence it would not be expected. The Presbytery of these bounds, instead of encouraging by their approbation such a person as Mr Lachlan, opposed him with their utmost might. The fact was that his prayer meeting fostered a spirit with which they had no sympathy, and which exposed their own coldness and unfaithfulness.

While Mr Lachlan taught the parish school of Lochcarron, the present manse was built; and as he was one evening passing that way he entered the manse when it was nearly finished, and as prayer was his vital breath, and the element in which he lived, he took advantage of the privacy of one of the rooms while the workmen were away, to pour his soul before the Lord, when that passage of Scripture, Psalm 60:6, 'I will mete out the valley of Succoth,' took hold of his mind and would not depart. He inquired what is the meaning of this, and in the course of time he was led to suppose that, as Succoth was a hilly country, the Lord might have some work for him to do at least among the hills and valleys of the Highlands, if not in the place in which he was then residing. That Lochcarron should be the scene of his labours was very unlikely at that time, for there were three members of that Presbytery who tried every means for the purpose of frustrating the hope of his being licensed at all. The ground of their opposition could not have been anything faulty in his character or qualifications, but the hatred they bore to his pious life and evangelical doctrines, with a mixture of jealousy at his constantly increasing popularity.

He was kept back more than a year from getting licence, but when the Lord's time came, all these obstacles were soon removed, and that in a way not to have been expected. These three ministers who led the opposition were suddenly and within one year called to go the way of all the earth, and give their account. Mr Lachlan was immediately licensed without any further opposition, and after all, a testimony was recorded in the minutes of Presbytery to his high acquirements and character. The people of that neighbourhood, who knew and heard of the whole circumstances, got the impression that it is not safe to treat unjustly any of the true people of God.

Thomas Mackenzie, Esq. of Applecross, was friendly to Mr Lachlan, as well as to the people upon his own property, and soon procured for him the Crown presentation to the parish of Lochcarron. When this report reached Lochcarron, the people were greatly delighted, and to their great joy, Mr Lachlan was ordained their pastor, and a door of usefulness was opened for him in the vineyard of the Lord among the hills and valleys of Lochcarron.

He then commenced to labour in the means of divine appointment, with intense desires for the best interests of his people, but, as has been the case with the most successful ministers, he now felt more than ever that nothing less than the power of God can make people willing to accept of salvation through free grace. He now began to feel how difficult it was for a minister of Christ to put down the barbarous practices which then prevailed in the Highlands, such as Sabbath profanation, excessive drinking, and other vices. But wild as was Lochcarron in those days, it was greatly reformed from the state in which Aeneas Sage found it. A brief ministry of three years intervened between Mr Sage and Mr Lachlan. By all accounts, Mr Sage was a faithful minister of the Lord—a bold, impartial, and uncompromising reprover of sin—an evangelical preacher of the gospel—and withal a man of immense physical strength. Often did he bear testimony for the cause of God, and reprove sin in Lochcarron, where his combined strength and piety alone could command respect and dread. It is to be regretted that the obituary Mr Lachlan wrote of this great and useful man has not been published.

Soon after Mr Lachlan came to Lochcarron he drew out and prevailed upon the people to sign the following regulations, which were no doubt a good preliminary step for improving the state of morality at that time, for after signing the rules they did not wholly break through them during his lifetime, and they were more orderly than before in going to Church and returning home on the Sabbath, as well as at burials and on sacramental occasions:

A brief memoir of the Rev. Lachlan Mackenzie

CHURCH OF LOCHCARRON, *26th September 1792*

Whereas it is the duty of all who name the name of our Lord Jesus Christ to depart from iniquity, and, as we are desired to abstain from all appearance of evil, we, the after subscribers, conscious that, it is our duty to have the cause of God and the interests of religion and morality at heart; finding that great irregularities are practised at burials and other meetings, and even on sacramental occasions; and as we know that other people make an excuse and take an example from the conduct of those who are reputed religious, and observing with regret that the Sabbath is shamefully profaned by idle talk in the churchyard, have come to the following resolutions, which we are determined, in the strength of God, inviolably to adhere to, *viz.*:

1. That none of us will taste a single drop of spirits at a burial after the body is interred; but, if the corpse is carried a good distance, and if the day be so coarse as to make it necessary to take a little on the road, that we shall do so at a decent distance from the churchyard, and only take a very little, if necessary, to refresh nature; but, if the day be good, that we shall not take any liquor but what we take at the house from whence the corpse shall be taken; and that, when the body is consigned to the earth, we shall immediately come to our respective homes. And however willing a poor widow may be, from a mistaken principle, to spend a good deal of whisky at the burial of her husband, we are determined that we shall not lay such a burden upon our consciences as to spend wantonly at the burial what might afterwards be of service to the widow and orphans. Whereas any of us singly, from slavish fear, might be afraid to break from this absurd and wicked practice, we hereby resolve, unanimously, to join together in breaking through it, so as that the world cannot be able to lay the blame upon an individual, but upon the whole of us taken collectively.

2. We hereby resolve, and promise solemnly and faithfully, in the sight of God, that, if we see or hear of any communicant being the worse of liquor at any meeting, especially a burial or sacrament, we will inform against him, so that he may be proceeded against according to the rules of the Church.

3. That every one of us shall go home immediately after sermon, and not stay in the churchyard conversing on idle or worldly topics.

4. That if any habit or practice, contrary to the Word of God, shall be observed in the parish, we shall do our utmost to suppress it.

5. That if any of us, through slavish fear, or a desire to gratify an appetite, shall break through any of these resolutions, he shall be reckoned infamous.

6 and lastly. That, to the utmost of our power, we will endeavour to observe the utmost regularity at our sacramental occasions.

Mr Donald Kennedy, Kishorn, father of the late eminent Mr John Kennedy of Redcastle, was the first name of the hundreds that signed the resolutions.

There were other regulations which he urged upon the people to comply with, such as public baptism, three regular proclamations of banns before marriage, and that every young man and woman in Lochcarron would know the questions of the Shorter Catechism before asking him to marry them.

When a party became displeased and would refuse to obey, Mr Lachlan would say, 'I do not prevent you from taking another minister.' So, taking another minister, or lifting the token off the table instead of getting it out of his hand, was what few or none liked to do, and when it was done, it was well known to be their own fault.

Outward reformation alone was not what Mr Lachlan aimed at chiefly in relation to the people, but the conversion of their souls and preparation for eternity. God often favoured him with visible tokens of the success of his ministry, and that given not in Lochcarron alone, but in many other parts of the county of Ross and Inverness. Many have been known to have come from Sutherland and Argyle, on sacramental and other occasions, to visit Lochcarron for the sake of the gospel, and it will not be known until the great day how great the benefit received by multitudes from the doctrines and prayers of Mr Lachlan.

There were many instances of people attending the fishing at Lochcarron, who were wonderfully caught in the net of the gospel: two instances of this kind took place by means of Mr Lachlan being directed to mention secret sins they committed, and one of them, from being a notorious sinner, turned out to be afterwards an exemplary Christian.

Lochcarron was the place where the Lord granted more visible marks of the success of his labours in the ministry, even to people who came from other distant parts of the land. He was often observed to mention and to plead the fulfilment of that promise, Psalm 72:16, 'There shall be an handful of corn in the earth upon the top of the mountains; the fruit thereof shall shake like Lebanon.'

The seed of the kingdom, sown by means of Mr Lachlan's preaching, has borne fruit in various respects. His preaching was the means of awakening, building up, and comforting many. It was a means of disseminating sound evangelical views of the gospel in that dark part of the land. He was a moral lighthouse to the Western Highlands and Islands, and there need be no doubt, as Dr Begg remarked at the Assembly of Inverness, that his doctrines were a means of leavening the minds of the people with those principles which in that part of the Highlands paved the way for the Disruption.

The people of the Highlands saw those principles exemplified in the life as well as doctrines of Mr Lachlan. As he was alone in the Presbytery, they sometimes laid a duty upon him that he felt difficult to accomplish, such as the settling of an unacceptable presentee, for the policy of those days was to appoint an influential minister for the purpose of keeping the people quiet and peaceable at the settlement. On one occasion that this task was imposed upon him, he felt the responsibility so great that he delayed obedience, waiting to get light upon the proper path. And although he felt exceedingly grieved on the occasion, the Presbytery had so little consideration and sympathy with him that the clerk issued a letter to him, threatening to take the legal steps for his deposition. Now, although such conduct was tyrannical on the part of the Church, and contrary to the spirit of the law, Mr Lachlan viewed his ordination vows in that light that he could not disobey the Presbytery without first separating from the Established Church. He therefore did obey, and, writing afterwards to his valuable friend, Dr Ronald Bayne of Kiltarlity, about that matter, he said, 'I was that day like blind Samson in the temple of the Philistines. It is true, the presentee to that Gaelic parish did translate a chapter in Isaiah to Gaelic.' The fact of Mr Lachlan's doing this, however, occasioned great uneasiness to him in his latter days.

Instances are still remembered of the efforts of his co-presbyters to thwart his labours for the suppression of sin and promotion of true religion. When Mr Lachlan was sorely tried any time in that way, he would lift his heart in prayer to the Lord, and sometimes send a message to a godly minister to pray for him. On occasion of the Presbytery dining with a rich and influential offender whom Mr Lachlan was subjecting to discipline, when they arranged to defeat his efforts, Mr Lachlan sent a special messenger to the Rev. Charles Calder of Ferintosh, requesting that great and pious minister to sympathize with him and to lay his case before the Lord. It was no wonder that a godly minister was so treated in a Highland Presbytery in those days, when Mr Calder himself had once to appeal from his own Presbytery to the Synod, to prevent a member of that Presbytery, a Roderick Mackenzie, from suppressing a parish by annexation, in order to increase his own emoluments. These were not the days of church extension. Mr Lachlan supported Mr Calder's appeal by a poetical effusion that recorded the event on the minds of his countrymen, and after the Synod of Ross had reversed the deed of the Presbytery suppressing the parish, Mr Lachlan commemorated the circumstance by adding the following stanza:

> The Synod, as it is reported,
> Their character for grace supported;
> And if aright we heard the story,
> None took the Devil's part but Rory.

It was good for these godly ministers that the public usually supported them when their grievances were made known. The weight of public opinion was almost the only protection of the feeble Evangelical minority in the church courts.

Mr Lachlan possessed great powers of satire and repartee, which he thought it his duty on suitable occasions to use in his Master's service. He could employ in the most solemn manner, and in Scripture words, the most cutting irony, and in this he thought himself justified by the example of the prophet, 1 Kings 18:27.

Mr Lachlan's large-hearted patriotism compelled him to lift his voice against other acts than those strictly ecclesiastical. He witnessed, with deep concern, that process of depopulation in the Highlands, and the impoverishment of those who were not expatriated. Mr Lachlan alone, of all his brethren, publicly protested against the system. He fearlessly raised his voice against the custom of depopulating parishes for the purpose of making room for sheep walks. He held forth that the soil was intended by the Creator for the maintenance of the human race, and that it was against his law to oppress man to make room for brutes or the inferior creation.

He preached a series of sermons at one time from Isaiah 5:8, 'Woe unto them that join house to house, that lay field to field, till there be no place, that they may be placed alone in the midst of the earth! In mine ears said the LORD of hosts, Of a truth many houses shall be desolate, even great and fair, without inhabitant.' The honest boldness of this man of God was unpleasant to the sheep farmers, and some of his remarks, on that occasion, were as unwelcome to some farmers and proprietors as Micaiah's faithful prophecies were to Ahab.

Mr Lachlan, however, continued to deliver the message he was directed to give, whatever obloquy [condemnation] it drew upon himself. He said that the system would be altered, or that the sheep would be destroyed in a way that was not expected in Scotland. He did not take upon him to determine the times or the seasons of the great alteration which he predicted. But when one in private conversation mentioned to him that many thousands of sheep had been lost in a snow storm, and took occasion to say that Mr Lachlan's predictions were thus in the way of being fulfilled, Mr Lachlan replied that it was not in this way that he anticipated a change; he was not looking to present appearances—it was neither the snow of winter, nor such heat as would dry the tongue of the raven, that would bring deliverance from the system of oppression, and grinding the face of the poor. But, added he, if the people of God be earnest and faithful in prayer, the deliverance will come sooner than it arrived to the children of Israel in Babylon. This was said in the year 1816, when the new leases were making great changes in Lochcarron.

The people of Lochcarron, besides many others, firmly believed that Mr Lachlan had some special gift or mode of prophecy. Many instances might be mentioned—*inter alia*, the following example. Mr Lachlan solemnly said from the pulpit, in the hearing of my informant, *viz*: 'Lochcarron young men, go to your knees this evening, and be earnest at a throne of grace. Great is your need to be so. A great breach is to be made upon you. There are five young men present here today that shall be in eternity before this day six weeks, and none of them above twenty-eight years of age.' There was one stranger present that day in the church of Lochcarron, who was a native of Easter Ross, and was then a road contractor in Lochcarron, and he thought with himself, if he lived, that he would mark how this prediction would be verified. It turned out, however, that it was fulfilled in a way he did not look for. There were three young men working for himself at the high road that died suddenly; the rest died in other parts of the parish, within five weeks of the time mentioned. They were all present that day in the church—none of them above twenty-eight years of age. This road contractor was at their burials.

There were many in the Highlands that placed great confidence in what Mr Lachlan would be directed in such a manner to say. They believed him to have been a person who obtained nearness of access to the Lord, and to whom the secrets of the Lord were manifested in a wonderful and uncommon degree.

As an instance of the confidence many had in what Mr Lachlan would say, it occurred near Inverness that two gentlemen were crossing in the boat at Kessock Ferry during the time that the parish of Redcastle was vacant, before Mr John Kennedy came to it. One of them was a clergyman, and said to the other that the law was decided, and that a certain person was to get the presentation.

Another passenger in the boat replied, 'That is impossible.'

The minister asked, 'How do you know?'

The person answered. 'Because Mr Lachlan said that the gospel would come to Redcastle.'

The minister asked, 'What did Mr Lachlan know?'

The other person replied, 'If you speak in that way about such a great and faithful servant of the Lord as Mr Lachlan, I will in the meantime drop the subject, but I call upon you to expose him as much as you can if what he said will not be verified.'

So that minister had not in his power to expose Mr Lachlan on that occasion, for the person that minister mentioned did not get the presentation. And some time thereafter, a minister, of whom he said that the Holy Spirit made a minister of him, was presented to it—the Rev. John Kennedy—who was such an eminent preacher of the everlasting gospel, and countenanced by his divine Master for being so useful in his day and generation, and particularly in the parish of Redcastle.

Mr Lachlan lived singularly above the world while he lived in it. He beheld through faith the glory of spiritual and eternal things to be far greater than the objects of time and sense. There was no man in his generation known to us that so much resembled the life of Elijah or John the Baptist. He was never married, and did not engage in the cares of the world, wishing to be at liberty, as an ambassador of the Lord, to give himself wholly to his service. In writing the statistical account of Lochcarron, he said about himself:

> The parson has no horse nor farm,
> Nor goat, nor watch, nor wife,
> Without an augmentation, too,
> He leads a happy life.

So he was a living testimony in his day that religion can render a man happy, although he may have but a small competency of the things of this life. He said that the proprietor kindly offered to him a large portion of the district for a farm, but that he refused it, well aware that he could be far happier without it.

Mr Lachlan did not give to his people that which cost him nothing: he was always careful and conscientious in his preparation for the pulpit. But during the first part of his ministry, and at the time he enjoyed the greatest enlargement and liberty, and that he was constantly engaged in public duties in his own parish and in many other places throughout the counties of Ross and Inverness, his chief preparation was meditation and secret prayer. It was believed by others, and felt and acknowledged by himself, that the doctrines he was delivering at that time were falling like the dew upon his own soul. And what made this so credible to others was how troubled souls particularly would get their cases and trials so clearly told to them.

For example, a woman in Inverness, who was labouring under great temptations, heard on Saturday that Mr Lachlan was to preach the next Sabbath at Kiltarlity, a distance of more than a dozen of miles from Inverness. She went that distance to hear him. Soon, in the course of the sermon, Mr Lachlan said, 'There is a poor soul here whose temptations are very peculiar. You did three things,' he said, and he mentioned them. 'At last, you desperately put your hand on the sneck [latch] of the door.' She was amazed by hearing what no fellow creature knew, and the direction he gave was blessed for consolation as great as her former temptations had been, and to which she was previously a stranger.

There is no evidence that during the first part of his ministry Mr Lachlan wrote out any of his sermons. But towards the decline of life, perhaps feeling more straitened, he began to write his sermons and lectures. This is one reason why his writings are not so rich as the sermons he sometimes delivered in preaching, before he began to write them. His writings contain chiefly, perhaps, the leading ideas on which he preached. After he began the practice, he frequently wrote on the Monday or Tuesday, particularly if he felt a degree of liberty on the Sabbath.

Mr Lachlan was laid aside by a stroke of paralysis fourteen months before his death. Within two or three months before his death, he could not rise or walk without support, but his remarks showed that even then he was feeling that man does not live by bread alone, but by every word which proceedeth out of the mouth of God. Upon the occasion of a person asking him one day how he did, his reply was, 'I am taking a faith's look into heaven.' He departed this life at 11 a.m., 20th April 1819, being the sixty-fifth year of his age, and thirty-seventh of his ministry.

(Signed) ANN MACKENZIE
Edinburgh, 1849

ᘓᘔ

Inscription on tombstone

The following is the inscription on Rev. Lachlan Mackenzie's tombstone in Lochcarron Churchyard

Here are deposited the mortal remains of the Revd. Lachlan Mackenzie, minister of Lochcarron, who died on the 20th April 1819, in the 37th year of his ministry.

A man whose simplicity of manners presented a picture of apostolic times, whose heavenliness of mind still spurned the vain objects of time and sense, whose vivid imagination shed a bright lustre on every subject which he handled, and whose holy unction in all his ministrations endeared him to the people of God, and embalmed his memory in their hearts.

His praise is in the churches. His parish mourns.

MDCCXXIV.

The life and times
of the Rev. Lachlan Mackenzie

IT may be of interest to those who have read the account of the life and ministry of Mr Lachlan Mackenzie to know something of the religious life of the community and the ministry of his predecessors in Lochcarron, and in particular of Mr Aeneas Sage. The following notes are taken from *The Days of the Fathers in Ross-shire*.

The immediate predecessor of Mr Lachlan Mackenzie in Lochcarron was Mr Donald Munro. 'He was an agreeable man, and preached the gospel in its purity,' is Mr Lachlan's account of him—a tribute not kept back by recollections of his unkind treatment of himself when he was pursuing his studies for the ministry. Unable to appreciate his schoolmaster, and regarding his eccentricity as a proof of his being below and not above the average of intellectual power, he had always dissuaded Mr Lachlan from aspiring to the ministry, and refused him all aid against his enemies in the Presbytery.

Mr Munro was preceded by the famous Mr Aeneas Sage—a man of undaunted spirit, who did not know what the fear of man was. He had, however, the fear of God and great zeal for the good cause in its highest perfection. He was the determined enemy of vice and a true friend of the Gospel. Such, according to Mr Lachlan, was the character of Mr Sage, the first minister who is known to have preached the gospel in purity and with success in Lochcarron. At the time of his induction, the state of the parish was very much the same as it was found by the Presbytery to be in 1649, when, after visiting it, they reported that there were no elders in it, by reason of malignancy [disaffection to the Church]. Swearing, drunkenness, cursing, Sabbath profanation, and uncleanness prevailed. As to the

Church, there was found in it 'ane formal stool of repentance', but no pulpit nor desks.[3] The stool, if the only, was truly the suitable seat for all the people in Lochcarron in these days, but the more it was required, the less power there was to make it aught else than 'ane formal' thing, as the solitary occupant of the church.

Matters continued in this state till the induction of Mr Sage nearly eighty years after. He was just the man for the work of breaking up the fallow ground of a field so wild, and a rich blessing rested on his labours. On the night of his first arrival at Lochcarron, an attempt was made to burn the house in which he lodged, and for some time after his induction, his life was in constant danger. But the esteem he could not win as a minister, he soon acquired for his great physical strength. The first man in Lochcarron in those days was the champion at the athletic games. Conscious of his strength, and knowing that he would make himself respected by all if he could only lay big Rory on his back, who was acknowledged to be the strongest man in the district, the minister joined the people on the earliest opportunity at their games. Challenging the whole field, he competed for the prizes in putting the stone, tossing the caber, and wrestling, and won an easy victory. His fame was established at once. The minister was now the champion of the district, and none was more ready to defer to him than he whom he had deprived of the laurel. Taking Rory aside for a confidential crack [conversation], he said to him, 'Now, Rory, I am the minister, and you must be my elder, and we both must see to it that all the people attend church, observe the Sabbath, and conduct themselves properly.'

Rory fell in with the proposal at once. On Sabbath, when the people would gather to their games in the forenoon, the minister and his elder would join them, and, each taking a couple by the hand, they would drag them to the church, lock them in, and then return to catch some more. This was repeated till none was left on the field. Then, stationing the elder with his cudgel at the door, the minister would mount the pulpit and conduct the service. One of his earliest

---

[3] Sloping book-boards to support Bibles. [RJD]

sermons was blessed to the conversion of his assistant, and a truly valuable co-adjutor he found in big Rory thereafter. Mr Lachlan thus describes the result of his ministry: 'Mr Sage made the people very orthodox. They seem to have a strong attachment to religion. There is a great appearance of religion in Lochcarron; and as the fire of God's Word is hereafter to try every man's work, there is cause to hope that some of it will bear the trial.'

Such was the state of Lochcarron at the time of Mr Lachlan's induction. Taught to respect a godly minister, the people cordially welcomed Mr Lachlan as their pastor. His fame as a Christian was already great, they had experience of his gifts as a speaker, and he occupied at once the place of an approved ambassador of Christ in the regard of the people.

He was of a peculiarly sensitive temperament, rendering him susceptible of the deepest impressions. Were it not for his powerful intellect, he would have been the creature of impulse, driven by his feelings rather than guided by his judgment. It is seldom so much mind and heart are found in one man. The light of a heartless intellectualism or the fire of an impulsive sentimentalism are often the alternatives in the case of those who have risen above the crowd. But in him the clear head and the warm heart were connected. Capable of forming a vivid conception of a subject, his imagination never failed to furnish him with metaphors by which aptly to illustrate it. He was no poet, though he often rhymed. But if he could not form those pleasing combinations of natural objects which, by their novelty and beauty, attest the working of poetic genius, he had the power of tracing analogies between the things of intellect and the things of sense. This to a preacher is the more useful endowment, and the imagination is more safely employed in such an office than when scattering the gems of poesy over the treasures of truth.

His Christian experience was singular. Early taught to know the Lord, one would have expected his course to have been unusually even. But the very reverse was the case, for few Christians ever experienced such marked changes of feeling. Now on the brink of despair under the power of temptation, and soon again in a state of rapturous enjoyment, shade and sunshine alternated in abrupt and rapid succession during the whole of his life. Ardent and imaginative as he was, the fiery darts of the wicked one flashed the more vividly and pierced the more deeply into his soul, and the joy that came to him from heaven the more violently excited him.

His prayerfulness was the leading feature of his Christianity. Much of his time was spent on his knees, and many a sleepless night he passed, sometimes wrestling, as for his life, against the assaults of the tempter, and at other times rejoicing in the hope of the glory of God. The nearness to the mercy seat to which he was sometimes admitted was quite extraordinary. Proof of this might be given, because of which we cannot wonder that he had the fame and the influence of a prophet among the simple people of the North, although the record of the proof would cause much incredulous nodding of the wise heads of the South. Avoiding the extreme of a superstitious credulity on the one hand, and of the formalist's scepticism on the other, it is altogether safe to say that Mr Lachlan enjoyed peculiarly familiar intercourse with God, and received such distinct intimations of his mind, in reference to the cases which he carried to the mercy seat, as but very few of God's children have obtained.

His preaching was always remarkable. His great originality of thought and manner, his apt and striking illustrations, his clear and emphatic utterance, the unction and authority with which he spoke, his close dealing with the conscience, his dexterous and tender handling of the cases of the tempted, his powerful appeals, his solemn earnestness, and his frequent outbursts of impassioned feeling, could not fail to win for him a measure of acceptance, as they gave him a measure of power beyond that of any other of his brethren. His was preaching to which all could listen with interest. His striking illustrations, often homely, though always apt, would arrest the attention of the most ignorant and careless. There was an intellectual treat in his sermons for such as could appreciate the efforts of genius. The scoffer was arrested and awed by the authority with which he spoke, and every hearer seeking the bread of life hung upon his lips.

A congregation was always eager to hear what Mr Lachlan had to say. A large crowd once gathered in Killearnan to hear him. So many had assembled that the church could not contain them, and the service was conducted in the open air.

When the text was announced, a rude fellow, sitting in the outskirts of the congregation, called out in the excitement of his eagerness, 'Speak out; we cannot hear.'

Mr Lachlan, not disconcerted in the least, raised his voice and said, 'My text is "Ye have need of patience,"' which the man no sooner heard than he was fain to hold his tongue and hide his face with shame.

The minuteness with which he described the feelings and habits of his hearers, and the striking confirmation of his doctrine often given by the Lord in his providence, gave him an extraordinary influence over his people. Preaching on one occasion against the sin of lying, he counselled his people to refrain in all circumstances from prevarication and falsehood, assuring them that they would find it their best policy for time, as well as their safest course for eternity.

One of his hearers, conscious of having often told a lie, and finding it impossible to believe that it could always be wise to tell the truth, went to speak to the minister on the subject. He was a smuggler, and, while conversing with Mr Lachlan, he said, 'Surely, if the exciseman should ask me where I hid my whisky, it would not be wrong that I should lead him off the scent.'

His minister would not allow that this was a case to which the rule he laid down was not applicable, and advised him, even in such circumstances, to tell the simple truth.

The smuggler was soon after put to the test. While working behind his house by the wayside on the following week, the exciseman came up to him and said, 'Is there any whisky about your house today?'

Remembering his minister's advice, the smuggler at once said, 'Yes, there are three casks of whisky buried in a hole under my bed, and if you will search for them there, you will find them.'

'You rascal,' the exciseman said, 'if they were there you would be the last to tell me,' and at once walked away.

As soon as he was out of hearing, and the smuggler could breathe freely again, he exclaimed, 'Oh, Mr Lachlan, Mr Lachlan, you were right as usual.'

On another occasion, he was bearing testimony against dishonest dealing, assuring his hearers that, sooner or later, the Lord would punish all who held the balance of deceit. As an example of how the Lord sometimes, even in this life, gives proof of his marking the sin of dishonesty, he repeated an anecdote which was current at the time. A woman, who had been engaged in selling milk, with which she always mingled a third of water, and who had made some money by her traffic [trade], was going with her gains to America. During the voyage, she kept her treasure in a bag, which was always under her pillow. There was a monkey on board the ship that was allowed to go at large. In course of its wanderings, the monkey came to the milk-woman's hammock, in rummaging which it found the bag of gold. Carrying it off, the monkey mounted the rigging, and seating itself aloft on a spar, opened the bag and began to pick out the coins. The first it threw out into the sea, and the second and third it dropped on the deck, and so on, till a third of all the contents of the bag had sunk in the ocean, the owner of the bag being allowed to gather off the deck just what she had fairly earned by her milk.

One of Mr Lachlan's hearers remembered, while listening to this anecdote, that he had in his trunk at home a bundle of banknotes, which he had got by the sale of diluted whisky. Feeling very uneasy, he hurried to his house after the sermon was over. It was dark before he arrived, and, kindling a pine torch, he hastened to the place where he kept his money, afraid that it had been taken away. Holding the torch with one hand, while he turned over the notes with the other, a flaming ember fell right down into the midst of the treasure, and before the man, bewildered as he was, could rescue them, as many of the notes were consumed as exactly represented the extent to which he had diluted the whisky.

Never did a sudden death occur in the parish during his ministry without some intimation of it being given from the pulpit on the previous Sabbath; and sometimes warnings would be so strikingly verified that one cannot wonder he was regarded as a prophet by his people. Such instances of the minute guidance of the Lord could not fail to make a deep impression on a simple-minded people, and should not fail to make some impression on any people.

Reminiscences and anecdotes

The secret of the Lord is with them that fear him.

REV. LACHLAN MACKENZIE used to assist the Rev. Hugh Mackay, minister of Dalarossie, Strathdearn, Inverness-shire. At the conclusion of the service on Monday on one occasion, while Mr Mackenzie was detained in bidding farewell to some friends, Mr Mackay went away to the manse. When Mr Mackenzie came in, and had waited tor some time without seeing Mr Mackay, he called the housekeeper and asked her where he was. She answered that he had gone out.

When he asked whether it would be long before Mr Mackay came back, she replied that he sometimes did not return till night came.

'Do you know the way he usually goes?' he asked.

She replied that she did, and, taking him outside, she proceeded to show him a footpath going into the wood beside the manse.

Mr Mackenzie followed the path, and came to a green spot in the wood, where he found Mr Mackay rolling himself on the ground, weeping bitterly. He enquired after the cause of his anguish. The answer was 'I had a promise from God's Word that some would be converted during the Communion season that is now past, and I was deceived, for none has been converted. I was as sure in my own mind that I got that truth as I was of the truth upon which I build my hope of being saved, so I have been deceived in the one as well as in the other.'

Mr Mackenzie said, 'If that is the cause of your weeping, you may take comfort, for you have taken two out of the kingdom of darkness yourself, and I took three out of it.'

At the next Communion, the five appeared before the Kirk Session and were received to membership in the congregation. This shows that the secret of the Lord, which is with them that fear him, was in an eminent degree with Mr Mackenzie.

ℰℛ

Rev. Lachlan Mackenzie asked his servant, after family worship one morning, to bring his horse saddled to the manse door, and that he was to prepare himself to accompany him. When the servant had done so, Mr Mackenzie mounted, and turned the horse's head towards Glencarron, the servant following. When they had gone about six miles, he turned into a mountain track, which strikes northward, near the present railway station of Achnashellach. Onwards they went until they came to the summit of a ridge. On the top of an opposite ridge, a woman came in sight, with a burden on her back. Mr Mackenzie turned round and said to his servant, 'I see now what brought us here.' At the bottom of the valley between the ridges, there runs a river, and it was here that they met. The woman waited on her side of it until the horseman should cross the ford.

When Mr Lachlan got across, he asked her where she was bound for, and for what purpose.

'I am going,' she said, 'to Lochcarron to see if the Rev. Lachlan Mackenzie will baptize this child which the Lord has given me, and which I have on my back.'

He enquired then as to where she had come from, and when she told him, he wished to know why she did not get her child baptized by the minister of her own parish. She said that it was not her habit to tell every man what she might have to say against ministers, because it might damage the cause of Christ.

'I am', he said, 'Lachlan Mackenzie, Lochcarron.'

'Will you baptize my child?' she asked.

'First of all,' said Mr Lachlan, 'you must tell me why you did not get him baptized by your own minister.'

'If you will ask the servant to go away so far as he will not hear me, I will tell you.'

When the servant had retired out of earshot, she explained every-thing to the worthy minister. Then Mr Lachlan called the man, told him to take the child off her back, performed a solemn, brief service, and baptized the child with the water of the river. When this was done, the servant replaced the child on her back, and she set off home again. Mr Lachlan returned to the manse of Lochcarron.

The writer received this story from an old man in Lochcarron over thirty years since. This man served Mr Lachlan as a lad. It is evident that Mr Lachlan must have been led by a portion of God's Word, or by an inward impulse, to go all these miles to meet the woman; for he did not know, until he saw her in the distance, where they were going, or for what purpose. One thing is quite plain, and that is that the Lord's hand was manifestly seen by the mysterious way He took to help the poor, godly woman in her effort to keep back the hands of an ungodly minister from administering to her child the sacrament of baptism.

ଚ୍ଚେ

It is related concerning Mr Lachlan that on a certain day, he was told that one of his elders, whom he appreciated very much for his piety, was very sick. When he went to see him, and saw that he was very seriously ill, he went on his knees beside the man's bed, and prayed God to spare the man to them in Lochcarron a while yet, as they had great need of him, and if death should have one at that time from their midst, that there was a fat mouthful for him at such a place. Shortly afterwards, the poor man began to recover, but a fat south-country farmer in the neighbourhood died suddenly.

A son of this farmer, who was an officer in the Army, came home to the funeral. He was told of Mr Lachlan's prayer, so he took his sword with him, and went towards the manse in a great rage. He met Mr Lachlan taking a walk on the public road. The officer asked him whether he was the minister of the parish. He replied that he was. The officer immediately drew his sword, and told him that he would have his life for having killed his father. The minister denied that he had killed his father. The officer repeated the words he had used in prayer for another man, adding that, as it was on account of that prayer his father died, he would therefore take his life.

Mr Lachlan said to him, 'Surely you will allow me to pray before you will do that.' He agreed that he would allow him to pray. Mr Lachlan said to him, 'Now, if the Lord will not answer my prayer, and that you will kill me, my soul will be singing in glory before you pass the churchyard' (which was only about a hundred yards off), 'but if he will answer my prayer, you will die on the spot, and your soul will be wailing in hell before I am at the manse door.'

The officer placed the sword in the scabbard, and went off quick march, without saying a word.

ഇാരു

In the year 1816, Mr Lachlan invited three of his brethren to assist him at his communion, namely, Dr Macdonald, Ferintosh, Mr Kennedy, Redcastle, and Dr Ross, Lochbroom.

Dr Macdonald received the following letter: 'I hear that you keep a large store of powder, which you use in blasting. I wish you to come to try your skill in breaking the hard rocks of Lochcarron.'

He accepted the invitation, and reached the manse of Lochcarron on the evening before the Fast day, along with Dr Ross of Lochbroom and Mr Kennedy of Killearnan. Mr Lachlan had been looking forward with great delight to the prospect of their visit and their services. He said to his sister a few weeks before, 'I have sent for Mr Macdonald with the Law, and for Mr Kennedy with the Gospel, and for Dr Ross with the Learning, and I will come after them myself with prayer, and I think we shall have a good time of it.'

But at the eleventh hour, his courage gave way. The Tempter persuaded him that they would not come, and when they arrived he was in bed in one of his fits of unbelief. When his sister told him that they had come, he refused to believe her till she had sent Mr Kennedy to his room. He then got up at once, came down in an ecstasy of joy to meet them, gave them a most fervent greeting, and hurried to the press [larder] for some refreshments to give them after their long journey.

Having placed the food on the table, he said to Mr Macdonald, 'You are the stranger, and you must ask a blessing.'

'No,' he replied, 'if you are to give us your good things, give us a prayer with them.'

This he did at once, in these words, in Gaelic. 'Tha fhios agad a Thighearna gun robh an nàmhaid ag innse dhuinn nach tigeadh do sheirbhiseach, agus gum biodh ball dubh air d' adhbhar, ach glòir dhut a-nis gun do chuir thu clach na chraos. Amen.'[4]

These words being the first Mr Macdonald heard Mr Lachlan utter in prayer, made a deep impression on his memory, and often did he repeat them afterwards. His opinion of Mr Lachlan he gives in a letter to Mr Sinclair, Thurso, written soon after his first visit to Lochcarron.

'Mr Lachlan,' he writes, 'is worth going miles to see. He is a dear servant of God, and lives near him at his footstool. He has failed much in body, but his mind is almost as vigorous as ever. He is truly a spiritually-minded Christian. He feels disheartened over the impenitence of Lochcarron sinners, and, indeed, there are not many of a contrary description in his parish. Yet he cannot believe but the Lord has a design yet to do good to Lochcarron, and he charged us who assisted him, and all the Lord's people, to carry Lochcarron on our spirits, and to pray much for his poor people. Worthy man, little

---

[4] 'Thou knowest, O Lord, that the enemy was saying to us thy servants would not come, and that there would be a black spot on thy cause, but now, glory be to thee, thou hast thrust a stone in his mouth. Amen.'

did he seem to know that some of those whom he thus charged had more need that he should pray for them.'

ഇരുജ

All Mr Lachlan's talents were laid at the Saviour's feet. Well might he say with the apostle Paul, 'Whose I am and whom I serve,' for his absorbing desire was God's glory and the salvation of sinners. It is recorded of him that he had stated that he never brought the cause of a sinner before the mercy seat but the Lord revealed to him the sinner's condition and what he was to do with him. True godliness takes cognisance of realities, and Mr Lachlan's practical mind, ever on the alert to find the joints in the sinner's armour, not infrequently feathered the arrow of reproof with the poetic touch.

Before the passing of the Forbes Mackenzie Act, the public-houses in Scotland were open on the Sabbath Day.[5] Midway between the farm of Tulloch and the Lochcarron Inn stands the old church. Two young men from the farm were in the habit of frequenting the inn, and Mr Lachlan on several occasions observed them through the windows, passing the church shortly after the service began. It deeply grieved the heart of the man of God to see men thus trampling on the Lord's Day and destroying their own souls. Being at the farmhouse one day, when both the young men were present, he struck off the following couplet in Gaelic:

> Thèid Iain agus Eoghainn a dh'òl;
> Agus iarraidh iad stob ma seach;
> Agus ma thèid an dithis do ghlòir
> Thèid Peadair agus Pòl a-mach.

---

[5] William Forbes Mackenzie (1807–1862) was a Conservative politician and temperance reformer. He entered Parliament as MP for Peebles-shire in 1837 and later became an MP for Liverpool. In 1853 he introduced the Public Houses (Scotland) Bill to the House of Commons. The Bill, commonly known as the Forbes Mackenzie Act, forced the closure of Scottish public houses on the Lord's Day and at 10 p.m. on weekdays. [RJD]

It may be translated thus:

> John and Ewen do drink;
> They order half-mutchkin about;
> If both will go to glory
> Peter and Paul will go out.

The arrow pierced the conscience of one of the young men: his sin and danger brought home to him in the light of Scripture wrought a great change within him; change of mind led to change of conduct and company, and henceforth the Sabbath found him, not in the public house, but in the house of prayer. In due course, he became an exemplary Christian, but his companion, as the couplet hinted, heeded not the warning, but, 'hardening his neck' in the ways of sin, passed on as he that is ready to be 'destroyed without remedy', thus fulfilling what had been revealed to this great watcher for souls. 'One shall be taken and the other left.'

§℃℞

The inn having become vacant on one occasion, a certain man in the village entertained thoughts of becoming its lessee, but his mind not being quite at ease as to the respectability of the innkeeper's calling, he decided to ask advice of Mr Lachlan. On meeting the minister, he unbosomed himself to him, the conversation taking place in Gaelic, when he received the following figurative and arresting reply: 'Gu bith nad òstair tha feum agad air trì nithean—earball cù, goile na muic, agus cridhe cloiche—agus mura bi na trì nithean sin agad, cha dèan thu òstair math a-chaoidh.' ('To be an innkeeper you need three qualifications—a dog's tail, a sow's maw, and a heart of stone—and without these three things, you will never make a successful innkeeper.') We leave the reader to solve the riddle.

§℃℞

Nestling at the foot of the hills on the south side of Lochcarron lies Attadale. Mr Lachlan visited this township at intervals to preach to the people, the passage thither being across the loch by boat. On such occasions, it was customary for a number of the Lord's people to accompany their pastor.

On one of these occasions, a larger company than usual, several of which were women, went with the minister. The boat was over-loaded, but the day being fine, no danger was apprehended. When, however, they were about the middle of the loch, a sudden storm arose. As on the Galilaean lake of old, the waves rising higher and higher under the fury of the wind, dashed over the deeply laden boat. The rowers plied their oars with all their might, but the pro-spect grew more and more alarming. They would never reach the shore! They would be swamped! So reasoned many of the occu-pants. The women began to weep. At length, the minister himself, like the disciples of old, showed manifest signs of fear. Again the cry arose, 'Lord, save us; we perish.'

The rowers strove manfully at their task, and at last the boat, getting under the shelter of the land, was safely beached. Among the rowers was one of Mr Lachlan's elders. Having helped to secure the boat, he turned to the minister and said, 'I wonder at so godly a man as you, Mr Lachlan, being afraid.'

'Oh,' replied the minister, 'although the Lord promised me that he would not cast me to hell, he did not promise me that he would not drown me.'

ဆာၛ

When Scriptural authority is cast aside, one of the first institutions to suffer in its sanctity and its claims is the Sabbath, the great bul-wark of true liberty, the day on which worldly ties being severed and worldly distinctions being laid aside, master and servant, peer and peasant, appear on equality before God, to take part in worshipping him.

At this period, a company of English tourists arrived at Lochcarron one Saturday evening, on their way to view the beauties of Skye. In those days Lochcarron was the embarking point for the 'Misty Isle'. Paying no regard to the claims of the Lord's Day, the Englishmen tried to secure boatmen to ferry them across to Skye on the morrow. Wherever they pressed their enquiries, however, they were reminded of their duty to 'sanctify the Sabbath'. This they determined not to do. Yet no one offered them his services. Neither pleading, scoffing, nor the temptation of a liberal supply of English gold availed to entice the boatmen, who stoutly maintained that they would not engage in work of any kind on the Lord's Day, except work of necessity and mercy, and that they would do without reward.

The Englishmen now urged the usual plea of the Sabbath-breaker when cornered—necessity. This the boatmen refused to accept as true, but at last yielded so far as to suggest that they (the tourists) lay their case before the minister, and they (the boatmen) would abide by his decision. This the tourists disdained to do, scorning the very thought of submitting to a Highland minister in anything. But the boatmen were adamant, and they themselves were impatient.

At last, after consultation, they sent a letter by a boy to the manse. The letter was handed to the minister.

He read it in silence, re-folded and enclosed it in the envelope, called for the boy, and when he entered the study, handed him the letter, addressing him thus, in Gaelic, 'Seo, thoir an litir sin gus na flaithe-anais, cha leams' a tha an t-Sàbaid idir.' Or in English, 'There, deliver that letter in heaven; the Sabbath is not mine at all.'

During that Sabbath, the Englishmen perforce 'rested according to the commandment'.

ഇറങ്

There was in Lochcarron a gracious woman, one of the excellent of the earth, who was afflicted with a bad memory. Her inability to carry away with her the precious things she heard, as she sat under Mr Lachlan's ministry, caused her great distress. Deeply dejected in mind, she went to make known her case to the minister.

Having heard what she had to say, the worthy man, in order to break the snare and to impress upon her the superior blessing of receiving fresh supplies of grace to the possession of a good memory, took the following way to reassure her.

'Take', said he, 'a bottle. Fill it with fresh water, cork it, and lay it aside carefully. Take another bottle. Put it in the clachan burn [village stream], and leave it uncorked, so that as the water flows into it, it flows out again. Go back at the end of a year and examine the bottles, and you will find that the water in the bottle which flowed out as it flowed in is fresh, whereas the water in the bottle which did not lose a drop is rotten.'

෪෪

Mr Lachlan wore at times homespun, and preached on several occasions while thus attired. This gave umbrage to some who were more concerned about orthodox clerical garb than about orthodox and savoury doctrine. The matter was reported to the Presbytery, with the result that Mr Lachlan was required to appear before that Court to answer for his conduct.

The preaching of borrowed sermons by lazy and incompetent ministers is no new thing, and among the Presbytery members, it would appear, were some addicted to this unorthodox practice. To it Mr Lachlan gave a shrewd blow in his defence. 'I can go into the pulpit', said the worthy minister, 'in a homespun suit and preach an English sermon, and I can go into the pulpit in an English suit and preach a homespun sermon.'

The hit was too palpable. The pressing of all-round conformity might have had very unexpected consequences for his persecutors, so they let the matter drop.

෪෪

But the man of God did not always get off so lightly at the hands of the worldly-minded among his brethren. The Lochcarron Presbytery in those days usually met at New Kelso, near the head of the loch. When the hour appointed for one of its meetings had come, Mr Lachlan had not put in an appearance. The brethren, however, decided not to proceed until he should arrive. The Moderator was the minister of Glenelg—a typical 'Moderate'.

On Mr Lachlan's arrival, the Moderator, impatient of the delay, saluted him in Gaelic thus. 'An do ràinig thu, Lachlainn, na casan fada?' ('Have you arrived, long-legged Lachlan?') (Lachlan was a tall, spare man.)

To this unseemly salutation, the minister of Lochcarron retorted, 'An tusa a th' ann, amadan na Clèire?' ('Is that you, the fool of the Presbytery?')

The Moderator, turning purple with rage, and springing to his feet, shouted that he would have Lachlan expelled from the ministry for calling him a fool, an expression forbidden by Scripture. The assembled brethren were amazed, the Evangelicals among them deeply grieved. The attack upon Mr Lachlan was wholly uncalled for: if the retort was sharp, the provocation was great; further, all knew that Mr Lachlan had only voiced the commonly held opinion regarding the Moderator. Yet, superficially at least, the Moderator appeared to have some ground for objecting to the epithet cast at him. Accordingly, a meeting of Presbytery was fixed, when the matter would be threshed out.

As the time drew on, Mr Lachlan fell under a fit of unbelief; fear filled his mind that the worst would happen. On the morning of the day appointed for the Presbytery meeting, having visited a member of his congregation, who was a great wrestler at the throne of grace, he expressed himself as dreading the Presbytery's decision. Being advised, however, to 'stay himself upon his God', with much trepidation, he proceeded to the meeting.

When he arrived, the New Kelso meeting house was crowded. All the members were present, and such of the godly in Lochcarron as could attend, fearing the treatment which might be meted out to their minister, came to witness the issue.

The Rev. Roderick Mackenzie, Torridon (the only minister ever settled in that place since the days of the Columban missionaries) was

Moderator. As Mr Lachlan entered, he was offered a chair by the Moderator.

'Nì sinn ùrnaigh an toiseach,' ('We shall pray first') was Mr Lachlan's reply, and without further ado, he (Mr Lachlan) began to pray.

Very soon, the meeting house became dark, as with approaching night; a terrific tempest of wind and rain descended upon the building, as though to overwhelm it. Next, a low, rumbling noise, as of earthquake, was heard, the house began to rock, and all present feared their last hour had come.

At this point, Mr Lachlan, still praying, cried with a loud voice, 'An can mi e? An can mi e? An can mi e?' ('Shall I say it? Shall I say it? Shall I say it?'), stopped abruptly, picked up his hat, and walked away home.

As soon as he stopped praying, the darkness passed away, the tempest and the earthquake ceased, and Rev. Roderick Mackenzie, the Moderator, having somewhat recovered from the general alarm, broke the silence by saying, 'Whoever will be against Mr Lachlan, I won't.'

But the Glenelg minister, now that the danger had passed, like Pharaoh of old, hardened his heart and demanded that, as Mr Lachlan had not answered the charge, he be made to appear before the Presbytery again. There was nothing for it but to appoint another meeting to hear the case. It may here be added that at the village of Lochcarron, about three miles away, nothing unusual happened. The sun shone brightly, and the people continued without interruption to work on their crofts: the strange happenings at New Kelso were confined to the vicinity of the meeting house.

In proceeding to the second meeting of Presbytery, Mr Lachlan was as buoyant in spirits as he had been depressed when on the way to the first.

In answer to the charge of calling a brother minister a fool, he replied, 'He who created my legs is he who created all things, and he has himself pronounced concerning all that he did create that he saw that it was very good, and none but a fool would find fault with anything he did create.'

The reply was unanswerable; the mouth of the wicked was stopped. Confusion fell upon the head of the adversary, who was now branded a fool, not by the opinion of man only, but in accordance with that Word which he had sought to employ as a cloak for his malice and an instrument to further his fell [cruel] design. 'The wicked are ensnared in the work of their own hands.'

The writer had the foregoing notes from his uncle, who in turn heard them from William Beaton, Slumbay, who was for a considerable period manservant with the Rev. Lachlan Mackenzie.

ॐ

Mr Lachlan, by his courageous stand for the oppressed and his out-spoken denunciation of the ruthless practice of clearing crofters off the land to make room for sheep, brought upon him much persecu-tion. The owner of a certain farm adjoining the manse was so very covetous that it was commonly reported among the people that he never saw a green spot of earth but he coveted it as his own. When covetousness and power meet together in a man, justice and right-eousness are too often forgotten, and harsh measures resorted to when a desired end is to be accomplished. This was painfully mani-fest in the former's conduct. And Mr Lachlan did not spare him.

Smarting under the pungent criticism of the worthy minister, he met him on one occasion, and began to threaten that he would turn his church into a sheep fank [sheepfold] and his manse into a smearing shed.[6]

To this threat, Mr Lachlan retorted, 'Ma chuireas mise fios gu Iain Mòr a' Chaisteil Ruaidh agus gu Robastan Chinn a' Ghiuthsaich agus ma nì iadsan casaid ort rin athair, chan eil ann an neamh no air

---

[6] A building where sheep were treated with tar and grease. See footnote on p. 100. [RJD]

talamh na chumas tus' à ifrinn.' ('If I send a message to Big John of Redcastle (Rev. John Kennedy) and Robertson (Rev. Mr Robertson), Kingussie, and if they report your conduct to their Father, there is not in heaven or on earth that can prevent you being cast into hell.'

He further added that, despite the farmer's boundless covetousness and great wealth, his grandson would die in the poorhouse. This was fulfilled as foretold, the farmer's grandson dying in the Inverness Poorhouse about the year 1890.

ഇൗര

In Mr Lachlan's day, the Church of Scotland groaned under the twin evils of 'moderatism' and 'intrusion'. Mr Lachlan repeatedly informed his hearers from the pulpit that deliverance from these evils would be forthcoming in a shorter period than that which measured the captivity in Babylon, but warned them that the deliverance would be comparatively brief and would be succeeded by a great falling away from the faith, when the plague of graceless ministers in the land would be more grievous than the plague of locusts in Egypt, of which we read that it was 'very grievous'.

Shortly after discoursing on this doleful subject, he was one day met by one of his parishioners, who, referring to the approaching gloomy day of which the minister had spoken, remarked, "S cinnteach anns an latha sin nach bi aon Chrìosdaidh ann an Lochcarrainn.' ('Surely in that day there will not be one Christian in Lochcarron.'), to which the worthy pastor, who had so much of the 'secret of the Lord', gave the reassuring reply, 'Cho fad 's a bhios tuinn a' bualadh air creag bidh Crìosdaidh ann an Lochcarrainn.' ('While the waves continue to dash on the rocks, there will be a Christian in Lochcarron.')

ഇൗര

Readers of the tract *Muckle Kate*, whose conversion in her old age after a life spent in gross sin was an answer to years of 'prayers and supplications, with strong crying and tears unto him who is able to save' on the part of Mr Lachlan, know how, at a communion service in the open field at Lochcarron, where thousands were present, that trophy of grace, blind by weeping over her sins, was led forward by the minister to the Lord's Table for the first time, where she sat alone; and how, in serving the table, speaking from the words, 'Not a hoof of them shall be left,' Mr Lachlan's address was so blessed to the assembled multitude that it is computed that two hundred were awakened to a sense of their lost estate. That memorable table has been called 'Muckle Kate's Table'.

Referring to it, Mr Lachlan said that another occasion would occur in Lochcarron, when the Lord's Table would be served having only one person sitting at it, and that, he added, would be a sign that the great declension, of which he had so often forewarned the people, had already begun.

This took place, as foretold. The writer's father and uncle were present when this table was served. The one individual who sat at it was the late deeply exercised and greatly respected Malcolm Kennedy of Kishorn, who finished his course in Inverness.

The incident happened thus. The service, as usual, was in the open field. Judging by the number of members present, the officiating ministers considered that three tables would be required to hold them all. To the first and second table members came forward very readily, and those tables were more than ordinarily full, so that when the invitation to the third table was given out, only Malcolm Kennedy came forward, and it was served with him alone sitting at it. The writer was not informed who the officiating ministers were, nor the year when the incident occurred. All he could ascertain is that it was about 1880.

ଈଔ

In instructing the people, Mr Lachlan, like his divine Master and the prophets of old, made frequent and effective use of 'similitudes'. By the wayside, and some distance westward of the church, he dug a well, which he called 'Tobar Suthainn'—the everlasting well—adding that it would be so called while the world lasts.

Some time afterwards, one of his people called upon him, requesting baptism. Before granting this privilege it was the practice of evangelical ministers in those days to examine applicants as to their knowledge of man's ruined state by nature and the way of gospel salvation, the ignorant being refused until they became better acquainted with the Scriptures.

The first question the minister asked the man was, 'Càit' a bheil tobair suthainn?' ('Where is the everlasting well?') (Jeremiah 17:13).

'Eadar an clachan agus an taigh-òsta.' ('Between where the church is and the inn.')

'Chan fhaigh thu am baisteadh.' ('You won't get baptism.')

The man went away crestfallen, but on meeting one of the elders, to whom he unbosomed himself, he was advised to go to the catechist for instruction. Having been under the tuition of that worthy functionary for some time, he returned to the minister, who repeated his former question. This time, however, the correct answer was given, when Mr Lachlan added, 'Tha mi a' faicinn gun robh thu a' coimhead air Iain MacDhonnchaidh' ('I see you have paid a visit to John the son of Duncan'—the catechist.) Other questions having been satisfactorily answered, baptism was duly administered.

On another occasion, when another of Mr Lachlan's people came for baptism, the first question asked him was, 'Cò às a thàinig uisg' a' bhaistidh?' ('Where did the water of baptism come from?') (John 19:34; John 5:5, 6, 8: Zechariah 13:1).

'Às Allt a' Chlachain.' ('From the Clachan Burn.')

'Chan fhaigh thu am baisteadh' ('You won't get baptism.')

There was nothing for it but to go for instruction to the obliging catechist, whose efforts at imparting knowledge brought about the desired result.

The above two notes were told by the Rev. Lachlan Mackenzie's niece, Mrs Mackenzie, who lived at Strome, the worthy lady adding that on

one occasion, when visited by two ministers, she told them these notes
and asked them to answer the questions, but they had to confess they
could not. We have surely reached a woeful pass when the shepherds
lack the knowledge which in former days was required of the meanest of
the flock.

୫୦୯୪

The last child baptized by Mr Lachlan was the future eminent Rev. Alexander MacColl, who finished his course on earth in Lochalsh, than whom there was no greater preacher of the Evangel in his day. His father at the time was a shepherd in Lochcarron. As showing how Mr Lachlan had the secret of the Lord, it is recorded that, as the father was handing back the child to its mother, after being baptized, Mr Lachlan said, 'Thoir an deagh aire air an leanabh, bidh e fhathast na lochran deàlrach leis an Tighearna.' ('Take good care of the child; he will yet be a shining light of the Lord.')

୫୦୯୪

When on his deathbed, Mr Lachlan realised that the end was at hand, he sent his manservant for the Rev. Roderick Mackenzie, Torridon, a truly gracious minister, for whom Mr Lachlan had the highest regard. Before his manservant set off for Torridon across the hill, he advised him, when returning with the minister, to observe the well near the top of the pass above Lochcarron—Fuaran Cath an Rididh—and if the water in the well was low, they were to make haste, as that would indicate that he (Lachlan) was still in life, but if the water was high, they might proceed at their leisure, for he would have departed this life.

As the manservant, making all haste on his way to Torridon, passed the well, he observed the water in it to be exceptionally low. Having stated his errand, he and the minister of Torridon hastened back together. When they reached Fuaran Cath an Rididh, they found it overflowing; nevertheless, they did not slacken their pace, but held on for the Lochcarron manse. On their arrival, they found that the saintly minister of Lochcarron had entered into the joy of his Lord shortly before their arrival at the well.

57

The Rev. Roderick Mackenzie here referred to is he who was Moderator at the memorable Presbytery meeting held at New Kelso, recorded above. He was also present at an induction service where Mr Lachlan preached a remarkable sermon, when, among other pointed things, in warning both the minister and the people of their responsibility before God, he said that there would be streets in hell paved with the heads of graceless ministers. This saying did not please Mr Roderick, who, after the service, accosted Mr Lachlan, asking him what he had to say for using such language. 'Nothing,' was Mr Lachlan's emphatic rejoinder, 'but take you good care that your own big head won't be in it.'

ℴ)ъ

Regarding his successor, Mr Lachlan told the people of Lochcarron that he would be a 'dumb dog that would not bark' (Isaiah 56:10). This proved to be the case. In warning the people of Lochcarron of the preciousness of gospel truth and the great privilege of sitting under the ministry of such as declared the 'whole counsel of God', he stated that, as a proof that he had never delivered to the people but what he received from the Holy Spirit, two trees would grow, one on each side of the spot where his pulpit stood, and that nowhere else would there be found precisely the same kind of tree; that when they grew up and their branches intertwined above the pulpit, they would fall to the ground: that would be a sign that the apostasy of the latter days had already begun.

All this occurred as foretold. The church, being small and old, a new and larger building—the present Parish Church—was erected a short distance eastward of the burying ground in which the old church stands. The trees grew, nobody knows how, as two witnesses to the truth of the doctrine delivered by the man of God to the people, and when their branches intertwined, they fell over on the ground, where they lie in a decaying condition, but still there.

Lectures

Matthew chapter 2: verses 1 and 2

WHEN mankind fell from God by the great apostasy of Adam, they were recovered again by the word of his grace. At the very time that the sentence was given against man, he was informed that the seed of the woman would bruise the head of the serpent.

The promise of the Messiah

Mankind were long, by this mystical promise, cheered and comforted. It was opened up gradually by succeeding promises, and revealed by degrees in the different ages of the Church. This truth was the substance of the doctrine of the prophets and the sacred meaning of the sacrifices, the ceremonies and the types of the Old Testament Church. Many prophets and good men longed for this day, but they only saw it by faith at a distance, and greatly rejoiced at the sight.

This glorious vision spoke at the appointed time, but the Church waited till four thousand years rolled their round, before the wonderful person made his appearance, in whom all the families of the earth were to be blessed. And though that may be dark to us, no doubt the wisdom and the goodness of God will appear in the long delay. The apostasy of man was deep, and the distance between him and God was so great that the divine wisdom saw meet to open up his great design to him gradually. Mankind were not prepared to receive this great truth all at once, and therefore God did not reveal it soon. We do not speak to children about the highest points in philosophy or about some abstruse points in natural science. We speak to them as their weak capacities and intellects are able to bear. And if God had revealed clearly everything that happened to our

Lord Jesus Christ, there is cause to believe that many of depraved mankind would act a still more shocking tragedy than they did in putting him to death. The same judicial blindness which made the Jews to reject and crucify him would have made them do so had the prophecies been never so clear. God promised his people a King. He also promised them a suffering Saviour, and as they could not reconcile them, they would have acted the very part they did, and perhaps with more aggravated wickedness; and to prove this, it may be asked, can any prophecy be more clear than what our Lord says of his resurrection? Can anything be more certain than the accomplishment?

The Jews refuse to believe, and we know that, though all the Old Testament prophecies had been never so clear, the wickedness and unbelief of the Jews would have resisted their accumulated evidence. Had they examined them without prejudice, they were clear, and accordingly our Lord appeals to them as bearing witness to the whole of his life and miracles.

The genealogy of Jesus

In the former chapter, we have the genealogy of our Lord by a long train of ancestors up to Abraham, the founder of the Jewish nation, as we have it in the 3rd of Luke, up to the first of the human race. And though we cannot readily obviate all difficulties that may occur in these and in other dark passages of Scripture, there are several arguments that may satisfy an honest believer and serious enquirer after truth.

1. First, the manner and customs of the East, and more especially with respect to adoption. Thus, for instance, after Jacob had adopted the two sons of Joseph, had some Jewish historians given us the genealogy of the tribe of Joseph, and that one said, 'Manasseh, the son of Joseph, the son of Jacob,' and the other had said, 'Manasseh, the son of Jacob,' they had been both right. The sacred historians give the genealogies of our Lord just as they found them, and it seems there was no fault found with them: they proved that

Jesus Christ was descended from David and Abraham. They both inform us that our Lord was born in Bethlehem, in the tribe of Judah, and this was the accomplishment of an ancient prophecy.

2. Second, the Jews were the bitter enemies of Christ, and if there had been anything wrong in these genealogies, they would gladly have caught hold of it, which it seems they did not. Had they been able to prove that there was a flaw in his genealogy, and that he was not descended from David, they would have got a victory and proclaimed their triumph. This they never attempted, and though they may object to the manner the Christians explain and quote prophecies, they cannot deny but these prophecies exist.

3. Third, whatever pains learned men and commentators have been at to reconcile dark passages in the Old Testament that had to their view the appearance of error, the darkness was in their own minds and not in the sacred pages, and this will appear very clearly from the following great consideration. Our Lord was the great Prophet of the Church whom God sent into the world. He often appeals to the writings of the Old Testament, and recommends their perusal to his hearers. He desires the Jews to search the Scriptures, and they will find several prophecies of Christ there. Now, if there had been anything really wrong or dark in the Scriptures of the Old Testament, would not our Lord point out such errors? As he did not, we may infer that there were none. We may conclude, then, that the darkness is in our minds, and not in the Scriptures of truth. And should some slight mistake occur, owing to the oversight of transcribers in a copy in manuscript, it can be corrected by comparing it to other manuscripts. Our Lord saw nothing in the original Scriptures worthy of animadversion [criticism], and where he did not, we ought not. As to the Septuagint version, it may be considered rather as a short paraphrase than a literal translation, and where it differs from the Hebrew, it may be corrected by it. Accordingly, the inspired writers of the New Testament quote Scriptures agreeably to that version.

In a word, the seeming inconsistencies that appear in the Old or New Testaments are only apparent, and not real. And if this had not been the case, Christ and his apostles would have pointed them out.

I now proceed by divine assistance to explain to you the prophecies of Scripture and the history of our Lord, as delivered by the Evangelist Matthew.

The birth of Jesus

> Verses 1–2. *Now when Jesus was born in Bethlehem of Judaea in the days of Herod the king, behold, there came wise men from the east to Jerusalem, saying, 'Where is he that is born King of the Jews? for we have seen his star in the east, and are come to worship him.'*

The wonderful circumstances that concur about the time of Christ's birth will strike the mind with astonishment. In the preceding chapter we read of his conception by the Holy Ghost, and the witness which God Almighty bore to that signal event by sending an angel to acquaint Joseph thereof, and to confirm him, and to confirm mankind in the belief of this important truth, wise men from the East, a heavenly light to the shepherds of Bethlehem, both announcing the birth of the Prince of Peace.

Now is fulfilled the prophecy, Psalm 132, 6th verse. Wonderful news is heard in Ephratah, and the shepherds heard it in the fields of the wood. Heaven and earth, learning and ignorance, wisdom, and simplicity, unite in bearing witness to this astonishing event. Infidelity itself will not dare to say that wise men of the East and the shepherds of Bethlehem fabricated such a story, or that Joseph and Mary suborned them so to do. The star that directed the wise men is new and wonderful. As they were philosophers and had studied the wonders of nature, this surprising phenomenon excited their attention. They concluded that it portended the birth of some illustrious personage. Some such opinions prevailed among the heathen, for we read of Caesar's star. Even among ourselves, the common people

64

think that a sudden flash of lightning signifies the death of a great man.

And here we may admire the manifold goodness of God in the different ways by which he reveals himself to people. Philosophers are directed by a star, the shepherds are instructed by a vision of angels, and Joseph by a dream—and to this day he takes several ways to lead sinners to his Christ. The wise men came from the East—very probably from the Happy Arabia,[7] as this country afforded the presents which were offered to our Lord.

We read in Genesis that Abraham sent his children by the second marriage to the East, that is, to Arabia, which lay south-east of Judaea. Besides, we read in Psalm 72:10 that the Kings of Sheba and Seba shall offer gifts, and we know that this is a part of Arabia. In their journey, however, they lost sight of the star—or, what is probable, perhaps they thought they would find the Prince they were in quest of, as they were now in the land of Judaea. Accordingly, they directed their course to Jerusalem, the capital, where they naturally expected to find the royal babe. They wish to see him, that they may worship him, and it is highly probable that the worship meant here is something more than that homage which is due to an earthly sovereign. But it seems that the birth of the heavenly babe did not excite the same sensation in the metropolis of his ancestors as it did in the wise men of the East.

---

[7] *Arabia Felix* was the Latin name for the southern part of Arabia, corresponding approximately to present-day Yemen. The Latin term was a translation of an earlier Greek name. *Felix* means 'happy', 'blessed', or 'fertile', in allusion to the productivity of the land in those days. [RJD]

Matthew chapter 5: verses 21 to 48

AS the Christian religion exceeds all other religions in the splendour of its miracles and the sublimity of its doctrines, it proves likewise its heavenly original by the superior purity of its morality.

The Jewish teachers in our Lord's time had perverted the moral law by their perverse glosses and unwritten traditions. They thought a man was safe if he was free from outward scandalous and gross sins. The doctrine of our Lord, on the contrary, is the spirituality of the law. It is holy, just and good. It reaches the thoughts of the heart and the most secret motives as well as the outward act. In regard to sin and duty, it is very different from the opinions of men. Many think that their lives are blameless if men have nothing to say to their conduct, and that they perform duty if they do things that are specious [Scots: splendid] in the sight of men. The language of Scripture is very different indeed. Holy oracles inform us that the thoughts may be sinful and criminal. And nothing is reckoned duty in the divine presence but what proceeds from a desire to glorify his name. Actions that please men may be an abomination in the sight of God. Our Lord spake as never man did, and he is the true commentator to explain his own Law.

I shall, therefore, speak upon the words you have heard, and conclude with some practical remarks.

The spirituality of the Sixth Commandment

Verses 21–26. Ye have heard that it was said by them of old time, Thou shalt not kill; and whosoever shall kill shall be in danger of the judgment: but I say unto you, That whosoever is angry with his brother without a cause shall be in danger of the judgment: and whosoever shall say to his brother, Raca, shall be in danger of the council: but whosoever shall say, Thou fool, shall be in danger of hell fire. Therefore if thou bring thy gift to the altar, and there rememberest that thy brother hath ought against thee; leave there thy gift before the altar, and go thy way; first be reconciled to thy brother, and then come and offer thy gift. Agree with thine adversary quickly, whiles thou art in the way with him; lest at any time the adversary deliver thee to the judge, and the judge deliver thee to the officer, and thou be cast into prison. Verily I say unto thee, Thou shalt by no means come out thence, till thou hast paid the uttermost farthing.

In these words, our Lord rectifies a mistaken notion that prevailed among the Jews. They acknowledge that manslaughter was a crime that deserved punishment, but they thought little or nothing of anger, malice, and opprobrious language. On the contrary, our Lord informs us that causeless anger and bad language deserve punishment in the world to come.

In allusion to the different courts among the Jews, he shows us that there are different degrees of punishment in the world to come for sinful anger and malignant expressions. 'Raca' and 'fool' are expressions of great contempt and abhorrence. They showed great disrespect for the persons to whom they were applied, but the Jews did not suspect that they would expose the persons that used them to everlasting punishment. But rancorous expressions betray a darkness and malignity of soul, befitting only the companions of reprobate spirits and devils. Bitter invective and poisonous expressions and epithets cannot have place in the kingdom of Christ and of God. Let reason speak. Did ever we observe two persons scold, and did we mark their expressions? May we not then ask whether their language is more like the dialect of devils than the songs of angels and the hallelujahs of the saints in light? Reason will not demur what answer to make. If people then live and die under the influence of such diabolic passions, they are fit companions only for the spirit of darkness.

Our Lord, therefore, assures us that anger showing itself in such harsh epithets exposes sinners to the pains of hell. And the expression he uses is very strong. He alludes to the valley of Hinnom. There was an abominable heathen idol there, a large figure of brass in the shape of a man, where their forefathers burnt their children to a devil and drowned the cries of the poor mothers by the sounds of musical instruments. The bodies of malefactors were thrown into the valley of Hinnom and burnt in the constant fire that was kept up there, together with the filth that came from the city of Jerusalem. And though the valley of Hinnom was naturally a beautiful place, these things made it a type of hell. And in like manner, though the soul of man should be a beautiful temple consecrated to the service of God, if it be filled with angry passions, it will become a habitation for devils and a cage for unclean and hateful birds.

Accordingly, our Lord advises every man that is angry with his brother without a cause not to offer his gift upon the altar of God till he is first reconciled to his brother. And, indeed, no man ought to come to the house of God with rancour in his heart against his fellow creature. How can he expect that God will hear the prayer that proceeds from a malicious heart? How can such a man repeat the Lord's Prayer? It is said that witches pray to the devil. And it may be asked, 'How can an angry man pray to the God of love when he feels hatred to his brother?' And therefore our Lord, in allusion to well-known practice at law courts, advises every man to be reconciled to his brother in time, lest he be cast into the prison of hell, from whence there is no redemption. And we are told that a man cannot get out till he pays the uttermost farthing.

How awful, then, a thing it is to fall into the hands of the living God and be exposed to everlasting punishment for the gratification of an ugly passion: the very gratification is attended with pain and misery. The angry man, by glutting his vengeance, cannot fail to make himself unhappy. Believing that the friends of his victim will make reprisals, his mind is always upon the rack. And if he lives and dies in this condition, he falls from one hill into another. And this shows the great propriety of our Lord's advice to conquer the malignant passion of anger in this world, before it be for pain and punishment in the next.

The spirituality of the Seventh Commandment

Verses 27–32. *Ye have heard that it was said by them of old time, Thou shalt not commit adultery: but I say unto you, That whosoever looketh on a woman to lust after her hath committed adultery with her already in his heart. And if thy right eye offend thee, pluck it out, and cast it from thee: for it is profitable for thee that one of thy members should perish, and not that thy whole body should be cast into hell. And if thy right hand offend thee, cut it off, and cast it from thee: for it is profitable for thee that one of thy members should perish, and not that thy whole body should be cast into hell. It hath been said, Whosoever shall put away his wife, let him give her a writing of divorcement: but I say unto you, That whosoever shall put away his wife, saving for the cause of fornication, causeth her to commit adultery: and whosoever shall marry her that is divorced committeth adultery.*

As he had explained the sixth commandment, he now proceeds to comment upon the seventh also. The Jewish teachers thought that adultery was a sin, but it seems, however, they thought little of heart sins and indulging unclean thoughts. Our Lord forbids the unchaste look and the immodest behaviour. And, in truth, persons may be very guilty though they do not proceed to gross acts of sin. In the time of the antediluvian world, Scripture observes that the imaginations were only evil continually.

And the apostle observes some persons had eyes full of adultery that could not cease from sin. And to show the danger of such sins, our Lord commands to pluck out a right eye and cut off a right hand if they endanger our everlasting happiness. The wandering of the eyes will hurt the soul. This was King David's snare and the ruin of his happiness and the loss of the purity of his mind for a long time. And this made him cry to heaven to create in him a clean heart and renew a right spirit within him.

And if the eyes betray us into sin, the hands are still more dangerous. In such cases, the sure—the only—remedy is to avoid all temptations and snares. Job says that he made a covenant with his eyes, and Solomon advises his readers not to lust after beauty in their hearts. The very touch of some women is poison to the soul, and therefore it is said, when the harlot kissed the young simpleton, that he went after her as an ox to the slaughter, and was not aware of his danger till a dart struck through his liver. The sinner is like a bird that hasteth to the snare and knows not that it is for his life. Our Lord shows that it is much better to conquer corrupt affections than be punished everlastingly for the indulgence of fleshly lusts. Women should not make their beauty incentives to sin in our guilty natures.

He likewise explains to us the doctrine of marriage. The Jewish teachers were very lax in that part of morality. They permitted men to turn off [dismiss] their wives for very trivial causes. On the contrary, he assures us that marriage is a union for life, and that nothing can dissolve it but uncleanness or infidelity in the one party. And though the innocent party may insist for a divorce and marry again, it does not by any means appear from our Lord's doctrine that the guilty has the same privilege. And here we may observe how much mankind are indebted to our Lord, and how much he consulted our happiness by bringing marriage to its original state. How unhappy was the fate of the Jewish women by the constant abuse of the doctrine of divorces!

The spirituality of the Third Commandment

Verses 33–37. *Again, ye have heard that it hath been said by them of old time, Thou shalt not forswear thyself, but shalt perform unto the Lord thine oaths: but I say unto you, Swear not at all; neither by heaven; for it is God's throne: nor by the earth; for it is his footstool: neither by Jerusalem; for it is the city of the great King. Neither shalt thou swear by thy head, because thou canst not make one hair white or black. But let your communication be, Yea, yea; Nay, nay: for whatsoever is more than these cometh of evil.*

After our Lord had explained the doctrine of the seventh commandment, he returns to the first table and speaks of the breach of the third commandment. The very heathens, as well as the Jews, saw the great sin of gross perjury, and believed that it would be punished. How little do parents consider this in the oath they give when their children are baptized, and foolish young people who give rash promises of marriage and confirm them by an oath, and afterwards break such promises. These sins are very great, and such as fall into them should be deeply humbled in the sight of God. But our Lord here shows us there was great danger in common swearing, however trivial some people may reckon the sin. By a constant habit of swearing, a person is prepared for the gross sin of perjury. He becomes so familiar with the name of God that he feels no reverence at least for an oath.

Among the Jews, some swore by heaven and others by earth; some by Jerusalem and others by their own heads. And among those called Christians, some swear by their souls—how fearful the pledge!—others by saints and angels, and some by God himself. How awful to take his holy name in vain in the most trifling conversation! They use their Maker worse than they would dare to use an earthly superior. But can such people, upon rational grounds, hope to escape the just judgment of God? He is merciful and long-suffering and does not inflict sudden vengeance, but though his vengeance is slow, it is sure.

Having mentioned the awful sin of common swearing, may I hope that those who profess religion among us, and are called communicants, are free from such deep guilt? If they are not free, dangerous is their case indeed. It seems such persons are determined not to go to hell alone. Their example is the ruin of many. When these people arrive at the kingdom of darkness, they will not have the language of the devils to learn, for they learn it in this same world.

In common conversation, then, the people of God are to use plain language in their ordinary conversation, without an oath. Whatever exceeds this is from the evil one, and therefore to be avoided by Christians. If these are the fruits, the trees are barren, twice dead,

71

and therefore to be cut down and cast into the fire. If reason, if common sense have any weight with those who are given to common swearing, we might ask them, what pleasure or profit do they reap from their sin? The drunkard and the unclean person and the thief have some sinful delight in what they do, but what pleasure has the swearer, unless it be in insulting the name of God, and this is the pleasure of devils?

Do you ask where is the great harm of small oaths? Christ will answer your question. He says that whatever exceeds yea and nay proceeds from the evil one. All sin proceeds from Satan. And do you really ask where is the great harm of being with the evil spirit for ever? If you are a common swearer, you wear his livery, and you may expect the reward he gives his faithful servants. You are volunteers in his service. Other sinners have some kind of reward from Satan in this same world, but you serve him for nought. But you may be sure of your reward when you come to his kingdom. The man that sells his soul, though he got the world, is but a fool, but the one that sells it without anything at all is one of the greatest fools in the creation.

As a substantial exchange for such abuse of language as swearing and ribaldry, I would recommend to you to commit to memory some of the most precious of David's Psalms and the most pleasant stories in the Old and New Testaments.

Christian meekness

Verses 38–42. Ye have heard that it hath been said, An eye for an eye, and a tooth for a tooth: but I say unto you, That ye resist not evil: but whosoever shall smite thee on thy right cheek, turn to him the other also. And if any man will sue thee at the law, and take away thy coat, let him have thy cloke also. And whosoever shall compel thee to go a mile, go with him twain. Give to him that asketh thee, and from him that would borrow of thee turn not thou away.

In order to throw some light upon these expressions, let it be observed that in all ages and in all languages, there are phrases that are not to be understood in the exact literal meaning. Many of the strong hyperbolical expressions used in Western Asia are dropped in the Holy Scriptures. And our Lord, as a public teacher, might use phrases that were well understood in Palestine. Every teacher may use the figurative and parabolical language of the country in which he resides. Our Lord and Saviour here forbids private revenge, and taking our cause out of the hands of the magistrate. Instead of this, we are to bear many injuries rather than repel force by force.

But that our Lord's advice is not to be used in the literal sense is clear from his own conduct. When a man struck him upon the cheek, he did not turn the other cheek to him. But though he did not show revenge, he observed a proper spirit by the rebuke he gave him upon this trying occasion. And as he forbids private revenge, he also forbids our struggling in vain and seeking sinful redress or vengeance when oppressed by law courts or by the violent and oppressive instruments of government. Better give the cloak with the coat; better go two miles instead of one than sin against charity, hurt our fellow creatures, or be provoked by private revenge to commit a great sin and bring upon ourselves a much greater loss than the want of the coat and cloak and the inconvenience of travelling two miles.

And it is likewise much better to lend a little to a poor man, even though there is danger that he would not pay again, than send away one poor brother with a heavy heart when perhaps we could relieve him at the time. But perhaps our proud and covetous hearts might object to this doctrine of our Lord, that by literally following his doctrines in these things, we might encourage wicked people to trample upon us, and covetous worldlings to impose upon us and hurt our temporal interest.

To this it may be replied that the figurative language of our Lord was well understood by his hearers, and we are certainly required to observe the spirit of his doctrines. And by so doing, we consult our own happiness, and it shall be found at last by such conduct that we do not injure even our temporal interest in the least. In many cases, we rather promote it. When the herdsmen of Abraham and Lot did quarrel, we find that the father of the faithful was of a quieting, conciliatory temper, and gave Lot his own choice, and yet we read that Abraham was rich in cattle, in silver, and in gold. And Isaac, though he yielded to the force and ill nature of the Philistines, was thriving in spite of them. And it will surely be acknowledged that this was better than that his pride would be the occasion of shedding human blood. Humble and obliging behaviour will have an effect upon the most rugged and tyrannical tempers.

Let it also be observed that in many cases, nothing can be more foolish than resistance. We not only suffer loss, but disgrace for our pains. Persons should well consult and foresee the consequences before they disturb the peace or shed the blood of their fellow creatures. It is often observed that the Quakers who literally followed these rules were the richest and most thriving sect in the world. Nothing is lost by Christianity, and though it does not absolutely forbid the use of the law or of the sword, if we can possibly do without them, it is still better. It was a good advice which a man gave once to his friend, not to draw his sword till he prayed thrice. The profit or pleasure a man can have by revenge is but short-lived at best, and the hurt he may do is incalculable, whereas the meek and humble Christian may fully depend upon the promise of his Lord and Master that he will inherit the earth.

Verses 43–48. Ye have heard that it hath been said, Thou shalt love thy neighbour, and hate thine enemy. But I say unto you, Love your enemies, bless them that curse you, do good to them that hate you, and pray for them which despitefully use you, and persecute you; that ye may be the children of your Father which is in heaven: for he maketh his sun to rise on the evil and on the good, and sendeth rain on the just and on the unjust. For if ye love them which love you, what reward have ye? do not even the publicans the same? And if ye salute your brethren only, what do ye more than others? do not even the publicans so? Be ye therefore perfect, even as your Father which is in heaven is perfect.

Our Lord in these words is calling upon his true followers to imitate his own glorious example. There was never such a perfect character; never a man that had so many enemies. And yet our Lord not only loved his enemies, and prayed for his enemies, but even laid down his life for them. The doctrine of the Jewish teachers was to love their neighbours and hate their enemies. Now, there is no great virtue in loving our friends and well-wishers. The most dissipated characters may do so. But our Lord requires of us to imitate the divine love and goodness which is universal and disinterested. He maketh the sun to shine and the rain to fall upon all. He makes no distinction between friends and enemies. In this sense, he may be said to love all mankind. By imitating God, loving and doing good to our enemies, we prove that we are his children, for it is an undoubted fact that none but the children of God can perform these hard and difficult duties. And indeed, we may complain even of these, how defective they are in this duty, though we are here required to be perfect like our heavenly Father.

But here it may be asked, 'Is this practicable? Can any man be thus perfect? Does not our Lord seem to require an impossibility?' The perfection our Lord requires is such as the parents of John the Baptist had. It is said of them that they were both righteous before God, walking in all the commandments and ordinances of the Lord blameless. It is said of Job that he was perfect and upright. And the Psalmist desires us to mark the perfect man and behold the upright, for the end of that man is peace. The perfection of the people of God is perfection of sincerity and holiness. This is their honest aim and endeavour, that the will of God may be done on earth as it is in heaven. And though they fail, they are accepted in the beloved. He yielded absolute obedience to the law. And we read in Scripture that they are complete in him. Thus there is the perfection of the people of God in all ages: their faith is as the shining light that shineth more and more unto the perfect days.

Practical remarks

I conclude with some practical observations.

1. If anger and bad language are punished in the world to come, if the indulgence of unclean thoughts send people to hell fire—what will come of murderers and unclean persons? You may read their doom in 1 Corinthians 6:9–10 and Colossians 3:5–6. Such persons should fly immediately to the fountain that cleanses from all sin.

2. If the looks are infectious, should not young people be cautious about their dress and behaviour? The wise man Solomon speaks of the attire of a harlot, and in no age, perhaps, was that attire so common. And should not modest persons beware of imitating the dresses of the worst part of their own sex? The eyes of a chaste woman are like the eyes of a dove. They look to Christ.

3. Lastly, if we would avoid all sin and the consequence of all sin, let us imitate God and have an eye to his glory. If all ranks did so, we would not have such complaints through the nation as we have of murder, uncleanness, and all manner of sin. When God arises to shake terribly the earth, our nation must be punished. Instead of imitating the Saviour, we imitate one another, and the man that looks to the Scripture and follows his duty is reckoned a singular character. Let us, then, follow God as dear children.

May God bless his Word. AMEN.

Matthew chapter 6: verses 1 to 21

OUR Lord here proceeds in his valuable practical discourse. In this chapter, he speaks of the duties of alms, prayer, fasting, forgiveness of injuries, and in an absolute trust in God alone as the surest antidote against carking [distressing] cares, and the immoderate love of the world, and overmuch attachment to the things of time. Instead of this, he recommends to his followers to secure the riches of eternity, with a promise that if they do so, they shall be provided with a competent portion of the good things of this life.

I shall speak of the several duties he recommends, and conclude with some useful remarks.

Almsgiving

Verses 1–4. *Take heed that ye do not your alms before men, to be seen of them: otherwise ye have no reward of your Father which is in heaven. Therefore when thou doest thine alms, do not sound a trumpet before thee, as the hypocrites do in the synagogues and in the streets, that they may have glory of men. Verily I say unto you, They have their reward. But when thou doest alms, let not thy left hand know what thy right hand doeth: that thine alms may be in secret: and thy Father which seeth in secret himself shall reward thee openly.*

In these few words, our Lord showeth us that people may spoil the most precious and useful duties, and make them of no avail to themselves by the manner in which they perform them. As dead flies spoil the ointment of the apothecary, the desire of vainglory, in like manner, may spoil the duty of almsgiving. The most exquisite dish may be spoiled to the guest by mixing some nauseous thing in the dish before him that his stomach abhors. And this sacrifice which we offer may be lost if our great aim is to be seen and praised by men. This will be all our reward.

Many acts of generosity and hospitality are performed merely to extort some popular applause. The rich man, who fares deliciously every day and gives sumptuous entertainments very often has no other view than to hunt after the praise of men. And the man who subscribes to public charities, as well as the man who gives alms in presence of a few, may have the same poor end. What a pity that duties so bright and so brilliant—that acts of beneficence, so useful to their fellow creatures—should be useless to those who perform them, merely owing to the motive from whence they proceed. In fact, persons may perform the divine will and fulfil the divine decree, and yet have no reward from God. So did Nebuchadnezzar, so did Jehu, and so did the greatest scourges of the human race. And our Lord and his apostles teach us that persons may perform very useful duties and yet lose their reward. And as they may spoil the duty of almsgiving, they may likewise spoil the duty of prayer. N.B., Joshua and Caesar contrasted.

Prayer

Verses 5–13. *And when thou prayest, thou shalt not be as the hypocrites are: for they love to pray standing in the synagogues and in the corners of the streets, that they may be seen of men. Verily I say unto you, They have their reward. But thou, when thou prayest, enter into thy closet, and when thou hast shut thy door, pray to thy Father which is in secret; and thy Father which seeth in secret shall reward thee openly. But when ye pray, use not vain repetitions, as the heathen do: for they think that they shall be heard for their much speaking. Be not ye therefore like unto them: for your Father knoweth what things ye have need of, before ye ask him. After this manner therefore pray ye: Our Father which art in heaven, Hallowed be thy name. Thy kingdom come. Thy will be done in earth, as it is in heaven. Give us this day our daily bread. And forgive us our debts, as we forgive our debtors. And lead us not into temptation,*

*but deliver us from evil: For thine is the kingdom, and the power, and
the glory, for ever. Amen.*

Prayer is the most precious and the most solemn of all duties, by
which we cultivate communion with God, and draw down his blessing upon our souls. And yet it is possible to spoil this precious act
of worship. There were people in the Jewish Church who prayed to
be seen of men. And in every Church there are people of this
description. There are some people, when they go to their private
devotions, who are anxious that others should know what they are
about by their loud speaking. No doubt these people have the
reward they seek, for mankind call them pious and devout. Better,
however, be pious than have the name of being so. But loud speaking and long prayers are not of the essence of devotion. Our Lord
tells us that the heathen thought they were heard by their much
speaking. Indeed, there are some who seem to think that God is
ignorant of their wants, for they are of great pains to tell him of
them over and over again. But the misfortune is that, however agreeable their prayers may be to themselves, they weary mankind with
them. Our Lord assures us that these are not the prayers that avail.
He even informs us in another place that long prayers are worse
than being useless. Some that devoured widows' houses had long
prayers and therefore received greater punishment. Let not the
apostate, however, triumph, who may hear this, who has given up
prayer altogether, for he is many steps behind the hypocrite himself.
A Pharisee may be converted: a Sadducee seldom or never.

Fasting

Verses 16–18. *Moreover when ye fast, be not, as the hypocrites, of a
sad countenance: for they disfigure their faces, that they may appear unto
men to fast. Verily I say unto you, They have their reward. But thou,
when thou fastest, anoint thine head, and wash thy face; that thou appear
not unto men to fast, but unto thy Father which is in secret: and thy
Father, which seeth in secret, shall reward thee openly.*

Fasting upon some occasions is an important and necessary duty. The design of it is to afflict and humble ourselves, and bring down ourselves to the dust before our heavenly Father. It is used by the people of God upon extraordinary occasions, when they pray for a blessing or deprecate [plead against] a calamity or judgment. But whether the duty be public or private, it may be spoiled if people only wish to be seen of men. Our Lord forbids this by telling us to anoint our heads and wash our faces. There are not many rules respecting the duty of fasting in the New Testament, and when the Old Testament speaks of it, the fact is declared to be useless if we persevere in sin. Indeed, prudence and a man's own heart will direct him how to perform the duty aright, if he is acquainted with Scripture.

The duty of fasting is to be joined with prayer, for we are told that our Father is in secret, and seeth in secret, and will reward us openly. Though God is present everywhere, he takes notice of—and is peculiarly present in—secret prayer. In many cases, God shows more of his love in private duty and in private prayer than in the congregation. And this happens to show us that we are to be con-scientious in all duties. We should neglect no duty, but we should peculiarly delight in the duties of the closet. Though our Lord was very punctual in public duty, we find he had peculiar delight in pri-vate prayer, for we read that he spent a whole night in prayer to God. And in the extraordinary appearance upon Tabor hill, his prayer was rather private, for he had only three attendants to witness that glorious scene.

Laying up treasures in heaven

Verses 19–21. *Lay not up for yourselves treasures upon earth, where moth and rust doth corrupt, and where thieves break through and steal: but lay up for yourselves treasures in heaven, where neither moth nor rust doth corrupt, and where thieves do not break through nor steal: for where your treasure is, there will your heart be also.*

Our Lord, in these words, is showing us the difference between earthly and heavenly treasures. The one is precarious and uncertain: the other sure and permanent. Earthly riches are subject to many unforeseen accidents. They may be destroyed by fire, by water, by wind, by rain, by injuries of time, by friends, and by enemies. Our best furniture and finest clothes may be destroyed by the moth, and our gold and silver, as well as other metals, may be consumed by the rust. We may think our treasures secure if they are under lock and key, but alas! foreign thieves may break through, and even domestic thieves may steal.[8] The man to whom we trust our affairs may be a villain, and the man who has our money may break with the full hand and deceive us. The very bank may prove bankrupt, and the man who is rich in lands and money today may tomorrow be reduced to beggary and obliged to beg his bread. And if our treasure was consigned into his hands, we may be involved in the same ruin.

These are not idle speculations, but matters of daily occurrence. But if we turn our eyes to the other side, we shall behold a beautiful reverse. The riches of eternity, the heavenly treasures, are substantial and constant. If there are some spots upon this earth so very fertile that they pay the husbandman an hundredfold, how sure is his reward who trusts in his God, and who takes the promises as his sure portion? Such a man must be rich and must be happy, for the divine promises cannot fail any more than the pillars of heaven can break. You may lend your money to man, and he may fail, but if you trust your soul to God, you will be happy through all eternity. If your treasures are upon earth, your thoughts are constantly engrossed there. And how miserable is such a state! If he has any happiness, it is the happiness of intoxication, for the worldly man is in a constant hurry and turbulence of thought. If he has any lucid interest, it is when he is calculating upon some visionary scheme of augmenting his sinful self.

---

[8] Domestic thieves refer to people who live in the household where theft occurred. In this context, 'foreign' means 'from another district' rather than from a different country. [RJD]

The heart is like the troubled sea (Isaiah 57:20), when it cannot rest, whose waters cast up mire and dirt. This is what it cast up at best with ordinary storms, but if it is agitated with madness of tempest, it casts ashore the wreck of vessels and the bodies of men. Such is worldly happiness: such the fate of its votaries. What do they gather after all their pains? Mire and dung that will not feed an immortal soul. And if they proceed too far in seeking earthly treasures and setting their hearts upon them, they make shipwreck of faith and a good conscience, and thus forfeit the joys and riches of eternity. How poor their pennyworth! How beggarly their treasure! They hug their treasures, and thus the love of riches will pierce them through with many sorrows, even in this same life, and render the prospect of another very gloomy. They may well say at last, as a wicked great man said, that if they served God as they served the world, he would not forsake them at death.

But the man who seeks his happiness in God and whose treasure is in heaven is calm and content. Like a person dwelling upon a mountain in sight of the sea, he is in no danger from the storm or tempest below. The Christian is happy in the favour of God. The Rock of Ages is his support. He is happy in this world, and he looks forward with humble hope to the happiness of the next. Whatever may be the language of providence, the language of Scripture will speak peace and comfort to such a man. His treasure is in heaven, and though his earthly treasure were snatched from him, he can be patient and resigned: he can be even cheerful, for his portion is in heaven, his delight in God. And though every other fountain would become dry, the fountain of life will always run, and the water will always refresh his heart.

Practical remarks

We may observe from these words of our Lord that the best works may be spoiled by the motive from whence they proceed. In general, the end or motive with many is the love of praise. To this we are indebted for many great actions, for many signal instances of generosity, and for a constant course of hospitality. What a pity that men should content themselves with a reward so poor. And even poor as it is, it is very often denied them. Instead of praise, they meet with obloquy [condemnation] and reproach. They lose their reward here, and cannot justly expect any reward hereafter. It was not from any love to God that he performed these actions.

Before we can expect any reward, our actions must proceed from a divine principle. We must be born again, and then—and not till then—can we bring forth fruit unto God. The Scripture doctrine is that the tree must be good before it brings forth good fruit. The good actions of bad men will not meet with the divine approbation. In vain do they expect the favour of God by a few acts of generosity or relief afforded to their fellow creatures, if themselves are the slaves of sin and the apes of the fashion. Instead of a reward, the impartial judge will say, 'Depart from me, ye workers of iniquity; I know you not.'

And this should teach us, as we value the favour of our Judge, to pray earnestly for the saving influences of his Spirit, and that he would create us in Christ Jesus unto good works. The work that proceeds from faith in Jesus Christ will meet with the approbation of heaven, but the fire of his justice will devour the wicked and all their works. Let us then lay our hands upon our breasts, examine our hearts and our works, and if they have any weight in the balance of the sanctuary, let God have the glory. But if they are wanting, let us apply to our great Immanuel, that we may be found in his right-eousness, and then our works of faith and labours of love will be accepted in the Beloved.

As our Lord finds fault with long prayers, we should take notice of what he rebukes, and study more the substance than the length of our prayers. It is true our Lord tells us that hypocrites may have long prayers, but even good Christians are to blame in this respect. God regards more the piety of the heart than the length of the prayer. David, by a very short prayer, disconcerted his enemies and crushed a formidable rebellion that rose against him. The prayer our Lord taught is short, and if we repeat it with true devotion, we shall be heard. The prayer that will prevail must conquer every sinful and malignant passion that once did predominate in the heart. We must forgive our enemies and set our affections on heavenly objects.

Lastly, we see here the riches and happiness of the true believer. His treasure is in heaven. The revolution of time and the fall of empires do not affect his happiness in the least. Secure in the favour and friendship of his God, he can trust though the mountains were cast into the sea (Psalm 46). He is still and quiet, acknowledging the divine sovereignty, and trusts in the divine mercy.

AMEN.

Matthew chapter 6: verses 22 to 34

IN the words that we have heard, our Lord shows the evil and danger of being immoderately attached to the things of this life, and by several arguments calls his people to trust in God for all the things that they stand in need of. And as carnal arguments might induce them, such as provision for a family and the fear of poverty, he concludes with one argument sufficient, one would think, to silence all unbelieving thoughts. It is this: that if we secure the favour and friendship of God, we shall have as much of the things of this life as will serve our turn. And we shall find that this is by far the happiest life. Let us do the duties of our station without anxious thought about futurity. It will save us from many sinful shifts that people make up to get the riches that perish. It will engage divine truth to provide for us, and let us look up to himself for what we stand in need of.

Light and darkness

Verses 22–23. *The light of the body is the eye: if therefore thine eye be single, thy whole body shall be full of light. But if thine eye be evil, thy whole body shall be full of darkness. If therefore the light that is in thee be darkness, how great is that darkness!*

The eyes are to the body what windows are to a house. They transmit the light. Now, when the eye is in good condition, we see what we are doing, and are directed to perform every duty in life. But when a person loses the use of his eyes, he is rendered useless, very often to himself and to others. But our Saviour here, it is clear by a proper similitude, speaks of the eye of the mind. The judgment and conscience enlightened by the Word and the Spirit of God is the eye of the mind doing its duty and directing the man's actions to the glory of God and his own good and the good of others.

The judgment debased and corrupted by sin and terminating all its actions in the black dead sea of self is the evil eye. That eye is blind as a mole in the things of God, and sees nothing but the advancement of his own poor temporal interest. And to show how awful such a state is, when the light of the mind is extinguished, that it sees nothing but the gratification of its lust and passions, our Lord says, 'How great is that darkness!'

And to direct us to discover where this darkness predominates, the Scripture gives us some marks to point out such a state, and it is incumbent upon us to notice them.

1. They call evil good, and good evil. They put darkness for light, and light for darkness.
2. Their lost state is hid from them, and they see none of their danger, and are unwilling to see their duty.
3. The more pains are taken upon them to cure them, the disease becomes still the more inveterate, until at last it becomes past all cure.

And though these marks may apply to other sins and other sinners—for Solomon assures us that whoremongers and unclean persons seldom return from their vices—yet they are particularly applied to the sins of covetousness.

Those, then, who have the evil eye of covetousness:

1. Call evil good, and good evil: they put darkness for light, and light for darkness. They often confound virtue and vice. There are different classes of covetous worldlings. Some of them heap up money merely in order to enable them to be great and make a figure in the world. And what they gather by oppression in one way, they squander by prodigality in another way. And this they call generosity and hospitality, never considering that God says that he hates robbery for burnt offering. And when they exceed the bounds of sobriety, they call this good fellowship. Others of them are inclined to hoard

up money without bettering their friends, and this they call prudence. What the Holy Ghost in the Scriptures calls godliness, they call enthusiasm, precision, and singularity. Who derided Christ and persecuted the apostles? We are told it was the Pharisees, who were covetous. Who gave the hard names of winebibber, Samaritan, and devil to the meek Lamb of God? It was the covetous Jews. It is likewise the covetous nominal Christians who give hard names to the people of God. Like their predecessors of old, their tongue is their own, and who is Lord over them?

2. They see not their lost state nor their danger by sin, and are unwilling to see their duty. By practice in sin and constantly stifling their conscience when calling upon them to forsake sin and turn to God, they become callous, hard, and brawny. They are like the wild creature of whom Job speaks (chapter 41:27): 'He esteemeth iron as straw and brass as rotten wood.' By often hearing the Word of God they become sleepy and secure, and at last regard the threatenings as words of course [unremarkable words]. And as the mind becomes hardened in infidelity, they think because sentence against an evil work is not executed speedily, their hearts are fully set in them to do evil (Ecclesiastes 8:11).

3. The more pains are taken upon them to cure them, the disease becomes still the more inveterate, until at last it becomes past all cure. This was precisely the case of the covetous Jews in the time of Christ. Himself preached to them for upwards of three years, and yet the nation in general preferred their farms, their cattle, and their pelf [ill-gotten money] to all the treasures of grace and of glory which his heavenly doctrine opened up to them. The Jewish Church, which was the garden of God for several centuries, was never so well cultivated as it was by Christ and his apostles. And yet, after all the pains bestowed upon it, what is the result? It brought forth wild grapes. And the visible Church does so notwithstanding the cultivation and pains bestowed by his servants. Let us look round us, and even traverse the whole kingdom, and yet, after all that the gospel has done, we shall find that the majority are worse than Mohammedans or pagans. And the cause is obvious from the next verse.

God or mammon

Verse 24. *No man can serve two masters: for either he will hate the one, and love the other; or else he will hold to the one, and despise the other. Ye cannot serve God and mammon.*

The Jews of old were in a most awful delusion, as we learn from the prophet Jeremiah (chapter 7, verses 8–11). They were guilty of the most horrid crimes, such as murder, adultery, and robbery, and yet boldly appear in the house of God and tell that they were delivered to do these abominations.

Now, the delusion of the Jews in our Lord's time is still prevalent in the Christian Church. He tells us that no man can serve two masters: the generality of people are of opinion that they can serve God and the world. And yet in the nature of things, this is impossible. To work in the world and to make the world our master are two very different things. A man may easily know whether he serves God or the notions of his own covetous heart. What is his chief end? The glory of God or the gathering of money? It will easily appear that service done to two such masters is impossible.

1. Such service is incompatible.
2. In a short time, a man will see that he must part with the one or the other.
3. This is clear from the history of other worldlings recorded in Scripture.

1. Service to God and to the world is incompatible. They ask the very same thing, and it cannot be given to both. 'My son, give me thine heart,' is the language of God. 'Thou shalt love the Lord thy God with all thy heart, soul, and strength. Thou shalt love thy neighbour as thyself,' is the sum of the moral law. What says the world? If you love God with all your heart, you cannot do everything that I require of you. If you follow conscience and the Word of God, you cannot have every profit that I can put in your way. If you love your neighbour as yourself, how can you expect to make good bargains? You cannot enlarge your farm or increase your stock. If you heed

the awful expressions that you find in the Bible, how can you be like others that have done these things and are in a very respectable footing in the eye of the world? If Scripture and conscience are your directors, you will lose the esteem of the majority. Death and judgment and future punishment are melancholy subjects. Don't think of them. Come to me and I will give you other employment. These joyful sounds are the gospel of the covetous, and they bewitch him till death opens his eyes and eternity stares him in the face.

2. Again, a man will see that he must part with the one or the other. He must often be in such a pass. And when he is, if the world has his heart, he will do just as the young ruler did: he will turn his back upon Christ. We see daily instances of such characters before our eyes. And what comfort have these poor worldlings? It is only this, that they have made no open profession of apostasy like the young man. They only betray their Master with a kiss by keeping up the name. Which is the safest course we leave yourselves to judge. Awful is the case of both!

3. This is clear from the history of other worldlings recorded in Scripture. This is clear from the story of Gehazi. He was in the service of Elisha, a man of God. And he had every advantage that such a situation could give him. But he could not keep his place. A covetous heart and a lying tongue made him leave a house where he had the service of God and draw upon himself the plague of leprosy besides. The covetous young ruler made a flaming profession. He kept the commandments, and wished to do something more. But he parts with Christ and prefers his farm to him. Demas forsook the apostle Paul, and his name, though once a professor, is in the black list of apostates. In short, let a man examine himself, and he shall know whether his love to God or to his self is predominate. His heart can tell him what he would do in such a situation. But, indeed, our present set of professors clearly show what they are without any examination at all.

God's providential care

Verse 25. Therefore I say unto you, Take no thought for your life, what ye shall eat, or what ye shall drink; nor yet for your body, what ye shall put on. Is not the life more than meat, and the body than raiment?

These words were directed to the first followers of Christ, and it required great faith to live up to the spirit of them. By embracing the doctrine and following the footsteps of Christ, they were thrown upon the wide world, as it were. They lost the favour of their friends and were deprived of their means.

Now we are not in this state—we live in more peaceful times of the Church. But still, many of the followers of Christ are in poor circumstances, and are greatly in the power of others. The doctrine then applies to them. They are not to be overanxious about food and raiment. God will provide. He is the author of their life and the former of their bodies, which are of greater value than food and raiment. We are, therefore, to trust in him for both. God, who gave us our lives and our bodies, meant them for some purpose. And if we consecrate them to his service, there is no doubt but he will provide food and raiment for them.

Verse 26. Behold the fowls of the air: for they sow not, neither do they reap, nor gather into barns; yet your heavenly Father feedeth them. Are ye not much better than they?

It is highly proper for us to gather instruction from the works of nature, and this was our Lord's method of teaching. He here desires his followers to consider the birds, who have no storehouses in which to lay up their food, and, though they neither sow nor reap, are supported by the divine bounty. And will not God much more provide for his rational creatures, though they do not indulge any anxious solicitude or unbelieving care about the support of their earthly tabernacle?

Verse 27. *Which of you by taking thought can add one cubit unto his stature?*

And he shows them in verse 27 that this harassing distress, which people give themselves about the things of this life, is of no avail. Such sinful cares do not better our circumstances or increase our stature.

Many of the people of God are kept in low circumstances, but this proceeds from divine love. Had the Israelites in the wilderness cause to complain of the divine goodness that they were daily fed with manna, though they did not get a large quantity at once to lay by for future use? By keeping their circumstances low, they are kept humble, and are taught constantly to depend upon God. Their poverty is a great advantage to them, because it makes them spiritually rich. And though it be said (Proverbs 30:8) that poverty is an enemy to virtue, he will not suffer them to be pressed too much with it, for he promises to keep his people from shame (Isaiah 40:4). And if they knew the spiritual and temporal trials which others of the family in better and more affluent circumstances endure, they would not, it is very likely, in many cases at least, exchange stations with them. We should then calmly submit to providence in the disposal of our lot.

Verses 28–34. *Which of you by taking thought can add one cubit unto his stature? And why take ye thought for raiment? Consider the lilies of the field, how they grow; they toil not, neither do they spin: and yet I say unto you, That even Solomon in all his glory was not arrayed like one of these. Wherefore, if God so clothe the grass of the field, which to day is, and to morrow is cast into the oven, shall he not much more clothe you, O ye of little faith? Therefore take no thought, saying, What shall we eat? or, What shall we drink? or, Wherewithal shall we be clothed? (for after all these things do the Gentiles seek:) for your heavenly Father knoweth that ye have need of all these things. But seek ye first the kingdom of God, and his righteousness; and all these things shall be added unto you. Take therefore no thought for the morrow: for the morrow shall take thought for the things of itself. Sufficient unto the day is the evil thereof.*

The doctrine contained in these words is a caution against immoderate care and concern for the things of this life. And our Lord urges his doctrine by very strong arguments.

1. He urges his doctrine from the lilies of the field. Nothing is more beautiful or more short-lived than the lilies. They please our senses and refresh our hearts, and soothe our imagination for a few days. Mankind in all ages have been pleased with the beauties of flowers, and no wonder, for our Lord tells us that even the glory of Solomon was inferior to these beauties of the ground. But their beauty soon withers like the glory of all earthly enjoyments. They may be cut down and employed to heat the ovens. And if God arrays the grass of the field with such lustre and beauty, will he not provide the clothing that is necessary for his own people, however weak their faith in divine power and divine providence may be? He surely will.

2. Again, he tells them that it was the character of the Gentiles to seek earthly things with overanxious concern. But the children of God and the heirs of the promises should aspire after higher delights. Such as have their portion in this life alone may be taken up with the tinsel and glitter of outward things. They may seek their happiness in the gratifications of sense, and pant after white and yellow clay. Christians, however, need not be anxious about these things, for God their Father knoweth what they stand in need of, and will accordingly provide for them. They do not consider this world as their portion, and therefore a little of it serves them in their passage through the wilderness. They need not be anxious about futurity, for this life is checkered with good and evil. He informs them that they need not be anticipating evil before it comes, for when any affliction comes, it will be burden enough of itself. We need not therefore create a double burden to curse lives by premature concern and carking [distressing] care.

3. But the greatest argument of all is, if we have the one thing needful, that a competence of earthly things shall be secured to us. If we

secure the kingdom of God we shall then have enough. He that has Christ for a portion needs not add house to house and field to field. Such an addition to his happiness would be as foolish an attempt as if a man on a bright summer day should get a number of candles in order to show him more light. Instead of adding to his happiness, he only pierces himself through with many sorrows. The apostle Paul found Christ, the Pearl of great price, and his language is, 'Having food and raiment, let us therewith be content.' Demas is not content with Christ as a portion, and therefore goes over to his farm and seeks his happiness in the present world. There is but one Demas mentioned in the New Testament, but we have many. And I can appeal to yourselves whether you think the apostle Paul or Demas the happiest man now. The apostle is in heaven, but poor Demas could get none in that blessed place that would talk to him about the profits of his farm and the best methods of increasing.

Practical remarks

1. How poor is the condition of those miserable souls whose light is darkness! All their thoughts, all their desires, all their conversation is about earthly things. God has cursed them by giving them up to the desires of their own hearts. They hate the light, for the Word of God has no room within them. They have left the light, and they have, therefore, thick Egyptian darkness. The darkness is so gross that they do not see the enormity of their own conduct in the contrariety to the law of God. They see others in the broad way, and therefore foolishly think there is no harm in what they do. They are of those who rebel against the light, and though they gag the mouth of conscience, yet, like the giant said to be bound under the mountain, it sometimes makes an earthquake within them. And if they do not repent, oh, how fearful will the resurrection of conscience be! The convictions they have buried, and the opportunities they have abused, will meet them in the dark valley of the shadow of death. And though they should cry through all eternity for one of the sermons they have trampled under foot, their petition will be rejected. No saint or angel will pity them; no minister or Christian will pray

for them. When eternity will open their eyes, they will have a different view of the communion of saints from what the Devil, while they are bent upon the prosecution of their lusts, will give them now.

And now, ye deluded souls, if ye do not turn to the Lord, I shall pursue you to the very gates of that hell where you are hastening with the terrors of God. All your lusts, all your jokes, all your companions, and all your money cannot screen you from the day of wrath. In spite of all that yourselves and the master you serve can do, your consciences will bear witness that you hear the truth. The doctrines that you hear must curse or bless you to all eternity. And what an awful thought if all the pains that God and his servant are at are only ripening you for damnation. You are worse than madmen if you think that these expressions will fall to the ground. They are as firm as the pillars of heaven, and it will happen [befall] you at last, as it did to the ungodly king. When the fingers of a man's hand will write upon your consciences and pronounce your doom, your countenances will then change, your joints will be loosed, and your knees will smite one against another. And all this may happen when you are prosecuting your lusts and indulging yourselves in mirth. I have told you your danger, and if you die in your sins, your blood will be upon your own heads.

I have much greater pleasure in preaching the precious, comfortable, and refreshing truths of the gospel than in giving you the terrors of the law. I would dwell with much greater delight upon the love of Christ, the joys of heaven, and the songs of paradise than upon the lake of fire and brimstone. But, my dear friends, can anything be more awful than the doctrines of Christ himself to the wicked? Hear his very words: 'Ye serpents, ye generation of vipers, how can you escape the damnation of hell?'

I must preach the law as well as the gospel, for I will not flatter you in your sins. Scripture says, 'If a man loves the world, the love of the Father is not in him,' and if you do not love God, can you be admitted into his kingdom? Impossible! Even infidels tremble at death, and Felix trembled at terrifying doctrine. When you are sick, you call for the prayers of the Church—a proof that God is striving with you. Look up to heaven. The angels cease from their music and look down to see if you turn to God. Give joy to the angels; give joy to your minister. Give joy to Christ himself, and add more jewels to his crown.

2. From what we heard, we clearly see that the service of God and the service of the world cannot be performed by the same man. Love to God and to the world cannot predominate in the same heart. The thing is impossible. And though Christ could work miracles, he never attempted such a miracle as this. If people do not renounce the love of the world, they forfeit the love of Christ and the joys of heaven. The care of a family and provision for children are foolish excuses. We read in Luke 12:20 that God asks the foolish worldling the night he died, 'Whose shall those things be, that he had provided?' Notwithstanding the largeness of his barns and the extent of his possessions, we do not read that his great riches descended to his children. We daily see that children do not possess what their parents left. There is a curse left with them which wears away their riches as the thaw melts the snow. And how often have parents lost their own souls by loving the world better than God, and left money to their children to spend upon their lusts and teach them the way to perdition?

3. Lastly, by securing the kingdom of God, we shall have a sufficient portion of the good things of this life. The blessing of God will make our stock durable. And what a comfort to a parent in the near views of eternity when he can tell his children that what he lost is not mixed with a curse or with a groan. That he did nothing that would hinder his own salvation in providing for them, and if they follow his example, that they shall surely inherit everlasting life. Let the case of the soul be predominant, and it will moderate and sanctify every other care.

Let every Christian then come with his case and cast it upon God himself. Let him trust in the Lord and do good, and the divine promise is that he shall dwell in the land and that he shall verily be fed.

AMEN.

Matthew chapter 7: verses 1 to 12

THIS is the concluding part of our Lord's sermon upon the mount. In the words just read, he gives his hearers several precious advices, which we shall endeavour to explain, and then conclude as usual with some practical remarks.

Judging others

> Verses 1–2. *Judge not, that ye be not judged. For with what judgment ye judge, ye shall be judged: and with what measure ye mete, it shall be measured to you again.*

The judgments of God are a great depth, and we are sure they are according to truth. But in many cases we are blind and cannot properly judge of other people. We are all sinners, and we could have nothing to say, although God would strike us with the severest of his judgments. And how can we pretend to judge others when perhaps ourselves are often more guilty than those whom we judge? There are many who have been guilty of great sins, and yet a kind providence has concealed their enemies. And yet, instead of being thankful for such a mercy, they have the impudence to censure in the severest terms others who have been guilty of similar or even lesser crimes.

Our Lord found fault with those who supported the Galilaeans, whose blood Pilate mixed with their sacrifices. And the men upon whom the tower of Siloam fell, were they greater sinners than others? Judging in this way proceeds from ignorance or hardness of heart, or perhaps from both. Good King David in his worst state

96

adjudged a man to death and to fourfold restitution for taking a lamb from his neighbour. But when the charge came home to himself, he is struck dumb with accusing silence. Let the rash censurer therefore consider that if the world knew about him but a part of what his Maker does, that he would not presume to open his mouth. Besides, let us suppose that the judgments which befell our neighbour were what he richly deserved, yet they may be meant for his good, and may cure his soul of the disease of sin by leading his soul to Christ.

And if this has no effect upon the rash censurer, let him consider that the argument may come to meet him in another way. Has he self-love? Why, then, if he judges, he may be judged again. Adonizedek is judged by the top of his toes, the unclean person by the baseness of his wife or children, and the knave by having his spoils divided among the descendants of those he has robbed. And be it so that the punishment inflicted upon one neighbour or acquaintance is what he richly deserved. So was the judgment upon the Jews for their wickedness. And yet we find two prophets of the Lord finding fault with the inhumanity and want of feeling of the Edomites, in that they laughed and insulted the Jews instead of condoling with them in the day of their distress. But the judgment came round upon Edom in their turn.

Our Lord therefore cautions against indulging this censorious turn of mind, and speaking with pleasure of the misfortunes of others. Some people have a malignant pleasure in spreading and enlarging bad reports, never considering that, perhaps, their own turn will come next. At any rate, they may look for like measure when divine providence will see that their cup is full. Have people a pleasure in breaking the character of their neighbour's children? Let them reflect that a very slight cause may break and destroy the good name of their own family. They will then feel the misery they gave to others.

Verses 3–5. *And why beholdest thou the mote that is in thy brother's eye, but considerest not the beam that is in thine own eye? Or how wilt thou say to thy brother, Let me pull out the mote out of thine eye; and, behold, a beam is in thine own eye? Thou hypocrite, first cast out the beam out of thine own eye; and then shalt thou see clearly to cast out the mote out of thy brother's eye.*

Without entering critically into the simile made use of here, we may observe in general that our Lord as a public teacher made use of language just as he found it. Criticism was below his notice. He spoke to the common people, made use of their phrases, adapted himself to their ideas and capacities, and spoke so as to be understood and, therefore, to be useful.

Our Lord came from heaven to save sinners, and he clothed the sentiments of heaven with the language of men. He spoke in a way that common people and children could understand him. He didn't come to refine the language but to refine the morals of mankind. He told perishing sinners their danger, and taught them their duty in plain language. He made use of the phrases and similes that were current in the country where he taught. If he had spent his time in useless criticism upon language, his labour had been lost. Our Lord never said a useless word or made use of an improper simile, and the more we imitate, the more useful shall our doctrine be. He knew that there never was and never will be a perfect character upon this earth but himself.

The doctrine he lays down, therefore, in these few verses, is not to be ready to censure others for smaller faults when ourselves are faults all over. The royal penitent, before his conscience was thoroughly awake, saw the story of the lamb very bad, though himself was guilty of much greater crimes, which, it seems, he did not see. A great thief or a great villain can talk with impunity, forsooth, of a poor thief that steals to satisfy his hunger, but this same thief never considers how many he has defrauded and robbed, and that he lives only upon the spoils of others. He can see the mote in his poor brother's eye, but does not see the beam in his own eye.

A gentlewoman who lived in her younger days in the grossest crimes of uncleanness, when she was past childbearing, had a servant maid who carried on a courtship with a young man and gave him his dinner at her mistress' expense. For this fault, her mistress gave her all the bad names which herself deserved years before. The true way is first to forsake sin ourselves, and we can then with propriety rebuke others. But if our own step is not even in the path of morality, we shall be answered as the crab answered her mother who rebuked her father's awkward motion. She begged of her mother to show her a good example, and she would follow her.

A good advice from a bad man is heard with prejudice, if not with disdain. Advices respecting our moral conduct are but ill-received, coming even from good characters. The Baptist himself, and even the Head of the Church, when they rebuke sin, are found fault with. The one is said to have a devil, and the other is called the friend of publicans and sinners. And it often happens that very irregular people greatly exaggerate and magnify the faults of others. But until we forsake sin ourselves, we cannot with propriety give a good advice or censure the misconduct of our neighbours. A certain worldly man raised a laugh against himself by calling a young man who had views upon the ministry Demas, because he gave up the Church for a more lucrative employment.

Verse 6. *Give not that which is holy unto the dogs, neither cast ye your pearls before swine, lest they trample them under their feet, and turn again and rend you.*

The wise man justly observes that by rebuking a scorner—that is, a wicked man who ridicules religion—a person loses his pains. The scorner is an unclean animal, and will continue in his wicked course, though you show him his danger and prove your argument by reason and Scripture. The apostle desires Titus to reject a heretic after the first and second admonition. And we might only ask what profit or pleasure a man can have in disputing with a professed infidel, deist, or atheist. Such a wretch, if he be not a perfect dunce, must be conscious that himself is in the wrong.

The Jews were commanded to give the flesh of beasts that died, being torn to pieces in the field, to dogs. And as much as we can avoid it, we should not give the mysteries of our religion to profane persons. Our Lord shows the danger of it. The dog and the sow would trample pearls under their feet, because they do not know their value. Though people get the privileges of the Church, they abuse them, as these unclean animals would stamp pearls in the dung. They may do more. When the dog or sow finds that pearls are a morsel they could not feed upon, they are enraged and run upon the persons that throw them to them in order to hurt them.

To prove this, observe human life. The very next day after the habitual sinner takes the sacramental cup in his hand, he returns to his sins and gratifies his passion, and if the good Christian rebukes him, we know what language he is likely to get. Instead of laying up the precious promises, the calls, and the pearls of the gospel, he tramples them under his feet. But if he gets the husks of worldly conversation, he feeds upon them. He is then in his element. Like a certain gentlewoman upon the evening of a Communion Sabbath, who, instead of talking about the Pearl of great price, conversed about a ball. Are you shocked at their conduct? Draw near them and you shall hear greater abominations. Do you observe that group? These are a company of gentlemen farmers. They sat at the Lord's table a little ago. Go now and hear their conversation. They have exhausted the whole subject of sheep-smearing.[9] There is scarcely any disease to which that animal is subject, but they have discussed and for which they have not found a cure. If you were to talk to them about the diseases of their souls, your words would be received with a sneer. And it may be asked, if a number of professed infidels were gathered together upon the evening of a Sabbath, could they take a more effectual method to profane the Lord's Day? As to the vulgar communicants, their conversation is still more coarse and more indelicate. We may, therefore, say that there is great propriety in the doctrine of the text.

---

[9] The practice of treating a sheep's fleece with a compound of tar and grease to protect it against damp and parasites. This procedure was rendered obsolete after the introduction of sheep-dip. [RJD]

This text likewise rebukes some of the people of God. They talk sometimes about their precious experiences even before worthless people who betray them and make a bad use of what they say. And this will hurt their feelings. Though our Lord rebukes rash judgment, he clearly shows by the words just now read, that we are to make a distinction between sinners. Our advice, like the preaching of the gospel, should be general, but when we find that they are not likely to do good or to mind the sinner, we may as well forbear any advice.

Some sinners are like dogs: they bark against good advice. Holy things are lost upon them: they not only do not receive them, but they speak against them. Others are like swine: though they do not bark, they disregard what they hear and go on in a sinful course, wallowing themselves like the sow in the mire. There is danger that they may proceed further than mere contempt: they may become persecutors. There have been such characters in all ages of the Church. It is not rash judging to tell people the danger they are in when we see them going on in a sinful course, whether they take it well or ill, whether they become our enemies or not. But if we really have cause to believe they are hardened in sin at the time, we may well spare an advice. After all (2 Timothy 2:25), we should not give them up entirely, for perhaps God may give them repentance, and as we do not know those who are desperately wicked, let us even entertain some hopes of the very worst. Who can say what sovereign grace may do!

Asking, seeking, knocking

Verses 7–11. *Ask, and it shall be given you; seek, and ye shall find; knock, and it shall be opened unto you: for every one that asketh receiveth; and he that seeketh findeth; and to him that knocketh it shall be opened. Or what man is there of you, whom if his son ask bread, will he give him a stone? Or if he ask a fish, will he give him a serpent? If ye then, being evil, know how to give good gifts unto your children, how much more shall your Father which is in heaven give good things to them that ask him?*

In these verses, the Lord teaches us the duty of prayer:

1. A sense of what we need, namely, the new heart and communion with God, will make us ask.
2. A sense of what we lost, namely, the image of God, will make us seek.
3. A sense of our distance from him will make us knock at his door for mercy on our souls.

1. A sense of what we need, namely, the new heart and communion with God will make us ask. We may feel that we have an old heart, and the old heart seeks its happiness in carnal pleasures and the possession of the world and of the creature. The new heart seeks its happiness in God, and till we return to our rest in him, we cannot be happy. We find there is an emptiness in our souls, and we sometimes think that the creature would fill it up, and we ask this in our prayers. This is often denied in mercy, and though it were granted, it would not fill up the large desires of an immortal soul. The creature—all creatures, even the whole world—could not fill it up. And there will be always a want; nothing can fill it but God alone.

But the heart will not ask this happiness till it gets a new turn, and when the heart is new, it will seek communion with heaven. And this blessing is promised in the covenant of grace. God promises to write his law in our hearts. He wrote his own law on tables of stone and delivered them to Moses. And this was a type of what he does to his people. Our hearts are stony, but we should do as Moses did. He hewed him out the tables and God wrote upon them. God commands us to make ourselves new hearts. This we cannot do: we should, therefore, come with our hearts, that himself may write his laws upon them. We are constantly to plead that he would give us such a heart as will delight in God and make him our portion here and hereafter. Let us ask this crowning blessing above all things, that he would be our God.

2. A sense of what we lost, namely, the image of God, will make us seek. A person under concern for his soul will naturally be looking into his heart and watching over his life. But, alas, what can he find in his heart? Scripture informs us that we lost the divine image by our fall in Adam, and we feel in our disagreeable experience that this is the case with ourselves. And this will make us solicitous to recover our original holiness.

But, alas, all that we can do will not recover the divine image. The Scriptures inform us of the manner in which this can be effected. The Son of God by becoming man has healed our nature, and we find a fountain of holiness in him. We wish to find this in ourselves, but we must go out of ourselves to him. We are seeking what we lost, and it is to be found only in the Mediator. He is the Tree of Life, and it is his fruit alone that can cure our distempered souls.

3. A sense of our distance from him will make us knock at his door for mercy on our souls. Sin has bred enmity, but himself has made overtures of mercy, for God is in Christ reconciling a lost world to himself. But though willing to be reconciled, and though ready to give the blessing, he will convince the sinner that grace is precious, and therefore worth the asking with importunity and perseverance. He will be enquired of by the house of Israel to do it for them. People like Jacob must not only run for the blessing, but wrestle and pray for it also. And whatever their spiritual feelings may be, and whatever fears they may have of a repulse, they must continue at the gate like the poor man at the pool of Bethesda till such time as they get a gracious answer. Whatever time he comes, they are to wait, and they are not to go to any other door for help till he comes. And whatever he does with them, they must wait at the door of mercy, and still continue knocking. Whether we cry from the depths with the Psalmist, or from the belly of hell with Jonah, we are still to cry till we are heard and obtain a gracious answer. And we ask sincerely.

There is here a gracious promise that we shall receive. And as unbelief may suggest awful things as to spiritual and temporal things we may be asking, we are here informed of the contrary. Unbelief may say that instead of grace, we shall at last have awful terrors of conscience; instead of the temporal good things we have been asking, that we shall obtain either a curse or a cross. Our Lord here informs us that even a sinful earthly parent would not so use his offspring. If a son ask bread, he will not give him a stone; if he ask a fish, he will not give him a serpent; and if he ask a good thing, he will not give him what is bad. And if we ask good things—the graces of the Holy Spirit—he will surely be readier to give them than sinful earthly parents to give their offspring the things they ask of them.

Making righteousness our rule

Verse 12. *Therefore all things whatsoever ye would that men should do to you, do ye even so to them: for this is the law and the prophets.*

And if God deals with us as we would wish, we ought to deal in the same way and manner with our fellow creatures. We wish God to hear, and we should deal with men as we wish they should deal with us, for this is the law and the prophets.

Practical remarks

1. Though we are to avoid rash judgment on the one hand, we are to take heed that we do not go to the contrary extreme. We have no right to judge people, it is true, but it is a duty to censure and rebuke what is amiss. To tell sinners where a wicked course will end is not rash judging, but plain honest dealing. And if we perform this duty from love and pity to souls, it may be blessed for their good.

2. Lastly, prayer is a general duty, and we should pray for what we feel we stand in need of. Sin has made a breach upon our souls, and Christ is a healer of the breach. And this breach is the wider in proportion as we have gratified our predominant passion. In some, it may cost a long time before they receive an answer, and this is owing to the strength of their corruptions. Prayer is a commanded duty,

and though the means was unlikely, Moses was commanded to strike the rock in order to obtain water.

May God bless his Word. AMEN.

Matthew chapter 7: verses 13 to 29

IN the words just read, our Lord gives us the following doctrines. He shows the necessity of entering the strait gate and travelling the narrow way. He gives a description of false prophets and of false professors in general, and the uselessness and danger of a false profession, and concludes with a proper advice about laying a proper foundation for our religion and future hopes of happiness. After speaking upon these points, I shall conclude as usual with some practical remarks.

The way to destruction and the way to life

Verses 13–14. Enter ye in at the strait gate: for wide is the gate, and broad is the way, that leadeth to destruction, and many there be which go in thereat: because strait is the gate, and narrow is the way, which leadeth unto life, and few there be that find it.

In these words, by a strong and beautiful comparison or simile, our Lord points out to us the necessity of conversion and holiness. Regeneration or conversion is compared to a strait gate, and holiness to a narrow way. It is true they are strait and narrow to our corruption. They are strait to the wicked who have no pleasure in holiness. When persons are advanced in virtue and piety, so far is religion from being narrow that her ways are said to be the ways of pleasantness, and all her paths are peace.

But Scripture talks agreeably to the opinions and language of men. The way of holiness is hedged on each side by the law of God, but there is plenty of room in it for travellers bound for Sion. The Garden of Eden was but small in comparison to the whole globe of the earth beside. But while Adam continued in a state of innocence, there was room enough in paradise for him, and he would not seek to leave it for any other place on earth. And when we begin to recover our spiritual taste, and set our face toward that place of which Eden itself was only a type, we shall not reckon ourselves abridged of our liberty by walking in the way of holiness. Virtuous and religious characters think themselves happy in being confined within the rules of purity and moral honesty, and they have much greater happiness than sinners can have in the gratification of their lusts and passions.

But observe, where does the narrow way lead us? It brings us to everlasting life. In Scripture, every bright idea, every happy thought is expressed by life, as everything that is gloomy is expressed by death. Death is the punishment with which Adam was threatened in case of disobedience, and everlasting life in heaven was to be the reward of his obedience. And he had a type of this constantly before him in the tree of life. And this tree was a type of the tree of life, Jesus Christ, who is in the midst of the true paradise of God in heaven. We receive this life in our conversion or effectual calling, and whenever holiness shall be perfect and complete, we shall be admitted to paradise. Is it surprising, therefore, that our Lord desires us to strive to enter in at this strait gate and narrow way?

And he makes use of another strong argument to induce us: that the wide gate and broad way lead to destruction, and many find it. But few find the narrow way. They walk in the broad way because it is agreeable to the corruption of their natures. They do not find the narrow way, but it is because they do not wish to find that way. It is disagreeable and irksome to them. If they miss the way, it is owing to their wickedness and blindness and folly. The road to heaven and happiness is clearly pointed out to us in the Scriptures of truth. But however pleasant to corrupt nature the broad way is, it terminates in destruction.

We find, then, that in spiritual things it is not the surest way to follow the opinion or the example of the majority. Though hand join in hand, the wicked shall not go unpunished. The eight persons who made choice of the ark in Noah's time were in a much safer state than the many thousands who perished in the flood. And we shall be more inexcusable than these. If we perish, it is not for want of knowing our duty. It is a dangerous opinion to believe that the majority are in the right when Scripture asserts the contrary. The Word of God is true, and those who oppose it will be found liars and destroyers of those who believe them, and of their own souls also.

A tree and its fruits

Verses 15–20. *Beware of false prophets, who come to you in sheep's clothing, but inwardly they are ravening wolves. Ye shall know them by their fruits. Do men gather grapes of thorns, or figs of thistles? Even so every good tree bringeth forth good fruit; but a corrupt tree bringeth forth evil fruit. A good tree cannot bring forth evil fruit, neither can a corrupt tree bring forth good fruit. Every tree that bringeth not forth good fruit is hewn down, and cast into the fire. Wherefore by their fruits ye shall know them.*

Our Lord in these words gives us a description of false teachers and the manner in which they appear, and the marks by which they are known. Like their predecessors of old, they wear a rough garment to deceive.

It pleased God in time of old to make known his holy will to poor men who could not afford to buy fine clothes, and sometimes were very scarce of the necessaries of life. They led a mortified and austere life for the most part. But that this mean garb was not essential to the office is very clear from several parts of Scripture. Very great men were prophets, such as Abraham, Isaac, and Jacob; kings were prophets, such as David and Solomon. Some polite courtiers, such as Joseph and Daniel, had the spirit of prophecy without the garb. But as this mournful garb was one of the marks of the prophets of the Lord, false prophets wore them in order to deceive the people.

Our Lord taught by parables, and he informs us here that false prophets or teachers would assume the appearance of sheep, merely in order to devour, for that they were ravening wolves. And the apostle informs the presbyters of Ephesus to feed the flock over which the Holy Ghost had made them bishops [overseers], for after his departure, ravening wolves would rule the Church and tear the flock to pieces.

False teachers, in order to impose upon the simple, assumed the appearance of good, though their principal aim was filthy lucre. A false heart will naturally produce false doctrine. And false doctrine will bring forth bad fruit. And though it is a general truth that a bad tree will produce bad fruit, and a good tree wholesome fruit, our Lord applied this general truth to a particular purpose. Though it be true in all cases, it is more eminently so in regard to false teachers. Though a wolf were dressed in a sheep's skin, he is naturally an enemy to the sheep, and would devour it up. All good Christians are the sheep of Christ, and they naturally find pasture for their souls in his word and gospel. Now the gospel is not the doctrine of the wolf, but something else. And as the wolf knows that the true sheep can relish nothing but the true gospel, the wolf wishes to destroy that. It is true he wears the sheep's skin, and makes use of some peculiar phrases to decoy the simple and the weak. But he wishes to introduce doctrines diametrically opposite to the truth. And when these doctrines begin to take root and to bear fruit, that fruit will have the taste of wormwood and gall. Instead of feeding souls, it will poison them.

The doctrines that oppose justification by faith and the merits of Christ alone have a specious appearance. They pretend to advance good works, and seem very zealous for the interests of morality. The most virulent heathen persecutors could bear to hear the moral precepts of the gospel, but were bitter enemies to its peculiar doctrines. The false teachers in the Christian Church were actuated by this very spirit. And their genuine descendants to this very day show regard for mere moral discourses, but are enemies to the doctrine of Christ crucified, advising them to build their hopes of future happiness upon the foundation stone which God did lay in Sion. Such doctrine they oppose privately or publicly just as it suits their interest so to do. The most effectual method they take now is to preach their doctrines with bold effrontery without, however, mentioning the doctrines they wish to oppose. And if any preach the peculiar doctrines of the gospel, they are sure to hear with indifference, if not with contempt. And these prophets may be known by their fruits. These advocating morality are often known by their immoral practices. They have neither personal or family religion. Their belly is their God, and they mind earthly things.

We wish that this was only a picture of the higher and more dignified clergymen in the Romish Church. But, alas! it will apply likewise to clergymen in the Protestant Churches. And these bad fruits will appear not only in their own lives, but in the bad lives of their hearers. The thing is too glaring to require a proof. Let any person go to those parts where the peculiar doctrines of the gospel are not preached, but something else in their stead, and he will find the people dead in trespasses and sins, without any regard to religion or concern for their souls. Or if they have been once acquainted with the gospel, and now miss the preaching that gave life, they lament the loss, and long for the precious blessing.

Great is the propriety of our Lord's advice to beware of false teachers, for our everlasting happiness or misery depends upon the doctrines that we hear. The fruits of the tree of life and the apples of Sodom are very different indeed. The gospel is the life of the soul, but mere dry harangues without life or power terminate in destruction. The doctrine that does not lead souls to Jesus Christ must lead them to destruction. If the doctrine is dead, how will it put life in a soul? Dead doctrine will leave but dead souls, and dead souls at last will be buried in the pit of everlasting destruction and misery. And as it is true in particular of preachers that a rotten tree will not yield good or wholesome fruit, it is true in general of all, that every tree that does not bear good fruit will be hewn down and cast into the fire. It does not secure us from danger, as some foolish people think, that we may be free from gross sins. We must bring forth fruit to

God. And we cannot bring forth good fruit till we are first made good trees.

Let this then be our first concern, that we experience a work of grace upon our own hearts. Let us ask the influences of the Spirit, the oil from the true olive tree. He can put life in us, and we can then bear fruit; he can revive our hearts and water our branches. Whether, then, we are teachers or private Christians, let us examine what fruits we bear. If they are such as the Great Gardener will approve of, we shall have comfort and happiness hereafter.

Jesus Christ discerns false professions of faith

Verses 21–23. *Not every one that sayeth unto me, Lord, Lord, shall enter into the kingdom of heaven; but he that doeth the will of my Father which is in heaven. Many will say to me in that day, Lord, Lord, have we not prophesied in thy name? and in thy name have cast out devils? and in thy name done many wonderful works? And then will I profess unto them, I never knew you: depart from me, ye that work iniquity.*

That mere professions will never do, we learn from the words we just now heard. We all call Jesus Christ our Lord and Master, and we are so far right, for so he is. But we see that many call him Lord who do not study to do his will. We cannot plead ignorance of his will, for it is clearly revealed in the Old and New Testaments, in the law and in the gospel. We are to study universal obedience, and the law is our rule. As we can only yield universal obedience, we are called upon to believe in him who did obey the law and bore the curse universally. And when we do so, our sincere obedience is accepted, for we are justified by his obedience. We are not under the law as under a vigorous and strict covenant of works. But though we obtain pardon of sin, and a right to eternal life by complete right-eousness, and such was only the righteousness of Christ, we are made meet and fit only by our own holiness or righteousness. And this is always growing more complete, till at last it becomes perfect. And God graciously rewards our obedience and good works.

On the other hand, he is offended when we offer him a mere profession instead of substantial holiness. That we may not deceive ourselves, we are here told that people may make a splendid profession and yet be the slaves of their own lusts and passions. Though people could cast out devils and do other wonderful works, it would avail them nothing if Christ will deny them at last, because they are the workers of iniquity. We are to obey God's revealed will, believe in Christ, and deny all ungodliness and worldly lusts. Bare leaves will not please him; we must have fruit, and for this purpose we must be trees of his own planting.

The parable of houses built on different foundations

Verses 24–27. *Therefore, whosoever heareth these sayings of mine, and doeth them, I will liken him unto a wise man, who built his house upon a rock: and the rain descended, and the floods came, and the winds blew, and beat upon that house; and it fell not: for it was founded upon a rock. And every one that heareth these sayings of mine, and doeth them not, shall be likened unto a foolish man, who built his house upon the sand: and the rain descended, and the floods came, and the winds blew, and beat upon that house; and it fell: and great was the fall of it.*

Our Lord, in the conclusion of his sermon upon the mount, advises his hearers to build upon a proper foundation. There are many false and sandy foundations which the Scripture points out to us, but it only mentions one sure foundation upon which it is safe to build. No name is given under heaven by which we can be saved but the name of Jesus of Nazareth. This is the stone which God hath laid in Zion. This is a tried stone, and we may safely build upon it, for it is firm as the rock. Christ is the Rock of Ages, upon whom we may safely build for eternity. In old times it was usual for people to build their fortresses and strongholds on rock. A fortress upon a rock, especially when there was a well of water, had every advantage which could be devised. It is a good foundation, it is difficult of access for an enemy, and can very easily annoy the besiegers. And in a spiritual view, Christ is all this to his people. He is the Rock, his work is perfect, his righteousness is complete, and therefore well may the inhabitant of the Rock sing.

But those who build upon Christ have their enemies here compared to rains and floods and winds. But they make no impression upon a building fixed upon a rock. People will meet with trials and temptations, whether they be Christians or not, whether they build their house upon the rock or upon the sand. Some build upon superficial morality and imaginary self-righteousness, some build upon imaginary faith without any morality at all, and some upon a profession of religion and a slight attendance upon the means. But whatever sandy foundation they build upon, the storms and tempests will beat down the house. Some, like the foolish woman, break it down themselves (Proverbs 14:1). They do not give the devil the trouble to batter it with his temptations; they beat it down to his hand. If they had a kind of appearance of religion, they act the life of it, and sap the foundation by the indulgence of their lusts and the deceitfulness of riches. These floods break down the building, and when death comes, the flood carries the building away.

But the man who builds upon a Rock has made Christ his portion, and therefore neither the lust of the eye, nor the lust of the flesh, nor the pride of life draw away his heart from God. Neither the allurements of the world nor the evil example of company make him flinch from his duty. The Scripture is his rule, and he follows his Saviour. Like Noah and Daniel and Job, he can be singular in his opinions and in his practices, and his Rock will support him. Nothing can shake him, and when death arrives, though he had his failings as he did his duty, his Lord and Master saw the integrity of his heart, and will therefore receive him into his kingdom. His Judge is his Friend, and his complete obedience is his plea at the judgment seat. A good life is the forerunner of a happy death. Let it, however, be observed that there can be no good life but what derives its support from Jesus Christ.

The authority of Christ's teaching

Verses 28–29. And it came to pass, when Jesus had ended these say-ings, the people were astonished at his doctrine: for he taught them as one having authority, and not as the scribes.

This is the concluding part of our Lord's sermon upon the mount. It struck the hearers with surprise. It was accompanied with power. It was not like the cold, dead, dry discourses of the scribes. And sermons which have a little of the Spirit of Christ in them have in proportion some of his power accompanying the doctrine. They leave marks upon the consciences of the hearers which render them inexcusable.

Practical remarks

1. If we have entered the strait gate, we surely walk in the narrow way. To pretend to the one without the other is but delusion and self-deceit. And it is still greater delusion to suppose that we can possess the joys of heaven without the one or the other. Now this delusion is very common. Many persons would be very uneasy if their children died without baptism, and if themselves are kept from the Lord's Table who never had searching thoughts lest themselves would die without grace. Our Lord said, 'Strive to enter in at the strait gate,' but we do not read, 'Strive to go to the Lord's Table.' The present set of Christians make a great struggle to go to the Lord's Table who never give themselves any trouble to enter the strait gate. Some snatch the token out of the minister's hand. The true Christian is often afraid to take a token at all.

2. If we have fears about the reality on entering the strait gate, let us examine the cause. Real Christians are sometimes afraid about their state. Their hearts condemn them for what they have done, and though they have forsaken sin long ago, and struggle and pray against it, yet as they find the motions of sin, they are full of doubts. The fighting Christian, however, is safer than the sleeping Christian.

As to many hearers, doubting is the best that they can do. They are too strong in the kind of faith they have. Confidence, while persons live in the slavery of sin or in the friendship of the world, is a suspicious thing. When Samson put his head upon the knee of Delilah, notwithstanding his presumption that he would go and shake himself, he fell into the hands of his enemies and lost his eyes to the bargain.

3. Lastly, have we each such a foundation for our religion as is likely to weather the storm? Some begin seemingly well, but they do not count the cost. Some people that are married for a short time are full of stark love and kindness. But as the passion was not founded in rational affection and the fear of God, it often degenerates into coldness and even sometimes into hatred. In like manner, the love of many to religion is like the love of some to women whom they believed had a large portion [share of an estate]. When he finds that he was disappointed, the love that he pretended to have will soon die. When people do not find satisfaction in religion because it cannot live with sin, they return back again to the world and to their lusts. The young ruler would follow Christ, and Demas would follow Paul, if they got a large farm in addition to what they had, but when they felt disappointed in their hopes, they make shipwreck of faith, and goodness ceases.

If, assisted by the influence of the Holy Spirit, you have delivered your souls to Christ, you have built your house upon the Rock, and your house will stand. But if your house is upon the sand, and you are still destitute of true faith and the influences of the Holy Spirit producing holiness and good works, your case is dangerous. Are you so far deluded as to suppose that taking the sacrament while you remain strangers to Christ will bring your souls to heaven? Himself informs you of your delusion and danger. Unless Satan had deluded you, you might easily find that your religion is unsound. When the work of God is in a neighbouring parish, your souls are so dead that you stay at home weeding your potatoes when you should be at the mount of ordinances in order to get your lusts subdued and your pardon sealed. The trifling things that keep you from Christ will hereafter make you weep. Rouse yourselves, then; rise from your sins; begin just now; begin anew, and build your house upon the Rock.

May God bless his Word. AMEN.

Matthew chapter 8: verses 1 to 17

WE read in the book of Exodus (7:9) that when Pharaoh, the king of Egypt, demanded a miracle as a proof of the divine mission of Moses, that he was empowered to work such astonishing works as struck Pharaoh and the Egyptians with terror and dismay. Now, Moses was a type of the great Prophet who was to come into the world. He was to be like Moses in many things, more especially in the splendour of his miracles. Accordingly, when our Lord began to preach, he gave full proof of his heavenly mission by a continued series of the most salutary and beneficial miracles. The works recorded in this very chapter prove to us beyond contradiction that he was the Son of God with power. The first miracles of Moses were turning his rod into a serpent and the water into blood. The first miracle of Christ was turning water into wine.

We shall speak a little upon this precious portion of Scripture, and conclude, as usual, with some practical remarks.

The cleansing of a leper

Verses 1–4. *When he was come down from the mountain, great multitudes followed him. And, behold, there came a leper and worshipped him, saying, Lord, if thou wilt, thou canst make me clean. And Jesus put forth his hand, and touched him, saying, I will; be thou clean. And immediately his leprosy was cleansed. And Jesus saith unto him, See thou tell no man; but go thy way, shew thyself to the priest, and offer the gift that Moses commanded, for a testimony unto them.*

The leprosy was a very loathsome disease, and more particularly so in warm climates. In many cases it was perfectly incurable. The miserable victims of the disease were in very distressed circumstances. They were obliged to sequestrate themselves from society, and were avoided by their nearest and dearest friends. As the disease was very loathsome, it would appear that it was likewise very infectious. And in this respect, it was a true emblem of sin. That spiritual malady excludes people from the presence of God and the society of the saints. A person labouring under this disease made application to our Lord immediately after his descent from the mount. Though our Lord veiled his divinity, it sometimes, nay, oftentimes, broke forth through his humanity in the glorious works he performed. The leper worshipped him, and this he did not refuse, for it was his essential right. He thought it no robbery to be equal with God. Though he did not appear with that outward glory which he showed in the Shechinah and in the pillar of cloud and fire, yet he showed as much of it as drew the attention of mankind. Numbers from the neighbouring countries flocked after him, and were cured of their several diseases.

Among the rest, a leper presented himself before him. And if we observe his language, it is such as will arise in the heart of the sinner who gets a view of the plague and leprosy of his heart and life. The poor leper was nauseous in his own sight, and he might probably think that his very appearance would offend the eyes of the Saviour, and accordingly he had some doubts in the willingness of the Saviour to cure him. And how often have we doubtful thoughts, either of his goodwill, or of his ability, or of both? And this arises from the nature and malignity of our disease.

But behold the event. He had compassion upon him, raised his hand and cured him immediately. And from this circumstance we may see that no disease, however malignant, can stand before the touch of Christ. He cured him instantaneously, and thus showed his divine power. His cures were not partial, for he perfectly healed him. How soon the leper was healed, our Lord desired him to conceal the cure for the time. Our Lord commanded some to conceal for a time the benefit they received, and he commanded the demoniac that was cured to publish his cure abroad. He was best judge of what was for his own glory and the good of souls.

What may be a duty in one man may be a sin in another, according to the circumstances in which they may be placed. In general, it is a duty upon every Christian to pray privately in his closet. But it was Daniel's duty to show publicly that he prayed to the God of heaven. Some persons whom our Lord commanded to conceal his miracles sinned by their disobedience. He surely meant to cure some wrong bent in their minds by giving them such injunctions. It is the sinful infirmity of some that they can conceal nothing they hear. And this might be the sin of the persons mentioned in the gospel. It is the credit of a man and of a Christian to conceal a thing delivered to him under the seal of secrecy. If he tells the secret, he ought to be avoided by every honest man. A person in anguish of spirit for his sins may tell his case to a man he looks upon as a Christian. How, then, will it wring his soul with distress if he hears his secret has been divulged? The person that can be capable of such breach of trust is guilty of a crime for which I have no name. When he breaks a trust, he generally tells a lie, and no man should trust him hereafter.

But though he desires him to conceal his cure for the time from the public, he desires him to go and tell it to the priest, and to offer his gift according to the law of Moses. And this was to be a testimony to them. Our Lord performed several such cures. And this evidence of the divine mission of our Lord and Saviour would come with irresistible force upon the consciences of the priests. They could not but confess the divine power of the Saviour, and thus they became his followers. And if they resisted the remonstrances of their own consciences, they were self-condemned. In either case, the offering of the leper served for a testimony. In like manner, every sinner that is converted is an evidence of the truth of Scripture. It proves the truth of Scripture to his own soul, for conversion is the greatest of all miracles mentioned in the gospel. If the gospel converts a man, he has the same proof of its divinity which the leper had.

The centurion's faith

Verses 5–13. *And when Jesus was entered into Capernaum, there came unto him a centurion, beseeching him, and saying, Lord, my servant lieth at home sick of the palsy, grievously tormented. And Jesus saith unto him, I will come and heal him. The centurion answered and said, Lord, I am not worthy that thou shouldest come under my roof: but speak the word only, and my servant shall be healed. For I am a man under authority, having soldiers under me: and I say to this man, Go, and he goeth; and to another, Come, and he cometh; and to my servant, Do this, and he doeth it. When Jesus heard it, he marvelled, and said to them that followed, Verily I say unto you, I have not found so great faith, no, not in Israel. And I say unto you, That many shall come from the east and west, and shall sit down with Abraham, and Isaac, and Jacob, in the kingdom of heaven. But the children of the kingdom shall be cast out into outer darkness: there shall be weeping and gnashing of teeth. And Jesus said unto the centurion, Go thy way; and as thou hast believed, so be it done unto thee. And his servant was healed in the selfsame hour.*

We have here the remarkable history of the centurion. Some years before this time, Judaea was reduced into a Roman province. And though the Jews were in a state of servitude, some of their rulers used them with humanity. The centurion here was a man of an excellent character. And though in the former part of his life he seems to have been an idolater, it would appear from what we read here about him that he had read the Scriptures of the Old Testament, and that he had correct sentiments of the Messiah whom the Jews expected. It is said of him that he loved the nation of the Jews and had built them a synagogue. At any rate, he made good use of the light he had, and this prepared him to receive the gospel. He had heard about Christ, and it would seem not only that he looked upon him as a great man, but that he looked upon him to be something more than man from the manner in which he addressed him.

The centurion's servant was sick of a palsy, and in great torment with his sickness. He, therefore, sent word to our Lord to come and heal him. When our Lord consented to come and heal the servant, the centurion acknowledged with humility his own unworthiness that Christ would come under his roof. He believed that Christ could as easily cure him with a word of his power as it was for him, who had some little authority in the Roman army, to command one of the soldiers or servants to do such or such a thing. The faith of the centurion struck our Lord with wonder, and he acknowledged that he did not find such faith, not even in Israel. The visible Church at that time, from Dan even to Beersheba, or at any rate the kingdom of the ten tribes, did not produce such an instance as the Roman centurion.

Upon this, our Lord observed that he was to collect a Church from the four corners of the earth, who were to be partakers of the privileges enjoyed by the great ancestors of the Jewish nation. And that the Jews themselves, who are here called the children of the kingdom, were to be excluded. They were to be cast into outer darkness, where was weeping, wailing, and gnashing of teeth. They had a foretaste of that awful state for upwards of seventeen centuries. At this very time, they are in the case emphatically described by the prophet (Isaiah 8:21): And they shall pass through it, hardly bestead and hungry: and it shall come to pass, that when they shall be hungry, they shall fret themselves, and curse their king and their God, and look upward.'

In the misery and straitness the Jews experience in their own country, instead of being humbled for their national sin of crucifying the Son of God, their custom is to curse and blaspheme the Lord Jesus Christ. The awfulness of their rejection and thick spiritual darkness is an emblem of the place of torment. They are excluded from the light of heaven and the comfort of grace. It is likely that the reprobate shall be on the outside of the creation, where they shall not enjoy any kind of light.

Let those, then, who reject and despise the gospel consider the strength of this awful argument. The day is coming when the bodily organ called the eye will not yield them light. And if their souls shall then be destitute of the light of grace, what can they expect but that

121

they shall deplore with unavailing sorrow their own misery for ever. Their state shall then be like the unhappy gentleman upon the bed of death, who acknowledged it would be a relief to him if the flames of hell would hide him from the presence of God. And we may learn from Scripture that the presence of God hereafter will frighten the wicked more than the flames that will consume and destroy the world around them. Alas, what pleasure can their feasting, their music, and their dancing afford the wicked in that day?

After our Lord had given the awful doctrine to the wicked, he turns with comfort to the centurion, and assured him that his prayer was answered, for his servant was healed in the selfsame hour. From these words, we see the great benefit and blessing of faith. The faith of God's people is serviceable, not only to themselves, but also to others, for 'the effectual fervent prayer of a righteous man availeth much'. And why are such instances recorded in holy Scripture but to encourage the faithful in all ages to be assiduous and persevering in prayer?

The centurion was heard, and so shall we, in proportion to our faith. And if our Lord was willing to hear his people when praying for a cure to bodily diseases, how much more willing is he to lend a gracious ear to their prayers when they pray for a cure to the spiritual diseases of sinners? Stephen prayed for his persecutors, and the next thing we hear is the conversion of Paul. And such spiritual miracles we are encouraged to expect in every age of the Church. And blessed be God, we now and then see such cures.

Is there any here of the people of God who has any near relations or friends sick of a spiritual palsy? Is he unable and unwilling to turn to God and serve him? Is he a glutton or a drunkard, or a Sabbath-breaker? Yet do not despair. Go and lay his case before your Saviour with very great humility. You have heard that the graceless children of godly parents have been converted. And why would you not hope that God may cast an eye of pity and sympathy upon your wicked child also? Go and try.

Healing Peter's mother-in-law

Verses 14–15. And when Jesus was come into Peter's house, he saw his wife's mother laid, and sick of a fever. And he touched her hand, and the fever left her: and she arose and ministered unto them.

We read in the beginning of the chapter that our Lord cured a loathsome disease, the leprosy, and that he cured the palsy, a disease that weakens the body and renders a person unfit for the duties of his calling. He now cures Peter's mother-in-law of a fever. And sin is like a complication of diseases, but our Lord cured all manner of diseases. He did so instantaneously, and this was different from what a physician could do. We know that after persons cool, and are upon the mending-hand, it takes them some time before they fully recover. But this woman recovers all at once, and is able to conduct the ordinary business of the house. And these instances should encourage us to pray to our Lord for a cure, whether we look upon our sin as a leprosy, a palsy, or a fever, or a complication of the three. A touch or a word can cure us. He cured the centurion's servant with a word, because the centurion had great faith.

Healing many

Verses 16–17. When the even was come, they brought unto him many that were possessed with devils: and he cast out the spirits with his word, and healed all that were sick: that it might be fulfilled which was spoken by Esaias the prophet, saying, Himself took our infirmities, and bare our sicknesses.

We learn from pagan writers that the power of Satan was very great in the heathen world. He had the impudence to get temples erected for himself and for other unclean spirits, his followers. And they gave answers that astonished them to their poor, deluded votaries. And Scripture informs us that they took violent possession of the souls and bodies of several miserable objects whom they greatly distressed. But our Lord cured them, and cast out the devils with a word.

They came with these objects at an unseasonable hour, as the sun was setting. Some think that it was the Sabbath day, and that it was not over till the sunset, and then another day began in the evening. But, however unseasonable the hour, our Lord did not refuse to cure those who were brought to him. And is not this encouragement to us to go to our Saviour, even when the sun is setting? We should not despair of old sinners or of great sinners. Even persons possessed with devils are cured. And we see some people furiously bent upon the prosecution of their lusts. The language of hell is in their mouth, and they seem to strive who will serve the world and the devil most. As if God was like the dumb idols of the heathen: they do not worship him in their families, and they sin as if they were not to give any account hereafter. And some sinners seem as if they bid defiance to heaven. The Sabbath is their day for bargaining, for journeying, for visiting, and feasting. These desperate sinners are very near the curse mentioned in Isaiah 22:14. The devil has got full possession of them, and yet we should not despair of God's mercy. Jesus Christ cast out devils. And who knows but he may reserve mercy for such characters, though their case is very desperate indeed.

It is likewise said that our Lord healed any that were sick, and this was an accomplishment of a prophecy of Esaias concerning him, namely, Isaiah 53:4: 'Himself took our infirmities, and bare our sicknesses.' Now, he did this in two respects. First, he bore our sins, and sin is the cause of every trouble and affliction that can befall us. He was a man of sorrows, and acquainted with grief, and his life all along was a suffering life. His sufferings were necessary from the cradle to the cross. Second, again, he bore the sickness of the people by the trouble he was at in curing them. He felt as a man, and it must be a prodigious burden to him, the healing of so many nauseous and awful diseases. This must have been a burden to him, as he was a man, and here we are told he bare the burden of our infirmities and sicknesses. However much fatigued he may have been by preaching and curing diseases, no sooner did new objects present themselves but he immediately waited on them without murmuring, and cured them of their diseases.

Practical remarks

1. The miracles of Christ are one proof of the divinity of the gospel.

It was prophesied of him (Isaiah 35:5–6): 'Then the eyes of the blind shall be opened, and the ears of the deaf shall be unstopped. Then shall the lame man leap as an hart, and the tongue of the dumb sing.' We know that these happy effects were produced by the gospel. And thus we have a double proof of the truth of the gospel prophecy and miracle. And if we wish for the greatest proof of all, let us earnestly pray for that. He promises the new heart, and when this is accomplished, our eyes shall see spiritually and truly that Christ is the Pearl of Great Price. Our ears shall hear his voice, and our feet shall cheerfully run the way of his commandments. Let us ask this precious faith.

2. We have seen the efficacy of faith in procuring blessings for others, and this should induce us to pray for ourselves.

Though Scripture does not encourage us to look for miraculous cures for our bodies, it encourages us to pray for a cure to the spiritual maladies of our souls. And though we should feel doubts of his goodwill or ability to save, as the poor leper or blind persons did, yet let us come with our sinful doubtings, that he may remove them, and let us throw ourselves at the feet of our Saviour, that he may cure us of all our diseases.

3. Lastly, it is great encouragement to us that he has cured others, and he can heal us also.

We are surrounded with a cloud of witnesses. The gospel assures us that he has cured many of their diseases. And every age of the Church informs us that he has sanctified and saved great sinners. And he is calling upon us to believe. It animated a poor blind man when it was said to him, 'Be of good comfort, rise; he calleth thee' (Mark 10:49). Let us, then, imitate the blind man by casting away the garment of unbelief and the darling sin, and let us rise and come to Jesus Christ.

May God bless his Word to our souls. AMEN.

Matthew chapter 8: verses 18 to 34

I PROCEED to explain the rest of the chapter.

The cost of following Jesus

Verses 18–20. *Now when Jesus saw great multitudes about him, he gave commandment to depart unto the other side. And a certain scribe came, and said unto him, Master, I will follow thee whithersoever thou goest. And Jesus saith unto him, The foxes have holes, and the birds of the air have nests; but the Son of man hath not where to lay his head.*

The splendour of his miracles and the power of his doctrine brought many after our Saviour. We are, however, here informed that when he saw great multitudes about him, that he gave commandment to depart unto the other side. This, at first sight, might seem a little strange. The business of our Lord [coming] into the world was to save lost sinners, and to do good to the souls and bodies of men. And one would think when he saw a vast crowd gathered round him, that he had a great field for doing good. Instead, however, of waiting to preach to them, he left them abruptly, and went to the other side of the lake. Mark observes it was in the evening (Mark 4:35). But he knew where his duty lay at the time. He said once to Peter, 'What I do thou knowest not now; but thou shalt know hereafter.' And this is the language of every dispensation of providence which we do not comprehend at the time.

Our Lord saw further than men did. There were two miserable objects on the other side that were possessed with devils. To heal them immediately was the first and the great duty. And as to the multitude whom he left behind, they suffered no loss, for their desire after his heavenly doctrine was rather increased than diminished by his leaving them for a short time. And though there may be delay in the answer to our prayer, we suffer nothing by the delay. God will come to us, time enough. There are others of his people that stand more in need. If we saw a house on fire, we might leave the duties of public worship and give our help. Such was the state of the possessed.

Meantime, a certain scribe accosted our Lord with an offer of his services. Our Lord, who saw his motives, answered him according to what was in his heart. The current doctrine at that time was that the Messiah was to be a great worldly conqueror. It was believed by their public teachers that he was to bring the world under subjection to his countrymen, the Jews. Full of these carnal ideas, this man applied to our Lord and told him he would follow him. And many would still follow him if they thought he would make them rich and powerful. But he who came to enlighten mankind and make known to them the divine will would not suffer him for a moment to labour under such a mistake. He told him at once that he need not expect posts and pensions from him—that as his kingdom was not of this world, he did not promise his followers riches or honours in the world. Himself was a poor and suffering Saviour. The foxes had holes, and the birds of the air had nests, but the Son of man had not where to lay his head. If they did not, therefore, wait with patience till he introduced them into the kingdom he promised his followers, it was in vain for them to follow him, expecting a kingdom of earthly delights.

And this may teach us one essential duty and truth. It is this: that we should weigh what we are doing before we take up a profession or promise that we shall follow the Saviour. This same scribe blindly promised to follow him. And how many foolishly do so to this day. But when the trial comes and the old lusts and love of the world begin to solicit attention, they begin to repent of what they promised. They break their promises and tell lies. They grudge the Saviour the self-denial and attendance of all the means of grace which their salvation requires at their hands. When he heard what he had to expect, he left his religion there, for anything that appears in the gospel concerning him. Alas! what an enemy to the soul is the allurement of riches. There are many such instances: there are many professors of this man's spirit.

Verses 21–22. *And another of his disciples said unto him, Lord, suffer me first to go and bury my father. But Jesus said unto him, Follow me; and let the dead bury their dead.*

The care of the soul is the first duty, and to this we should attend above all things. At first view, we would naturally think that what this man asked was a duty which the very light of nature would dictate to him, namely, to bury his father. But we find our Lord forbade him, and surely he saw danger to the man's soul, else he would not give such a command. Our Lord saw farther than man could do, and therefore he gave him the necessary caution. He knew the character and sentiments of those who would meet him at the burial, the language they would have, and the arguments they would use. And he saw the weakness of the man's mind to resist such temptation, and therefore forbade him to go.

And this part of our Lord's doctrine may teach us this necessary duty, that when anything whatever is likely to prove a snare to our souls, we ought to avoid the snare and the temptation (Leviticus 21:10). And if persons venture beyond their strength, it is just that they would be permitted to fall. Our corrupt nature is ready like a tinder-box to take fire at the slightest temptation, and we should therefore avoid great temptation, and especially if it has a strong fleshly argument to support it. If a rich man of very bad practices solicits the beautiful daughter of a poor man to engage in his service, telling her that if she does so, he will take care of her poor, old, weak parents, the temptation is strong. But when her godly relation, who sees the snare which she did not suspect, tells her not to go upon any account, but to lean her old parents on the care of that kind providence who hitherto took care of them, she takes his wholesome advice and saves her soul. Some such danger our Lord saw, and warned his disciples.

Jesus calms a storm

Verses 23–27. *And when he was entered into a ship, his disciples followed him. And, behold, there arose a great tempest in the sea, insomuch that the ship was covered with the waves: but he was asleep. And his disciples came to him, and awoke him, saying, Lord, save us: we perish. And he saith unto them, Why are ye fearful, O ye of little faith? Then he arose, and rebuked the winds and the sea; and there was a great calm. But the men marvelled, saying, What manner of man is this, that even the winds and the sea obey him!*

Since our Lord appeared in a public character as the teacher sent from God and the Saviour of the world, there is scarcely a step he takes but is attended with some wonderful or good thing. When he entered the ship, some of his disciples followed him, and we find that such of his disciples as follow him in the most difficult duties see more of his wonders, though they meet with greater trials. No sooner do they enter the ship than a great storm arises. If we venture our all upon Christ, our main interest will be safe and secure. But storms and tempests may arise, and seem to endanger everything. And what is very remarkable, our Lord acts as if he were without any concern about them. He was asleep, and did not seem to know the trouble his poor disciples were in. But his providence watched over them. And his Church has been often in a similar situation. His Church has been often overwhelmed with the waves, and her Lord as if he had been fast asleep. And here one cannot help being a little angry at the disciples. Why are they afraid, and Christ so very near them in the vessel? Alas, we are as often to blame for such unbelief! As he is God, he is always near us in trouble, and he never slumbers nor sleeps, but how often does unbelief sink us as if he never did anything for us! But the disciples were perfectly right in applying to him alone.

And here we may observe that, however high the wind, however boisterous the waves were, the ship in which our Lord was could not sink, but came safe to land. And in a spiritual view, this will happen to all his people. He has promised and engaged to his Father to bring them all safe to port. It is said the captain of the vessel, in which the Doge of Venice goes to be married to the sea, gives such a promise about his vessel and crew. However foolish the promise in the one case may be, it is certain that our Lord Jesus Christ is able to save to the uttermost all that come to God through him, for he ever liveth to make intercession for them. And when they came safe to land, well might they all say, 'What kind of man is this, that even the winds and the sea obey him!'

And when our Lord brings his people safe to heaven, well may they say, 'What kind of man is this?' He is the great man—the God-man—whom the redeemed shall celebrate with songs of praise through all eternity. How shall they adore him with gratitude and love for the great work of redemption and the salvation of their souls for ever!

Another observation arising from the words is this. Though our Lord was asleep, the disciples were awake. And while the watchmen in Israel are awake upon the walls of Zion in the night, and while the people of God pray, the Church, however oppressed, cannot sink. Though our unbelieving fears might point out the Saviour as if he were asleep, let us cry to him to help, heal, and save. It is the complaint of the Church of old that he was asleep. And when he has this appearance in his providence, the business of faith and prayer is to awaken him. And when he awakens, he will arise, he will strike his enemies and help his friends.

Jesus heals two men with demons

Verses 28–34. *And when he was come to the other side into the country of the Gergesenes, there met him two possessed with devils, coming out of the tombs, exceeding fierce, so that no man might pass by that way. And, behold, they cried out, saying, What have we to do with thee, Jesus, thou Son of God? art thou come hither to torment us before the time? And there was a good way off from them an herd of many swine feeding. So the devils besought him, saying, If thou cast us out, suffer us to go away*

131

into the herd of swine. And he said unto them, Go. And when they were
come out, they went into the herd of swine: and, behold, the whole herd
of swine ran violently down a steep place into the sea, and perished in the
waters. And they that kept them fled, and went their ways into the city,
and told every thing, and what was befallen to the possessed of the devils.
And, behold, the whole city came out to meet Jesus: and when they saw
him, they besought him that he would depart out of their coasts.

The place where this miracle was wrought was in the neighbourhood of the two cities, Gadara and Gergesa. This miracle accounts
for the haste our Lord was in to cross the lake. As to the other miracles we read of, it may be said that our Lord was solicited to perform them. But in the present case, he was moved only by his free
and sovereign grace.

It may be said that many are converted after many prayers are put
up to heaven in their behalf. And this has happened to the wicked
children of good men. But others have been converted who were
the children of the wicked, and themselves mere devils incarnate.
Perhaps none ever prayed for them, and yet sovereign grace plucked
them like brands out of the fire. They could not and would not come
to Christ, but he came to them.

Such was the case of the poor demoniacs of Gadara or Gergesa.
They were objects of terror in their dwelling in the tombs. But Jesus
knew where they were, and pitied them. The blind men put themselves in his way, but he himself went the way of the poor demoniacs
to meet them. He meets some of his elect people in the use of the
means of grace. But others he saves by his sovereign mercy. He is
found of them that sought him not, and such was the case here.

The devils had taken strong possession of them, and were very
unwilling to leave their habitations. When the Saviour came, the
devils trembled and suspected, and asked if he came to destroy them
before the time. But, understanding their fate and that they were to
be expelled, rather than be without anything, they ask permission to
enter into the swine. Permission is granted them to punish the covetousness of their greedy owners. If they were heathens, they

deserved this for ridiculing the law of God and keeping swine. If they were apostate Jews, they deserved it still more, for they knew the sow was an unclean creature and not fit for food, though greed made them feed swine to make profit of them among the neighbouring nations.

The design of all the miracles of Christ was to do good to the souls and bodies of men. The cure of the poor demoniacs and the story of the swine must have struck all that heard it. And, however petrified with the love of the world the owners of the swine were, their consciences must have told them that they got what they deserved. And whatever stroke wicked men get for the punishment of their sins, whether they acknowledge it or not, something within them must whisper to them that this is but an earnest of more, unless they repent.

But some have an incorrigible spirit. Instead of turning to God, the men of the city beg of the Saviour that he would leave their coasts. And this is the language of the hearts of many covetous men to this day. It would give them pleasure if the places of worship and kirkyards were folds for sheep, and that there were no faithful teachers to terrify their consciences for their sins.

The unhappy Gadarenes or Gergesenes (Luke 8:37) beg of the Saviour to leave their coasts. Their unhappy prayer was granted. How many Gadarene or Gergesene prayers are this day in Scotland? And God is granting in judgment an answer to such prayers. There were many townships in the Highlands of Scotland where the voice of prayer was heard, where we see nothing but sheep. Christ has left the place at their desire. But now it may be asked, What did the Gadarenes gain by parting with Christ? They turned off [dismissed] Christ, and they also lost their swine. The profit they make by substituting the bleating of sheep for the sound of prayer will have the fate of the swine of the Gadarenes. Such profit will perish in the waters. Though people do not believe the Word of God, they must believe their eyes and their ears.

In a certain district of praying people in Scotland, a certain man turned them adrift, and it is well known that he died a beggar and a fool (Jeremiah 17:11 and Luke 12:20), and this verifies both the Old and the New Testament. And if persons had not been hardened by the devil and by the love of the world, they would be afraid to turn poor families adrift. The rising generation will see the history of the Gadarene swine awfully verified. The profit made at the expense of poor families shall last but short, and run down headlong, and be drowned in the waters.

Whatever profit is made by sacrilege and oppression will have a bad end. The Gadarenes might remember the day they bade farewell to Christ. And worldlings will remember with terror the day they bought the groans of the poor, and brought the curse of God into their families. It would appear that God raised them up as he raised Pharaoh, that the justice of God might be seen in their punishment. Their money shall perish, and their memory shall rot.

Practical remarks

1. We see the danger of a superficial profession. Many promise very fair, like the scribes, because they do not know their own hearts. They are strangers to the strength of their corruptions, and still more to the nature of true religion. No wonder though such turn their backs upon Christ and his service. Let us then examine our motives, and see if we have a heart for his work.

2. Again, we see the danger that people may sometimes be in of being led into sin under the appearance of duty. The man that wished to bury his father thought he was doing his duty. Christ saw otherwise. And this shows us the necessity of prayer, watchfulness, and self-diffidence. We must look up for direction in everything, great or small. Have we delivered ourselves and our interest, temporal and spiritual, to Christ? If so, whatever may be the appearance of providence, we are secure. The ship Christ was in was as safe when covered with the waves as when it came to shore. In the cold, piercing month of December, we believe that we shall soon experi-

ence the warm and pleasant breezes of spring. Such is the faith of the Christian.

3. Matthew calls this the country of the Gergesenes; Mark and Luke, the country of the Gadarenes. It was the same country the three evangelists meant, but it was in the neighbourhood of the cities of Gadara and Gergesa. And it seems that the whole district, city and country, solicit Christ to leave their coasts. How awful, how ominous their prayers! What a judgment upon them to grant their request! And here we may see what are the sins people indulge when they wish for the removal of the gospel. Mere love of the world, when people, like the swine of the Gadarenes, can relish nothing but the trash of this world, and cannot endure to entertain any serious thought about eternity. Security in the kind of happiness they enjoy, as if it was to last for many years, like the fool mentioned in Luke 12:19. Sensuality, also much indulgence of bodily pleasures (Job 21:11–13, and Isaiah 22:12–14).

4. Lastly, a dumb kind of despair (Ezekiel 33:10). They have gone on in a course of sin, and, therefore, now think it vain to repent and turn to God. Like the devils, they are afraid the gospel would torment them before the time. They love their swinish lusts better than Christ.

May God bless his Word. AMEN.

Matthew chapter 9: verses 1 to 38

THE gospel is always attended with power, less or more, to this day. Where it is believed, it is sure to do good to the souls and bodies of men. Though we have no ground to expect bodily miracles, we may always look for power to heal cuts and to cure their distempers. And we are sure that if people lived up to the rules of the gospel, it would prevent many bodily diseases, and make our lives easy and comfortable. Serenity of mind, contentment with our lot, and peace of conscience proceeding from the love of God in Jesus Christ would conduce to our health and long life. And surely this is one of the blessings of the gospel.

I proceed, then, in the usual manner to explain the words, and conclude with some practical remarks in the way of improvement.

Christ heals the man sick of the palsy

Verse 1. *And he entered into a ship, and passed over, and came into his own city.*

In consequence of the awful request of the Gadarenes, who loved their swine better than the gospel, he left them in a deplorable condition. How dreadful the case to be deprived of Christ and of the world at the same time. This is one of the bitter fruits of despising the gospel.

'He came to his own city.' We read in the 4th chapter of Luke of the usage he met with from the people of Nazareth. He left them, therefore, and came to dwell in Capernaum. We might naturally say, 'Happy city which was chosen by the Son of God as his habitation.' And the people of Capernaum might have been happy if the fault had not been in themselves. What particular reason induced our Lord to dwell there, it is not for us absolutely to say. Whatever was the reason, we know it was a good one. The district in which Capernaum was situated was one of the most pleasant and fertile and happy spots upon earth. Near Capernaum there was a pleasant and wholesome fountain of clear water.

Now, we know that our Lord, like the prophets of old, who were types of him, taught by emblems, types, and parables. We are told that he sent the man, upon whose eyes he put the clay, to wash in the Pool of Siloam. And John informs us that the interpretation of Siloam is 'sent' (John 9). Now, our Lord in Scripture is called (Song of Songs, 4th chapter, 15th verse), a fountain of gardens, a well of living waters, and streams from Lebanon. And might not our Lord teach them by dwelling in Capernaum that he himself, and not the beautiful fountain of Capernaum, was the true well of living waters? But he was not long in Capernaum when he was applied to for a cure.

Verses 2–7. *And, behold, they brought to him a man sick of the palsy, lying on a bed: and Jesus seeing their faith said unto the sick of the palsy; Son, be of good cheer; thy sins be forgiven thee. And, behold, certain of the scribes said within themselves, This man blasphemeth. And Jesus knowing their thoughts said, Wherefore think ye evil in your hearts? For whether is easier, to say, Thy sins be forgiven thee; or to say, Arise, and walk? But that ye may know that the Son of man hath power on earth to forgive sins, (then saith he to the sick of the palsy,) Arise, take up thy bed, and go unto thine house. And he arose, and departed to his house.*

People came from all quarters to see the Saviour, and to be healed of their different diseases. A poor man sick of the palsy, who could not come himself, was carried by his friends in his bed, and laid before the Lord. Our Lord saw their faith, and their faith was not put to shame. We are not to suppose, when so much is ascribed to faith in Scripture, that faith itself is the cause of such extraordinary effects, but that faith is the channel or organ by which such cure, bodily and spiritually, was effected. And it is a sure fact that when

God works the faith, he will work the cure. If we believe, he will work. If we pray with faith, something will follow.

Our Lord tells the sick man some very cheerful news, that his sins were forgiven. He first cures the soul, and then the person. But we see that our Lord is found fault with, and accused of blasphemy. The best things we can do or say are blamed by the wicked. Such is the malignant nature of sin that it is only offended with what God does, for he always does good. Their minds were blinded with prejudiced thoughts against our Lord, and therefore some of the scribes spoke against him, not considering that the prophet Nathan told King David that his sin was forgiven. And if they considered him only as a prophet, he would have this power. But he had much more, for he could pardon sin. And to convince them that he had this power while he was conversant upon earth, he proved that he healed and pardoned his soul by healing his body. Accordingly, he ordered him to rise, take up his bed, and go to his house. And this he did immediately. Before he performed the miracle, they might be persuaded of his all-seeing eye, for he told them the thoughts of their hearts, as he was God. And he now convinced them of his power, by bestowing health and strength upon a poor paralytic.

Verse 8. *But when the multitudes saw it, they marvelled, and glorified God, which had given such power unto men.*

Though the faith of the multitude did not ascend as far as it ought, yet they could not but acknowledge that God had given him the power of working miracles. But they might have observed that a divine power resided in this man, which they never saw or heard of before. There was no such power in Moses, or in any of the old prophets. They could not prophesy or work miracles any time they pleased, as our Lord could. The Shechinah was in him continually, and this they might observe.

We may likewise observe that the multitude did not glorify God for hearing that the paralytic's sins were pardoned. This they could not see, but when they saw him take up his bed and go home to his own house, this struck them with astonishment, and therefore they glorified God. Something similar to this will always happen. Men cannot see the work of the Spirit of God upon a Christian's soul, and they cannot discern faith and repentance in his heart. But they can see the effects of faith and love in his life and conversation. They can see and experience his good works, and for these they can glorify God, and give him credit for his profession of religion. Faith does good to a man's own soul, and works will do good to the souls and bodies of others.

The calling of Matthew

Verse 9. *And as Jesus passed forth from thence, he saw a man, named Matthew, sitting at the receipt of custom: and he saith unto him, Follow me. And he arose, and followed him.*

Our Lord wrought several miracles upon the bodies of men, and it was with a view to the good of their souls. Indeed, his miraculous cures of the bodies of men were comparatively of little value. The cure made them comfortable and happy for a few years. But what was this in comparison to the health of the soul, which was to last for ever? He converted persons and healed their souls with a single word. He said to Matthew here, 'Follow me.' The call was instantly obeyed, for it came with power, and was, therefore, effectual. The covetous worldling, the sinful publican, in a moment becomes a saint and a follower of Christ. He left his bags of money, and whoever knows the heart of a worldling will acknowledge that the power which effected this change was as great as the power that raised Lazarus from the dead.

Christ's meal with publicans and sinners

Verses 10–13. *And it came to pass, as Jesus sat at meat in the house, behold, many publicans and sinners came and sat down with him and his disciples. And when the Pharisees saw it, they said unto his disciples,*

Why eateth your Master with publicans and sinners? But when Jesus heard that, he said unto them, They that be whole need not a physician, but they that are sick. But go ye and learn what that meaneth, I will have mercy, and not sacrifice: for I am not come to call the righteous, but sinners to repentance.

Matthew gave a proof of the sincerity of his conversion, for he made a feast for Christ and his disciples, at which were present a number of publicans and sinners. The convert was now indifferent to the world and to all the profits arising from his plan. He had the world about him just as Elijah had his mantle, ready to part with it at the least call from Christ. And this is the great thing the gospel requires (Acts 5:4). We may believe this was a happy feast, a dinner at which Jesus Christ did preside. Here was nothing irregular or wrong, and yet the Pharisees, the inveterate enemies of Christ, find fault with Christ for being the table companion of such characters. With his usual dignity, mixed with the most perfect humility, he soon silenced their unjust, illiberal cavil. He appeals to the writings of their prophets (Hosea 6:6, and 1 Samuel 15), men for whom they pretended to have great respect (Jeremiah 7:22).

The doctrine of the prophets is that God prefers mercy to sacrifice. Though the ceremonial law was of great authority, yet mercy was a greater duty. The necessity of hunger made David break the ceremonial law. It was a duty to save himself and his followers from death. But it was an act of still greater mercy in our Lord to save the souls of poor publicans from spiritual death. Though they were publicans and sinners, he saw that they were disposed to hear his heavenly doctrine. Not so the Pharisees, for they were hardened with the love of the world, and despised Christ. And however exceptionable the characters of people might have been formerly, if they now show any symptoms of penitence and attachment to religion, we ought to receive and encourage them. And we may naturally conclude that they had something good about them when they could relish the company of Christ. When wicked people relish the company of the people of God, there is some cause of hope of reformation about them. They were sick, it is true, but they had still greater need of a physician. And he was the Physician of souls, and though the Pharisees, believing themselves to be in health, saw no need of Christ, poor sinners did; therefore they applied and were healed. And though there may be danger of infection by associating with wicked men, the danger ceases when they show that they are willing to confess and forsake their sins. If good men, therefore, associate with sinners, merely to bring them back to God, there is no danger in their society. But if they keep their company merely for a social turn, there is danger that evil communications may corrupt good manners. And this has often been the case. But if good men, in the exercise of the duties of their calling, should fall into any company, let them only prove true to God, and they may do good to others without getting any hurt to themselves.

Christ's answer to John's disciples

Verses 14–17. *Then came to him the disciples of John, saying, Why do we and the Pharisees fast oft, but thy disciples fast not? And Jesus said unto them, Can the children of the bridechamber mourn, as long as the bridegroom is with them? but the days will come, when the bridegroom shall be taken from them, and then shall they fast. No man putteth a piece of new cloth unto an old garment, for that which is put in to fill it up taketh from the garment, and the rent is made worse. Neither do men put new wine into old bottles: else the bottles break, and the wine runneth out, and the bottles perish: but they put new wine into new bottles, and both are preserved.*

It may occasionally happen that good men join the wicked against the good cause. The disciples of John and of the Pharisees used to fast (Mark 2:18), and they both join here and come to Christ, thinking they would carry a victory. Both parties plumed themselves upon the multitude of their duties and religious services. They used to fast; so did not the disciples of Christ, and it would appear they thought themselves far before them. The answer of our Lord would all at once satisfy the disciples of John, who would learn from their master that Christ was the Messiah. As such, he was the bridegroom of the

Church, and while the bridegroom was present, it would be highly improper to fast. But the day was coming when he would be removed from them, and then they would mourn and fast.

Our Lord did not lay a great burden at once upon the shoulders of his followers. He trained them gradually, so that they would not feel the discipline. And he illustrates this by the two similes: the piece of new cloth and new bottles.

The bottles in the East, as many of them are still, were made of skins. New wine, therefore, put in old bottles would destroy both. As the disciples were novices in religion, he did not wish to put too great a burden upon them at once. The Pharisees needed not to boast of their fasting, for some of them did so often, merely to obtain a pleasant dream or to avert an ominous one. It is customary in some parts of England for young women to fast for a husband. They think by fasting they will see him in their sleep. Some people think there is merit in abstaining from flesh upon Fridays, though they eat other food. In our Church, following the doctrine and example of Scripture, we have occasional fasts. Though free from the yoke of ceremonies, we have fasting mentioned in the New Testament. Though we fast, we do not pretend to impossibilities. We have no pretended fast or Lent for forty days in imitation of Christ, who fasted forty days. To abstain from flesh during that period, while people deal in other foods, is a kind of farce which no single text of Scripture can support.

The ruler's daughter raised

Verses 18–26. *While he spake these things unto them, behold, there came a certain ruler, and worshipped him, saying, My daughter is even now dead: but come and lay thy hand upon her, and she shall live. And Jesus arose, and followed him, and so did his disciples. And, behold, a woman, which was diseased with an issue of blood twelve years, came behind him, and touched the hem of his garment: for she said within herself, If I may but touch his garment, I shall be whole. But Jesus turned him about, and when he saw her, he said, Daughter, be of good comfort; thy faith hath made thee whole. And the woman was made whole from that hour. And when Jesus came into the ruler's house, and saw the minstrels and the people making a noise, he said unto them, Give place: for the maid is not dead, but sleepeth. And they laughed him to scorn. But when the people were put forth, he went in, and took her by the hand, and the maid arose. And the fame hereof went abroad into all that land.*

In these words, we have two miracles recorded at once, struggling, like the twins mentioned in Genesis, which shall be first performed. A certain ruler applied to our Lord about his daughter. As he went to the house in order to cure her, a woman who laboured under a disagreeable and nauseous disease, and who was therefore ashamed to come into his presence as she was legally unclean, came behind him and touched the hem of his garment. She believed that the Saviour was endued [endowed] with power to heal all diseases. But as we learn from Mark, though her faith was great and praiseworthy, she seems as if she thought that a miracle could be, as it were, stolen from the Saviour. But whatever mixture may be with the faith of the people of God, at last it will prove victorious. Our Lord accordingly praises her faith, and dismisses her with comfort and peace.

When he came into the ruler's house and saw the minstrels, and heard the noise the people made, he told them that the maid was not dead, but sleeping. As they did not understand our Lord's meaning, they laughed him to scorn. Our Lord called the death of Lazarus and of this young woman a sleep. The death of the righteous is called a sleep in Scripture. It is but short, like the sleep of Lazarus and the ruler's daughter. As the people who were present were actuated by a spirit of murmuring and unbelief, and were therefore unworthy to witness the miracle, they were turned out. And then he raised her to life in presence of her father and mother and some of the followers of Jesus himself. He took her by the hand and snatched her from the jaws of death. When her soul returned, her health and appetite returned also. Accordingly, he ordered to give her food. The evangelist Mark observes that he desired to conceal the miracle. And he did this, no doubt, to avoid the suspicion of ostentation, and because a more proper opportunity would soon occur for publishing it, namely, his resurrection from the dead.

Two blind men healed

Verses 27–31. *And when Jesus departed thence, two blind men followed him, crying, and saying, Thou Son of David, have mercy on us. And when he was come into the house, the blind men came to him: and Jesus saith unto them, Believe ye that I am able to do this? They said unto him, Yea, Lord. Then touched he their eyes, saying, According to your faith be it unto you. And their eyes were opened; and Jesus straitly charged them, saying, See that no man know it. But they, when they were departed, spread abroad his fame in all that country.*

After he had raised the ruler's daughter to life, two blind men cried after him, 'Thou Son of David, have mercy on us.' This was one of the names of the Messiah. After they had thus expressed their faith in him, they followed him to the house, and he asked them if they believed he could do this for them. And sometimes it is not an easy matter to believe in the goodwill or in the power of Christ. They said they did, and immediately he opened their eyes according to their faith. But after he performed this miracle, he gave them a strict charge, with some degree of vehemence or anger, not to divulge the cure. He was above vainglory, and the blind men did wrong in spreading abroad the miracle at the time. He awaited his Father's time for spreading abroad his glory and publishing his great works of power.

A dumb man healed

Verses 32–34. *As they went out, they brought him a dumb man possessed with a devil. And when the devil was cast out, the dumb spake, and the multitude marvelled, saying, It was never so seen in Israel. But the Pharisees said, he casteth out devils through the prince of the devils.*

Among the cures our Lord wrought, he cast out a dumb devil. There are many dumb devils in our day. They are dumb in the things of God, and the devil has tied up their tongues that they cannot pray. Though these cures are seldom performed, we now and then hear of such instances. When a man is converted, the dumb devil is cast out, and then the man prays in his family. But notwithstanding such a glorious cure, the Pharisees allege it was wrought by the help of the prince of devils. These wretches were guilty of the most malignant blasphemy, and their punishment is declared in the 12th chapter. They could not but know that our Lord was a good man and full of good works, which proceeded only from the good Spirit of God.

Little, therefore, do the wicked think how awful their danger is when they talk contrary to the conviction of their own minds concerning good Christians. They must know that they are doing their duty when attending the means and promoting their own salvation. The wicked may think their tongue is their own, but they shall find hereafter how fearful a thing it is to fall into the hands of the living God. Scripture informs us that men shall be rewarded according to their works, and what reward can they expect that persecute the people of God for doing their duty?

Jesus teaching, preaching and healing

Verse 35. *And Jesus went about all the cities and villages, teaching in their synagogues, and preaching the gospel of the kingdom, and healing every sickness and every disease among the people.*

Let the people of God, however, follow the example of their Saviour (verse 35), for we are told that, notwithstanding the calumny of the foul-mouthed Pharisees, he went about all the cities and villages, teaching in their synagogues, and preaching the gospel of the kingdom, and healing every sickness and every disease among the people. In doing his duty, he did not pay attention to the flattery of his real or pretended friends, or the bitter invectives of his cruel and bitter enemies. He only studied the glory of God and the salvation of men, and nothing could divert him from his glorious purpose till the moment he said upon the cross, 'It is finished.'

> Verses 36–38. *But when he saw the multitudes, he was moved with compassion on them, because they fainted, and were scattered abroad, as sheep having no shepherd. Then saith he unto his disciples, The harvest truly is plenteous, but the labourers are few; pray ye therefore the Lord of the harvest, that he will send forth labourers into his harvest.*

The gathering of souls to God and to Christ is here compared to the time of harvest. Our Lord, we are told, saw a number of souls, and few or none to take care of them. This excited compassion in the tender-hearted Saviour. The people were like sheep without a shepherd. The harvest was great, and though there were many thousand souls in Palestine between Dan and Beersheba, he saw a still greater sight in the Gentile world. And he directs his disciples to pray for the glorious event. This was what his heart was bent upon. He asked the Church from God the Father as the payment for the labour of his soul. And when we pray for success to the gospel, we only join the Saviour in his prayer. God has promised him the heathen for his inheritance and the utmost bounds of the earth for his possession. And however unpromising such appearance was at the time, he desired his disciples to pray for the event. We see unlikely things happen in the natural world, and unlikely things will happen in the spiritual world. In the days of 'Saint' Columba, when two Christians met, one of them took his New Testament from his pocket, read a chapter, sang a Psalm and prayed. And that happy day will yet dawn upon the Church, when the memory of the graceless wretches who now call themselves Christians and would laugh at so much devotion shall perish, and their memory shall rot. They shall have no part or lot in this matter. But the seed of those who are now praying for such a resurrection of the good cause shall enjoy the fruits of their fathers' prayers.

Practical remarks

1. From these words, we are called upon to follow the bright example of Christ. He did his duty in every possible case and circumstance. He always had his eye upon what was duty, and followed that. He did everything that promoted the glory of God and the good of souls. When called by the Spirit of God and the leadings of providence to perform duty, however difficult, he immediately obeyed. The flattery or praise of men did not exalt him, nor did their frowns or bad language discourage him. Let us follow his footsteps.

2. Lastly, it is the duty of all Christians to pray for success for the gospel. The salvation of sinners was the business of our Lord in the world. And this ought to be the subject of our prayers. For where two or three are gathered together in his name, he is present in the midst of them. Our Lord admitted all people to hear his heavenly discourse. But he had private meetings with his disciples, where he explained difficulties to them and gave an ear to their several petitions. We ought to follow them.

Matthew chapter 10: verses 1 to 27

Verses 1–10. And when he had called unto him his twelve disciples, he gave them power against unclean spirits, to cast them out, and to heal all manner of sickness and all manner of disease. Now the names of the twelve apostles are these; The first, Simon, who is called Peter, and Andrew his brother; James the son of Zebedee, and John his brother; Philip, and Bartholomew; Thomas, and Matthew the publican; James the son of Alphaeus, and Lebbaeus, whose surname was Thaddaeus; Simon the Canaanite, and Judas Iscariot, who also betrayed him. These twelve Jesus sent forth, and commanded them, saying, Go not into the way of the Gentiles, and into any city of the Samaritans enter ye not: but go rather to the lost sheep of the house of Israel. And as ye go, preach, saying, The kingdom of heaven is at hand. Heal the sick, cleanse the lepers, raise the dead, cast out devils: freely ye have received, freely give. Provide neither gold, nor silver, nor brass in your purses, nor scrip for your journey, neither two coats, neither shoes, nor yet staves: for the workman is worthy of his meat.

The call and ordination of the twelve apostles

IN the words you have heard, we have an account of the call and ordination of the twelve apostles. He had been advising his disciples to pray the Lord of the harvest that he would send forth labourers into his harvest, and we learn from the evangelist Luke that our Lord Jesus Christ spent a night in prayer to God previous to the ordination of the apostles. And his prayers gave effect to the call and preaching of the apostles and their successors, for he will be with them to the end of the world. He endued them with ample powers to heal diseases and cast out devils, as well as to preach the gospel.

148

Their names are also recorded, and the name of the traitor among the rest. And this is done, among other reasons, to be a beacon to the clergy, that they might pray earnestly to God to keep them from the rock upon which he split. A covetous clergyman is a bad character, and I do not think it probable that God will employ him as an instrument to convert souls. But what the sovereignty of God might do, I shall not take upon me to determine. And there I must leave the matter.

This thought must be a searching one to a clergyman. I believe, if we do our duty conscientiously, that some good effects will follow, though they should not happen in our day. Our Lord did sow the good seed, and there was a great harvest of conversions in Judaea before the commencement of the siege of Jerusalem. When he gave his commission to his ambassadors, the first offer was to be to the lost sheep of the house of Israel. The apostles were to be gradually instructed in the precious secret that the Gentiles were to form a large part of the flock of Christ. Although our Lord is the Saviour of all the ends of the earth, his commission as a preacher of the everlasting gospel was confined to the Holy Land. But he, now and then, gave more than obscure intimations that he intended to call the Gentiles, for he cured the centurion's servant and the daughter of the woman of Canaan. He likewise praised the faith of both. But the time of their calling was not yet come. It was necessary that he should suffer and die and rise again before the apostles could bear witness of him to the Gentiles. They could not be furnished with sufficient arguments till these events took place. To prepare them for executing this large commission, their labours for this time are confined to the narrow bounds of Palestine. And they were to inform the Jews that the kingdom of heaven—that is, the gospel dispensation—was at hand.

In order to procure credit to their doctrine, they are empowered to work astonishing miracles. They were to heal the sick, cleanse the lepers, raise the dead, and cast out devils. They received those powers freely, and freely they were to communicate them. It was a delegated power they received, and they were to use that power for the good of others.

They were also required to express an unlimited trust in divine providence (verses 9 and 10). They were not to provide gold or silver or brass in their purses; they must not have two coats or shoes, or even staves. And this conduct would prove unfeigned trust in God and disinterested benevolence toward men. And if we showed more of this spirit in ourselves, we would live more happily than we generally do. Though we are not literally called to the duties required of the apostles, the followers of Christ are to show this spirit to the end of the world.

If the Lord Jesus has use for the service of any man in the gospel, that man needs not to speak to the patron[10] before the death of the incumbent. He says himself that the labourer is worthy of his hire. And if we labour honestly in the vineyard, we will surely get our penny in the day. He will provide bread in this world, and a crown of glory in the next. Those who turn many to righteousness will shine as the stars for ever and ever.

> Verses 11–15. *And into whatsoever city or town ye shall enter, enquire who in it is worthy; and there abide till ye go thence. And when ye come into an house, salute it. And if the house be worthy, let your peace come upon it: but if it be not worthy, let your peace return to you. And whosoever shall not receive you, nor hear your words, when ye depart out of that house or city, shake off the dust of your feet. Verily I say unto you, It shall be more tolerable for the land of Sodom and Gomorrha in the day of judgment, than for that city.*

Let us now attend to the advices our Lord gives them in the discharge of their duty as his ambassadors. When they came to any town, city, or house, they were to make enquiry into the character of the inhabitants. This they would soon know. When they entered a house, they were to salute it. If the house or city had a relish for

---

[10] The chief landowner in a parish, who had the right to present a minister to a vacant congregation. [RJD]

their doctrine or message, they would make them welcome; if not, they would grudge to receive them.

After saluting the house—that is, wishing it prosperity and peace—if the house was worthy, the peace of God would remain in it. But if the house was not worthy, the blessing they prayed for to the house would fall upon themselves. Thus we learn in the 49th chapter of Isaiah that though the labours of Messiah were in vain with respect to unhappy Israel, that himself would be glorious in the eyes of the Lord. And this happens to all faithful clergymen. Though their hearers should remain in their wickedness and unbelief, their well-meant labours will be accepted by God. And their doctrine will raise its head years after they return to God.

If they were ill-received, they were desired to use a significant ceremony: they were to shake off the dust of their feet against them. Those who rejected or despised their message could not forget what they saw. And however much people may despise or ridicule the gospel, they will find to their cost that this is a sin of the deepest dye. Sodom and Gomorrah were destroyed by fire from heaven, and yet their punishment will be small in comparison with those who despise the gospel. And yet the people of the world reckon this as only a venial sin. What infidels we are in fact! If a clergyman in a great town, after having witnessed the execution of a murderer, were to tell his hearers that the civil and honest part of his congregation would be more severely punished in the world to come than that murderer, how would his doctrine be received? Perhaps with a smile. But the doctrine may be true. Owing to the wicked depravity of his parents, the murderer might be ignorant of the gospel. And though he died in his sins, he was not so guilty as those who were sermon-proof, who refused the gospel, and bade defiance to religion.

Our Lord was in true earnest in the things which he spake. The punishment of the people of Sodom will be less than the punishment of those who refuse the gospel. And it is evident that great numbers of people who are not grossly immoral do so. From this appears the malignity of unbelief. We know from Scripture that some of the most shocking characters that ever existed upon the face of the earth are now in heaven. And how did this happen? They turned from their sins, and were washed in the blood of the Lamb. Thousands of decent characters in the eyes of the world rejected the atonement, and therefore perished in their sins. The most inveterate diseases of the souls of men were cured, the filthiest crimes were washed, when they applied to the Physician. All are sinners, and how awful is the condition of those who refuse him!

And wherein does the malignity of unbelief consist?

Answer: 1, in making God a liar; 2, in rejecting the only remedy for sin.

1. It consists in giving the lie to God himself. Unbelievers give him a challenge, and therefore they must fall before him. Giving the lie has always been resented in every age and country, as an insult that must be punished. And God will severely punish those who refuse to believe after getting every proof laid before them that reason could ask of the truth of the gospel.

2. And the malignity of it will further appear from this, that they reject the only remedy for sin. Though sinners had destroyed themselves, God provided a remedy in the gospel. If a man had a bodily disease and refused a cure that was offered him, still he might be cured by some other means. But for the diseases of the soul, there is no cure in the whole creation but one, and that is the blood of sprinkling. Those who refuse this cure must die in their sins, and this shows the awfulness of this sin.

Predictions of trouble

Verse 16. *Behold, I send you forth as sheep in the midst of wolves: be ye therefore wise as serpents, and harmless as doves.*

The apostles were sent forth to preach the gospel without any defence or armour of proof. They were surrounded by enemies on every side, and therefore they are here enjoined by the Saviour to join the wisdom of the serpent to the simplicity and innocence of the dove in their intercourse with men.

Since the earliest accounts of mankind, the wisdom of the serpent is taken notice of. The best things only about the serpent are here recommended. The serpent, above all things, takes care of her head. Before the serpent drinks, it spues the poison, lest it should hurt herself. It renews her age by casting off her skin. It refuses to be charmed by the voice of the enchanter. In this manner we ought to imitate the commendable things that we may find, even in bad men.

We must have also, as true Christians, the innocence of the dove. The wisdom of the serpent, if there is no more, is a poor account of a man professing Christianity. And it must be inconvenient for a Christian in this world, though his life were innocent, if he is entirely destitute of the wisdom of the serpent. But by blending both, we may make our way through the thorny paths of life in a way somewhat tolerable.

> Verses 17–27. *But beware of men: for they will deliver you up to the councils, and they will scourge you in their synagogues; and ye shall be brought before governors and kings for my sake, for a testimony against them and the Gentiles. But when they deliver you up, take no thought how or what ye shall speak: for it shall be given you in that same hour what ye shall speak. For it is not ye that speak, but the Spirit of your Father which speaketh in you. And the brother shall deliver up the brother to death, and the father the child: and the children shall rise up against their parents, and cause them to be put to death. And ye shall be hated of all men for my name's sake: but he that endureth to the end shall be saved. But when they persecute you in this city, flee ye into another: for verily I say unto you, Ye shall not have gone over the cities of Israel, till the Son of man be come. The disciple is not above his master, nor the servant above his lord. It is enough for the disciple that he be as his master, and the servant as his lord. If they have called the master of the house Beelzebub, how much more shall they call them of his household? Fear them not therefore: for there is nothing covered, that shall not be revealed; and hid, that shall not be known. What I tell you in dark-*

153

ness, that speak ye in light: and what ye hear in the ear, that preach ye upon the housetops.

He desires them to beware of men, for they were like wolves. And a wolf will devour a sheep without any fault at all in the poor, innocent animal. Our Lord, therefore, bids his followers to take care that they do not give them just cause of offence. And he tells them what they might expect from them. They were to deliver them up to the councils and scourge them in the synagogues. He informs them that they were to be brought before governors and kings for his name's sake, for a testimony against them and the Gentiles. When the followers of Christ pleaded their cause before kings and before pagan governors, if they rejected the gospel, it was at their peril. They could not but hear what would condemn them if they remained in unbelief.

And it must be so to this day in regard to the hearers of the gospel. They cannot forget before the great judgment seat the great and tremendous truths which they heard. These truths must appear for or against them. Now, it might occur to a person that the terrifying truths which our Lord here spoke might discourage them entirely, and almost entirely sink their spirits. But let such reflect that the prospect of a battle wherein so many thousands are likely to fall will not damp the courage of good soldiers, though the General promises only temporal rewards to those who may survive. But our Lord promises a crown. And we find that the crown animated them in all that they did and suffered for Christ. He does not feed them with temporal promises, but to the eye of faith he holds forth the promised reward.

And in case they might fear lest they would be at a loss what to say when called upon to defend the truths of Christianity, they were here told that they need not study beforehand what they would say. He promises them a large share of the Holy Spirit to assist them. As their trials would be great and extraordinary, they would get new and extraordinary assistance. The nearest relations were to betray one another. This happened often on account of religion. But to animate them they are told that he who would persevere to the end would certainly be saved.

And however furious the persecution might rage, there was to be some respite, and they had liberty to flee from one city to another. And before they traversed the whole land of promise, the Son of man would come. His coming does not necessarily imply his coming to judgment. But it certainly implies some great work of power to be performed by him.

Our Lord said to the centurion applying for his servant, 'I will come and heal him.' This did not imply his bodily presence to heal his servant, but his powerful spiritual presence. Our Lord may be said to come when he does glorious works of power in the gospel, or when he punishes his enemies in the ordinary or extraordinary course of his providence. And he set up a Church for himself in Judaea, and these churches were in a flourishing condition in the days of the apostles, and long before his coming to punish wicked Jerusalem by the sword of the Romans.

Now, lest it should surprise or even offend his disciples that they should suffer so much for doing good to the souls and bodies of men, our Lord obviates this objection. He tells them that the disciple was not above his master or the servant above his Lord. If they gave reproachful names to the Master of the house, what surprise or wonder need it excite if they ill-used the servants of the family?

He guards them against fear on account of the gospel. It was now dark and obscure, but the day would soon arrive when it would arise superior to all the power that could rise against it. It was now a secret, but it would soon come to light. It was customary in the East for a great teacher to have an interpreter. What the Master said in the interpreter's ear, he spoke aloud to all the scholars. The meaning then would be that the gospel would not be any longer confined within the narrow limits of Palestine. It would soon spread like lightning, and shine upon the whole Gentile world. And this came to pass a few years afterwards. Before the apostles died, it spread through a great part of Asia, Europe, and Africa. And the day is fast approaching when it will enlighten the whole habitable globe.

Practical inferences or remarks

1. How precious is the gospel! We are all desired to pray for the success of the gospel. The apostles prayed for it, and we ought to follow their example. This is the reward that Christ is to have for the labour of his soul. Our Lord not only prayed for it, but we are told he spent a whole night in prayer to God. And our Lord will be with all the faithful followers of the apostles to the end of time.

2. The danger of refusing the gospel. Sodom and Gomorrah are punished with signal vengeance, but Capernaum and the cities of Galilee are threatened with worse. And we daily hear the doctrines which they refused. Poor is the pennyworth—though great is the punishment—of those who reject the Saviour. Whether a man gets a large farm with Demas, or the young ruler a purse of silver with Judas, or plenty of meat and drink with the rich glutton—alas! What has he when he loses his soul?

May God bless his Word to us. AMEN.

Matthew chapter 10: verses 28 to 42

I N the remaining part of the chapter which we heard just now read, our Lord gives several useful doctrines and directions to his apostles, which we shall explain in order.

The fear of man and the fear of God

Verse 28. *And fear not them which kill the body, but are not able to kill the soul: but rather fear him which is able to destroy both soul and body in hell.*

How contrary is this doctrine to the spirit and practice of the world. The fear of man is a most powerful principle in the human heart. When Nebuchadnezzar set up his golden image in the plain of Dura, among the great multitude gathered upon that occasion, none had the courage to oppose him but three Hebrew youths. In the pagan and popish persecutions, alas! how many yielded through the slavish fear of man! In matters of less consequence than denying the faith, what a powerful charm is in the breath of a superior! And why? He can hurt the body and blast a man's temporal interest. In many cases, men had often the power of life and death in their hands, and they have made a bad use of it by punishing the innocent and putting the body to death. Even in our own day, the pride of a superior, or what we call a laird [landed proprietor], removed a young man from his estate because he rebuked him for breach of the Sabbath.

But our Lord contrasts the two fears: that of those who can kill the body, and of him who can destroy both soul and body in hell. And when these are put in opposition, reason will tell which is the proper choice. And if the principle of the slavish fear of man was not very powerful in our hearts, our Lord would not use the most powerful argument in the creation to counteract its influence.

There is here laid before us the frown of man and the anger of God as opposites, and yet we daily find that owing to the depravity of our hearts, the fear of man will often sway our actions. We act against principle, reason, and conscience. The language of the world is, 'If thou let this man go, thou art not the friend of Caesar.' Now, as it is a duty to follow Christ even to the cross, and lay down our lives for his sake if called to do so, this teaches us to pray earnestly for his Spirit to enable us to perform such a difficult duty, for of ourselves we can do nothing.

Let us look to the cloud of witnesses that surround us. Persons as weak in body and mind as ourselves have suffered for Christ, and he can enable us to do likewise when we depend upon his assistance and grace. Our timorous hearts and our unbelief may suggest to us that if matters came to a trial, we might act the part of Pilate and crucify the cause of Christ. In answer to these fears, it may be observed that the apostles were afraid that they might be tempted to commit a crime their souls did abhor. It is well known that many soldiers who were terribly afraid before the battle have behaved valiantly after the engagement began. Let us do our present duty, whatever it may be, and if called to more difficult duties, we shall receive additional strength and courage. According to our day, so shall our strength be.

We may be, and often are, afraid of things that will never come to pass. We should cast our care upon the Lord, and leave things to come in his own hands. Why should we be troubled if we find ourselves destitute of the courage of a general or the wisdom and talents of a Secretary of State? God is glorified if we act in proportion to our present strength. Let us trust in the Lord, for in him is everlasting strength. By persevering in the way of the Lord, we shall become stronger and stronger. If we resist smaller temptations to sin with the strength we have at present we may hereafter be able to overcome more powerful ones, like Joseph and David. 'Shall I do this great wickedness and sin against God?' is the language of the one; 'The Lord forbid that I should stretch forth mine hand against the Lord's anointed,' is the resolution of the other. And yet their temptations were strong and powerful. The strongest of all temptations is the fear of death. The practice of doing their duty made them strong against strong temptations to sin. God will not suffer us to be tempted above what we are able to bear, and his grace will be sufficient for us in all our struggles.

God's providence

Verses 29–31. Are not two sparrows sold for a farthing? and one of them shall not fall on the ground without your Father. But the very hairs of your head are all numbered. Fear ye not therefore, ye are of more value than many sparrows.

The divine providence overrules the actions of creatures through the whole extent of creation. Not only the highest seraph in glory is the object of his regard, but the most insignificant creatures upon earth are under his care and inspection. And if his providence reaches the minutest concerns of the minutest of his works, how much more does he regard the actions and interests of his people. The very hairs of their heads are all numbered. A sportsman cannot bring down a sparrow to the ground without divine permission. Nor can the enemies of his people be permitted to hurt or touch them unless it be for their own good and the good of others, and for the divine glory. Men do not count but things they reckon valuable, and his people are so precious in the sight of God that the hairs of their heads are all numbered. And if the people of God formerly had a favour for the dust of Zion, we believe that God has a regard for the bodies of his people when reduced to dust. It is precious dust, and God will raise it to life and glory.

Confessing Christ or denying Christ

Verses 32–33. *Whosoever therefore shall confess me before men, him will I confess also before my Father which is in heaven. But whosoever shall deny me before men, him will I also deny before my Father which is in heaven.*

One would think that these words would prove like a thunderbolt to those smooth, slippery Christians that are so pliant as to be of the religion of any company they happen to be among. If religion is despised or ridiculed in their presence, they have not the courage or the honesty to stand up in its defence. Is not this denying Christ before men? And how awful is this threatening! He says he will deny them before God. He will not acknowledge them as his own before God and his holy angels. Great and good men have felt the importance of these awful truths. That pious man, Archbishop Cranmer, burnt his fingers in the candle because he signed a paper at the desire of the Papists in the bloody reign of Queen Mary. And it cost a still greater man, the apostle Peter, many tears because he denied Christ. Let us, then, be faithful to our religion, and hold fast our profession before men.

Not peace, but a sword

Verses 34–36. *Think not that I am come to send peace on earth: I came not to send peace, but a sword. For I am come to set a man at variance against his father, and the daughter against her mother, and the daughter in law against her mother in law. And a man's foes shall be they of his own household.*

The Jews, and many besides them since the days of Christ, have made a bad use of these words, merely because they did not understand them. Our Lord is the Prince of Peace, and to those who embrace and believe his gospel, he giveth a peace that passeth understanding. How, then, does he say in these words that he did not come to send peace on earth? Our Lord foresaw the effects the gospel would produce in the wicked. They would oppose and persecute the followers of Christ. Those who did not believe would betray and punish their nearest relations. And thus the gospel of peace would be the cause of disturbance, owing to the perverse, malignant wickedness of mankind.

It is so to this day, for the apostle tells us that all that will live godly in Christ Jesus will suffer persecution. The generality of professing Christians have conformed so much to the spirit of the world that the world does not persecute them. The Christian world is now as wicked in many cases as the pagans were in the days of the apostles. And how few are there so true to the cause of Christ as to rebuke them. The tiger, the wild beast of persecution, may be now asleep, but the revival of Christianity would awaken him. Let a true Christian rebuke a wicked, great man or rich man for his uncleanness, his breach of Sabbath, his intemperance, and his oppression, and if he cannot hurt his temporal interest, he will at least attempt to break his character: he brands him with the epithet of bigot, enthusiast, fanatic, and twenty other odious names. But the man who drinks with them and winks at their practices is a decent, honest fellow, and is therefore permitted to sleep in a safe skin. And it is cause of regret that even some true Christians are defective in their duty in this respect.

Honouring God

Verse 37. *He that loveth father or mother more than me is not worthy of me: and he that loveth son or daughter more than me is not worthy of me.*

The divine commandment is that we should honour our parents, and love and cherish our children. But it sometimes happens that parents may be wicked and unnatural, and may oppose us in things that belong to God. In such cases, it must be observed that our duty to God must have the preference. Parents may desire us to commit sin. This we are not to do to please or humour any parent, friend or benefactor. A very heathen could say, 'Plato is my friend, Socrates is my friend, but the greatest friend is truth.' Parents and children may interfere with our duty and prove a snare to our souls. We may love and obey them too much. Eli preferred his children to God, and Micah, by the advice of his mother, set up idolatry in his family, as we read in the book of Judges. The children of popish parents who have been converted to God and to a purer religion could not be prevailed upon to desert the true faith, notwithstanding the threats and the displeasure of their parents and friends. A wicked parent may encourage and even advise his children to steal and to break the law of God. But they may lawfully refuse to obey, and by doing so, they do not break the Fifth Commandment. We are to obey God rather than man. And if parents stand by their children in wickedness, take their excuse and pretend they are innocent when appearances say they are guilty, do not such parents show clearly that they love their wicked children better than their Saviour, and do they not prove themselves unworthy of the Saviour and of his love?

Verses 38–39. *And he that taketh not his cross, and followeth after me, is not worthy of me. He that findeth his life shall lose it: and he that loseth his life for my sake shall find it.*

Self-denial is the great duty of the Christian, and by comparing this with other parts of the Scripture, our Lord seems here to prepare his followers for suffering persecutions for the sake of the gospel. But though this may be the principal scope of the words, they refer to the ordinary state of Christians in whatever particular case they may happen to be. We are not to murmur or rebel against God for his dispensations. They may be severe, but they are less than our iniquities deserve. Shimei cursed and gave bad language to King David, but he submitted. We may meet with ungrateful returns from men. What then? So did many good men before us. Our present state is the best for us at the time, and he will give a good account of everything delivered into his hand. Let us then give ourselves and our condition without reserve to him. Let us wait his time. Let us surrender ourselves to him in the way of duty, and though we should even lose our lives for his sake, we shall be gainers at last. What is a man profited should he gain the world if he loses his soul? Let us not be like the bankrupt, who said that whatever would come of the soul, he took care of the body. This is the morality of the villain, but it is a morality that is very much in vogue. We are, therefore, to follow the Saviour, and submit to the cross and to the present duty. If we resist *that* and flee from the presence of the Lord, our iniquity may find us out, and we may be punished like Jonah, or like the brethren of Joseph.

Rewards

Verses 40–42. *He that receiveth you receiveth me, and he that receiveth me receiveth him that sent me. He that receiveth a prophet in the name of a prophet shall receive a prophet's reward; and he that receiveth a righteous man in the name of a righteous man shall receive a righteous man's reward. And whosoever shall give to drink unto one of these little ones a cup of cold water only in the name of a disciple, verily I say unto you, he shall in no wise lose his reward.*

Little do sinful mankind who hear the gospel consider what they do when they hear the gospel with indifference. By so doing, even though they should not go so far as to persecute or punish the preacher, they forfeit the joys and the reward of heaven.

We are informed here that such as receive the messengers of Christ receive himself. By believing his messengers, it is the same thing as if they heard the doctrine from his own mouth, and yielded to him the obedience of faith. By believing, we receive the gift of eternal life. And even by receiving a prophet in the name of a prophet or a righteous man as such, we receive a share of the rewards of such good men. Nay, even a cup of cold water given to one of the poor followers of Christ as such will be sure to receive a suitable reward.

Cold water, though very plentiful in our cold climate, is not so in Eastern or Southern countries. There it is a luxury, and we better understand the force of the expression if we happen to travel in extreme sultry weather. What a comfort, what a refreshment is the cold stream! Water is bought and sold in the East to this day. Moses offered to pay to the King of Edom money for the water the army of Israel would drink in passing through his country, and this was cruelly refused him. The Moabites and Ammonites are blamed because they came not with bread and water to the children. The plain meaning is that the least favour done to one of the followers of Christ as such will be amply rewarded. And this sometimes happens, even in this same world as well as in the next.

Matthew 13: verses 1 to 23

OUR Lord Jesus Christ was the great Teacher sent from God, who spake as never man spake. He is the great Prophet of the Church, who hath revealed to us the great doctrines of grace and the mysteries of our salvation. As he was in the bosom of the Father, and is his interpreter and counsellor, he knew the whole will of God respecting his Church and people.

It is said that, though a son (as he was a man), and did not know letters, his soul was furnished with more learning and knowledge than the children of men. And we must believe that this was the case by virtue of his union with the divine nature. Grace was poured into his lips, and he was anointed with the oil of joy above his fellows. Though this was eminently true of him, it does not appear from Scripture that he employed the power of a gesture, or the charms and beauties of fine composition in the heavenly discourses he preached. He adapted his doctrines to the meanest and rudest capacities. He taught by apt similitudes or parables, so that they could scarcely forget his doctrines. We learn from Scripture that people understood his parables, and if the doctrines he taught were hid from any, it was owing to their own wickedness and unbelief. We then ought to say to every man, 'He that hath ears to hear, let him hear.'

I shall, therefore, by divine assistance, endeavour to explain to you the portion of Scripture which was read to you with as much regard to perspicuity as possible, and conclude with some practical inferences by way of improvement.

Jesus' teaching by parables

Verses 1–2. The same day went Jesus out of the house, and sat by the sea side. And great multitudes were gathered together unto him, so that he went into a ship, and sat; and the whole multitude stood on the shore.

Our Lord was an indefatigable preacher—he never wearied of doing good. You heard the doctrine he taught in the former chapter, and now you hear that upon the same day, he went out of the house and sat by the sea side, and as great multitudes were gathered together, he taught them again. It was his meat and drink to do the will of God, and bring immortal souls to a sense of their duty. He did not excuse himself from his delightful employment by what he had done in the former part of the day. Like the sun that enlightens every part of the earth, he went about through all Palestine and executed the commission his Father gave him. He went about constantly doing good, enlightening dark souls by his heavenly doctrines and confirming his commission by the most astonishing and most salutary miracles.

As all Christians should follow his holy example, so ministers of the gospel are called upon in a particular manner to proclaim his name, and follow him in the assiduity with which he prosecuted the work of the ministry. The apostles were so struck with a sense of the importance of their work that they appointed others to superintend the temporal concerns of the Church, that they might devote all their time to prayer and the work of God.

Are ministers of our day better than the apostles, and can they do what the apostles would not and should not do? A minister is the soldier of Christ, and he cannot entangle himself in the affairs of the world—he cannot serve two masters. The apostle Paul says, 'Who is sufficient for these things?' Does not the conduct of a minister who meddles in the world tell us that he is more than sufficient for these things—that he is sufficient for the world also? Can we do what the apostle could not venture to do? I leave you to answer this question. The Saviour was a lover of souls, and we ought to love them above all other concerns.

The propriety and decorum of the Saviour's parables

Verses 3–8. And he spake many things unto them in parables, saying, Behold, a sower went forth to sow; and when he sowed, some seeds fell by the way side, and the fowls came and devoured them up: some fell upon stony places, where they had not much earth: and forthwith they sprung up, because they had no deepness of earth: and when the sun was up, they were scorched; and because they had no root, they withered away. And some fell among thorns; and the thorns sprung up, and choked them: but other fell into good ground, and brought forth fruit, some an hundredfold, some sixtyfold, some thirtyfold.

As I mean to explain the parable more particularly when I come to the 19th verse, I shall from these words observe the following things: first, the propriety and decorum of our Saviour's parables; secondly, why he taught the people by parables.

First, the propriety and decorum of our Saviour's parables. In a parable, the particular scope or intention of the person that propounds it is what we are to pay attention to. We are not to apply every particular part of a parable, for this will not hold always in the parables of the gospel. The principal thing is what we are to pay attention to.

The parable plainly points out to us the reception the gospel would meet with. There are many kinds of heavens, and this is the scope of the parable. When we compare the parables of the ten virgins, the talents, and the sower, we find that their principal and only scope is to show that mankind in general would not receive or believe the gospel when it was propounded to them. It does not signify, as some would have it, the proportion the good bear to the bad—if this was the case, one parable would contradict the other. It signifies only that some were good and some bad. When our Saviour in plain terms informs us that many are called and few chosen, this throws sufficient light upon the doctrine of the parables.

Why the Saviour taught the people by parables

Second, why he taught the people by parables. He did this, in the first place, because allegory or parable is a plain, familiar way adapted to all capacities and what every person can understand. If he made use of abstract reasoning, or if he employed the finest composition, very few could follow him. The learned only would understand him, but the bulk of his hearers would go home without edification. Again, he employed this method because it was the best calculated to strike the attention and be retained in the memory. Children would remember similes borrowed from the works of creation, and they are not below the attention of men of the most exalted genius. Lastly, he made use of parables because the doctrine couched in them is, in general, better received than what is given in plain language. The sinner is reproved, and, like the royal penitent, is made to understand himself.

Verse 9. *He that hath ears to hear, let him hear.*

It is the duty of all that hear the gospel to take heed what they hear, for they cannot hear it with indifference but at their everlasting peril. This word is the savour of death or of life to all that hear. Scripture speaks of people uncircumcised in heart and in ear. 'To whom shall I speak,' says the prophet Jeremiah, 'and give warning, that they may hear? Behold their ear is uncircumcised, and they cannot hearken.' And in another place he complains that the house of Israel were uncircumcised in the heart. God promises to circumcise the heart of his people, and that he will remove the stony heart and give a heart of flesh. We cannot hear with profit to ourselves till this is the case. Is our Saviour's advice, therefore, in vain, or will the stony heart or the uncircumcised ear excuse people? It will not. This aggravates their condemnation. When people hear the Word of God, there are some things in their power to do, and if they do them, they are inexcusable, and their punishment will be just. First, they can examine whether what they hear be the Word of God. And they may know this by the purity of the doctrine, the prophecies, and the miracles that support it. They may know by the hold it takes of their conscience, so that they humble themselves at the thought of the judgment to come. Though the will revolts, conscience says 'Yes.' The Word of God shines by its own light and brings such conviction as will render sinners inexcusable. It must be so, for they will be judged by the Word.

2. Again, it is in their power to hear with attention and impartiality. They may purge their minds from prejudice and forsake many of the sins that blind their minds and harden their hearts. Why does not the Word profit them? They refuse to give it admittance and make truth a prisoner of unrighteousness. They do not give the Word an impartial hearing, for if they did, it would condemn their practices and terrify their souls. They do not wish to know that such and such truths are in the Word. They are willingly ignorant, and as to the knowledge they have, they rebel against the light. Now, they could help and avoid all this.

3. They have it in their power to pray to God for his sanctifying and enlightening influences to guide them in the right path, and make them believe and obey the gospel. And when people honestly ask this, reason as well as Scripture will say, 'Ask, and ye shall receive; seek, and ye shall find; knock, and it shall be opened to you.' When people, then, come to hear the Word of God, is this their uniform practice? Do they hear with reverence, examine with impartiality, and pray with sincerity? 'He that hath ears to hear,' let him do this, and the Word will profit his soul.

Verse 10. *And the disciples came, and said unto him, Why speakest thou unto them in parables?*

From these words we may see the character of those who are truly willing to learn. His disciples heard many things which they clearly did not understand. They took the first opportunity of being better informed, and we also find that our Lord was ready to explain his doctrines to any that were of a teachable disposition and were willing to learn. Ignorance could be no excuse to those who could have heard Christ, and it can surely be no excuse to us. And our Saviour informs us of this in the following verses:

Verses 11–12. *He answered and said unto them, Because it is given unto you to know the mysteries of the kingdom of heaven, but to them it is not given. For whosoever hath, to him shall be given, and he shall have more abundance: but whosoever hath not, from him shall be taken away even that he hath.*

Our Lord answers their question by recurring to the free and unmerited grace of God to his disciples, and as for the rest, he lays the blame to the account of their own wickedness and unbelief.

'Unto you it is given.' From these words we see that some are distinguished by free grace. If any are saved, they are saved by grace, and to those who improve their grace more shall be given, and they shall increase abundantly. The great doctrines of the gospel are mysteries, and none can know them till God reveal them to their souls by his Spirit. 'The natural man knoweth not the things of God', and though the word strikes the ears of the body, the mind is blind and the heart hard. By nature we are enemies to God, and if people nurse and cherish this, natural enmity will grow. And our Lord shows us the danger of this state in the following verses.

Verses 13–15. *Therefore speak I to them in parables: because they seeing see not; and hearing they hear not, neither do they understand. And in them is fulfilled the prophecy of Esaias, which saith, By hearing ye shall hear, and shall not understand; and seeing ye shall see, and shall not perceive: for this people's heart is waxed gross, and their ears are dull of hearing, and their eyes they have closed; lest at any time they should see with their eyes, and hear with their ears, and should understand with their heart, and should be converted, and I should heal them.*

Parables strike the attention and excite curiosity. If we had never heard any of the parables of the gospel till this day, they would make a great impression on our minds. Now, our Saviour's parables are so striking that they carry light and conviction to the mind. Some of them might be dark and at first not easily understood by ignorant people, but such as were of a teachable disposition might easily have access to get them explained. Parable or allegory were frequent in the writings of the Eastern authors, and if persons carped at their literal meaning, they betrayed either ignorance or wickedness or both. He alludes to practices and customs to which they were not strangers, and therefore could not mistake his meaning. If they were ignorant, therefore, they were wilfully ignorant, for they shut their eyes upon the truth.

Our Saviour therefore uses parables as the fittest method of teaching for all ranks of his hearers. Such as were willing to learn could not forget a beautiful and significant parable. A principle of curiosity and a principle of conscience would excite them to get the doctrine explained to them. Such as hardened themselves in their sins must have offered violence to their own consciences and to all the feelings of their hearts if they did not search after the meaning. If they remained ignorant, they must have done so from mere malignity of heart. In them, therefore, and in all such is fulfilled the prophecy of Isaiah, 'Hearing, ye shall hear ... ; and seeing ye shall see, and not perceive: for the heart of this people is waxed gross; their ears are dull of hearing and their eyes they have closed; lest they should see with their eyes and hear with their ears, and should be converted and I should heal them.' The doctrine was calculated to heal them. If people are not brought to God by the gospel, the cause is obvious: they have eyes but do not see; they have ears but do not hear, and while they remain such, they can never be healed or pardoned.

The gospel, and the Author of the gospel, are the most precious guests that ever visited our benighted world. If we refuse to give the gospel access to our hearts, great must be our condemnation. Let us not provoke God by such wicked conduct. It is said in Scripture that Pharaoh hardened his heart, and afterwards it is said that God hardened Pharaoh's heart. He left him to the hardness and malignity of his own heart. It would appear that many of the Jews in our Saviour's time were in this very state. This is an awful state, and this is the state in which people may fare by despising the gospel. It is the way in which God punishes them, and it is the most awful of all punishments.

Though this is a most dangerous state, almighty grace can cure the malignant disease. And that it has been cured may appear from the following reasons.

First, our Lord informs us that all manner of sin shall be forgiven to men, and one of his apostles informs us that the blood of Christ cleanses from all sin. Our Lord does not accuse them of the unpardoned sin.

Secondly, people would not have committed such a great sin as the crucifixion of the Lord of glory unless they had been hardened by other sins and brought to a state of insensibility, and it is clear from Scripture that many of those sinners were washed and pardoned.

Lastly, Manasseh, to name no more, was hardened in sin, and by all appearance was given up to a reprobate sense. Otherwise, how could he have been guilty of actions so black, so contrary to Scripture, to reason, and to humanity? His actions were even blacker than the actions of Pharaoh, whom God himself is said to have hardened. Now, we know that black actions proceed from a black and wicked heart, and yet Manasseh was pardoned and saved.

If our hearts are hardened, let us labour to get them softened. Let us apply to the Saviour for his blood and Spirit. We have heard of the danger of this awful state of mind, and though Manasseh was brought out of this state, you see that Pharaoh was left to perish in his sins. And if you harden yourselves against the doctrines you hear—if you perish, it shall be your own fault. By opposing a doctrine of Scripture, you are like a wave of the sea dashing itself against the ROCK. People may despise and even laugh at the doctrines of the gospel, but they shall think differently of them when the rattle is in their throat and their souls are hovering upon the borders of an unseen world. If people come to hear the Word with a view to getting some word to carp at or to laugh at, let them laugh at the following Scripture: 'Ye serpents, ye generation of vipers, how can ye escape the damnation of hell?' If people have a turn to joke, they should at least show more common sense than to laugh at things that are verily connected with everlasting happiness or misery. Let them not crucify Christ afresh.

Verses 16–17. But blessed are your eyes, for they see: and your ears, for they hear. For verily I say unto you, That many prophets and right-eous men have desired to see those things which ye see, and have not seen them; and to hear those things which ye hear, and have not heard them.

After showing the awful state and danger in which the Jews lay by their obstinacy and unbelief, he turns his doctrine to such of his hearers as were of a teachable disposition and heard the truth with impartiality and sincerity. 'Blessed are your eyes, for they see: and your ears, for they hear.' And to show of what importance the truths of the gospel were, he informs them that many prophets and right-eous persons desired to see and hear what they saw and heard.

Our Saviour pronounces them happy, not merely because they heard them with the ears of their bodies, but because they embraced them with a true and lively faith. The greatest men under the patri-archal and Jewish economies rejoiced at the prospect of gospel days. The Word of God was then confined to a small spot of the earth, and the heavenly doctrines were couched under a load of ceremo-nies and dark parables. They rejoiced at the thought that Messiah was to reign from sea to sea, and from the river to the ends of the earth. And if we likewise make a good use of the gospel, our happi-ness is unspeakable. We have privileges which were not granted to the greatest and most respectable characters under the Old Testa-ment. It was not their worldly prosperity or honour that made these great men to rejoice, but a view of the day of Christ which we enjoy. Let us beg of God to give us grace to improve our great and glorious privileges.

The parable of the sower

Verses 18–19. *Hear ye therefore the parable of the sower. When any one heareth the word of the kingdom, and understandeth it not, then cometh the wicked one, and catcheth away that which was sown in his heart. This is he which received seed by the way side.*

We may easily know the literal meaning of the simile—the birds of the air devoured the seed that fell by the wayside, and the wicked one taketh away the Word from persons that do not understand the value and import of what they hear.

The high road is hard by the feet of passengers, so that the Word could not get hold of the earth, and though the Word of God may drop for a moment into the heart that is rendered callous by the love of the world or the indulgence of some sinful passion, the enemy of their souls catcheth it away immediately. The Word finds no room in a heart rendered hard by sin. And if some slight impression should occasionally be made upon the surface of the heart, it does not go deep enough. Satan and his emissaries soon wear off the impression, and when the man goes among his sinful companions, he soon drowns his convictions in the bowl[11] or suffocates them by the commission of some new sin.

Or perhaps the miserable sinner may be so far forsaken by God as that he may fall into the company of false teachers who have a living for preaching the gospel, and laugh secretly at the most serious truths contained therein. These are the most dangerous companions for a man's soul. They are the black birds of hell, who devour the precious seed. And when people delight not in the truth, God may give them up to strong delusions, to believe a lie. It is no wonder though you should see these false teachers, the bosom companions of those who are delivered up by God to a reprobate sense and the plague of a hard heart. They mutually blind and harden each other, and when the blind lead the blind, both fall into the ditch.

---

[11] A drinking vessel. [RJD]

The greatest curse that can befall any man in this world is to prefer falsehood to truth, and this never happens till the heart becomes as hard as the high road. In that case any temptation that passes by may carry off the Word from him. And you may easily see that if his heart is not ploughed by the law of God, he must die without grace and have a distressed eternity.

Verses 20–21. But he that received the seed into stony places, the same is he that heareth the word, and anon with joy receiveth it; yet hath he not root in himself, but dureth for a while: for when tribulation or persecution ariseth because of the word, by and by he is offended.

'And that which was sown in stony places.' In these words, we have a lively picture of many professors. At first, they seem to glow with affection. They hear the Word with joy, and continue for a while. Their hearts are not so hard by the practice of sin as those who are compared to the high road; they have some kind of regard for it: they hear it, and seem to have a relish for what they hear. But, alas! they have no root, for the first trouble or persecution that arises on account of the Word gives them offence. And this supposes that trouble of some kind will rise, for all that will live godly in Christ Jesus will suffer persecution. They cannot avoid it, for there is enmity between the seed of the woman and the seed of the serpent.

Now, as those persons have no root in themselves, they cannot bear persecution—they fall away and decline. They are offended—they do not relish a religion that exposes them to contempt or ridicule. And as they get no spiritual view of the beauty of religion, or experience in a saving manner the joys that flow from the one thing needful, they abandon what they do not think worth the keeping.

If great people or rich people countenance religion, they can then put on the outward garb of holiness, but if the common people hear Christ gladly, they ask, 'Have any of the rulers or of the Pharisees believed on him?' When rich or learned people laugh at religion, they give it up. But if all the rich or learned men in a kingdom would say that health of body or the light of the sun are not good, no man in his senses would believe them or part with his health or eyes to please them, and yet people often part with their religion, which is the health and light of the soul, for fear they should be the laughingstocks of fools. This, however, is a proof that they have no root in themselves, for if religion is the one thing needful, they should part with everything to retain it. How poor and contemptible is the character that sells his religion for a smile! And yet such characters are common, but their state is awful and dangerous.

Verse 22. *He also that received seed among the thorns is he that heareth the word; and the care of this world, and the deceitfulness of riches, choke the word, and he becometh unfruitful.*

From these words, we see the danger of covetousness, worldly ease, and overmuch attachment to the things of this life. Mark mentions likewise the lusts of other things. Now, the lusts of the flesh, as well as covetousness and the deceitfulness of riches, choke the Word and render it unfruitful. If a field is full of thorns, and they are allowed to grow, they prevent the seed from coming to any perfection.

Our Saviour informs us that it is easier for a camel to pass through the eye of a needle than for a rich man to enter into the kingdom of heaven. And he explains to us who are the rich men he means— even those who trust in riches. The love of riches is a deceitful and a bewitching passion. It often alters his sentiments and manner of life. The desire of these is never satisfied. Riches blind the eyes and harden the heart. He sees that riches procure for him all the pleasures and luxuries of life. He observes that honour and respect are attached to riches, and therefore pursues them with all the bent of his soul. Now, it is impossible that the grace of God can dwell in a heart where any grovelling lust or passion bears sway. The love of the world and the love of God cannot dwell in one heart.

Verse 23. *But he that received seed into the good ground is he that heareth the word, and understandeth it; which also beareth fruit, and bringeth forth, some an hundredfold, some sixty, some thirty.*

Here we are taught the effect the Word has upon those whose hearts are made good ground by the grace and Spirit of God. They receive the Word in a good and honest heart, and bring forth fruit with patience. They yield some thirty, some sixty, and some an hundredfold.

We need not be surprised at the extraordinary fruitfulness of Palestine and other warm climates when we sometimes experience surprising fruitfulness in our own country upon some occasions. Now, the Word has a similar effect upon some good men. The apostles and primitive Christians were wonderfully fruitful. They yielded an hundredfold. And blessed be God in all ages of the Church, there have been instances of people bearing some sixty and some thirtyfold. They have been remarkable for their fruits of faith and labours of love. Some spots of God's vineyard have been very fruitful. They have flourished like Sharon and Carmel. They have been like a watered garden and their fruit like Lebanon. If it be a pleasant sight in the eyes of men to see fields in the highest state of cultivation, waving with corn and repaying the husbandman's labour and attention, how inexpressibly pleasant is his garden to the Saviour, wherein grow all manner of pleasant fruits. The trees of righteousness bear fruit in old age.

Inferences and improvements

How awful is this doctrine to careless and indifferent hearers! Two sorts of people are in great danger—those who neglect and despise the means of grace, and those who enjoy the benefit of them and live in sin.

If people come to hear with a malignant intention, they are only sealing their own condemnation. Their disease must indeed be very virulent when they convert the food of their souls into the most deadly poison. Take heed, then, how you hear, and beware lest you provoke God to give you up to a reprobate sense and hard heart upon whom all means will be lost.

From these words, we see the different effects the Word of God has upon different hearers. And should not this effectually provoke us earnestly and importunately to cry to heaven for his enlightening and sanctifying influences upon our souls? We cannot hear with profit if we do not believe, and we cannot believe while the heart is hard. And as God has promised to give the new heart, let us plead his promise, for he has not excluded us. Let us look to his power and promise. He can, for he created heaven and earth, and nothing is too hard for him. He will, for he sent his Son to the world, and this is his work—to destroy the work of the devil and give repentance.

Some poor soul will ask, 'What if I be in this sad condition—"having eyes, ye see not"?'

Answer: Read over the awful state of the Jews in the Saviour's time. Though this is a most dangerous state, almighty grace can cure the malignant disease. And that it has been cured may appear from the reasons annexed to verses 13, 14 and 15.

May God bless his own Word. AMEN.

Matthew chapter 13: verses 24 to 43

I N this parable, our Lord gives us a description of the state of the visible Church, and the different states that await good and bad men in the world to come.

I have already informed you of the propriety of instruction by parable or allegory. Parables are easily remembered, and if people despise or neglect the doctrines couched under them, they do so to their own unspeakable hurt and misery.

I shall, by divine assistance, endeavour to explain this portion of Scripture to you, and conclude by giving some sound, practical inferences in the way of improvement.

Parable of the tares

Verse 24. *Another parable put he forth unto them, saying, The kingdom of heaven is likened unto a man which sowed good seed in his field.*

Our Lord himself, in the explanation of the parable, informs us who it was that sowed the good seed in the field. It is the Lord Jesus himself. The gospel, and those who are influenced by the gospel, are the good seed, and this seed is sown in the world. This is the great field, and though the greatest part of it is still a wilderness, the time is coming when it shall be brought under cultivation, for God promised the heathen to his Son for his inheritance. A great part of it that was once cultivated is now wild, being destroyed by the boar from the forest and the wild beasts of the field. Places which were once enlightened with the gospel of Christ are now under the power of Mahometan delusion.[12]

But the parable has respect in particular to those parts of the field which are cultivated and where the good seed is sown. The gospel is the good seed, and those who embrace it are the children of God and the seed that serve him on earth. When they are born to God by the gospel, they are a spiritual seed, and this seed is sown here and there in the earth, and sometimes a handful of the precious seed is sown upon the top of the mountains, and the fruit of it becomes like Lebanon.

Verse 25. *But while men slept, his enemy came and sowed tares among the wheat, and went his way.*

When the gospel was first preached, there was no impure mixture with the precious Word of God. The apostles did not handle the Word deceitfully, or lay any other foundation than Jesus Christ as the head corner stone. And for some short time, none durst join the society of Christians but true and genuine believers. The rest were afraid, as we read in the Acts of the Apostles. But in a short time, things took another turn. Even in the times of the apostles, though they could discern spirits and could distinguish between the true and the false, hypocrites and false teachers crept into the visible Church, and much more so in the times of their immediate successors.

The parable observes that it was while men slept that the enemy came and sowed the tares. Charity thinketh no evil, and as the primitive teachers and Christians were men of upright hearts and sincere intentions, they believed that others were actuated with the same sentiments as they were themselves when they professed Christianity. In the following ages, real spiritual sleep seized pastors and their flocks, and this made them an easy prey to seducing spirits. They were not so sharp-sighted as the apostle, who observed a spirit of

---

[12] This is an archaic term denoting Islam. [RJD]

ambition entering the Church in his own day, which he foresaw would one day overspread the Church.

By tares, then, we may understand false teachers and false profession. Learned men observe that tares are very like the wheat, and hypocrites pretend to be like Christians. They come to church, attend the worship, and partake of the sacraments. But they are destitute of true faith and the love of God. They live in the practice of some sin which, like the worm at the root of Jonah's gourd, eats out religion from their souls.

Verse 26. *But when the blade was sprung up, and brought forth fruit, then appeared the tares also.*

In the book of Job, we are informed that when the children of God met to worship, Satan appeared among them, and, we may believe, not with a good intention. And it has been the fate of the Church to have bad men and hypocrites mixed with true believers. However, though we cannot always judge of hypocrites, it appears from the parable that they can be known in many cases even before the harvest. It is expressly said that the tares appeared also.

False doctrines and false professors may be known, the one by their tendency and the other by their fruits. False doctrines may have a fine outward appearance and the semblance of worth and substance. As the tares are like the wheat, they may appear like the wheat; also, like the food of life, till they are handled and felt. For instance, justification by works has the appearance of promising virtue and holiness, but this they can never promote unless they proceed from faith in the Lord Jesus Christ. Doctrines that recommend our own good works and the merits of Christ also as the procuring cause of our salvation have a strong appearance at a distance. But when we handle them, we find that, in fact, they make Christ of none effect to us.

If we are justified by faith in Christ, we are justified antecedently to any good work or qualifications of our own, for he justifies the ungodly. As such we must receive Christ, and if we do not see our misery and lost, undone state, we cannot and will not apply to Christ for justification. A first-rate saint observes that all our righteousnesses are but filthy rags. And, it may be asked, what kind of justification will filthy rags procure for us? If it be said that we are only properly justified when we sew together by our own endeavours our own filthy rags to the bright robes of our Redeemer's righteousness, and that this is what constitutes our justifying righteousness, the saints in light say, 'Not unto us, Lord, not unto us.' And if we have grace to perform any good work, who procured us this grace? We cannot call it our own—it is the gift of God through Christ.

And these specious doctrines that have the appearance of truth, but in reality are false and hollow, produce but hollow and empty Christians, like tares. The tares, however like in appearance they may be to the wheat, are empty of substance. False Christians are void of piety, and entertain principles and produce practices contrary to holiness. And as false doctrines are known by their tendency, false professors are known by their fruits. Our Saviour mentions this as the only criterion. 'By their fruits shall ye know them,' says he. That tares may be distinguished from the wheat and false professors from the true is clear from the next verses.

Verses 27–28. *So the servants of the householder came and said unto him, Sir, didst not thou sow good seed in thy field? from whence then hath it tares? He said unto them, An enemy hath done this. The servants said unto him, Wilt thou then that we go and gather them up?*

They are surprised at the growth of the tares, knowing that it was good seed that was sown in the field, and accordingly ask permission to pluck up the tares. May not this language represent the spirit of the zealous servants of God, the faithful ministers of the gospel? They are surprised and grieved at the small success of the gospel and the quick growth of pestilent opinions and wicked practices among professing Christians. They wish to reform the Church, and their honest zeal hath sometimes carried them too far. They wish to pluck up the tares. Even the apostles James and John would call down fire from heaven, and Peter draws the sword in his Master's cause. They

have shown an example in this which has been but too much followed in the Church. Good men have often gone too far in endeavouring to pluck up the tares and to reform the Church. They have
employed carnal weapons in the spiritual warfare. And as the best
of them are but men at the best, there is a danger in allowing them
to pluck up the tares. And this is clear from verses 29 and 30.

*Verses 29–30. But he said, Nay; lest while ye gather up the tares, ye
root up also the wheat with them. Let both grow together until the harvest: and in the time of harvest I will say to the reapers, Gather ye
together first the tares, and bind them in bundles to burn them: but gather
the wheat into my barn.*

The master of the field does not give permission to gather the tares
before harvest, lest the wheat should be plucked up also. And does
not the history of the Church throw light upon this truth? Have not
even saints persecuted saints, thinking them to be sinners? Did not
one Christian take up the sword against another? If a committee of
the most godly and learned clergymen and Christians in the kingdom were armed with secular and spiritual power to reform the
Church after the most diligent scrutiny, what would be the consequences? The consequences would be that, in many cases, they
would spare the smooth, polished, specious, well-spoken hypocrite,
and in some instances would break the bruised reed and quench the
smoking flax. Men have not the spiritual skill and address of our
Saviour to reject such characters as the amiable young ruler, and
receive the Samaritan and the thief.

And does the doctrine of the parable forbid the discipline of the
Church? It does not. It only supposes that, notwithstanding the
strictest attention to discipline, there will be tares among the wheat,
and that it will be best to permit this to happen in many cases, and
that spiritual rulers should ask spiritual wisdom to direct them in
their duty. What we cannot cure, we must endure.

Both must grow together till the harvest, and then the tares will be
gathered in bundles for the fire. They are gathered together in bun-

dles, and their punishment will be answerable to their sin. They have often gathered in companies to oppose the interest of Christ and the gospel. People that have jarring interests in other respects can unite in opposing the gospel. Herod and Pontius Pilate, though enemies before, became friends when Christ was to suffer. And in Church politics, when his cause is to suffer, how often has this cemented the friendship of the wicked? The tares, however, shall be gathered in bundles and burnt. But the wheat shall be gathered into the barn. All God's jewels shall be brought into one place, and, oh, how bright shall their united light shine! What a beautiful group! What a bright company! They shine like the stars for ever and ever; they even shine like the sun in the kingdom of their Father.

I reserve what I have further to say upon this parable till the inferences, and proceed to speak a little about the other two parables— the grain of mustard seed and the leaven.

Parable of the mustard seed

Verses 31–32. *Another parable put he forth unto them, saying, The kingdom of heaven is like to a grain of mustard seed, which a man took, and sowed in his field: which indeed is the least of all seeds: but when it is grown, it is the greatest among herbs, and becometh a tree, so that the birds of the air come and lodge in the branches thereof.*

In these words, we see the wonderful success of the gospel from small and unpromising beginnings. Mustard seed is one of the smallest seeds that is sown in the earth, but in warm climates it arrives at a great and wonderful growth. The fowls of the air lodge in the branches, and it provides a shelter to them.

When the gospel made its first appearance, it was despised and rejected of men, like its divine Author. To the Jews it was a stumblingblock, and to the Greeks foolishness. In a short time, however, it became a great tree, like to that which King Nebuchadnezzar saw in his dream. The gospel soon spread. The great apostle of the Gentiles preached the joyful tidings all the way from Jerusalem to Illyricum. He spread the news through a great part of Europe and Asia. It would appear that the Ethiopian eunuch, mentioned in the Acts of the Apostles, carried the gospel to Africa, and we learn from Church history that churches were planted in every quarter of the globe, even in countries that were not subdued by the Roman armies. And this happened in the first and second centuries, long before Christianity was the religion of the State. And when God shall give command, it shall spread still further, and be the religion of all the world. And this appears from the next verse.

Parable of leaven

Verse 33. *Another parable spake he unto them; The kingdom of heaven is like unto leaven, which a woman took, and hid in three measures of meal, till the whole was leavened.*

It is the property of leaven that, as the apostle expresses it, a little leaven leaveneth the whole lump. It is said in the parable that a woman hid the leaven in three measures of meal till the whole was leavened. By three measures, divines understand three-quarters of the globe—Europe, Asia, and Africa—the three-quarters of the then-known world. Now, the truth is that the gospel leaven is to leaven the whole lump. The whole earth is to be converted to the faith of Christ. And this shall happen not by power or might, but by the gospel itself. The State cannot make Christians; the sword cannot convert men to God. The Church once made crusades, or what they called holy wars, to recover the Holy Land from the hands of infidels. As this was the work of men, it came to nought, and infidels still possess the land of Canaan. But when God gives the Word—the gospel which now lies hid will exert its natural energy, and subdue all nations to the obedience of Christ.

Parabolic teaching

> Verses 34–35. *All these things spake Jesus unto the multitude in parables; and without a parable spake he not unto them: that it might be fulfilled which was spoken by the prophet, saying, I will open my mouth in parables; I will utter things which have been kept secret from the foundation of the world.*

God promised his people that he was to raise up a great prophet among them, who was to declare his will to them. And a part of his doctrine was to be given in parables, as we learn from the Psalmist. All the ancient prophecies centre in Christ, and it was necessary that the very minutest of them should be exactly fulfilled. On this very account, it was necessary that he should ride upon an ass's colt, and that his very clothes should be divided among the Roman soldiers. Our Saviour gave his doctrine in dark parables and revealed heavenly truths that were hid from the beginning of the world. Was not the doctrine of the ancient patriarchs and the whole Jewish religion a dark parable till our Saviour explained it by his gospel? The gospel revealed what was hid for ages and generations.

> Verse 36. *Then Jesus sent the multitude away, and went into the house: and his disciples came unto him, saying, Declare unto us the parable of the tares of the field.*

Our Lord, like a wise and compassionate physician, applies his medicines according to the spiritual state of his patients. The multitude he taught by parables which, though they could not fully understand, they could well remember.

Now, as medicines do not always work an instantaneous cure till some time after they are taken, the doctrines of our Saviour did not produce their full effect till afterwards. In some few, such as his disciples and immediate followers, they produced conviction all at once. And these had the benefit of his heavenly conversation and familiar discourses. What they could not understand of his public doctrine was explained to them in private, as we learn from this parable. The multitude, however, who were benefited by his instructions but in part, remembered the doctrines they heard. After his resurrection from the dead, the seed that was sown in their hearts, being quickened by divine influences, began to show itself by their conversion to the faith. In a short time, they saw and understood the meaning of his parables. They saw the parable of the sower and the tares of the field exemplified in their countrymen, the Jews, and the conversion of the Gentiles. The mustard seed and the leaven they understood when the gospel began to spread.

We see in the words of the text, the disciples asked him to explain the tares of the field. The few that followed him were prepared for what was to follow by his private instructions. There was a necessity for our Lord's teaching by parables and explaining them privately during his own ministry. If he had plainly explained his doctrine all at once, he would have offended his friends as well as his enemies. And this we learn from the rebuke which Peter gave him when he spoke about his sufferings.

> Verses 37–43. *He answered and said unto them, He that soweth the good seed is the Son of man; the field is the world; the good seed are the children of the kingdom; but the tares are the children of the wicked one; the enemy that sowed them is the devil; the harvest is the end of the world; and the reapers are the angels. As therefore the tares are gathered and burned in the fire; so shall it be in the end of this world. The Son of man shall send forth his angels, and they shall gather out of his kingdom all things that offend, and them which do iniquity; and shall cast them into a furnace of fire: there shall be wailing and gnashing of teeth. Then shall the righteous shine forth as the sun in the kingdom of their Father. Who hath ears to hear, let him hear.*

Practical remarks

From the doctrine we heard and the explanation our Saviour gives of the parable, the following remarks are offered as worthy of your attention and care.

1. First, our Lord taught by parable, and there was a necessity for this method of instruction. The Jews were taught to believe from the writings of Moses and the prophets that the Messiah was to come into the world. From the description given of him in Scripture, they justly concluded he would be a great personage, but they falsely supposed that he would set up a great earthly kingdom, not considering that he must suffer before he was to reign. The prejudice in favour of an earthly king was so strong that the notion must be gradually opposed and the true doctrine offered by parable and allegory. And next to the power of God, nothing but the sufferings of Christ, of which they were eyewitnesses, could persuade his most faithful followers of the nature of his kingdom.

2. Secondly, there is a kingdom of heaven upon earth, but all that profess to be members of it are not in the interests of their Prince and King. The language of the hearts and practice of many is, 'We will not have this man to reign over us.' The tares, though like in appearance, in substance, however, are unlike to the wheat. Though false professors agree in some opinions and practices with good Christians, they differ with them in the main points. The Jews would submit to Christ if he came as a great king and earthly conqueror. They would own him to be the Messiah if he bestowed upon them riches and pleasures and power.

And if Jesus Christ granted liberty to his followers to pursue their favourite passions, that they might live as they pleased, and that he promised earthly pleasures in a heavenly world, the multitude would follow him. Devils and infidels would commence to believe it. We should hear no more complaints of the gospel. But such a Messiah and such a kingdom would be unworthy of God. If God erect a kingdom upon earth, it must be pure and spiritual and heavenly.

Now, whatever they may profess, the bulk of mankind will not submit to such a kingdom. They may have several reasons for professing to be members of his kingdom, but they hate his kingdom in their hearts. His kingdom never had greater enemies than those who professed to be its true and only subjects.

That all professors are not of this kingdom, but tares among the wheat, is clear from the following reasons. Christ's subjects are a willing people, made so in a day of power. Can those, then, who have no will to his work and favour, be called a willing people? And much less can those be so called who ridicule and hate every appearance of seriousness. His subjects are a free people. They are not the slaves of their own passions—they are kings and priests, for they rule over their sins.

Now, sinners cannot be members of his kingdom. His subjects are zealous of good works. Their measure of grace at first may be small, like the grain of mustard seed, and they may be obscure in the world, like leaven hid in meal, but they have a catholic spirit, and wish to disseminate the gospel. Their profession is not merely in word but in power. And though they are in the world like wheat among the tares, they do not mix with the world, but oppose its corruptions, and keep from its bad example and practices.

3. Lastly, from the different lot of bad and good men in the life to come, we may learn the important lesson of fleeing from the wrath to come and avoiding the place of torment. With what care ought we to avoid sin and prepare ourselves for that kingdom where the righteous shall shine like the sun! And should it not quicken our diligence to gain souls to Christ when Scripture informs us that they who do so shall shine as the stars for ever and ever. What bright promises! What scenes of happiness in the world to come! Behold the righteous, how they shine! Would you wish to be with them? Follow their faith and patience. The world takes no notice of you now: they must look at you when you shall shine like the sun and stars. Endeavour, then, to shine here. 'Whosoever hath ears to hear, let him hear.'

AMEN.

Matthew chapter 13: verses 44 to 58

OUR Lord still continues the parabolical method of instruction as the best adapted to the bulk of his hearers. Having already showed the beauty and propriety of this method of teaching, I proceed to the illustration of his other parables, and the reception he met with in his own country, and conclude with some practical inferences.

Parable of hid treasure

Verse 44. *Again, the kingdom of heaven is like unto treasure hid in a field; the which when a man hath found, he hideth, and for joy thereof goeth and selleth all that he hath, and buyeth that field.*

As the bulk of mankind place their happiness in riches, Scripture speaks of unsearchable riches and treasures to be found in Christ. The people of the world seem to think that all kind of happiness is to be found in riches. When a man finds a treasure hid in a field, he conceals what he got, and as he believes there is a great deal more if the field was his own, he should have a right to the treasure. Accordingly, he sells his all and buys the field for the sake of the treasure. The treasure, he supposes, can make him rich, and can procure him all the delights of the children of men.

Happiness is the great object of every rational being. And whatever species of happiness he pursues, he would forego everything to obtain that. If a man sees his happiness in the enjoyment of anything, he surmounts all difficulties to obtain that thing. The creature is seeking happiness in this and the other vanity. At last, he comes to the field of the gospel. He is advised to dig there, and that he shall find a treasure. He does so, and the treasure satisfies him. He was in quest of happiness, and here he finds what fills all the desires of his soul. And as the worldly man with joy will hide the treasure that he may engross it all to himself, in like manner he hides the Word of God in his heart, and receives it now as his treasure. He sells all that he has; he foregoes every treasure that would stand in competition with the gospel. And this clearly points out the superlative love and esteem we ought to have for the truth.

We are desired in Scripture to buy the truth, and to buy milk and wine. Christ is in our offer, and we ought to prefer him to our chiefest joy. He is a treasure hid in the field of the gospel, and we are to sell everything to procure the treasure. Have we other treasures, and do we seek our happiness in other enjoyments? We are to remember that they who are Christ's crucify the flesh with the affections and lusts. We are likewise to remember that the treasure is hid in the field. We are therefore to dig for it. This shows us our duty. We are certainly to struggle to come to Christ—we must strive to enter in at the strait gate, and do our diligence to be found in him at last, without spot or wrinkle.

The Pearl of great price

Verses 45–46. *Again, the kingdom of heaven is like unto a merchant man, seeking goodly pearls: who, when he had found one pearl of great price, went and sold all that he had, and bought it.*

We all know the value which mankind put upon precious stones, pearls, and jewels of every kind. But as mankind put a value upon them, the trade has become interesting and profitable. Now, a person dealing in this branch of commerce might meet with one pearl, the value of which is so great that he would give all the riches he had in order to procure it. He knows it is a valuable acquisition and that this alone will make his fortune. And Christ is the Pearl of great price, and therefore more valuable than every other pearl, than every species of happiness in which people seek happiness and satisfaction to themselves. Christ is the Pearl of great price because all fulness is in him alone. Why are people in quest of pleasure, of riches, and of honour, but because they think they confer happiness? Now, all happiness is to be found in him alone.

We can suppose a case that may occasionally happen. A rich man might travel in disguise in a foreign country. He may have papers and notes to the value of many thousands about him and but an inconsiderable quantity of small money about him. As he passes for a poor man in a strange country, he may pass some part of his time with apparent inconveniency, but he is happy, notwithstanding, for he knows himself to be a man of fortune, and he carries a great share of riches about with him. He may live happily, though his travelling in disguise and the want of small money may occasion inconvenience. If a man has the Pearl of great price, he is inconceivably happy, and he sees his own happiness. As he travels in disguise in this world, he may want some things, but this does not affect his happiness; he knows he is rich, and will be happy when he comes to his own country. Let us secure this Pearl.

Parable of the net cast into the sea

Verses 47–50. *Again, the kingdom of heaven is like unto a net, that was cast into the sea, and gathered of every kind: which, when it was full, they drew to shore, and sat down, and gathered the good into vessels, but cast the bad away. So shall it be at the end of the world: the angels shall come forth, and sever the wicked from among the just, and shall cast them into the furnace of fire: there shall be wailing and gnashing of teeth.*

In this parable, we find a description of the visible Church and the different states of good and bad men at the consummation of all things. In the net there are good and bad fishes, and notwithstanding the care and vigilance of the ministers of the gospel, wicked men will make their way into the Church. But at the end of the world, we find that sinners shall be cast into a furnace of fire, where there will be weeping, wailing, and gnashing of teeth.

But perhaps our carnal reason will object to this, and reply, 'How is it consistent with the goodness of God to inflict such terrible punishment for momentary crimes?' To this it is answered that though God has no pleasure in the death of sinners, yet, as he has bestowed immortality upon the human soul, he has informed his creatures that misery must be the result of following their own sinful will and happiness. They are outwith the will of God.

It appears clearly from Scripture that the soul is immortal, and in spite of all the arts of infidels, in spite of their endeavours to become brutes, when they are in distress they believe the doctrine. Now, the hell mentioned in Scripture is being given up to unsanctified passions and the reflections of their own minds. If the thoughts are foul and unholy, to be given up to them is the greatest punishment. Now, the sinner can blame none but himself, for he got fair warning of his danger. The Judge of all the earth will surely do right, and it will be found hereafter that the criminals themselves will acknowledge the sentence to be just.

New and old treasures

Verse 51. *Jesus saith unto them, Have ye understood all these things? They say unto him, Yea, Lord.*

It is not enough that we hear doctrine and attend ordinances. It is necessary for us that we understand what we hear and reduce it to practice. If we understood what we heard, we would believe, and if we believed aright, we should naturally obey. And this question may be proposed to all hearers. How many come to the house of God and hear the gospel for many years, who remain stupidly ignorant and cannot give a reason of the hope that is in them, or give any solid argument why they believe the Christian religion? Ignorance is a common and deadly disease, even among those who pretend [claim] to have knowledge.

Verse 52. *Then said he unto them, Therefore every scribe which is instructed unto the kingdom of heaven is like unto a man that is an householder, which bringeth forth out of his treasure things new and old.*

From this comparison, we see the necessity there is for setting old and precious truths in a new light, that they may strike the mind and procure attention. It is necessary that the people should often hear something new. Unless the attention is kept up, people are very ready to forget what they hear. It requires prayer in a clergyman for direction to preach, not only useful truths in general, but likewise the particular truths that their spiritual wants more specially require.

We read in sacred history that Goliath was struck in the forehead; we read in profane story that Achilles was wounded in the heel. However much a sinner may be entrenched in infidelity, he is vulnerable somewhere. The great art is to hit the mark, to strike so as to wound, to wound so as to make the sinner fall, and who is sufficient for these things? If he hears what he has often heard before, he seems to be prepared for the attack. To bring the truth with irresistible force to the mind, it must come in a new dress and be set in a new light, to gain attention and pierce the conscience. Such as are conversant in history know that a battle has been gained by a new kind of armour and a new method of fighting.

Jesus rejected at Nazaraeth

Verses 53–58. *And it came to pass, that when Jesus had finished these parables, he departed thence. And when he was come into his own country, he taught them in their synagogue, insomuch that they were astonished, and said, Whence hath this man this wisdom, and these mighty works? Is not this the carpenter's son? is not his mother called Mary? and his brethren, James, and Joses, and Simon, and Judas? And his sisters, are they not all with us? Whence then hath this man all these things? And they were offended in him. But Jesus said unto them, A prophet is not without honour, save in his own country, and in his own house. And he did not many mighty works there because of their unbelief.*

In these words, we see the force of prejudice and the natural power of unbelief. The Jews were taught to look for a carnal Messiah and a glorious conqueror, who, they expected, would raise their nation to the highest pitch of dignity and honour. As Christ made a lowly appearance among them, they could not therefore see the divine power in his miracles, or the accomplishment of prophecy in his person. Deny his miracles they could not, but they despised them as performed by the reputed son of Joseph. His nearest relations are poor, and this is the great objection to their perceiving the hand of God in his work. Fraught with ignorance and pride, and petrified [turned to stone] with the love of the world, they despised such a meek and lowly Saviour. They forgot that David, his predecessor, was advanced from the sheepfold to the throne. Jacob, their great predecessor, passed over the Jordan with only his staff in his hand when he fled from his brother Esau, and Elijah, their great prophet and the restorer of the law of God, was so poor that he was fed, first by the ravens and afterwards by the widow of Sarepta. And these men, notwithstanding their poverty and low circumstances, were high in the favour of God, and one of them wrought astonishing miracles.

There is but one God, and the Old Testament, as well as the New, speaks of the Son, and commands us to worship him; and Christ wrought miracles to prove that he was that Son, and therefore the object of divine worship. If Christ wrought miracles to draw men from the worship of the one God to idolatry, the Jews had been in the right to accuse him; but he taught people to worship one God, who is a Spirit, in spirit and in truth. He taught that there were three persons in the divine essence, and the very first verse of the first book of the Old Testament speaks of God in the plural number. And as his countrymen rejected the method which infinite Wisdom saw meet to employ to bring them to repentance and reformation, he did not work many miracles among them on account of their unbelief.

Practical inferences

I shall conclude this lecture with some practical inferences.

1. If Christ is the treasure hid in the field of the gospel—if he be the Pearl of great price—it is our duty, like the wise merchant, to sell everything to buy the field and purchase the Pearl. This treasure, this precious jewel, can enrich our souls. Here happiness is to be found. In him are hid all the treasures of wisdom and knowledge. In him dwelleth all the fulness of the Godhead bodily. If we seek our happiness here, we need not go anywhere else in quest of it. He is the fountain of life, and the sun that enlightens the spiritual world.

2. If there is a spiritual state, as reason and Scripture assert, we should examine whether our conduct is such as gives us room to expect that it will be well with us hereafter. Have we fled for refuge to the Saviour to secure us from the wrath to come? Did we forsake sin, and is our peace made with God? If so, we are safe—we are happy: if not, we should flee without delay from the wrath to come. In Noah's time, there was a reprieve and delay of one hundred and twenty years given people to repent of their sins. How many years have you to work out your salvation? Do we understand what we hear? Do we believe the tremendous truths of Christianity? Do we understand that we have souls, and that our souls are destined for immortality? If we do not understand, how criminal is our ignorance! If we do, how guilty is our conduct before God if we do not! If ministers are to have things new as well as old, it is the duty of the people to pray for them that they may be directed to the doctrines necessary for their spiritual state, whether for instruction, reproof, or consolation. Brethren, pray for our souls as well as for your own.

3. Lastly, we see from these words the malignant nature of unbelief. The most powerful miracles to convince them had no effect, even upon Christ's countrymen. Unbelief, then, is the great sin, the capital crime of the Christian world. It resists all the means of grace; it renders of none effect all the arguments, all the promises, threatenings, and precepts of the Word. We ought to pray to God with earnest-

ness against the prevalence of this malignant, this deadly disease. Let us entreat God that he would enlighten our minds and soften our hearts, that we may see the glory of Christ in the gospel.

Matthew chapter 14: verses 1 to 21

MIRACLES are one of the proofs of the divine authority of Scripture. They were designed to convince unbelievers, and if they always remain in unbelief they must be inexcusable. Miracles will naturally gain attention—they are calculated to gain authority to a doctrine.

Accordingly, as Moses had a new doctrine and a new dispensation to reveal to mankind, and was a promised leader to lead the people out of Egypt, he supported his pretensions by miracles. What was the doctrine of Moses? That there is but one God—that the seed of the woman would bruise the serpent's head—that this seed was to be of the tribe of Judah, and would appear when the sceptre would depart from that tribe.

What was the doctrine of Christ? That there is but one God—that the seed of the woman is come—that he was the Messiah promised—the incarnate God. He proves his divine mission by miracles. Now, miracles have an effect upon mankind, else God would not work them. They had an effect upon Pharaoh, hardened as he was, and at last he let the people go. And though our modern sceptics laugh at the idea of miracles, it seems their predecessors had more modesty. They did not pretend to deny facts that were attested by thousands of witnesses and spectators. Even wicked Herod acknowledged the truth. And as the scribes and Pharisees could not deny facts, they ascribed them to magic. But the malignant insinuation confutes [refutes] itself. Let common sense speak. Can evil spirits—can anything short of almighty power—perform such works of wonder as are mentioned in the gospels?

The works wrought by our Saviour came to the ears of Herod, and, though they did not work repentance in his soul, they roused his

198

guilty conscience, for he was afraid it was John the Baptist risen from the dead. The piece of history respecting Herod and the miracle of the loaves shall form our meditation for this day, and I shall, in a word, conclude with some practical inferences.

The martyrdom of John the Baptist

Verses 1–2. At that time Herod the tetrarch heard of the fame of Jesus, and said unto his servants, This is John the Baptist; he is risen from the dead; and therefore mighty works do shew forth themselves in him.

The power of conscience is great. However great the power of the wicked may be, however secret their crimes, guilt lying upon the conscience will occasionally terrify their souls. Instances similar to this occur in the history of every kingdom and country. No state, however dignified, can hide a man from his own thoughts. Vengeance pursues the sinner, and several circumstances bring his sin to remembrance, and make him uneasy amidst apparent ease and happiness.

We sometimes think people happy because they have a polished outside, and they seem to have the smile of happiness upon their countenance. But if we saw their minds, they are often racked with misery and despair. Misery is the portion of wickedness, even in this same life. Great crimes are attended with great torture, and the sinner reaps a part of what he sows in this same world. Murder and robbery are dreadful sins.

Will not your own reflections tell you that if a man, to enrich himself and family, will turn a number of poor families adrift upon the wide world, he must feel pangs of guilt? Some of these poor creatures die of cold and diseases contracted in bad lodgings and starved circumstances. And are not the authors of their misery guilty of murder in the sight of God? Tyrants can establish iniquity by law and give it all the authority of human laws. We leave this to the stings of their own conscience. And that murder, committed directly or indirectly, will raise and leave very uneasy reflections, is clear from the history of

Joseph. His brethren thought he had been dead, and that his blood had been required. And if people are accessory to the death and temporal misery of their fellow creatures, their thoughts will make them unhappy.

> Verses 3–4. *For Herod had laid hold on John, and bound him, and put him in prison for Herodias' sake, his brother Philip's wife. For John said unto him, It is not lawful for thee to have her.*

We learn from another of the evangelists that Herod, before this time, had paid great attention to the doctrine of John the Baptist, and did many things. The king had some appearance of seriousness, and it is likely he had given up some other sins. But the Baptist, faithful to God and to the souls of his hearers, would not, through flattery or false complaisance, wink at sin in any man, and therefore rebuked the king for his wicked deeds. Offended at the courage and faithfulness of the good man, he added this to all his other wickedness, that he put him in prison. Herod, it is likely, could bear the faithfulness of the Baptist in other things, had he spared his darling sin, but here he could not bear control.

In the Baptist, we have an example of faithfulness and courage becoming the faithful ministers of Christ. John is not afraid of the frown of a worthless tyrant. By winking at his faults, he might procure favour and even respect for himself at Herod's court. But had he done so, he had betrayed his trust and forfeited the great character which he had supported before. Riches and respect at the expense of virtue are too dear a purchase. The Baptist's conscience would not stoop to flatter a strumpet [prostitute] or to encourage a tyrant in his vices. Had he lived in our days, possibly some of the polite clergy would have laughed at him as an accomplished rustic that had the bad manners to see the faults of the great.

> Verse 5. *And when he would have put him to death, he feared the multitude, because they counted him as a prophet.*

Though he imprisoned him, he was afraid to imbrue his hand in his blood, and this did not arise from any principle of honour or virtue, but merely from fear. Tyrants are often afraid of the people, and they have cause. They are always ready to rise if they had a fit opportunity and found a proper man to head them. Herod was afraid of some commotion if he had put him to death. He was a murderer in intention long before he put his design in execution. Many are guilty of great crimes in the sight of God, and we are indebted to his restraining providence that the wicked are not so bad as they would incline. The fear of the law, the shame of the world, or some prudential consideration prevented them.

Verses 6–11. *But when Herod's birthday was kept, the daughter of Herodias danced before them, and pleased Herod. Whereupon he promised with an oath to give her whatsoever she would ask. And she, being before instructed of her mother, said, Give me here John Baptist's head in a charger. And the king was sorry: nevertheless for the oath's sake, and them which sat with him at meat, he commanded it to be given her. And he sent, and beheaded John in the prison. And his head was brought in a charger, and given to the damsel: and she brought it to her mother.*

The tyrant has now a fit opportunity of putting his bloody design in execution, and gratifying the revenge of a base woman. His birthday is kept, and he stains it with the murder of an innocent person. One would think that a regard to character, to decency, and to propriety would keep his birthday free from murder at least. But sin blinds the eyes of the mind, and when people stifle the voice of reason and conscience, it is no wonder they should be deaf to every other consideration.

The daughter of Herodias came in and danced before the company, and pleased Herod so much that he promised with an oath to give her anything she asked. Instructed by her worthless mother, she asks the head of the Baptist. Strange infatuation! What could a young lady make of such a present? Why did she not ask a large sum of money, or something handsome that would have innocently promoted her temporal interest, a present that had been worthy of the royal dignity and worthy of the young lady's virtue and character? Instead of this, she stains her own soul with murder, and seals her mother's infamy. She verified the word that says, 'Like mother, like daughter,' and indeed, if free grace does not interpose, what can be expected from bad parents but bad children?

The king was sorry, and no wonder, but he pretends the conscience of an oath. And here we see the awful nature of sin: one crime begets another, and the wretched sinner seldom or never stops till he plunges his soul and body in misery and perdition. The young lady's request is granted her, and we would think she needed not to boast of her achievement. History says that her crime did not go unpunished, that afterwards, in passing over ice, it broke under her, so that she fell in and had her head separated from her body.

And here one cannot help remarking what a slavish and unmanly part all the nobles and great men of Galilee had acted upon this occasion. There is none found to plead the cause of oppressed innocence and virtue. None of them had the courage or virtue to remonstrate with the king upon the base and unprincely part he was acting, or with the young lady upon her shameful and unnatural petition. Base and worthless as Herod was, they might have prevented his bringing such an unlucky omen upon his birthday. They might put him in mind that King David altered his resolution, though he swore to put Nabal to death. How much more fit was it for Herod to break his sinful oath and spare the Baptist! But when great men go on in wickedness, they obtain evil counsellors and flatterers by way of curse.

> Verses 12–13. *And his disciples came, and took up the body, and buried it, and went and told Jesus. When Jesus heard of it, he departed thence by ship into a desert place apart: and when the people had heard thereof, they followed him on foot out of the cities.*

In these words, we find that after John's disciples had performed the last duty to their master, they returned and told Jesus. Upon this, he departed unto a desert place, and numbers of people followed him on foot from the cities.

When we read the gospel with attention, we find that Christ is true God and true man. We have lately heard that the fulness of the God-head dwelleth in him bodily, and, if so, why should he flee from Herod and avoid the fury of his enemies? Let it be observed that it was to suffer he came into the world, and his time for suffering was not yet come.

The wisdom of God did not see it meet that our Saviour be always working miracles on all ordinary occasions. His natural life was not supported by miracles: he wrought with his hands before he was called to the ministry; nor did he support himself by manna, or work wonders to procure food after he began to preach the gospel. When he could avoid the fury of Herod by leaving the place he was in, he did not exert his power to deliver himself. His name is Wonderful, for he united infinite power and human weakness in his own person. His enemies said by way of derision when he was upon the cross, 'He saved others; he cannot save himself.' They spoke truth: he was crucified in weakness. He could not save himself, for God cannot lie, and he promised to save his people by suffering in their stead.

Verse 14. *And Jesus went forth, and saw a great multitude, and was moved with compassion toward them, and he healed their sick.*

Here we see that if he chose, he could laugh at the impotent malice of Herod and all his enemies, for the person that could work such wonderful works could restrain the fury of his enemies. By a word of his power, he made those who came to apprehend him fall back-wards on the ground. When he saw the multitude, he was moved with compassion and healed their sick. Could a mere man do this, or can any power less than divine do such works as the evangelists ascribe to our Saviour? He relieved the miserable, and always granted their request.

Feeding of the five thousand

Verses 15–21. *And when it was evening, his disciples came to him, saying, This is a desert place, and the time is now past; send the multitude away, that they may go into the villages, and buy themselves victuals. But Jesus said unto them, They need not depart; give ye them to eat. And they say unto him, We have here but five loaves, and two fishes. He said, Bring them hither to me. And he commanded the multitude to sit down on the grass, and took the five loaves, and the two fishes, and looking up to heaven, he blessed, and brake, and gave the loaves to his disciples, and the disciples to the multitude. And they did all eat, and were filled: and they took up of the fragments that remained twelve baskets full. And they that had eaten were about five thousand men, beside women and children.*

In these words, we have an account of an astonishing miracle which our Lord wrought to relieve the necessity of his followers and prove the truth of his doctrine. As the evening drew nigh, his disciples inform him that the people, who had continued now a long time hearing his heavenly instructions, should be dismissed, for a number of them had come a distance. He told them there was no necessity to send them away, and ordered them to give them food. They informed him that they had but five loaves and two fishes, and this was far from being sufficient for such a multitude, consisting of five thousand men, besides women and children. By this account, it is likely the number of persons fed by the five loaves and two fishes amounted to ten thousand or twelve thousand at least. In large congregations we may say that the women and children make up more than one half.

And here we may observe the decorum our Lord observed on this and on every other occasion. He made them sit down by ranks in order upon the green grass. He intended to work a miracle before them. But it was necessary to prepare them, for though God can do everything, he only works in behalf of those who believe. Unbelief, cursed, malignant sin, ties up (as it were) the hands of omnipotence.

When Lazarus was to be raised, the people are prepared for what is to follow by our Lord's discourse and prayer, and by ordering to remove the stone from the mouth of the grave. At this time, likewise, he took the loaves and fishes in his own blessed hands, he looked up to heaven, he blessed the food, broke the loaves, and ordered his disciples to distribute them among the people. His implacable enemies, among their other wicked charges, alleged he kept correspondence with the spirits of darkness, and by the help of these performed his miracles. And therefore, partly to confute his malignant foes, and more especially to strengthen the faith of his followers and show us a holy example, he asked a blessing upon the food. His blessing wrought effectually, for the loaves began to multiply, and after feeding five thousand men, besides women and children, the fragments that remained were more than what was at first laid before them.

This great multitude did eat and were satisfied; they were all satisfied and left abundance. And here we cannot help observing the malicious and senseless insinuation of several unbelievers. They said that all this was but an illusion upon their senses. But several thousands could confute this senseless remark. An illusion upon the sight could never feed a hungry multitude. Evil spirits could not and would not work such miracles. A mere creature could not do these things. Wicked spirits would not destroy their own power, worship and influence. The doctrine of the gospel was their greatest enemy. It is a doctrine of strict purity.

Miracles, then, are the work of God, and he wrought them to confirm a pure and a holy doctrine. We may appeal to the common sense of any man, and ask him, 'What is his objection to the morality of the gospel?' We are taught to worship God and to live soberly, righteously, and godly in this world. If we are taught to believe mysteries, reason may tell us that the mystery must be true, for God cannot tell a lie.

Practical inferences

We conclude with some practical inferences.

1. From what we heard, we may learn the misery of the wicked. An evil conscience is a troublesome companion. He follows them, whether they will or not. Whether the sinner lives in a cottage or in a palace, he is an object of compassion. Herod, though surrounded by flattering courtiers, living in a palace and possessed of absolute power, is afraid of John the Baptist, even after his death. And whatever sins people are guilty of, they occasionally fill them with terror.

2. We learn from these words a lesson of the infinite wisdom and goodness of God to sinners in general. People often are ready to complain of their lot, and to think how much happier they would be in a more elevated rank, or in more affluent circumstances. In these thoughts, people are greatly mistaken. God not only knows what is best for us, but also what we would do in such and such circumstances. Herod and Hazael may show us what unsanctified nature armed with power is capable of effecting. But instances of this kind are almost innumerable. It is the sinner's mercy that he is kept in low circumstances. If he continues a devil notwithstanding the cold blast of poverty, he would soon render himself a monster if he had riches and power.

3. We here see the malignant and awful effect of bad example. Children generally follow a good deal of what they see. Herodias had a bad mother, who trained her up in the school of sin. She was accessory to her mother's crime, and had a hand in the murder of the innocent Baptist. Had Herodias the benefit of a virtuous and religious education, she might have proved a very different character. We might hear her name mentioned among the saints, and her character might have a sweet savour to the end of the world. Instead of this, we hear her name with abhorrence, and young Herodias is nearly as nauseous [loathsome] as the infamous mother that bore her. And this may teach us how much is in the power of parents. They form the character of their children, and their example often has an influence upon their everlasting state. If they train them up

in a disrelish of the gospel, or if the children catch the infection of any of the bad habits, or vicious [immoral] or idle practices of their parents, they may seal their misery for ever. If parents gave a good and religious example to their children, they may be the means of their conversion to God. At any rate, they keep them from many sins into which they would otherwise fall, and by endeavouring to give them a relish for the gospel, they put them in a hopeful way of meeting the Saviour.

4. From the death of John the Baptist and the triumph of a wicked woman, we have one of the strongest arguments of a future state. God often permits his people to be poor, to live despised and persecuted, and to die in misery or obscurity. He allows the meanest and most worthless of mankind to rise to notice, to thrive in the world, to prosper in vice and wickedness, and to oppress the virtuous and innocent. Are we, therefore, to suppose that God is like an idle spectator, or indifferent about what passes in this lower world? He is not. If we got one peep into the invisible world and saw but one sight of John the Baptist this day, and of Herodias and her wicked mother, we would justify the providence of God, and say that he did all things well. Verily there is a reward for the righteous, and there is a God who judgeth in the earth.

5. Lastly, in the miracle wrought by Christ, we may learn one substantial lesson as Christians. We have no ground to look for miracles, nor is there any necessity for them. But we may look for a divine blessing upon our temporal concerns. We see our Lord blessed the loaves and brake them. The disciples had but few loaves, but they brought them to Christ. Let us do the same. Our loaves may be few and our circumstances straitened. Let us bring our loaves to the Saviour that he bless them. A righteous person may have but little, but that little is better than the great riches of the wicked. If the poor man brought his loaf to the Saviour, he would find the blessed effects. Instead of this, many wish to increase their loaves by sinful means, or at any rate by their unbelieving industry. Many trust more in their own exertions than in the blessing of Christ. So fare many of them: their exertions miscarry, and their

unbelief brings leanness upon their souls. Christians, if you trust your souls to Christ, you may trust him with the loaves to bless them. This is a sure way to thrive in your souls and circumstances.

May God bless his Word. AMEN.

Matthew chapter 14: verses 22 to 36

WHEN we compare the Scriptures of the Old and New Testament, we find that the same works that are ascribed to God are ascribed to our Lord Jesus Christ.

Among other things, we read in the book of Job, 9th chapter and 8th verse, that God treadeth upon the waves of the sea. 'He maketh Arcturus, Orion and Pleiades, and the chambers of the south. He doeth great things past finding out; and wonders without number.' But the greatest wonder he hath done is his assuming the human nature and working our redemption. Men of great learning inform us that the earth moves round about the sun. And we may venture to affirm that several minute philosophers,[13] who are infidels about the gospel, are infidels also about this part of natural philosophy,[14] or if they do believe it, they believe it as the vulgar [ordinary people] do, upon the authority of others.

The reports of philosophers may justly stagger our reason, and yet we believe things upon their authority. And may we not equally believe the astonishing truths of the gospel, since reason may assure us that God will not—and indeed cannot—deceive his creatures? For hear the God of truth—and he wrought great miracles to gain our belief.

We shall speak a little of what you heard, and conclude with some practical inferences.

---

[13] Philosophers who are very precise about very small matters. [RJD]
[14] The philosophical study of nature and the physical universe. [RJD]

Jesus walking upon the sea

Verses 22–23. *And straightway Jesus constrained his disciples to get into a ship, and to go before him unto the other side, while he sent the multitudes away. And when he had sent the multitudes away, he went up into a mountain apart to pray: and when the evening was come, he was there alone.*

After our Lord had wrought the miracle in feeding several thousands with five loaves and two fishes, he sent his disciples away, and he himself retired into a mountain to pray. Our Lord dealt much in prayer, and what was the subject of his prayers? He prayed for himself and for his people. The apostle to the Hebrews informs us that he offered up prayers and supplications with strong cries and tears to him that was able to save him from death, and was heard in that he feared. The great work he undertook required strength and assistance. In the prayers, therefore, of our Lord, we have an example of the petitions that succeed at a throne of grace.

Our Lord prayed from a sense of need: his petitions were not the language of form and ceremony, but the genuine dictates of the heart. He felt his need, and prayed for assistance. That he was supported by the arm of omnipotence we learn from the 42nd chapter of Isaiah. Now, our Lord's prayers, like his great sacrifice, were offered through the eternal Spirit, and his divine nature gave a dignity and savour to both that rendered them acceptable.

But we are told that Christ is God, and what need had he to pray? Answer: He was man, and as such, he prayed that his human nature would be enabled to support the great burden he had to bear. And he was supported, as he was man, to suffer for all his people. And he often took opportunities to pray. Profane worldlings may think that the people of God spend more time than they need in prayer at religious duties. Like graceless Pharaoh, they may say and think they are idle and have little to do. Christians, however, will find use for their prayers at death. Christ saw what was before him, and he prepared himself by prayer, and so ought we.

And would not you think yourself happy if you thought yourself one of those for whom he prayed in the mount? Did you, and do you, put a value upon his prayers? And do your prayers, like his, proceed from a sense of need or a strong desire to be found in Christ and have an interest in his prayers?

And as our Lord prayed for himself, that he might obtain strength to perform the great work of redemption, I have no doubt but he prayed for all his people by name. He undertook for them all: they lay upon his heart and were engraved upon the palms of his hands. And if there is such astonishing efficacy in the prayers of his poor people, though mixed with many weaknesses, imperfections, and blemishes, how powerful must the prayers of our great high priest have been! It was his prayers that put life and vigour in every prayer that ever ascended to heaven and found acceptance at the throne. His prayers were valid upon earth. He knew to whom he was praying, and they never returned empty. Happy are the souls for whom he is praying in heaven: they shall be sure to obtain his help, though he should delay coming to their assistance to the fourth watch of the night.

But some poor soul will say, 'How will I know whether he prays for me, as my prayers are so weak and worthless?' Answer: Is it not your desire to put your prayers in the hands of the great Mediator, and to be accepted by his merits? If so, your prayers are heard and will be accepted.

I was reading in the last newspaper that there were three farthings coined in the reign of Queen Anne—they were so valuable, because so few, that a poor man who found one of them obtained £400 sterling for a single farthing. Now, your prayer, though of small value itself, will be found strong and powerful, because it comes recommended by the prayers of Christ. But though Christ was happy praying in the mount, we see his poor disciples in great distress by a storm at sea.

Verses 24–25. *But the ship was now in the midst of the sea, tossed with waves: for the wind was contrary. And in the fourth watch of the night Jesus went unto them, walking on the sea.*

Our Lord, we find, had ordered his disciples to go to the other side, and he went to pray in the mount. From these words, we make the following remarks.

1. Though our Lord knew all things and therefore that the storm was coming, he left them and went to pray in the mount.

2. Again, we see that though he knew their distress, he delays coming to their assistance till the fourth watch of the night.

3. That though they were tossed by winds and waves, they were perfectly safe, for he came to their assistance.

The ship that carried the disciples is a true emblem of his Church. We cannot exactly say what were the particular corruptions of his followers which this dispensation was calculated to cure. And he had causes best known to himself for delaying coming to their assistance to the latter end of the night.

The affections of his people are wisely ordered by our Saviour, as well as the time appointed for their relief. His prayers in the mount kept them safe on the sea, and his prayers in heaven keep his people safe upon earth. He came to their relief walking upon the sea. And his providence always interposes right early for his Church. He knew when he should come to their assistance. If he delays his help till the fourth watch of the night, so much the more signal shall be the deliverance. He came walking upon the sea, and sometimes his providence is wonderful, and his works and ways unsearchable. If there are remarkable prayers, there will be remarkable providences. Let us wait his time, and he will surely come to our deliverance.

Verses 26–27. *And when the disciples saw him walking on the sea, they were troubled, saying, It is a spirit; and they cried out for fear. But straightway Jesus spake unto them, saying, Be of good cheer; it is I; be not afraid.*

We may naturally believe that the disciples, when tossed by the waves and in danger of sinking to the bottom, lifted up their souls to heaven and cried for assistance. No doubt they were longing for their Lord and Master, and, like Martha and Mary upon another occasion, might think if he had been present, they had not been in such danger of their lives. It is likely that several distracting and unbelieving thoughts passed through their minds upon this trying occasion. Now, will they reconcile the present appearance of providence with the opinion they had formed of Messiah and the promises that he had given them? Their faith and their unbelief alternately preponderate, and they are allowed for a time to be tossed upon the waves before there is the least prospect of relief.

At last, when all hope was gone, and they had given themselves up for lost, they see a strange sight upon the lake—the appearance of a man walking upon the water. Struck with terror and astonishment, they cried out, for they supposed they had seen a ghost. It was a common opinion among all nations that there are spectres and visions of the night. Such they supposed the present appearance to be—they thought it a dreadful omen, and that it portended their death.

Our Lord cheered their drooping spirits and informed them that he was the Great Being, whom winds and waves must obey. He makes use of the same expression which Moses was directed to make use of to the children of Israel in Egypt: 'Be of good cheer—I am—be not afraid.' Our Lord, indeed, bids them be of good cheer, but he does not in plain language inform them, or even insinuate, that there are no spirits of the night. He leaves us in the dark as to that subject. He teaches, indeed, to be afraid of no being but that Great Being who has life and death at his command.

And here we may observe that the disciples were in the same situation of mind which many of his people before and since have been in, when he comes to their relief. A little before, he comes in a wonderful interposition of providence to relieve Jacob. We hear him exclaiming, 'All these things are against me.' When Moses meets with a repulse from Pharaoh, he complains to God, 'Thou hast not delivered thy people at all.'

And this is true also in a spiritual view. When he comes to make a work upon the souls of his people at first, and arrest them by the law before he relieves them, they are afraid of him, and think he means to destroy them. They are troubled with their corruptions, the body of sin which is in their members. They pray against it. The answer terrifies them. The way God purifies them is by giving them a strong feeling of unbelief, a sight of their corruptions, and a powerful flood of temptation. When they are tossed by these dreadful waves, their Redeemer comes in the fourth watch of the night, walking upon the waves, and he says to the winds and raging billows, 'Peace be still,' and there is a calm and serenity in the soul. They have joy and peace in believing.

Verses 28–31. *And Peter answered him and said, Lord, if it be thou, bid me come unto thee on the water. And he said, Come. And when Peter was come down out of the ship, he walked on the water, to go to Jesus. But when he saw the wind boisterous, he was afraid; and beginning to sink, he cried, saying, Lord, save me. And immediately Jesus stretched forth his hand, and caught him, and said unto him, O thou of little faith, wherefore didst thou doubt?*

Peter was a man of a bold and intrepid spirit and great love to his Saviour. Whenever he knew his voice, he begged leave to walk to him upon the waves. Our Lord, partly to reward Peter's faith, partly to show how little he could do independently of divine aid, bade him come forward. Peter, like many others, thought he had more faith than he actually possessed. Accordingly, he proceeded with some degree of confidence, but finding the sea rough and the waves high, for the wind was strong, he became afraid, and began to sink. Whenever he began to sink, he cried to the Lord to save him. Upon this, he reached his hand to him, supported his sinking faith and his sinking person, and at the same time rebuked him for his unbelief in that he was afraid when his Lord was so near him.

And is not this our own case? He bids us come to him. We scarcely make two steps when our faith begins to fail and, forgetful of all that ever he has done for us, our hopes begin to sink and unbelief to swallow us up. If we have the appearance of faith at some particular times, how soon does the trial show us how weak and inconstant we are! Unless the Lord reach his hand to us, we would soon sink in the waves of affliction and trouble. Have not our souls cause to bless his name that he has often proved our help, and that right early, when he saw our hope was gone and we had no other help?

Verse 32. *And when they were come into the ship, the wind ceased.*

Our Lord, who sometimes walks upon the wings of the wind, at this time walked upon the waves of the sea. Although Peter was afraid, the sea to him was as dry land. The storm and tempest did not affect him. He allowed the storm to rage till such time as he came to the ship, and then the wind ceased. And this happened merely for the sake of his disciples. While he was with them in the ship, they were safe, but while the storm continued, they had been terribly afraid, and therefore, to compose their minds, he silences the wind and waves. Though the ship was safe when Christ walked upon the sea to their relief, they did not see themselves safe and happy till they got him with them.

And is not this the case with us? When a person gets a sight of Christ coming upon the waves to his relief, he is perfectly safe, though he does not see himself perfectly happy. Nothing can do this but some degree of assurance, and this is like being in the ship with Christ. Where there is true faith, it labours after assurance, and where there is humble assurance, it pants after the full assurance of faith.

And if a person may ask, 'What is the difference between the assurance of faith and the presumption of many?' the text affords an answer. When Christ came to the ship, there was a calm, and when he comes to the soul, he breaks the power of sin. If people are tossed by their passions and are slaves to their lusts, they have the faith of presumption, and not the faith that purifies the heart. Even such of the people of God as are tossed with temptations and corruptions see only Christ coming upon the waves to save them. Others of them have him sleeping in the ship. They do not wish him to awake till he please. Should a storm arise against such, they have only to cry to him. He immediately rebukes the winds and the waves, and there is a calm. And no man should rest satisfied till he gets the faith that purifies the heart. Victory over the passions, lusts and affections will give peace and serenity to the soul. The blood of sprinkling will purge the conscience from dead works, and the spirit of prayer will give strength and power against corruption and sin. While the wind and tide of corruption are strong, endeavours are ineffectual: we can never be at ease till Christ comes to the ship, and then there is a calm.

Verse 33. *Then they that were in the ship came and worshipped him, saying, Of a truth thou art the Son of God.*

The great mystery of godliness is this, that God was manifested in the flesh, that the Son of God became man, that Jesus Christ was the Messiah promised in the Scriptures of the Old Testament. And how did Christ prove that he was so? By the great works he wrought. Now, these works carried such evident demonstration of divine power that they brought conviction to the mind all at once. If a man did not choose to shut his eyes, he could not refuse to acknowledge what he saw.

Now, the illiterate mechanic [manual worker] and the unpolished rustic were as capable of examining miracles and judging what they saw, and bearing honest testimony to the truth, as the most acute and learned philosopher. And is it not either stupid ignorance or gross partiality, if not both, in those who object to the truth of the gospel, that the bulk of those who embraced it were men without letters?

Now, it may be asked, can anything be more unreasonable than this objection? If two men claimed the greatest estate in the kingdom, would the witnesses adduced by either party be objected to because they are not scholars? I think not. When people are tried for treason or any other great crime, will their counsel take any exception against the witnesses because they are not philosophers and men of liberal education? No. Now, the men in the ship were competent witnesses of what they saw. They could tell they saw a man walking upon the water, that it proved to be the Lord Jesus Christ himself, that there was a calm whenever he came to the ship. And what would still more strengthen their faith, they could declare they saw Peter also walking upon the sea, and that he began to sink till Jesus reached his hand and kept him above water.

How silly, then, is the objection of an infidel. There cannot be such a thing as a miracle, and, therefore, he will not believe. Let us turn the tables upon him and examine his argument. I acknowledge, indeed, that an infidel is a wonderful phenomenon in the Christian world, but the spirit of prophecy takes notice of them and acquaints us they would arise. Let us, however, put the case that several persons in an island or remote corner had been trained up in the purest principles of Christianity till they became men. Some persons inform them that a wonderful king had appeared in England; that he denied the truths of Christianity and the miracles of the gospel. Let us now suppose that one or two of these good men exclaim, 'Impossible. There is no such monster in nature as the person you style an infidel.' He is informed by credible witnesses that there are infidels, that they saw and heard them, and that there are accounts in books of some few that were in England two hundred years ago. Would not these good Christians be thought very unreasonable if they refused to believe eyewitnesses and the authority of books that were known to be true and believed in the kingdom for two centuries? I dare say an infidel would reckon them very unreasonable in their unbelief. But he ought to consider that he himself is as great a curiosity to this same Christian as a miracle can be to an infidel.

And what hinders the Christian from believing that there is such a creature? Prejudice. Now, whether he believes such creatures are or are not, there are infidels. And whether infidels believe in miracles or not, there have been miracles, and people have been gained by miracles to the belief of the gospel. The men in the ship acknowledged that Jesus Christ was in truth the Son of God.

Verses 34–36. *And when they were gone over, they came into the land of Gennesaret. And when the men of that place had knowledge of him, they sent out into all that country round about, and brought unto him all that were diseased; and besought him that they might only touch the hem of his garment: and as many as touched were made perfectly whole.*

After our Lord had calmed the winds and the waves, they came into the country of Gennesaret. The people of that place acted as his followers do to this day. Our Lord had a great following, notwithstanding he had a great number of enemies. Now, enemies are never at a loss for expressions to vilify the characters of those whom they wish to hurt. His followers, however, knew that all their ill-natured and virulent invectives could not alter the nature of truth. His miracles were notorious [well-known] facts, and facts are stubborn things: they cannot be controverted. He has repeatedly cured the sick, opened the eyes of the blind, and raised the dead. The people of Gennesaret knew all this, and therefore they brought their sick and diseased to him in order to be healed. They had even such faith in him that when any of them touched the hem of his garment, they were healed.

And this is the case with all true Christians. Whatever unbelievers may say against the gospel, they have experience of the truth of it in the work which the Spirit of God made upon their souls. Infidels may laugh at this as the language of fools. The plain English of that is this: 'I do not understand what you say. You must be, therefore, a fool.' A man without learning comes to the library of a great scholar. A Latin or Greek author is put in his hands. He cannot read it, and therefore it is nonsense. And this is the logic of an infidel.

It is a fact that several thousands in the kingdom—men of sound sense and good behaviour, and a number of them men of great learning—could declare upon the word of honest men, that whereas they were blind, now they see. The Pharisees could not persuade the man born blind that Christ had not cured him. His simple reasoning overcomes their chicanery [subterfuge] and unbelief, and though confuted by the strength of his arguments, they had not the candour or honesty to acknowledge the truth, or see the hand of God in the miracle.

The people of Gennesaret were healed by touching the hem of his garment. And could any of these people be persuaded that this did not happen? Must they not have believed in his divine mission, and that he was the Son of God, of a truth?

It is true there are no miracles now in the Church. The bodies of men are not healed by a touch of the Saviour. Miracles, however, are wrought upon the minds of people. The unchaste are made clean; the dissipated, sober and honest; and the unbeliever, a saint. And this happens by having faith in the gospel wrought in your souls. They live such a pure and holy life as no infidel can live, and they obtain such comfort at death as surprises and delights the spectators. And this happened by touching the hem of Christ's garment. In plain language, they believed, and by doing so, they experienced the power of Christ in healing and sanctifying their souls. And how different is their life and death from the life and death of the votaries of pleasure and the promoters of infidelity! The death of infidels has often been awful; faith has healed the souls of Christians. Their lives have been useful, and their death edifying and pleasant.

Practical inferences

I conclude with some practical inferences.

1. First, if Christ went up into the mount to pray, how great is our need? He had a work to perform worthy of a God. He therefore prayed that his human nature might be strengthened to bear the burden and perform the work. And we have a work also to perform. We are desired in Scripture to work out our own salvation with fear and trembling, and to make our calling and election sure. We are not sufficient of ourselves for this work: we must therefore depend

upon the assistance of another, and look up for help to God. The constant struggle between virtue and vice in the soul, the solicitations of pleasure, and the evil example of the world around us are surely very powerful arguments to engage us to pray. If we slacken our diligence in prayer, we shall be like Moses when he hung down his hands. We must support the hands of faith and prayer that we may subdue our spiritual enemies. Let us retire from the world after the example of our Saviour, and spend some time in prayer in the mount. Our Saviour often retired to a mountain to pray and keep up communion with heaven. Did the success of his enemies, the suggestions of his friends or acquaintances, or any other avocation [diversion] whatever divert him from this necessary and delightful duty?

His prayers returned with a rich answer from heaven. His human nature became victorious. He satisfied the justice of God and bore our sins. He conquered our spiritual enemies and made a show of them openly. Would you gain spiritual victories? Retire from the world. Go up to the mount to your Saviour. Moses went up to the hill of Pisgah, and got a view of the promised land. Abraham got a glorious promise in the mount, and it was upon a mount that the three apostles got a glimpse of the glory of Christ, and a sight of Moses and Elijah. Let us follow their example.

2. Secondly, are we tossed by the waves of affliction and temptation? And is our Saviour now removed to the mountain of myrrh and the hill of frankincense, and therefore, in our own view, at a greater distance from us than he was from his disciples when in the ship? Let us then remember that though he is now in heaven, he is present with his people by his Spirit and by the sweet workings of his providence. Though storms arise and they are tossed with tempests, their vessel will be safe. The storm is sent for their good and for the trial of their faith and patience. Let us not complain because such and such things come in our way which God might easily prevent. Had our Saviour prevented the storm, the disciples had not had such comfort by a kindly breeze as they had by his seasonable appearance for their relief. The illustrious display of his power in walking upon

the sea must have naturally strengthened their faith and filled their souls with joy and astonishment.

3. Thirdly, from what we heard, we learn that troubles are often blessings in disguise. The people of God, when they see the trouble approaching, are ready with the disciples to cry out with fear. Guilt and unbelief may put awful constructions upon the dark dispensations of providence. But under this appearance, it is the Saviour coming to their relief.

And how does this appear? Answer: Afflictive providences are calculated to rouse the conscience and to make people fear in their hearts and examine their conduct. Conscience gets a calm and impartial hearing, and they begin to see for what they get the stroke. Affliction humbles the heart and makes people to forsake their darling idols, and come weary and heavily laden to Christ. And though unbelief may suggest that the dispensation is calculated to destroy them, it will be found to have a very different and contrary effect. And when they submit to sovereignty and know that he is God, their captivity is turned like streams in the south, and they know that the affliction has humbled and purified them, and given health and vigour to their spiritual constitution. When the peccant humours [sinful dispositions] are expelled, their spiritual appetite is restored, their strength returns, and they run the way of God's commandments with alacrity and vigour. They proceed from strength to strength, and never stop till they appear perfect before God in Zion.

4. Lastly, we find that a touch of the hem of Christ's garment brought health and cure to the diseased. And should not we imitate their example? It is more than probable that, in a great concourse of people following the Saviour, several individuals could not get access to come to speak to him and reveal their cases particularly. Necessity teaches them to take a short method. They touch the hem of his garment, and are immediately cured.

And this may happen to us. Several poor souls complain they cannot get access to the Saviour: they are so choked with unbelief, with temptation, and corruption. In this case, let them touch the hem of his garment. They heard about him. Let them, then, trust in his power. And though at a distance, like a person that could only touch the hem of the garment, let them wait in the means they enjoy, and let them believe. There is no person under the gospel but may have access to the hem of his garment. If people happen to have but a small degree of knowledge or have not full access to the means of grace, even then, let them attempt to believe and follow Christ, and this will effect their spiritual cure.

A person wishing to speak to Christ, and not able by reason of the crowd, found her health restored by touching the hem of his garment. He knew her wish and answered her desire. He knows when we wish to believe and have a desire to get sin broken. And though people cannot speak to him, he knows where the sincere wish and the honest desire is, for this will produce honest endeavours after holiness and obedience. The man does his duty according to the light he has, and Christ meets his wish and heals his soul. He can read the wishes of those who cannot speak, and the famished beggar in his extremity will draw virtue from Christ to feed and cure his soul.

May God bless his own Word. AMEN.

Matthew chapter 15: verses 1 to 20

THE Scripture in every part is in perfect harmony with itself. It was the same Spirit that dictated the whole. The doctrine of the prophets agrees in everything with the doctrine of the apostles. The design of the gospel is to sanctify the nature and reform the life. But as religion is designed for spirits that dwell in bodies, it must have something in it that will strike the senses. Accordingly, the religion of the Jews was full of pomp and parade, full of ceremonies and acts imposed upon them till the time of the gospel.

Such, however, has been the corruption of human nature that people in all ages have been taken up more with the ceremonial part of religion than with the substance and spirit. As it is this day, it has been in the time of our Saviour. Our Lord showed them the danger of false opinions and immoral practices, and the emptiness of that religion that can rest in ceremony and fall short of true Christian piety and the love of God. And there is cause to fear that we are more guilty in this respect than the Jews themselves. We have more light and knowledge, but what have we besides? Covetous as they were reckoned, they did not grudge to pay costly sacrifices. But a man of religion such as this will grudge any part of religion that will in the slightest degree thwart his temporal interest, or bid forsake what he reckons his ideal.

I shall explain the words in the order in which they lie, and conclude with some practical improvements.

Jesus reproves the scribes and Pharisees about tradition

Verses 1–2. Then came to Jesus scribes and Pharisees, which were of Jerusalem, saying, Why do thy disciples transgress the tradition of the elders? for they wash not their hands when they eat bread.

We often find mention made in the gospel of the scribes and Pharisees. The one was a sect among the Jews, and the other were their leaders and spiritual guides. Now, these persons were people that, under the mark of piety, not only neglected the duties of morality, but even were guilty of flagrant immoralities. They were full of covetousness, vainglory, and revenge. It is true they could make long prayers, but they did not scruple to devour widows' houses. They could take of the outside of religion as much as did not interfere with their temporal interest. If a man fell in with their views and extolled them for their superior sanctity, they would embrace him as a brother and cry him up for a good man. But when the Saviour exposed their principles and their practices, they endeavoured to make him feel the heaviest stroke of their resentment.

And if we investigate the character of people of the same stamp and spirit, we shall find they follow the same line of conduct, according to their power. We have a number of people among us that profess religion. They can pray in public, speak about divine things, and edify us with their own experiences. But if a man should talk ever so elegantly about meat and drink, if he seldom taste either and for the most part have an aversion to food, he will soon fall into sickness, and if he perseveres, it will end in his death. We see people attending means when it suits their temporal interest: if it does not, we must excuse them. Observe the conduct of your religious people. Follow them to the market, to the high road, and to the public house. Notice their conduct through the week, and if you are actuated by the spirit of your Saviour and rebuke them for the shameful inconsistency of their conduct, you will soon know what they shall do. The Pharisee is offended if you have the impudence to see the spot that is in his face. People that live in gross immoralities (if intemperance, dishonesty, and revenge deserve this name) will readily find fault with others for things of very little consequence. The scribes and Pharisees blamed our Lord and his disciples for eating bread with unwashed hands. The rulers of the Jews, who had no scruples to murder an innocent and holy person, would not go to the judgment hall for fear of polluting themselves. Such persons can strain at a gnat and swallow a camel.

> Verses 3–4. *But he answered and said unto them, Why do ye also transgress the commandment of God by your tradition? For God commanded, saying, Honour thy father and mother: and, He that curseth father or mother, let him die the death.*

In these words, we see the wisdom and the dignity with which our Lord met the accusation of his invidious enemies. As if he had said, 'Be it so that I have transgressed the tradition of the elders, that is a small thing in itself, and of no consequence as to the interests of morality. But why do you break the law of God?'

Our Lord here opposes question to question, and his enemies could give no answer but such as would condemn themselves. He taxes them in particular with a breach of the Fifth Commandment, but our Lord thought and acted very differently. He himself, though the Son of God and Lord of glory, yet as man was obedient to his poor parents and paid them respect, and even upon the cross recommended his mother to his beloved disciple. As the Fifth Commandment implies in it obedience of every kind, both civil and spiritual, our Lord by his example and doctrine inculcated this part of moral duty. He paid tribute himself and taught his hearers to render to Caesar the things that were Caesar's. He taught them to respect their spiritual rulers, for he went to the synagogue and desired his disciples to follow what was praiseworthy in their doctrine. This, however, was not the practice of those who asked the question, for our Lord tells us:

> Verses 5–6. *But ye say, Whosoever shall say to his father or his mother, It is a gift, by whatsoever thou mightest be profited by me; and*

honour not his father or his mother, he shall be free. Thus have ye made the commandment of God of none effect by your tradition.

It seems it was customary among the Jews to devote their substance to God by vow, and the practice was encouraged by the teachers, and redounded to their own advantage. The undutiful child pleaded exemption from the duty he owed to his parents, that he gave either his substance or his service to God. And the spirit of this very tradition of the Pharisees is still among many hypocritical professors. When required to perform the essential duties of religion and morality, they think they have done enough if they perform in a formal manner some of the easier duties of religion. Our Lord shows us the emptiness of such pretensions, and couches his rebuke to such characters in pretty severe terms.

Verses 7–9. *Ye hypocrites, well did Esaias prophesy of you, saying, This people draweth nigh unto me with their mouth, and honoureth me with their lips; but their heart is far from me. But in vain they do worship me, teaching for doctrines the commandments of men.*

In these words, the people that were led and the teachers that did mislead are equally reprehended. And they show us this useful and edifying lesson that people may have the form of religion and observe some dead ceremonies while their hearts and affections are not engaged in the work. We see here that people are often fonder of what is merely human in what concerns religion than they are of the vitals and life of religion in the souls. And this remark will apply to professors in the purest Church upon earth. Under every form of religion, people may satisfy themselves in that very form without the power. We find that half-professors (and these form the majority among all sorts of Christians upon earth) are more taken up with what peculiarly distinguishes them from other parties than they are with the essential doctrines and true spirit of Christianity. And it sometimes happens that people who contend for the orthodox faith and doctrines are not very remarkable for the orthodoxy of their morals. And will not the words of our Saviour to the scribes and Pharisees apply to such, that they are hypocrites who draw near to

God with their lips, while their heart is far from him? And our Lord rectified their mistake.

Jesus teaches the multitude about heart defilement

Verses 10–11. *And he called the multitude, and said unto them, Hear, and understand: not that which goeth into the mouth defileth a man; but that which cometh out of the mouth, this defileth a man.*

The doctrine of our Lord in these words is that the observation of a ceremony of mere human authority is not binding upon the conscience, and therefore indifference about it will not attach guilt to the soul. And this will apply to what is merely human in every Church upon earth. How awful, then, in churchmen to have put these things in a level almost with the articles of faith. It will apply to churchmen of all denominations. This is obvious to a judicious observer. Alas! we are guilty in this respect.

Verses 12–14. *Then came his disciples, and said unto him, Knowest thou that the Pharisees were offended, after they heard this saying? But he answered and said, Every plant, which my heavenly Father hath not planted, shall be rooted up. Let them alone: they be blind leaders of the blind. And if the blind lead the blind, both shall fall into the ditch.*

Pure and holy as the Saviour was in his nature and in his life, pure and holy as his doctrines were, they were far from pleasing all men. It is true, multitudes followed him when they saw his miracles and witnessed the glorious works and wonderful cures he performed. But though fairer than the sons of men, though grace was poured into his lips, and though he spake as never man did, his doctrine gave offence. No sooner did he begin to inform the multitude that his kingdom was not of this world, no sooner did he strike at the doctrines that were current among the teachers, at the opinions and practices of the multitude, than they began to cool, and many of them began to go back. When he pointed out the mere emptiness of external ceremonies and washings and the necessity of something more substantial in religion than mere outside, they took alarm, and he met with a very formidable opposition. The Pharisees were offended at the doctrines he preached: the blind leaders gave the alarm to the blind multitude, and the conspiracy at last turned very strong. When the disciples informed him of the offence his doctrine gave, he informed them that every plant not planted by his heavenly Father would be rooted up, and then showed them the danger of blind teachers and their deluded followers.

'Every plant not planted by my heavenly Father shall be rooted up,' and this remark equally affects doctrines as well as persons. And it affects this day as well as it did in our Saviour's time. The scribes and Pharisees were rooted out of the Church of God, as well as their empty and unsubstantial doctrines. And with regard to doctrines and opinions not founded upon Scripture, the remark will apply to many of the people of God. If there is any plant in them not planted by their heavenly Father, it shall—it must—be rooted up. Opinions and practices that are not agreeable to the sure word of revelation will be destroyed at last. The Word is what is to try both, and we should be cautious in admitting what can not be clearly proved from these lively oracles.

The danger of false doctrines and false teachers is clear from our Saviour's comparison. If the blind lead the blind, both will naturally fall into the ditch. People without concern for their souls, who are blind as to their best interests, cannot lead others. And when they do not lead, they must, of course, mislead, and an error here is of most fatal tendency. We should, therefore, be open to conviction, and earnestly and assiduously cry to heaven for the heavenly illumination of the Holy Spirit to lead us unto all truth. As the book of God is in our hands, we should pray that it may be also in our hearts. Christ is the way, the truth, and the life, and in his light we shall see light.

Verses 15–18. *Then answered Peter and said unto him, Declare unto us this parable. And Jesus said, Are ye also yet without understanding? Do not ye yet understand, that whatsoever entereth in at the mouth goeth*

*into the belly, and is cast out into the draught? But those things which
proceed out of the mouth come forth from the heart; and they defile the
man.*

Our Lord, in these words, after reprimanding Peter for his slowness
in understanding spiritual truths, informs his disciples in general
what defiles a man. Eating food without washing the hands is a matter of mere ceremony, and does not defile the man. What defiles
him is what proceeds from the heart. The heart is the fountain of
life or of death, and we may know whether the fountain is poisonous
or not by the waters that proceed from it. This is clear, for our Lord
says:

*Verses 19–20. For out of the heart proceed evil thoughts, murders,
adulteries, fornications, thefts, false witness, blasphemies these are the
things which defile a man: but to eat with unwashen hands defileth not
a man.*

Such as are acquainted with Scripture and human nature will readily
acknowledge that the plagues of the heart are so manifold that one
would think people need not add imaginary sins to the number of
sins that are really and truly such. Churchmen have found out the
way of imposing supernumerary duties upon the people, and have
made the breach of these duties a sin. Our Lord, however, informs
us what opinion to form of mere human authority in matters that
are spiritual and divine. We should know our liberty in things
wherein Christ hath made us free, and not be entangled again by the
yoke of bondage.

Our Lord, however, informs us what are the things that defile the
man—evil thoughts or reasonings. Now, thoughts and reasonings
defile the mind in several respects. People may be guilty in the sight
of God of many sins which they never get the opportunity or the
power to commit. It is at the heart that every sin begins. It is the
fruitful forge of every iniquity. The thoughts are polluted before
people proceed to actions. And not only do evil thoughts, strictly so
called, defile the soul, but also evil reasonings. While the reason is

sinful and unsanctified, it will produce evil reasonings. It is oft only by evil reasonings that people are kept from their duty, and are seduced to commit sin. The first reasoning was this, 'Ye shall not surely die.' The next reasoning was that the fruit was pleasant to the eye, fit for food, and calculated to make one wise, and by their combined force, the woman was tempted to her ruin. Her soul was polluted before she defiled her body by the outward act of sin. And this is the case to this very day. 'When lust hath conceived, it bringeth forth sin: and when sin is finished, it bringeth forth death.' Evil thoughts and false reasonings are the things that keep people in the snares of Satan and in the chains of sin all their days. These are the poisonous sources of all the false religions upon earth. These polluted vapours spread their baneful influence over all the human race, and produce all that flood of sin and misery of which we are the constant spectators while we sojourn in this world. (N.B. Mark 7:21).

Another of the things that defile a man is murder. And indeed, the grossest acts of this sin are so repugnant to the light of nature, as well as to the light of Scripture, that it is astonishing how it could be committed in a country where there are any traces of civilisation, and more especially in a country blessed with the light of the gospel. Scripture informs that a murderer hath not eternal life in him, and this shows us the dreadful nature of that sin, and the danger of sinful anger, malice, and wickedness of that kind. If we retain such thoughts in our hearts, we are not fit to receive the pardon of sin. Our Lord teaches us to pray, 'Forgive us our debts, as we forgive our debtors,' and informs us that if we do not forgive, we shall not be forgiven.

As Christians, we profess to be the royal offspring of heaven. Well might we, then, apply to ourselves what a heathen poet applied to his heathen gods: 'Dwells such resentment in heavenly minds?' If we are the followers of the meek and lowly Jesus, the disciples of the humble and heavenly Saviour, how comes it that we entertain thoughts of anger, hatred, malice, and revenge? These thoughts are but heart murder, and they greatly defile the soul, deprive it of its happiness, light and beauty, and transform it into a mere demon or spirit of darkness, for he that hateth his brother is of the devil.

But again, adulteries and fornications proceed from the heart and defile the man. Indeed, all these sins have such a tendency to defile the heart, the affections, and the life that they generally go by the name of uncleanness. It takes away the heart and sinks the soul into the grossest kind of idolatry. It forces the soul into the most abject state of slavery. And few of those who go on in this sin ever return to God or repent. This sin is so dangerous that one of the fathers of the Church said that it was as difficult to bring a dead man to life as to make a lustful man chaste and pure. King David was so sensible [aware] of the danger of uncleanness that he cried to God to create in him a clean heart and to renew a right spirit within him. Young people often flatter themselves that they will forsake sin and repent when they become old. In this hope, alas, they are fatally deceived. Old men are often as guilty in this respect as those who are young. A more awful spectacle does not exist upon earth than the old sinner who curses himself for the follies of his youth, except the stupid wretch who is judicially hardened and can talk no language but the language of hell, and can boast of no more glorious exploits than the actions of a brute.

How miserable is the portion of the old sinner who reflects that he gave his youth to the devil, that he has given his strength to the service of sin, that he has wasted his body and destroyed the faculties of his mind! He has no pleasure in life, and the thought of death and judgment must be awful to his soul! His thoughts are foul, and his impure soul is unfit for the pure pleasures of the heavenly state. He is an impure spirit, and a fit companion for the spirits of darkness. His dark and polluted soul must be miserable, for his unruly passions, his filthy thoughts, and his enraged conscience will be his tormentors for ever and ever. These are some of the sins that defile a man, make him abominable here, and miserable hereafter. May God awaken such sinners!

Theft is another sin that defiles the man. Mark mentions with theft, covetousness. And the covetous man is a thief, for Judas is reckoned a thief, though we do not read that he actually stole; but he was covetous, and therefore a thief in the sight of God. The desire of accumulating wealth defiles the soul and fills the heart with racking and uneasy thoughts, and pierces people with many sorrows. The love of money is the root of all evil. The covetous man defiles his own soul, makes himself unhappy, and others often miserable. And though he loses his soul to enrich others, his heirs will not thank him for what he has done.

Mark, after covetousness, mentions wickedness and deceit. And this may point at the different kinds of villainy and tricks that people use in order to overreach [cheat] their neighbours and enrich themselves. And these thefts greatly defile them and hurt their souls.

False witness defiles the soul, and this sin often proceeds from covetousness also. Why does one man sell his own soul but to hurt another? People bear false witness by going about as talebearers, by raising a lie to hurt their neighbours, or by swearing before a judge. These are awful sins, and defile the man's soul, and expose him to the curse of God.

Blasphemy likewise defiles the soul. And this is a great sin, whether it be against man or against God. We blaspheme man when we asperse [belittle] his character with a view to hurt him. We blaspheme God when we speak against him or against his Word and providence.

Mark mentions likewise an evil eye, pride and foolishness as things that defile the man. Now, an evil eye is a covetous eye, full of envy and ill-will at the good of our neighbour, proceeding from a heart that would wish to do him all the hurt we can. If I wished to gratify your curiosity, I might, upon this occasion, mention to you the opinion of the ancients with respect to the malignant influence of an evil eye. But we are a philosophical generation, and we pretend to more wisdom than our ancestors had. We laugh at the existence of witches and the influence of an evil eye. They are mentioned, however, in Scripture, and our Saviour mentions an evil eye as one of the sins that defile the soul. But though Scripture mentions these sins to us,

I pretend not to explain to you how, or how far, their influence may extend, or dare be wise above what is written.

Pride defiles the soul. It cast the devil out of heaven; it cast Adam out of paradise, and it will cast thousands and many tens of thousands into hell. To show how odious this sin is, Scripture assures us that God resisteth the proud. And even men, corrupt and wicked as they are generally, conspire against a man that is eminently proud, and wish to humble him. The sin of the proud man constantly defiles him, and makes him uneasy to himself and others. No man, he thinks, gives him that respect which he thinks is due to him. The soul of a proud man is like a skin abused [damaged] with the itch— you must dip a feather in oil and handle it gently, otherwise the least touch will hurt it. And if the proud man is not constantly flattered, you cannot please him. Strong common sense may cast a veil over pride and hide it from the superficial observer. But it is a fact that will always prove true that no man will sooner obtain favour from a proud man than a flatterer. And the wise flatterer, like the wise lover, will flatter in private, and is sure to succeed.

Pride is natural to the heart of man. It was our first sin, and the last, perhaps, that will be conquered and expelled. We may appeal to our own hearts whether flattery pleases us. Tell an ordinary man that he has all the qualifications of a hero, or a silly woman that she has all the accomplishments that adorn her sex, and if you have the address to give your words the appearance of sincerity, you gain their hearts and obtain their favour and friendship. Pride insinuates itself into everything we do. There is something in our natures analogous to what philosophers call attraction. Pride always finds or draws something to feed upon. Riches, learning, religion, intellectual abilities, and especially fine clothes, are the fuel that feed this fire. It makes us impatient of contradiction; it makes us look down with contempt upon those that differ with us; it makes us laugh at the follies and foibles of mankind; and it often exposes ourselves to the laughter of fools in our turn. Pride is the offspring of ignorance: no man would be proud if he knew himself. The more a man has of the grace of God, the more humble he is. Our Lord Jesus Christ had in him the fulness of the Godhead bodily. He was the humblest man upon the face of the earth. Satan, the prince of devils, is the greatest sinner that exists, and he is the proudest creature in all creation. The more we are puffed with pride or adorned with humility, the more we resemble the one or the other. In a word, pride defiles and debases the soul.

Lastly, foolishness leads up the rear of the sins that defile the soul.

Foolishness here, as in several parts of Scripture, signifies the folly of sin. 'Be not foolish, but understanding what the will of the Lord is,' says the apostle. We see some men astonishingly clever and alert in managing the affairs of this world, and availing themselves of every proper opportunity that offers to improve their means. But examine them as to the state of their souls—they are as blind as moles. Nay, there are some people would be thought wise and sensible persons that are perfectly ignorant and brutish as to the state of their souls.

Now, these sins which we have heard mentioned are the things that defile the man. The due observance of the ceremonial part of religion will not sanctify our souls, but the practice of sin is sure to defile them, and this is the doctrine of our Lord and Saviour, Jesus Christ.

Practical inferences

We conclude with some practical inferences. That professors are the greatest sinners—[they] occasion sins of others—Ezekiel 36:20.

1. First, how vain and empty, therefore, the religion of those who perform some easy and superficial duties, and neglect the first and leading duty of religion: the love of God, and the essential duties of morality, the keeping of the commandments.

2. Second, that it is a great sin in the rulers of the Church to put things of lesser moment upon a level with the great articles of religion and essential moral duties. And this sin is still more highly

aggravated when the one jostles out the other. Washing the hands before dinner was more essential in the eye of the Pharisee than obedience to parents and other weighty duties of the law.

3. Third, that the doctrine of our Lord gave offence to the Pharisees. Light is said to hurt the eyes of the mole. And to such as have the eyes of their minds blinded with prejudice or sunken in sin, the clear light of God's Word must be equally painful. They cannot bear the light because their deeds are evil. If we are of the light, we can bear the doctrines of the light, and have our deeds examined by the light. Such doctrines and deeds as cannot bear the light are not from God.

4. Lastly, we see that sin of every kind sinks and debases the soul. It should, then, be our main concern to avoid those things that spoil the beauty and lustre of our minds and sink them down in matter [material things]. Sin is the disease of our souls. We should come to the gospel for health and cure, and when we obtain this, the exercise of faith and holiness will always keep them bright and pure.

God bless his Word. AMEN.

Matthew chapter 15: verses 21 to 39

THE manifold wisdom of our Lord and Saviour is manifest as a teacher. He constantly went about doing good to the souls and bodies of people. He adapted his doctrine to the spiritual state and conditions of those that heard him. The proud and self-righteous he sends to the law, and by so doing, he condemns him out of his own mouth. The young ruler, proud of his duties and highly pleased with his own performances, he sends away sorrowful, and proved to his own conviction, and to the conviction of all succeeding generations, that he did not keep the commandments as he thought he had. By going away sorrowful, he showed that he loved his possessions better than his God, and that he had not yet kept the first command, much less all the commandments.

But our Lord observed another kind of language to the penitent that saw his sin and was condemned by the law. 'Be of good cheer; thy sins are forgiven thee,' is his language to such. He observed, likewise, a different conduct with respect to those who had a strong and a weak faith. The one gets an answer all at once: the other is made to wait and his faith put to the trial.

In the portion of Scripture just now read, we have the history of the woman of Canaan, from the 21st verse to the 28th; the accomplishment of the prophecy in Isaiah 35th chapter, in verses 29, 30, 31; and the miracle of the loaves from verse 32 to verse 39.

I shall speak to each of these points, and conclude with some practical inferences.

The faith of the woman of Canaan

Verses 21–28. *Then Jesus went thence, and departed into the coasts of Tyre and Sidon. And, behold, a woman of Canaan came out of the same coasts, and cried unto him, saying, Have mercy on me, O Lord, thou Son of David; my daughter is grievously vexed with a devil. But he answered her not a word. And his disciples came and besought him, saying, Send her away; for she crieth after us. But he answered and said, I am not sent but unto the lost sheep of the house of Israel. Then came she and worshipped him, saying, Lord, help me. But he answered and said, It is not meet to take the children's bread, and to cast it to dogs. And she said, Truth, Lord: yet the dogs eat of the crumbs which fall from their masters' table. Then Jesus answered and said unto her, O woman, great is thy faith: be it unto thee even as thou wilt. And her daughter was made whole from that very hour.*

And we have here, first, the history of the woman of Canaan, where we may observe what she was; the reception she met with from our Lord; the trial and victory of her faith.

First, what she was.

Scripture says expressly that she was a Syrophenician, and therefore, by birth, a Gentile. She was an alien to the commonwealth of Israel, had no right to the covenant of Abraham, and was excluded from the privileges of the people of God. Great were the privileges of the ancient people of God, as ours are also, who have succeeded them. The apostle mentions their privileges—they had the oracles of God; they had the promises; they had symbols of the divine presence among them. From all these, the poor Gentiles were excluded, and lived without God in the world. And as they lived without God, they were without the ordinary means of salvation. As they had no access to the means of grace, they could not hear the joyful sound, or any accounts of the great Messiah who was to save his people from their sins. This was the condition of the generality of the heathen world.

History, however, informs us that the Scriptures of the Old Testament were translated into the Greek language, and no doubt this paved the way for the gospel. Christ is called the desire of all nations, and there was a general belief among mankind that some great personage would appear at the time that our Saviour was born and some time thereafter. And they could learn this only from the writings of the prophets. And there is a strong probability that the nation bordering upon Palestine must have known something more of the true God than those who lived at a greater distance. And this opinion is confirmed by the history of this woman. Though a Gentile by birth, she knew the doctrine of salvation, and applied personally to the Messiah himself for a cure to her sick daughter. Her faith is extolled by the Head of the Church himself. She was like some in our day who, having occasional access to the gospel, embrace the call and obtain salvation to their souls; whereas those who constantly hear it, like the Jews of old, reject the great salvation, and thus perish in their sins.

Again, we have here the reception she met with from our Lord.

The poor woman had her daughter at home, grievously tormented by a devil. She had heard about the great prophet that appeared among the people of Israel, and of the wonderful and astonishing cures that had been performed by him. As she seems to have known the history of the Jews, for she called our Lord the Son of David, it was natural for her to think that, as Elisha had cured Naaman the Syrian, a man of another nation, that Christ would cure her daughter. Full of these thoughts, with the deepest humility, she came to our Saviour and set forth her piteous case.

Instead of a gracious answer, he continues silent. It would appear, by comparing Matthew and Mark, that he gave her no answer in the house. She came after and followed him. He does not say a word. 'Merciful Saviour, how mysterious are thy dealings with thy people,' she cries after him. 'Have mercy upon me, thou Son of David.'

The disciples interpose and plead for her. The answer they obtain is that he was sent to the lost sheep of the house of Israel. As a preacher and worker of miracles, this was the case, though not as a Saviour. And thus by partly concealing, partly revealing the truth, he exercised her faith. It was a great trial to her to hear that he was sent to the house of Israel, and this seemed to cut off all her hopes, for the words were said in her hearing and before the people. Though she meets with a repulse, yet she would not be put back. She came and worshipped him, saying, 'Lord, help me.'

The answer she gets, one would think, would have reduced her to absolute despair. 'It is not meet to take the children's bread, and cast it to the dogs.'

But observe in her answer and behaviour the nature, the power, and the victory of faith. 'Truth, Lord,' said she, 'yet the dogs eat of the crumbs which fall from their master's table.' She observed that the dogs under the table ate of the children's crumbs. She acknowledges the truth of our Lord's observation and, from his very words, makes an argument to carry her point. She pleads kindness, and insists that the dog is an animal belonging to the family and therefore entitled to the crumbs.

The compassionate Saviour, no longer able, as it were, to resist the faith his own Spirit had raised, told her that her faith was great, and instantly granted her request. And here we may observe that this is always the nature of faith. It makes an argument of everything which sense and reason and the dark appearances of providence would raise against it, in order to carry its point. It hopes against hope, and sees the kind hand of God in the darkest dispensations.

The event makes it appear that this woman was in reality a child, though she acknowledged herself to be a dog. And every child of God may do the same when he considers how the poison of sin has infected his nature and all his actions. But there is something in him that follows the Saviour notwithstanding. And this principle of faith keeps the people of God in the way of duty, and put a favourable construction upon all that the Lord does. They see something bright behind a dark providence, and at last they obtain deliverance. In the pillar of fire and cloud, there was a dark side to the Egyptian and a bright side to the Israelites, and it was the same pillar.

Afflictions, troubles and crosses are dark dispensations. But in the midst of judgments, faith sees mercy. And, in fact, there is mercy in the sharpest troubles, and it is our misery that we receive them with rebellious hearts. When we do so, we draw down more troubles upon our own heads. The Israelites are brought to the wilderness. By their murmurs, discontent, and rebellion, they bring down judgments, and at last provoke God, so that none of that wicked generation see Canaan except a few individuals that were resigned to the will of God. The way to remove an affliction is to submit to the divine will, and if the troubles continue long, the way to convert the poison into a wholesome medicine is to receive the stroke with meekness, humility and resignation.

Contrast to her—Ahaz—scribes seeking a sign—Herod—a miracle.

This good woman had a grievous affliction, a devil possessing her daughter. The appearance of providence would tell her that her affliction was likely to continue while she lived. Faith submits, waits upon the Saviour, and obtains a cure.

Job—Joseph—temporal prosperity—Ahaz.

The patriarch Joseph and that miracle of patience and resignation, the holy Job, had their great share of the afflictions of this life. By receiving them with humility and submission to the will of God, their faith rises triumphant at last. They obtain temporal prosperity, and their latter end is better than their beginning. Their souls also made great improvement in the virtues and graces of the spiritual life. They proved in every sense of the word the truth of that divine promise that they will not be put to shame who wait upon him. Sin is the cause of trouble, and God is the best judge what particular kinds of afflictions and troubles are most calculated to heal our perverse spirits and lead us to our duty. People are generally crossed in their darling lust and favourite pursuit. Is it not natural to suppose that, as Jacob, David and others have got their sharpest trials from their idols, that this good woman might have made an idol of her daughter? When she saw her possessed, her unbelief might have raised awful apprehensions. And had not her unbelief great advantage when she heard the Saviour himself say, 'It is not meet to give the children's bread to dogs.' She must have felt the force of the expression, as the Jews were wont to call the Gentiles by this name. She acknowledges the charge, and yet faith makes use of the very charge to plead kindness at the hands of the Saviour.

What a contrast to the faith of the people of God is Ahaz, the rebellious king of Judah, who refused a sign from heaven, and continued obstinate notwithstanding all the troubles sent to reform him! His rebellion and unbelief have fixed a stigma upon his memory that will continue while the Old Testament is read in the Church. The Pharisees and Sadducees, who asked a sign from heaven, as well as the impious Herod, who wished to see a miracle, form likewise a contrast to the humble faith of the people of God.

Our Lord never yet refused any person who came in earnest to ask his assistance. But the proud and presumptuous are always sent empty away.

And it should be our business, as man is born to trouble, to examine how we improve them. Do they lead us, like the woman of Canaan, to the Saviour, and do they empty us of sin and self? Do we come to the Saviour in the spirit of the poor publican and the woman of Canaan, or do we ask the removal of them with the self-conceited spirit of the proud Pharisee? Are we at the foot of the cross waiting for our answer, or are we like the wicked king of Israel, who proudly said, 'Why should I wait upon the Lord any longer?' The woman of Canaan did not go away in a pet [a fit of peevishness] because she was called a dog, but humbly and meekly acknowledged the charge, and still continues her suit, and obtained her request at last when every appearance was against her.

Jesus heals many

Verse 29. *And Jesus departed from thence, and came nigh unto the sea of Galilee; and went up into a mountain, and sat down there.*

The other part of the lecture is the accomplishment of the 35th Chapter of Isaiah, in verses 29, 30, 31.

In the 29th verse, we find that our Lord went up to a mountain. A mountain is a fit place for prayer and meditation. A person is then retired from the world, and has his thoughts collected and his mind upon heaven. There is a grand view of the works of creation, and the sight will raise the soul to God. If Moses went up to the top of Nebo to get a view of the holy land, is it a surprise that a 'greater than Moses' should occasionally retire from the multitude and go up to a mountain to pray and hold communion with heaven? The people sometimes thought of making him a king, but, oh, what a mere trifle did an earthly kingdom appear to his large and comprehensive mind! He had a view to the recompense of reward and to the kingdom that was waiting for him. The sweet savour of his heavenly doctrine and the fame of his miracles made even the multitude to follow him hither.

> Verses 30–31. *And great multitudes came unto him, having with them those that were lame, blind, dumb, maimed, and many others, and cast them down at Jesus' feet; and he healed them: insomuch that the multitude wondered, when they saw the dumb to speak, the maimed to be whole, the lame to walk, and the blind to see: and they glorified the God of Israel.*

Did ever a king, in the triumph of his conquest, bestow upon his poor subjects gifts like these? The blind see, and the lame walk, and the sick are returning in health. And should not the example of this great multitude be followed by the multitude of the people of God in every age and in every place? Though we are not to expect miracles, we may always look for answers to prayer and spiritual cures. They threw the blind and the deaf and the maimed at the feet of Jesus, and he healed them. We do not read that he refused to heal any of them—and there were many.

This is surely a lesson to us. How many blind and lame sinners are among us? Do we in reality throw them at Christ's feet? If we do not, do we not certainly fail in our duty? Can we say that the Saviour, who did not refuse to cure bodily distempers, would fail to cure spiritual diseases if we applied to him? Is not a spirit of grace and supplication among the people of God always accompanied with an answer? Our Lord Jesus Christ is a compassionate Saviour, and if we acted the part to dead sinners that Lazarus' sisters acted to their brother, we would see the happy effects.

When the multitude saw the astonishing miracles that were performed upon numbers of poor objects, they glorified the God of Israel. And we have the same cause they had, for miracles are one of the great proofs of the truth of the gospel and the divinity of our Saviour. But the great miracle which will make us effectually to believe is his almighty power exerted in converting and sanctifying our own souls. And when sinners are converted from the evil of their ways, they will then see cause to glorify God, and with grateful hearts to acknowledge his mercy in delivering their souls.

Feeding of the four thousand

Verses 32–39. *Then Jesus called his disciples unto him, and said, I have compassion on the multitude, because they continue with me now three days, and have nothing to eat: and I will not send them away fasting, lest they faint in the way. And his disciples say unto him, Whence should we have so much bread in the wilderness, as to fill so great a multitude? And Jesus saith unto them, How many loaves have ye? And they said, Seven, and a few little fishes. And he commanded the multitude to sit down on the ground. And he took the seven loaves and the fishes, and gave thanks, and brake them, and gave to his disciples, and the disciples to the multitude. And they did all eat, and were filled: and they took up of the broken meat that was left seven baskets full. And they that did eat were four thousand men, beside women and children. And he sent away the multitude, and took ship, and came into the coasts of Magdala.*

The faith of the people is further strengthened by being witnesses of another miracle which he wrought to feed their bodies. In the 32nd verse, we read that our Lord had called his disciples and informed them that he was touched with compassion for the multitude that had continued with him so long, and had nothing to eat—that he would not send them away fasting, lest they should faint by the way.

The answer of the disciples argues a wonderful weakness of faith. They had already seen so many specimens of his power in the works he had already wrought that one would think they would naturally look for some exertion of his power when he had given but the smallest hint of his unwillingness to send them away fasting.

We wonder at the unbelief of the Israelites in the desert, and that of the apostles, who were so long in the company of our Lord. Mark 6th, verse 52, assigns as the cause the hardness of their hearts. And if we examine ourselves, the cause of our not believing the gospel is the hardness of our own hearts. Our Lord asked them how many loaves they had. And when they informed him there were seven loaves and a few small fishes, he made the multitude to sit upon the ground. Upon this, he took the loaves and the fishes, gave thanks, broke them, and gave them to the disciples to be distributed to the people.

And here we may observe the wisdom, as well as the compassion, of our Lord. He used means in his condescension to the weakness of his faithful followers. Though he could create food to satisfy their hunger, he gives the blessing to the loaves. They increase by distributing them. He took the loaves and blessed them. And if we put our loaves—let them be never so few—in his hand, he can and he will bless them. When they are increased by him, there is a blessing in them. But if we increase them ourselves, they are in danger of leaving a curse.

And we may take notice as we pass along that no person will lose by following the Saviour and doing his will. He supports them, though it were by a miracle. In verses 37, 38, 39, we see that the whole multitude did eat and were satisfied, and left more than was set before them. And when the people were satisfied with food, he dismissed them, took shipping himself, and went to the coasts of Magdala.

He was unwearied in well-doing, and when he preached, wrought miracles, and did good in one place, he then went to another. And all the works of our Saviour were purely with a view to the glory of God and the salvation of souls.

Practical inferences

I shall conclude this lecture with some practical inferences.

1. First, there is encouragement here for those poor souls who seem in their own view to be excluded, who meet with deep silence from the throne, and have their prayer shut out like Jonah and Jeremiah. Let such wait, hope and plead, and not take delay for a refusal. The Lord's time is best, and though he afflicts, he will surely return and have mercy, speak peace, and give a gracious answer. Every man has something peculiar in his own case. But let him entertain kind hopes of the Saviour.

2. Secondly, let such as have burdens of any kind throw them at the feet of the Saviour. Whether we plead for ourselves or for others, let us go with our complaints to Christ. There is encouragement for the people of God, not only to pray for themselves, but likewise for others. They cast the blind and the lame at Christ's feet, and he healed them.

May God bless his Word. AMEN.

Matthew chapter 16: verses 1 to 20

B Y reading and hearing the history of our Lord Jesus Christ we may discover the malignity of that spiritual disease under which we labour, and the exceeding preciousness of our cure. If we wish to find out the poison that lurks in the human heart, and if we are desirous to be acquainted with the human character, let us read the gospel. Sin at its lowest stage is opposition to the will of God, and sin at its height is enmity to God and to everything that is good. We have a common expression among us, that is, when we speak of a perfect character. If such a person should appear among us, whatever our opinion of ourselves may be, we would not love him. The only perfect character that ever appeared on earth among mankind was hated and despised by men. Never man had so many enemies as our Saviour; never system had so many opponents as his gospel. That the doctrine is heavenly and the morality is pure will be acknowledged by all that examine it, our enemies themselves being judges. Whence, then, had our Saviour so many enemies, and why does his gospel still meet with such a cold reception among us? The cause is clear: they love sin better than the Saviour.

I shall endeavour to explain the words in the order in which they be, and conclude with practical inferences.

The sign of the prophet Jonas

Verse 1. *The Pharisees also with the Sadducees came, and tempting desired him that he would shew them a sign from heaven.*

The Pharisees and Sadducees in some points were diametrically opposite in their sentiments. But they both agree in one great

246

opinion—their opposition to Christ. Herod and Pontius Pilate had enmity among themselves, but they became friends when Christ was to be condemned.

And we may observe similar cases in this our day. There are people of various opinions in point of religion, and we may easily observe that they associate with, and have greater pleasure in the company of, libertines and infidels than in the society of pious people. Whatever set of opinions people may embrace, whatever Church they belong to, they join in one great opinion: they study to please themselves, and not the Lord Jesus Christ. They oppose strict godliness, and persecute those who follow the Lamb wherever he goes.

The Pharisees and Sadducees unite in tempting Christ by asking him for a sign from heaven. Not satisfied with the many and irrefragable [indisputable] proofs that he gave of his being the Messiah, they ask some sign from heaven to gratify a sinful and petulant curiosity. Had they done justice to their own consciences, they might remember the story of the shepherds, the history of the wise men from the East, and the public baptism at Jordan. He was there acknowledged by a voice from heaven as the Son of God, in whom he was well pleased. Our Lord knew well they were steeled with prejudice, and were resolved to refuse conviction; otherwise, his astonishing works might make them acknowledge the truth. Miracles and signs from heaven would be equally lost upon them, and therefore he refused their request.

Verses 2–4. *He answered and said unto them, When it is evening, ye say, It will be fair weather: for the sky is red. And in the morning, It will be foul weather to day: for the sky is red and lowring. O ye hypocrites, ye can discern the face of the sky; but can ye not discern the signs of the times? A wicked and adulterous generation seeketh after a sign; and there shall no sign be given unto it, but the sign of the prophet Jonas. And he left them, and departed.*

It is well known to any that choose to read and study the gospel with candour and impartiality that our Lord never refused his assistance to any that stood in need and made application. It is likewise a fact that when any person wishing to come at the truth made enquiry whether he was the promised Messiah, he gave such all the satisfaction he could naturally expect. John Baptist sent persons to ask if he was he who was to come. The answer our Lord made was an appeal to the glorious miracles he wrought as a proof of his divine mission and divine unction. It was by giving a proof of his omniscience that he convinced Nathaniel that he was the Son of God. But when his bitter and avowed enemies, with malignant intention, called for a sign from heaven, he absolutely refused their request. And at the same time showed them how inexcusable they were as to their affected ignorance of his being the true Messiah.

In Palestine, as well as in all other countries, many persons can prognosticate the weather from the appearance of the skies in the morning or evening. He blames them for their knowledge in natural things and their criminal indifference to things of infinite consequence to their souls. They were at no pains to discern the signs of the times. The Scriptures of the Old Testament were in their hands, and they might know the time of the Messiah's appearance. Daniel's seventy weeks were nearly run out, the sceptre was fast departing from Judah, for they were under the power of the Romans. A wonderful person had appeared among them, for both the purity of his life and the glory of his works and miracles. He was known to be of the tribe of Judah and the family of David.

In a word, all the character of Messiah centred in our Lord Jesus Christ. And as they might know this if they did justice to the Word of God and to their own consciences, he referred them to the sign of the prophet Jonas and then left them. Jonah was three days and three nights in the heart of the sea, and thus was a type of the Saviour.

Our Lord, by this answer, referred them to his resurrection as the last proof of his being the Messiah. Wicked and adulterous, therefore, as that generation were, they were to get an offer of salvation after his resurrection, and if this would not convince them, they were to be left as a prey to their incorrigible lusts and passions, and the hardness and deplorable obstinacy of their own hearts. Every method was tried to convince them: when all failed, they were at last cast off.

And it is to be feared that we are like the Pharisees and Sadducees in this respect. They were acute enough in discerning the face of the sky, but blind like moles in the things of God. And have we not many among us who show themselves to be men of prudence and good sense in managing worldly affairs, who are mere fools in the things of God? They have penetration enough to see and discern what makes for their temporal interest, but, alas! they allow their souls to lie uncultivated like the sluggards' gardens. Ministers of the gospel use every mean they can think of to better their spiritual condition, but instead of growing better, they become worse, and very often are more wicked and greater sinners than those that never heard the joyful sound. They come like the Jews to hear our Saviour, not with a view to get good to their souls, but that they may afterwards contradict and blaspheme what they hear, and thus accumulate guilt and damnation upon their own souls. They are convinced in their own consciences that what they hear is the truth. With regard to such, we may well ask the Saviour's question, 'How can they escape the damnation of hell?'

The leaven of the Pharisees

Verses 5–12. *And when his disciples were come to the other side, they had forgotten to take bread. Then Jesus said unto them, Take heed and beware of the leaven of the Pharisees and of the Sadducees. And they reasoned among themselves, saying, It is because we have taken no bread. Which when Jesus perceived, he said unto them, O ye of little faith, why reason ye among yourselves, because ye have brought no bread? Do ye not yet understand, neither remember the five loaves of the five thousand, and how many baskets ye took up? Neither the seven loaves of the four thousand, and how many baskets ye took up? How is it that ye do not understand that I spake it not to you concerning bread, that ye should beware of the leaven of the Pharisees and of the Sadducees? Then under-*

stood they how that he bade them not beware of the leaven of bread, but of the doctrine of the Pharisees and of the Sadducees.

In these words, we find that our Lord gave a caution to his disciples to avoid false doctrine. It is true he observes in another place that the scribes and Pharisees sat in Moses' chair, and he recommends them to follow what was wholesome in what they heard. As far as they followed the doctrine of Moses, they were to follow them. But here he bids them beware of what was false and poisonous in the doctrine of Pharisees and Sadducees.

From this advice of our Saviour, we see of what consequence it is to the comfort and happiness of our souls to hear fat and wholesome doctrine. The apostles were very anxious about the doctrines the people heard. And this absolutely condemns that senseless and foolish observation often made by the common people that, if they made good use of the worst doctrine they hear, they would be safe. This is not true, for they may hear what will prove poison instead of food or medicine to their souls. The observation proceeds from their insensibility of conscience and mere indifference about the state of their souls. All doctrines are much the same to them while they continue in that state. They would not, however, talk in this lukewarm style in drawing a comparison between different kinds of foods or of liquors. They will not say that if a man makes good use of the worst kind of bread and a scant measure of the same, and of the weakest liquor, that he is rendered as strong for bodily labour as the man that gets great food or plenty of good food and refreshing liquors. The cause is, they have tasted bodily food, but they are strangers hitherto to what will feed and invigorate, comfort, and strengthen their souls.

And our Lord here justly blames the weakness of his disciples' faith. They gave a wrong turn to his words—not, indeed, from malignity, but from simplicity and ignorance. Our Lord shows them, by putting them in mind of the miracles he wrought, that he could still feed them in the same way if there was necessity. They clearly perceived by this that he pointed at the doctrine of the Pharisees and Sadducees.

And here we may observe that friends, as well as enemies, sometimes give a wrong turn to the expressions of our Saviour. Our Lord, however, knew the heart, and made a great distinction between weakness of intellect and corruption of heart. The people of God, in some cases, may have sinful prejudices in smaller matters, but they are sins of ignorance. But our Lord did not nurse them in sins of ignorance or in any errors. But when he rebukes them, he has different language from what he uses to his implacable enemies. He did not encourage the errors of his friends, and he thus showed himself the great friend of their souls. And the people of God should cheerfully submit to every rebuke that is calculated for the spiritual and everlasting good of their souls.

Christ's conference with his disciples

Verses 13–19. *When Jesus came into the coasts of Caesarea Philippi, he asked his disciples, saying, Whom do men say that I the Son of man am? And they said, Some say that thou art John the Baptist: some, Elias; and others, Jeremias, or one of the prophets. He saith unto them, But whom say ye that I am? And Simon Peter answered and said, Thou art the Christ, the Son of the living God. And Jesus answered and said unto him, Blessed art thou, Simon Barjona: for flesh and blood hath not revealed it unto thee, but my Father which is in heaven. And I say also unto thee, That thou art Peter, and upon this rock I will build my church; and the gates of hell shall not prevail against it. And I will give unto thee the keys of the kingdom of heaven: and whatsoever thou shalt bind on earth shall be bound in heaven: and whatsoever thou shalt loose on earth shall be loosed in heaven.*

Our Lord was constantly going about doing good. We read in the former chapter that he was in the coasts of Tyre and Sidon, and here we find him in the coasts of Caesarea Philippi. The one is supposed to be a day's journey from the other.

It is true our Lord was the minister of the circumcision, and as a preacher was sent to the lost sheep of the house of Israel, but we see that he came to the borders of the heathen, as if he meant to show them that he was a light to enlighten the Gentiles, as well as the glory of his people Israel. The time of the calling of the Gentiles was not fully come till after his resurrection, and therefore he did not preach personally to them. But we find he gave them an opportunity of hearing him and seeing his miracles, and thus prepared them for the preaching of his apostles afterwards.

Upon this occasion, our Lord asked his disciples what was the opinion of the multitude concerning him. He did this not from any desire of vainglory or to gain the good opinion of the people, but merely to instruct his disciples in the truth concerning the promised Messiah.

The disciples told him that some looked upon him to be Elias; others as Jeremiah, or, at any rate, as one of the old prophets. When he asked their own opinion, Peter made a glorious confession of his faith—he answered and said, 'Thou art the Christ, the Son of the living God.' Our Lord, as a reward for his faith, pronounced him happy in having this mystery revealed to him by the Spirit, and told he would build his Church upon that Rock whom Peter had acknowledged for the Rock of his salvation, and that the powers of darkness would never prevail against it. At the same time, he promised to make Peter one of the principal pillars in his Church, and gave him the keys of discipline as well as doctrine, as he afterwards gave to all the apostles.

Now, in these words we may observe the following doctrines:

1. First, the divinity of our Lord Jesus Christ.
2. Secondly, the necessity of divine light and grace to see this truth.
3. Thirdly, that the gospel shall prevail against the powers of darkness.
4. Lastly, the privileges of the Church and ministers of the gospel.

Of these great truths we shall speak a few things as they be in order. From these words we see:

1. The divinity of our Lord Jesus Christ. Peter calls him Christ, the Son of the living God. As the Son of Man naturally signifies a man, in like manner the Son of God signifies one that has all the essential properties of the divine nature. Good men and angels are called the sons of God, but it is not said that the fulness of the Godhead ever dwelt in one of them. But when the Son whose throne is from everlasting is introduced into the world, all creatures are desired to worship him. We are to kiss the Son in token of honour and homage and subjection. And this subjection and worship can only be given to the divine nature. The divine nature in our Lord received worship from his creatures. It is according to the divine nature that he uses that remarkable expression, 'And now, O Father, glorify me with thine own self with the glory which I had with thee before the world was.'

2. The necessity of divine light and grace to see this truth. No man can come unto the Son except the Father draw him. Others, as well as Peter, had access to hear his doctrine and witness his miracles, but without effect. Thousands had heard his precious gospel and saw his works. But instead of believing on him, they rejected him as the Messiah, and the rock of salvation became to many a rock of offence. And this shows us the necessity of prayer for divine influences. (Mark 7:7; Luke 22:13).

3. The gospel shall prevail against the powers of darkness. The gospel shall prevail against the powers of darkness. And this will naturally happen because the Church is built upon a rock. The waves may dash themselves to pieces against the rock, but they will not prevail. All the enemies of God shall be put to confusion, and their fury shall fall at last upon themselves. And this may appear:

(1) From the nature of the gospel. It is a system of purity and calculated to promote the glory of God and the good of man. And as this is the end the gospel has in view, it must ultimately prevail. God will support his own glory, and punish all that persevere to the end in opposing him. His honour binds him to keep the gospel in the world.

(2) But again, we may reason from what has happened. The corruption of human nature has given it all the opposition possible from the beginning. Every art that the malice of hell, the strength of lust, and the power of the sword could make use of were employed to subvert it, and it still subsists. And from what has passed, we may reason as to what is future. The sun rose every day for 1000 years past: we may reason that it will rise also tomorrow. And people would show as much wisdom in arresting the sun and endeavouring to hinder his rising as oppose the power of God in the progress of the gospel. It did, and it will prevail in every place where the Spirit of God is determined to exert his power.

If God has determined that the gospel will be in a place, it will be sent there. It may leave one spot of the earth and go to another, but God will have a Church always to the end of the world. And let it be observed that this remark regards the operation of the Spirit accompanying the gospel, and not the mere outward establishment of Christianity. The one may be destroyed in a place: the other never can. The Church may be ambulatory in the wilderness, but it is always somewhere or other protected by the pillar of fire and cloud. Every opposition from enemies of all kinds serve only to illustrate and establish the gospel.

(3) And this appears from the several promises of the Word. We have a sure word of revelation. All the promises centre in Christ. They must be accomplished, for his Word cannot fall to the ground. There are various promises respecting the gospel, both in the Old and New Testaments. And God is faithful in accomplishing his promises. We see his predictions literally performed in things of less consequence. And in fact, the enemies of the gospel, contrary to their own intention, shall be found instrumental in accomplishing divine promises and exalting the Saviour.

4. The privileges of the church and ministers of the gospel. Lastly, we see the privileges of the Church and the ministers of the gospel. The privileges of the Church are great, and this is not the proper place to explain them. We shall only observe that all the privileges of the ministers of the gospel are given them in behalf of the

Church. What ministers, therefore, do in doctrine and discipline is for the edification and good of the Church, and to promote their salvation. What they bind or loose on earth is bound or loosed in heaven. When we authoritatively pronounce pardon of sin to the penitent, that is bound in heaven. The penitent is loosed in heaven, and he often feels the comfort upon earth. And if a wicked person is incorrigible and is delivered to Satan, he shall find to his cost that this is bound in heaven also, and if he does not repent, the sentence of the Church shall be executed by the sentence of judgment. How awful, then, is excommunication when it is pronounced against wicked and obstinate sinners! And it is your duty, my friends, to pray that sinners may be awakened to see the danger of their ways.

Jesus' charge to his disciples

Verse 20. *Then charged he his disciples that they should tell no man that he was Jesus the Christ.*

We read in the 20th verse that he charged his disciples that they should tell no man that he was Jesus the Christ.

The time of his sufferings was now drawing very near, and as his apostles were established in the truth of his divinity, he enjoined them at this time to conceal it. And there was good cause to do so for some short time. The faith of the apostles themselves had enough to do while he lay in the grave. The time for preaching this great truth was after his resurrection from the dead, when he was declared to be the Son of God with power. The resurrection, then, is the great proof of his divinity and of the truth of the gospel.

Practical inferences

Having thus explained the words, I shall conclude with some practical inferences.

1. First, if the Jews were guilty of criminal neglect in discerning the signs of the times, let us beware that we be not guilty of the same kind of neglect. There are signs of good weather and of bad weather, signs that precede the summer, and others that indicate the approach of winter. There are signs that may attend individuals and communities. If an individual lives in sin, and neglects the gospel and abuses golden opportunities of promoting his salvation, he carries about with him the signs of his own future misery. If he believes the gospel and forsakes sin, he has a presage [sign] of his future and everlasting happiness.

And with regard to communities, if there are great sins among them, as this is a reproach to any people, these are signs of their approaching dissolution. The long-suffering of God and the prayers of his people, like good and wholesome medicines, may prevent death, as it were, for some little time. But the disease may become too inveterate for a radical cure. Dissolution must therefore ensue. Great sins destroyed the empires of the Persians, Greeks, and Romans. And the sins of Christians are still greater, and must bring greater judgments.

On the other hand, if we saw a spirit of prayer poured out upon all ranks in Church and State—if we saw private and public prayer diets, and that virtue, honesty, purity, and all the Christian graces did prevail among us—these would infallibly prognosticate temporal and spiritual prosperity. And we may appeal to your own consciences which of these signs do you see among us.

2. Secondly, that good and wholesome doctrine is of the utmost consequence to people. The apostles stood in need of the caution they got: much more do we. And if people do not make good use of the doctrines they hear, God may permit poison to be mixed with their food. Good doctrine is your mercy, if you improve it—if not, it must prove your greater condemnation to hear it.

3. Lastly, we see how glorious are the privileges of the Church of Christ and the ministers of the gospel. The Church is secured from

all the powers of darkness. If a man remains, therefore, in the Church and is a true member of Christ, he is safe.

Ministers have great privileges. What they do is bound in heaven. The ambassador of an earthly sovereign, who represents his master, can propose terms of peace or war. To show you the nature of discipline, suppose a man from the camp of Israel had been excluded from the people of God, and had gone over to the Egyptians the night the two armies passed through the Red Sea, what would be the consequences? Death, undoubtedly, to the miserable man. How fearful is the deathbed of an excommunicated person! You know when we baptize a child, we pray to confirm in heaven what was done upon earth. And if people do not forfeit it, there is a blessing promised. In like manner, when we excommunicate, we deliver a man over to Satan. And we have power to do the one as well as the other.

What wretches must they be who can talk lightly about such an awful ordinance! How awful, then, is the excommunication pronounced against the wicked! 'Depart from me, ye cursed.'

May God keep you from knowing what it means, and bless his Word to your souls.

AMEN.

Matthew chapter 16: verses 21 to 28

AFTER our Lord had nearly finished his course of obedience, he now prepares himself for the course of suffering he had to undergo. As the great captain of our salvation, he was to be perfect through suffering, and thus open the door of heaven to those who believe and obey him. He had prepared his apostles by his heavenly discourses to hear this doctrine, and it was necessary that they should be instructed in the doctrines of his sufferings, as this was the great end of his coming into the world.

His disciples were tinctured [affected] with the false notions which the Jews entertained of the earthly kingdom of Messiah. It was, therefore, by degrees that our Lord opened up the leading doctrines of Christianity and the great mystery of our redemption. He now informs them of this great truth in plain terms, and tells them that this was the design of his journey to Jerusalem.

I shall, by divine aid, explain the words and make some practical inferences.

Christ's reproof of Peter

Verse 21. *From that time forth began Jesus to shew unto his disciples, how that he must go unto Jerusalem, and suffer many things of the elders and chief priests and scribes, and be killed, and be raised again the third day.*

In these words, our Lord shows himself to be great, and the Good Shepherd that was to lay down his life for the sheep. He was now called by his Father to drink the bitter cup, and, instead of declining to do so, he cheerfully met his sufferings. He saw the storm that was coming, and met it with firmness and courage. And as his sufferings would likewise prove a great trial to his disciples, he prepares them likewise, that they may not come upon them unawares. The sufferings of our Lord were to be very great, for he was to undergo a public trial, and be condemned and crucified. And this trial was to be carried on by the principal characters in the nation—the chief priests, elders, and scribes. But though he was to suffer death, he was to rise again on the third day. He was an innocent person, but he was to suffer for the sins of others. And as he suffered unjustly, for his judge acknowledged his innocence, God raised him from the dead. And this he informs his disciples of, to comfort them in view of his approaching death. It was necessary that our Lord should suffer for the glory of God. The truth, and the accomplishment of prophecy, and the salvation of men required this. But at the time he mentions his death, he also informs them of his resurrection, so that they might rest assured that the one event would happen infallibly as well as the other.

Verse 22. *Then Peter took him, and began to rebuke him, saying, Be it far from thee, Lord: this shall not be unto thee.*

From these words, we may make the following remarkable [noteworthy] observations:

1. First, the inconsistency of human nature.
2. Secondly, that Peter himself could not be the Rock upon which our Lord was to build his Church.
3. Thirdly, that it concerns the best of us to examine what spirit we are of.

1. First, the inconsistency of human nature. Peter, a little while ago, had made a most glorious confession that our Lord was the true Christ, the Son of the living God. He was then in the Spirit, and full of heavenly love to his Saviour. We see him now in a very carnal frame. He yields to the suggestions of carnal wisdom, self-conceit, and foolish pride. If Christ was the Son of God, how could he take upon him to contradict or advise him? If he was the wisdom of the

Father, the way, the truth and the life, could he possibly be mistaken himself or mislead others? And yet the holy and blessed apostle is guilty of this fault. Even the great Elijah fails in his courage, and the meek Moses is angry. And if such tall cedars fell, Lord, what is man? Weakness and folly—may thy grace be sufficient for us.

And is this the case with us all? At times, we think ourselves in a heavenly frame, and what would we not do for Christ and his cause? At other times, we are in a languid, carnal, and earthly frame, unfit and indisposed for any duty. Upon some occasions, we think we have got the victory, but anon we cry, like the apostle, 'O wretched man that I am! who will deliver me from this body of sin and death?' We are oppressed with lust, pride, or passion, or some other carnal affection.

We have no cause to boast, and this may teach us our weakness, and that we must depend upon free grace and the great and all-sufficient Saviour.

2. Peter could not be the rock upon which our Lord was to build his Church. It is true our Lord says to him, 'Thou art Peter,' and in allusion to his name, he says, 'I will build my Church upon this rock.' And does he not say to the Jews, 'Destroy this temple, and in three days I will build it again'? He does not mean the temple of Jerusalem in the one case more than he means the rock of Peter's faith in the other. Peter had strong faith, but he was permitted to fall into blunders and sins to show he was fallible, and that he could not possibly be the rock upon which the Church was built.

In the next verse, our Lord calls him Satan, and if he fell himself, how could he be the rock that supported others? There is, besides, another glaring absurdity in the supposition. If Peter was the rock upon which the Church was built, we may well ask, what was Christ himself? If Peter was the rock, then Christ must build upon Peter, and not Peter upon Christ, and if this is not an absurdity, what is so? The bare mention of it is enough to confute [refute] the sentiment. If it be asked, then, 'And what is here promised to Peter?' A great deal indeed.

(1) His salvation is here secured, for he built his hope upon a rock. Satan could not prevail finally against him—though he fell, he rose again.

(2) Again, he is here constituted one of the principal pillars of the Church of Christ, and one of the great instruments that procured the salvation of men.

3. That it concerns the best of us to consider what spirit we are of. Peter might think that he spoke from affection to Christ, but the event makes it clear that he was warped with carnal prejudices and worldly motives, for if he was right in his opinions and had the glory of God in view, he had not been rebuked. Two of the apostles wished to bring fire from heaven. Another complains that a person who did not follow them had cast out devils in the name of Christ. No doubt they might think their motives were pure, but there was something wrong lurking under all this seeming zeal. And if the apostles were wrong, are we not at least in equal, if not greater, danger? Lord, direct all our steps.

Verse 23. *But he turned, and said unto Peter, Get thee behind me, Satan: thou art an offence unto me: for thou savourest not the things that be of God, but those that be of men.*

When Peter got such a rebuke, couched in terms so very severe, we may well conclude that there was something awful in his advice, and that he was certainly guilty of a very great crime. Our Lord was not subject to unguarded sallies of passion, for he was free from all sin. He could not be mistaken in what he said, for he was the wisdom of God, and therefore infallible in all his doctrines and rebukes. And what was Peter's sin?

(1) He wished to divert our Lord either by worldly motives or slavish fear from the great work he had undertaken.

(2) He opposed the glory of God in the salvation of men.

(3) His advice would overthrow all the leading promises in the Old Testament.

All this being true, our Lord turned to him and told him that he acted the part of an adversary to him, and that instead of seeking to promote the glory of God, he gave him the greatest opposition. He was actuated by motives of ambition and pride, and wished to carry on an interest contrary to the interest of God in the world. Had the Saviour flinched from the work he undertook, hell might triumph, and the pillars of heaven would fall. Eternal truth would fail, and God Almighty be disappointed of the end he had in view.

It is true, Peter swerved through ignorance and folly, not knowing the import of his own advice. But as his advice was so diametrically opposite to God and the salvation of his people, the Saviour rebuked him as he deserved. He showed him his danger, and it would appear the good man did not proceed further. He saw his folly in the proper light, and that the foolishness of God is wiser than the wisdom of men.

The value of the soul

Verses 24–28. *Then said Jesus unto his disciples, If any man will come after me, let him deny himself, and take up his cross, and follow me. For whosoever will save his life shall lose it: and whosoever will lose his life for my sake shall find it. For what is a man profited, if he shall gain the whole world, and lose his own soul? or what shall a man give in exchange for his soul? For the Son of man shall come in the glory of his Father with his angels; and then he shall reward every man according to his works. Verily I say unto you, There be some standing here, which shall not taste of death, till they see the Son of man coming in his kingdom.*

After our Lord had given this sharp rebuke to his favourite and apostle, he comes to lay down some general doctrines respecting not only his immediate followers, but also all his followers to the end of the world. For though the first Christians were more exposed to persecution on account of religion than we are, the spirit of the doctrine is the same. It concerns us as much as it did them.

1. The first doctrine our Lord lays down here is self-denial for all his followers.
2. Second, is to take up the cross.
3. Third, is to suffer persecution to death rather than deny our religion.

The argument he uses is the danger, on the one hand, and the great reward on the other. And then informs them that some of those who heard him would not taste of death till they saw the Son of man coming in his kingdom.

I shall speak to each of these doctrines.

1. First, our Lord lays down self-denial for all his followers. Since the fall of Adam, the human will is in direct opposition to the will of God. Sin has spread over all the powers of the soul, so that a state of spiritual discipline and regimen is absolutely necessary. And we are averse from suffering of any kind. A gracious God appoints suffering of one kind or other for our spiritual good. He begins with the lowest kind and ascends to the highest, according as our disease and the state of our hearts and conversation may require.

We are to deny ourselves, because our will is corrupt and our desires sinful and contrary to the will of God. And even when lawful, we may exceed. We are to deny our sinful self. And this is absolutely necessary for the life of our souls. Sin of every kind is spiritual poison.

The gratification of our sinful passions is to the soul what strong food may be to the body in some dangerous diseases. A sick man will deny himself the pleasure of food and liquor which his appetite may crave, if his physician warns him there is danger in taking them. And no man in his senses will say that this self-denial is a cruelty to the patient. He denies himself, that he may have the greater relish for food after he recovers his health.

People in health deny themselves. If a man is invited to a feast tomorrow, he takes a light supper tonight and a sober breakfast in the morning, that he may have the greater enjoyment of the feast to which he is invited. And if we would relish the rich feasts of the gospel and prepare ourselves for the joys of heaven, we ought to avoid sinful joys, and taste moderately all lawful enjoyments, for fear we disqualify our own souls.

Our Lord forbids us nothing but what our reason will justify. Children are required to use a great deal of what they must reckon self-denial and even hardship. Their strong appetites and perverse inclinations would urge them to do a thousand things of which they would afterwards be ashamed. What they would think a hardship when children, they see very proper when they become men and women, and they avoid these things cheerfully.

Now, in our minority, we are fond of our own will, but when our souls are thoroughly sanctified, we see the great propriety of all the rules of self-denial laid down in the Word. What is chastity, temperance, and humility but so many exercises of self-denial? And this self-denial may be painful, but when we get the victory and enter upon the joys of heaven, we would naturally avoid these things that religion forbids. We then see in a clear light the wisdom of our heavenly Father and his goodness to our souls in giving us such a gracious command as self-denial. When we become men and women, our stomachs would have an aversion to all the trash of which children are so fond. We are, then, to deny ourselves, and not to seek our own will. There is such malignity in sin that it poisons all our enjoyments. We covet what is forbidden, and convert our very food into poison. The great aim of the Christian is to bring his will to the will of God, and, like his Saviour, to say, 'Not my will, but thine, be done.'

2. Again, we are to take up the cross. It is a truth which Scripture and experience may teach us that man is born to trouble. Sin will bring sorrow, and as we are sinners, we must suffer affliction of one kind or other. People must suffer, whether they be Christians or not. There is something in every man's lot that he must consider as a cross. But the doctrine of the text is that we must take it up and follow Christ. Now, if we take it up cheerfully and willingly, it will prove a blessing and a medicine to our souls. The profession of a

Christian, if he is truly such, will naturally expose him to trouble. If he follow Christ, he must have the cross. He will meet with opposition. The world, flesh, and devil meet him in his pilgrimage to the heavenly Canaan, and, like the Amalekites in the wilderness, will give him battle till the sun sets.

Now, we are to bear all that comes in our way for the sake of Christ. Providence will lay the trial or the sufferings in our way that is best calculated for our spiritual good. We must not flinch or go back from our duty. As far as we do so, we hurt our spiritual interest.

It was a cross to the apostles to receive Christ as a mere spiritual king, when they were taught to look for a mere temporal Messiah. They were stumbled at the idea of his sufferings. When we seek our happiness in anything but the favour of God, trouble is graciously sent to buy us back to a right way of thinking. We are to take up the cross, submit to the will of heaven, and follow the suffering Saviour. If suffering was necessary for him, it must be doubly necessary for us also. Whether the cross is sent (as we think) by man, or immediately by God himself, we are to take it up.

Joseph and David had their crosses from men. They considered them as instruments submitted to the will of God, and thus got good to their souls. The good man Job justified God in the midst of all his trials and afflictions, and still retained his integrity. The primitive Christians bore all the troubles to which they were exposed, for the sake of Christ, with humility and resignation. They did not throw off the cross, because this would be denying their profession. We ought, then, to bear the cross and go with our burden after the Saviour, for he will, sooner or later, loose every burden. Only let us await his time.

3. We are to suffer persecution to death, rather than deny our religion. This is no doubt an awful trial, but should it ever happen to us, God would be seen to be infinitely wise and good in the trial. Should his providence bring us to the stake, he would do us no injury. He would, according to our need, give us grace sufficient for our suffering. And this will further appear when we consider that it

is a Christian's duty to resign his life to God upon the bed of death. If God demands it, rather at the stake or gibbet, where is the great odds? Our future joy would be greater in the one case than in the other. If unbelief should tell us that we would faint and go back, or that we have no grace, and that we would lose the crown of martyrdom, let us go with such thoughts to the Saviour, and if we have no grace, let us go as we are to the fountain of grace for strength in duty and assistance in every time of need. The Saviour is always a present help in time of trouble.

The argument he uses is the danger on the one hand, and the great and unspeakable reward on the other.

The danger of apostasy is great, and we should carefully avoid all approaches towards that great sin. Let us not sin against conscience or indulge our own carnal appetites. Esau is an awful example to carnal Christians. Let drunkards, swearers, liars, and all other rotten professors consider this. The covetous worldling may here see for how much he would sell Christ and betray his cause.

On the other hand, the reward of constancy and perseverance is great. Eye hath not seen, nor ear heard, what joys await the true followers of Christ. The more we do and suffer for him, the more glorious our reward. In his presence is joy, and at his right hand are pleasures evermore.

And after our Lord had delivered this useful doctrine, he informed them that some of those who were present would not taste of death till they saw the Son of man coming into his kingdom.

Now, it is a fact that several of his followers lived till the Christian religion had spread far and near, and the crucified Saviour was worshipped in Europe, Asia, and Africa. Some few of them lived till the destruction of Jerusalem, when he came to take signal vengeance of the Jewish nation for the horrible sin they were guilty of in crucifying the Lord of glory. The destruction of Jerusalem was the great accomplishment of prophecy and the triumph of Christianity.

Practical inferences

I shall conclude with some practical inferences.

1. The sufferings of Christ are one great proof that he was the Messiah promised in the Old Testament. His sufferings are pointed out in the types, ceremonies, and prophecies. He is the Lamb slain from the foundation of the world. In spite of the Jews, sacrifices have ceased since the establishment of Christianity. As the great sacrifice has been offered, it was not for the honour of God that his providence should suffer sacrifices to be offered, after proof had been given to Jews and Gentiles that Christ had offered a sacrifice for the sins of his people.

By the time Jerusalem was destroyed, Christianity had been sufficiently spread and published.

2. If we are the faithful followers of Christ, it is incumbent upon us to offer up our bodies as living sacrifices to God, and to crucify the flesh with the affections and lusts. He suffered for our sins, and we ought to give up our lusts and sins to be nailed to his cross. And we are to do this willingly, for it is to be a reasonable service. Christ went willingly to death, and we must willingly part with sin. If our hearts, like the covetous young man in the gospel, go away sorrowful from Christ, we are yet in our sins.

Christianity is a religion come from heaven, and if we would enjoy the rewards of it, let us live up to the spirit of it, let us follow our divine leader, and if we suffer, we shall rest with him, high in salvation and the climes of bliss.

God bless his Word. AMEN.

Matthew chapter 17: verses 1 to 9

A S the sufferings of our Lord now drew very nigh, he saw proper to select three of his disciples, lead them to a mountain, and give them a view of his glory and a foretaste of heaven.

Without further preface I shall, by divine assistance, endeavour to throw some light on this delightful portion of sound writ, and conclude with some practical inferences.

The transfiguration

Verses 1–2. And after six days Jesus taketh Peter, James, and John his brother, and bringeth them up into an high mountain apart, and was transfigured before them: and his face did shine as the sun, and his raiment was white as the light.

Our Lord chose three of his apostles to be witnesses of his glorious transfiguration. Two or three witnesses are sufficient to attest any fact. And he was best judge what three were the most proper for his purpose.

To me it appears very probable that these three were more exposed to unbelief than any of the rest. Our Lord himself said to one of them, 'Simon, Simon, Satan hath desired to have thee, that he might sift thee like wheat.' To satisfy their minds, therefore, he gave them a sight of his glory, that the recollection of what they saw might keep up their hearts at the time of their greatest distress.

The two evangelists, Matthew and Luke, have a seeming difference: the one speaks of six days, the other about eight days. The one men-

tions the exact time; the other uses a round number—as we say
'about eight days' when we speak of the time between two Sabbaths,
we include the two Sabbaths as well as the six intervening days. And
let it be observed that the difference between the sacred writers is
rather seeming than real when examined.

He brought them up into an high mountain apart. He did this to
have the greater privacy and the more opportunity for heavenly contemplation. A mountain is a proper place for this purpose. Abraham
went to a mountain to worship, and Moses, a little before his death,
ascended the mountain of Nebo, and stood upon the top of Pisgah
to get a view of the Holy Land. Our Lord went often to a mountain
to pray. A mountain is a very proper place for devotion. The view a
person gets of the works of creation is calculated to raise the
thoughts to heaven, that we may seek communion with the ever-
present God.

It is likely the mountain our Lord ascended at this time was Tabor,
in Galilee. It stands alone in a great plain, and the view from the top
of it is inexpressibly beautiful. Here, then, it is thought our Lord
brought his disciples and gave them the most glorious sight that
could be seen this side of heaven. His face did shine as the sun, and
his raiment was white as the light.

Luke observes that this happened when he was praying. And here
we may observe that the greatest and most glorious actions of our
Lord, the great head of the Church, were accomplished by prayer.
When he was baptized, after prayer, the heaven was opened and the
Holy Ghost descended upon him like a dove. After prayer, he raised
Lazarus from the dead, and after prayer, he was transfigured on the
mountain. And if we are followers of the Saviour, we shall obtain all
our blessings, temporal and spiritual, in and through prayer. While
he sojourned upon earth, his glory was eclipsed, and he passed for
a poor man. But now he shows himself as something more than
man. He discovers himself as the Son of God and the brightness of
his Father's glory.

Verses 3–4. And, behold, there appeared unto them Moses and Elias talking with him. Then answered Peter, and said unto Jesus, Lord, it is good for us to be here: if thou wilt, let us make here three tabernacles; one for thee, and one for Moses, and one for Elias.

By comparing Luke and Matthew together, it would appear that this bright and glorious scene happened in the night. Peter and the other apostles were heavy with sleep. And as this happened in the night, it tended to make the scene still more glorious.

Now, we cannot help observing that the apostles, though valuable and good men, betrayed a great deal of human weakness. They did not watch with the Saviour, but fell asleep. He continued praying alone, though they did not join him, for they were asleep. But their sloth did not provoke the Lord to withhold from them the glorious sight of his transfiguration. And here we may observe that he did everything alone. His disciples did not join in prayer when he was transfigured: they were asleep—the spirit was willing, but the flesh was weak. When they awoke, what a glorious sight! Did ever man since the creation of the world get such a midnight vision before? A light as bright as the sun enlightens the midnight gloom. When the apostles awake, they see the sight. The poor and humble Saviour appears in his robes of glory. His face is like the sun, and his very garments bright as the light.

And to add to their astonishment, they behold Moses and Elijah appear in glory likewise with the Saviour. It would appear the conversation continued for some time, for the apostles knew when such exalted characters met together in such glory and majesty, what is the subject of their discourse? They do not talk of politics, the rise and fall of empires, and the great revolutions that happen in the kingdoms of this world. They have a much more sublime and heavenly subject. They talk about the Saviour's death and the redemption of mankind.

If the glorious spirits who surround the throne of God descend to this inferior world, their conversation is suitable to their character. The angels talk of the birth of the Saviour and benefits that accrue to mankind by such a gift. If wise men of the world met together, their discourse would not rise higher than the politics of the day, and the grandeur and riches of this earth. They would allow pious people to talk of the gospel, as a subject beneath the notice of philosophers. We find, however, that the most exalted beings in the creation of God consider it as their honour and pleasure to talk about the gospel. Exalted characters talk about exalted subjects, and would consider earthly conversation as the play of children, and entirely below their notice.

After Moses and Elijah had talked for some considerable time upon this glorious theme, they departed to heaven again. Peter, still willing to detain them, and wishing to prolong the conversation that pleased him so much, proposed to the Lord to make three tabernacles: one for Moses, and one for Elias, and one for him. Scripture observes that he knew not what he said. He wished to prolong the heavenly vision, but this sight is too glorious for the earth: he could not triumph till he first fought the good fight of faith. And this is too much the case with us also. We are much fonder of the privileges and comforts than of the duties of religion. In our present state, however, the one is more for our happiness than the other. Comfort is reserved for the life to come. This is the field of battle, and we must be content with cordials now and then till we arrive at the paradise of God, and are called to sing the song of Moses and the Lamb.

Verse 5. *While he yet spake, behold, a bright cloud overshadowed them: and behold a voice out of the cloud, which said, This is my beloved Son, in whom I am well pleased; hear ye him.*

Instead of gratifying him in this particular, we read in verse 5 that 'while he yet spake, behold a bright cloud overshadowed them; and behold a voice out of the cloud, which said, "This is my beloved Son, in whom I am well pleased; hear ye him."'

Under the Old Testament dispensation, the cloud was a symbol of the divine presence. The cloud appeared to temper the glorious sight they saw, and, perhaps, to check their curiosity and prevent their attempting to pry too much into a subject that was too glorious and sublime for mortal eyes to see. When the cloud overshadowed them, they hear a voice from heaven, and what is the language of the heavenly presence? The very language of the gospel. And though God should this day speak by a voice from heaven, he would not give a different advice from what is given already in the gospel. The advice is to believe and obey the Saviour. God is always consistent with himself, and the uniform language of the Old and New Testaments directs us to Christ as the salvation and hope of our souls.

But though the divine voice is full of mildness and grace, we find:

Verse 6. *When the disciples heard it, they fell on their face, and were sore afraid.*

The voice of God is terrible to sinful men, and if a Mediator did not interpose, his voice would strike us down to hell. Though Christ was near them, there is something terrible to conscience when God speaks. And if his voice, speaking in mercy to his friends, frightens them, how awful will the voice of his justice be when he speaks to his enemies! Let us employ Christ.

When God called after the first bold transgressor, 'O Adam, where art thou?' it was no wonder though he ran off. Conscious guilt had made him afraid, and sin had blinded him so far as to hide himself from the all-seeing eye of heaven. The congregation at Sinai trembled when the law was given, but this is the less surprising, as the sight was so very terrible. But how shall we account for the terror the apostles were in on the holy mount? They heard only the mild voice of the gospel, and the Mediator himself was standing beside them. And yet we read they were sore afraid.

This shows us that the best of men have cause to be afraid of God without a Mediator. They cannot depend on their own merits or performances. And wherever people ignorantly talk of the merits of human works while they are strangers to the corruptions of their own hearts, and the purity of the divine nature and divine law, when God begins to speak to them in terrible language in his providence or on the bed of death, they tremble through every nerve. And they have cause. And so had the apostles, as they were sinners; nor could they get comfort till they were cheered and encouraged by the Saviour.

Verse 7. *And Jesus came and touched them, and said, Arise and be not afraid.*

We find, then, that the voice of God speaking even to his people is terrible. But the Redeemer, like the pillar of cloud in the desert mitigating the great heat of the sun, interposes, stands between them and justice, bids them rise and not be afraid.

If we take a view of God as described in Scripture, he is to be feared even in the congregation of the saints, and nothing can dissipate our fears or remove our doubts but a believing view of our great Intercessor as interposing in our behalf. And if people approach now to worship that God, who said to Moses and Joshua that the ground whereon he spoke to them was holy, have we not cause of fear? The disciples were afraid, and if we have no fear that makes us apply to the Saviour when we come to worship in his house, it must arise from one of two causes—either that we had more grace than the apostles had, or that we are blind and ignorant of our spiritual condition. If we have our fears and our doubts, let us beg of Christ to touch us by the word of promise, and speak comfort to our souls.

Verses 8–9. *And when they had lifted up their eyes, they saw no man, save Jesus only. And as they came down from the mountain, Jesus charged them, saying, Tell the vision to no man, until the Son of man be risen again from the dead.*

Our Lord did not give them a longer continuance of the vision than they had strength to bear. Moses and Elijah were glorified spirits, and had bodies too bright to be fit companions for the apostles but for a very short time. When they were left alone with the Lord, he bade them conceal the vision till after his resurrection.

I observed a little before, that to me it appeared probable that the three apostles were the most exposed to unbelief. And this might consist very well with very strong faith. In the natural world, the greatest tide is always followed with the lowest ebb. Now, there is great wisdom and goodness in the caution they got to conceal the vision. Had the three apostles, in the fulness of their hearts, revealed what they saw to his other followers, some of whom, no doubt, had but weak faith, the consequence might be very disagreeable. God never gives his people trials but such as they are able to bear, and it seems he saw they were not prepared to bear this. This vision is concealed till after his resurrection, and the history of his resurrection and transfiguration, like two strong cordials given successively, revive their drooping hearts, and strengthen their faith against all future opposition.

Practical inferences

I shall now conclude with some practical inferences.

1. First, there is such a thing now and then among the people of God as being brought up to the mount. When good Christians are humbled in the sight of God, the Holy Spirit may enlighten their minds, so as to make them believe and embrace the promises of the gospel. When this happens, their joy rises superior to the pleasure that corn and wine can give to the people of the world.

If we are Christians indeed, we should beg of God to bring us to the mount, and give us a sight by faith of the heavenly Canaan. The more we are confirmed in the doctrine of a future state, the more our joy will abound. The pleasures of religion bring joy whether we look back or look forward. How poor are the joys of a worldling on the bed of death! Whereas the Christian looks back with pleasure, he looks forward with triumph.

2. If we have been in the mount, it should be known by us in our life and conversation. When people return from a wedding or feast, the good company and good cheer, and exhilarating liquors put

them in a stew [an excited state] of good humour. They are agreeable to themselves and others. And if we have tasted the pleasures of religion, they will surely make us better men and better neighbours and members of society.

If people love the Lord Jesus Christ, we can tell the effect. He loved sinners, and we know the consequence. He gave proof of his love, and so will we also. We shall promote their temporal and spiritual interest. Such as are actuated by religion show their attachment to the gospel. If grace opens the heart, it opens the purse and cellar and wardrobe to our poor fellow Christians. A mean or selfish, or a hard-hearted or narrow-minded Christian is a contradiction in terms. If people love God, they will love their brother also. And if they do not show this, they are mere strangers to religion, and have not yet been in the mount with the Saviour.

3. If people do not enjoy the pleasures of religion and are not taken up to the mount with the Saviour, they may blame themselves. If we seek our pleasures in the husks of this world, we are not qualified for enjoying the sublime pleasures of religion and devotion. A mere sensualist cannot enjoy the pleasures of a chaste mind, nor can a mere worldling enjoy the pleasures of a pious Christian. And if the heart of a professor is a workshop to the world or to the enemy, can he naturally hope to enjoy the visits of the Holy Ghost? If the proclamation in the churchyard[15] gives a man greater satisfaction than the proclamation of free grace in the house of God, is he not a painted hypocrite, and yet dead in his sins? We should examine, then, whether we are the chaste spouse of Christ, or live in whoredom and adultery with the world. God will never call you in such a state to the mount.

4. Lastly, if the sight seen upon Tabor was so glorious, how astonishingly grand and glorious is heaven! When the King of saints and Head of the Church gives a full view of his spiritual beauty to all the blest spirits above, how enchanting and unspeakable indeed is such

---

[15] It was a common practice to make public announcements in the churchyard after services. [RJD]

a sight! And should we not prepare for it by holiness and a good life? It is true all the people of God do not enjoy all the high and holy consolations included in the idea of being in the mount. But true it is that they must, in some degree, possess the reality of religion, for without holiness no man shall see the Lord.

Compare the joys of heaven with the joys of a worldling. If you would form a faint opinion of them, ascend Mount Tabor. How glorious your Saviour shines: his face like the sun, his very garments like the light! And if a short glimpse of his glory transported the mind of the apostle to wish for the continuance of it, oh, what is it now? Take up the glass [telescope]! Behold the glories of heaven and the land that is very far off! If you wish, then, to stand with him upon Mount Zion, follow the Lamb wherever he goes.

God bless his Word. AMEN.

Matthew chapter 24: verses 15 to 31

A S the prophecy of the destruction of Jerusalem is one of the arguments in support of Christianity, it is given in such clear and express terms as that he that runs may read it. We shall therefore endeavour to illustrate this part of the prophecy, and conclude with some practical inferences.

The abomination of desolation

Verse 15. *When ye therefore shall see the abomination of desolation, spoken of by Daniel the prophet, stand in the holy place, (whoso readeth, let him understand).*

The Jews had the holy oracles in their hands, and many of them could read the prophecies. He appeals in particular to Daniel, as he had clearly pointed out the time of Messiah's appearance and the subsequent destruction of Jerusalem. He speaks in particular of the abomination of desolation as appearing in the holy place. The Jews, since their return from the captivity at Babylon—though in other respects a very wicked people—had a very great aversion to idolatry. So much so that they could not bear an image or statue of any kind. They had the utmost abhorrence for idols in all places, and how much more so, had they seen them about the holy city.

If the idea of an army passing through their territory without any hostile intention was so very disagreeable to them, because they had idolatrous ensigns, how much more awful must the Roman army be! And that this is the meaning of the abomination of desolation, we learn from Luke 21:21. Jerusalem was invested with an army which had the Roman eagle upon their banners, and therefore abominable to the Jews. When this event was to take place, such as could read are desired to understand: the event will make prophecy clear, and those who have the Scriptures in their hands are inexcusable if they do not understand them. Infidelity in the leading points of Christianity is a crying sin, as the Bible is open for the inspection of all. The Jews might now read their sin in their punishment. The Saviour whom they refused comes to punish them for rejecting his gospel.

Verse 16. *Then let them which be in Judaea flee into the mountains.*

Such of the Jews as took the hint, and all the Christians, retired from the city and were safe. A little before the destruction of the city, the followers of Christ fled from Jerusalem to the other side of Jordan. They took the advice in proper time, for soon afterwards there was no egress from the city, as it was surrounded by the Roman army. As Lot was formerly ordered to hasten his flight from Sodom, the Christians are ordered to flee unto the mountains, and when we see the judgment of God upon earth, we ought to flee to our stronghold.

Verse 17. *Let him which is on the housetop not come down to take any thing out of his house.*

The houses in Judaea, as well as in all Eastern countries, were flat on the top, and there were stairs on the outside, so that a person might walk upon the tops of houses in great towns from one end to the other, till he came to the gate and there descended.

He is here warned not to come down to take anything out. What may be a duty at one time may be a dangerous snare and a great sin at another time. The people to whom this advice was given were in danger of their lives by staying in Jerusalem. If they saw the march of the Roman army from the tops of their houses, they should not go in, but flee immediately. Life was better than their household furniture, or even their money. To take care of both at another time was a necessary duty, but on this occasion life—precious life—was at stake. It was therefore their duty to flee.

It is the duty of Christians to take care of their temporal concerns, but if the call of providence and of their own consciences invite them to spiritual duties, and if they stifle the motions of the Spirit of God, they may neglect a duty and opportunity which can never be recalled, and thus endanger their own everlasting salvation. Lot was to hasten from Sodom; they were to hasten from Jerusalem, and we are to hasten from the wrath to come, and listen to the voice of God when he calls to present duty.

Verse 18. *Neither let him which is in the field return back to take his clothes.*

He might have use for his clothes, and the excuse is very plausible, but if a party of the enemy met him, he might lose his life, and thus he purchased his clothes too dear. When duty calls a man, he has this thing to do and the other thing to do, and he cannot attend to the duties of religion and the care of his soul. In the meantime, death may strike him unawares, and if he had obeyed the call of God and of conscience, he might be eternally saved. And by neglecting duty and engaging in the whirl of business, he may plunge himself into a situation similar to the danger which mariners are in when they approach a certain whirlpool in the North Sea. We often see ourselves surrounded by dangers and by death, and if it finds us in the hurry of business or the pursuit of pleasure, we may perish with the wicked world, as all did perish who continued in wicked Jerusalem.

Verse 19. *And woe unto them that are with child, and to them that give suck in those days!*

Sinful Jerusalem was a lively type of the world lying in wickedness. When the wrath came upon them, people in this critical situation were in the greatest danger among them. We read very awful stories of women eating their own children in the siege of Jerusalem. Now, the people burdened with the care of families and children and many worldly cares are in greater danger of perishing than others, and their punishment will be greater by continuing in a state of sin.

Verse 20. *But pray ye that your flight be not in the winter, neither on the sabbath day.*

If the Jews were obliged to fly in the winter, the weather was cold and the roads bad and heavy, and it would be peculiarly distressing to them to be obliged to travel on the Sabbath. And now we are called to leave the world lying in wickedness. We have health and strength and time and opportunity to do so, as the Jews had to leave Jerusalem. But if we neglect this till the winter of old age and trouble, and if the manifold breaches of the Sabbath will meet our consciences at death, how awful will our flight be then! It is the duty of every man that hears the gospel to leave the world lying in wickedness, but if people delay the work till the winter of old age, it will be doubly difficult. But if they continue in sin till their souls are surrounded by the terrors of death, they cannot escape, as they neglected the great salvation.

Verse 21. *For then shall be great tribulation, such as was not since the beginning of the world to this time, no, nor ever shall be.*

We have the history of the destruction of Jerusalem written by one of the Jews themselves, and the description he gives of the siege fully verifies this prophecy of our Saviour. They experienced all the terrors of famine and of fire, of butchering one another, and all the calamities that a very wicked people could inflict upon one another when rendered furious by despair. Indeed, the description is too horrible, nor have we anything like it in any history upon earth. And what makes it still more credible is that the Jews, by their religion, were obliged to attend the solemn feasts, and more especially the passover. And this occasioned their being contained in Jerusalem as in a large prison, and exposed to miseries which the ear of man never heard before or since.

Verse 22. *And except those days should be shortened, there should no flesh be saved: but for the elect's sake those days shall be shortened.*

The siege and destruction of Jerusalem were carried on in a short time. The city was so strongly fortified that it was naturally believed that it could only be starved to surrender. The Roman general, however, carried on the work with vigour, and, as he himself acknowledged, the hand of God was in it. He took the city in a short time. But for this circumstance, the whole body of the Jewish nation had been destroyed. The days were shortened on account of the elect. Many of the Jews embraced the Christian religion, and they escaped. Now, if the minds of the Roman army had been rendered bitter by a long siege and great reduction of their numbers, they might be provoked to that degree that they had cut off the Jews, root and branch. To save the believers, then, the days are shortened. Besides, Scripture informs us of the future conversion of the whole nation of the Jews. They are still preserved as a separate people, and many of them were preserved after the destruction of Jerusalem, because from these in future ages are to descend a considerable number of God's elect people.

> Verses 23–25. *Then if any man shall say unto you, Lo, here is Christ, or there; believe it not. For there shall arise false Christs, and false prophets, and shall shew great signs and wonders; insomuch that, if it were possible, they shall deceive the very elect. Behold, I have told you before.*

About the time that Christ appeared, and for several years afterwards, there was a general expectation among the Jews that their Messiah would now manifest himself. Our Lord found fault with them because they did not observe the signs of the times. Had they examined their own books with honest impartiality, they would have acknowledged the true Messiah. He is promised in several of the prophets, and the very time of his appearance is specified. The sceptre was to depart from Judah, and he was to come after seventy weeks, or 490 years from the date of the order to build the city.

Now, an extraordinary personage appeared, to whom all the characters of Messiah agree. As the Jews rejected him, this emboldened several impostors, such as Simon Magus and several others, to set up as being the 'great Prophet', and as the magicians, by the black art, wrought tricks imitating the miracles of Moses, these impostors also wrought false miracles, and brought after them many followers. Nay, the very elect, the true people of God, were in danger if they did not beware, and therefore in verse 25 he says, 'Behold, I have told you before.' They are put on their guard, and therefore had antidote against the infection. When a new prophet came, with new signs, the gaping multitude would stare, but their character is so minutely described in the gospel that the Christians might know and therefore avoid them.

Verse 26. *Wherefore, if they shall say unto you, Behold, he is in the desert; go not forth: behold, he is in the secret chambers; believe it not.*

Several of these deceivers led their deluded followers into the desert, where they were destroyed by the forces of the Romans. Our Lord preached and wrought some of his miracles in the desert, and as they rejected him, impostors led them to the desert to their ruin. Our Lord also wrought some of his miracles in the great city: other impostors brought their followers to secret chambers and places of security, and promised them signs of deliverance. Instead of this, six thousand perished by fire when endeavouring to escape the flames.

Verse 27. *For as the lightning cometh out of the east, and shineth even to the west; so shall also the coming of the Son of man be.*

The lightning comes on very suddenly and appears without giving any notice of its approach. A person need not ask, 'Where is the lightning?' for it appears everywhere. Now, the gospel flew like lightning and pervaded every corner of the earth, or Roman Empire, before Christ in his terrible judgments came to destroy Jerusalem. He sent his army, as he tells us in one of his parables, to destroy the murderers and burn up their city. Accordingly, the Romans marched from the East to Judaea, and overspread the land on their way to Jerusalem. Now, the flash of lightning is followed by an awful clap of thunder, and the Roman army brought the thunder of war to the gates of the city—and not only to the gates of the city, but wherever the Jews were gathered together.

Verse 28. *For wheresoever the carcase is, there will the eagles be gathered together.*

Our Saviour used to clothe his doctrine, as well as his prophecies, with proper and pertinent similitudes. The Jewish nation he compares to a dead carcase. Now, they were so in a judicial and in a spiritual sense. They were dead in trespasses and sins, without a proper sense of their guilt and danger. They had murdered their Messiah, and instead of repenting of this great wickedness, they continued in unbelief and rejected his gospel.

In consequence of this, in the just judgment of heaven, they are given up to the filthy lusts of their own hearts; and as they are a wicked generation from the highest to the lowest, the judgment overtook them to the uttermost. Wherever, therefore, this carcase was, the eagles were gathered to devour. The Roman army had the eagle in their standards. It was the bird of Jupiter, and in their opinion, the emblem of victory. The prophecy is so clear that it scarcely requires a comment.

The coming of the Son of man

Verse 29. *Immediately after the tribulation of those days shall the sun be darkened, and the moon shall not give her light, and the stars shall fall from heaven, and the powers of the heavens shall be shaken.*

In the pompous [magnificent] language of the prophecy, this means the great and wondrous revolution that was to take place in the Jewish republic. By the sun, moon, and stars, we may understand the great and principal persons in the state. This we may learn from Joseph's dream and several passages of the prophecies. Accordingly, the Jewish polity and religion are set aside to make way for the dispensation of the gospel.

Verse 30. And then shall appear the sign of the Son of man in heaven: and then shall all the tribes of the earth mourn, and they shall see the Son of man coming in the clouds of heaven with power and great glory.

We read in Josephus, the Jewish historian, of several signs that preceded the destruction of Jerusalem. Our Lord tells us that he would come in the clouds of heaven. We read in the old prophets (*i.e.* Isaiah 19:1) that God was to come in the clouds, when he was to execute some signal things in the course of his providence. And the destruction of the Jewish polity was such a signal instance of the power and vengeance of God, as if he came in the clouds of heaven, and in consequence of this vengeance, the families of the Jews would bewail their hard fate, and many of them, from the contemplation of these judgments, would be led to embrace the gospel.

Verse 31. And he shall send his angels with a great sound of a trumpet, and they shall gather together his elect from the four winds, from one end of heaven to the other.

The Jewish nation, the children of the kingdom, were to be cast out and forfeit their long-enjoyed privilege of being God's people. The Gentiles were to come in their place, and this event was to happen by the trumpet of the gospel, as the people of the Jews were called to worship by the sound of the trumpet. God was to collect his elect by the preaching of the everlasting gospel. The ministers of Christ were the angels employed for this purpose.

Practical inferences

1. First, we learn from these words that the Messiah was expected at the very time the Lord Jesus Christ made his appearance. Our Lord was born in the Augustine age,[16] at a time of general peace, when people had time and leisure for free enquiry. The Jews looked for their Messiah, and the Gentiles had it in their power to examine

---

[16] The time when Augustus Caesar reigned. [RJD]

their pretensions. The holy oracles spoke of such a personage, the time of his appearance, and his great works.

All these marks apply to Jesus of Nazareth, descended of the royal family of David, and born in the town of Bethlehem. He was the true King of the Jews, by birth and by title. He wrought a number of astonishing miracles, and crowned the whole by his resurrection from the dead and his ascension unto heaven. He was the Great Prophet sent from God, and as the Jews did not obey him, they were destroyed. He foretold the destruction of their polity [nation] and the appearance of false Christs and false miracles. These events came to pass. As God permitted the magicians to ape the miracles of Moses, false pretenders imitated the miracles of Christ. They were, however, the effects of delusion, and soon came to nought. The gospel can bear examination, and if we do not believe, we may see the fate of infidel Jerusalem. Similar will be the fate of all unbelievers, sooner or later, here or hereafter.

2. There are such strong expressions in this prophecy as might induce us at first view to suppose that our Lord speaks of the general judgment. To this it may be observed that though our Lord might intend it as a type of the general judgment, yet in fact its primary object is the destruction of Jerusalem. As to the strong expression, such as his riding on a cloud, we have a similar expression in Isaiah, 19th chapter, 1st verse, where it means a singular appearance of providence in that country. As to the shaking of the luminaries of heaven, it means an extraordinary revolution, such as happened to the Jewish nation.

Our Lord made use of the sober, established language of the old prophets, and this is an additional proof of the truth of the gospel. If the favourite nation were punished, what may we expect if we imitate their sins?

3. Lastly, if Christians are desired to beware that their flight be not in winter or on the Sabbath Day, is not this a strong advice to us? We should leave the city of destruction. Let us not delay till the win-

ter of old age. If a despiser of the gospel dies upon Sabbath, how awful his state! Pray that this may not be the case.

God bless his Word. AMEN.

Matthew chapter 24: verses 32 to 51

A S the destruction of Jerusalem is one proof of the truth of the gospel, it was proper that it should be delayed for some time, to give notice to all the nations that should hear the gospel, and to exercise the faith of God's people. It was also necessary that it should happen during the time of that generation, that their faith might not fail, and that the pagans might not have any cause to triumph. But though the destruction of Jerusalem is primarily meant, there can be no doubt that our Lord had something higher in his view than the destruction of that city. It was a type of the end of the world and the dissolution of all things, and therefore from the 36th verse the words will very properly apply to that awful event.

I shall therefore endeavour to illustrate this portion of Scripture, and conclude with some practical inferences, and may the dew of his grace and salvation descend upon our souls.

The parable of the fig tree

Verses 32–33. Now learn a parable of the fig tree; When his branch is yet tender, and putteth forth leaves, ye know that summer is nigh: so likewise ye, when ye shall see all these things, know that it is near, even at the doors.

The different signs that preceded the destruction of Jerusalem are mentioned in the former part of this chapter. And when they came to pass, they were as sure presages [forewarnings] of that event as the tender blossoms of the fig tree indicated the approach of summer, or of the spring, which is the beginning of the summer season.

Nay, when they saw some of them, such as the approach of the Roman army, they might infallibly believe the destiny of the city.

> Verses 34–35. *Verily I say unto you, This generation shall not pass, till all these things be fulfilled. Heaven and earth shall pass away, but my words shall not pass away.*

Now, this is a proof that the prophecy principally respects Jerusalem, though our Lord had something still higher in his view, as several prophecies of the Scripture relate to more than one event. Many of the people who lived in Judaea during our Lord's public ministry were to be witnesses of the fulfilment of this prophecy, and it was impossible it would fall to the ground; for he tells us (verse 35), 'Heaven and earth shall pass away, but my words shall not pass away.'

The meaning of this is that the frame of the universe would sooner be altered than that this prophecy should fail. And this may show us the desperate folly of those who do not believe, love, or obey the gospel. If the Word speaks against them, the threatening shall as surely be accomplished as were the threatenings against the Jews.

> Verse 36. *But of that day and hour knoweth no man, no, not the angels of heaven, but my Father only.*

He tells us in another place that the Son, as to his human nature, did not know this particular time. Our Lord, as he was man, grew in wisdom and knowledge, and consequently did not know all things. The knowledge of this might be given him when he was exalted at the right hand of God.

The time of the destruction of Jerusalem and of the general judgment are events which the wisdom of God did not see meet to impart to his creatures, that they might always live in a state of watchfulness and preparation. And our Lord informs us that the fate of the Jews, or of mankind in general, would be similar to that of the antediluvian world.

Verses 37–39. But as the days of Noe were, so shall also the coming of the Son of man be. For as in the days that were before the flood they were eating and drinking, marrying and giving in marriage, until the day that Noe entered into the ark, and knew not until the flood came, and took them all away; so shall also the coming of the Son of man be.

This was the case with regard to Jerusalem, and it seems it will be so at the time immediately preceding the general judgment. At the time of the flood, it was a time of general inattention to the great concerns of religion and eternity. They were immersed in the cares and pleasures of this present life, and though Noah was a preacher of righteousness, so stupid and dissipated was the generation that they did not dream of a flood till it came and swept them all from the face of the earth.

And we see from the words that when men became slaves, even to the lawful pleasures of this life, they immediately lose sight of the pleasures of the next. When people are slaves to their passions, there is great danger that they will proceed to unlawful pleasures and pursuits. The antediluvian world did so, for the earth was full of violence and oppression, of carnal pleasure and its usual attendant contempt of virtue and religion. And when these vices prevail and become general, they bring on national punishments.

At whatever distance the general judgment may be, it is certain that death will seal the fate of every man. It is of little consequence to the wicked whether they be alive at the Day of Judgment or die before it. Our great concern is to avoid their sins, that we escape their punishment. All ranks are involved, for he says:

Verses 40–41. Then shall two be in the field; the one shall be taken, and the other left. Two women shall be grinding at the mill; the one shall be taken, and the other left.

With regard to the lowest rank and the lowest offices, some would escape and some would be involved in the general calamity. It shall be so at the end of the world, and it shall be so at death. According to people's state and conduct in the world, so shall be their fate. If a good man, God will not neglect the meanest in the world; and if a bad man, he shall cry to the hills and the mountains to hide him from the face of the Judge. And therefore our Lord gives an advice, proper and necessary for all:

The need for watchfulness

Verse 42. *Watch therefore: for ye know not what hour your Lord doth come.*

This duty is to be practised at all times and upon all occasions. It is enjoined to all, more especially the ministers of the gospel. If Christians are off their guard, though it were but one night, for instance, they may fall into such sins during that night as may be a source of sorrow and vexation to them all their days. They may fall into sins that will defile their souls, blast their comforts, and mar their usefulness, and this should make them very cautious. And this caution must be exercised continually, for our Lord tells us so, to strengthen his argument.

Verses 43–44. *But know this, that if the goodman of the house had known in what watch the thief would come, he would have watched, and would not have suffered his house to be broken up. Therefore be ye also ready: for in such an hour as ye think not the Son of man cometh.*

Whatever time Jerusalem was to be destroyed, it was an undeniable truth that death was to overtake them at some time or other. And as the time was as uncertain as the time the thief would choose after midnight for breaking into a house, it was proper they should be always ready. A thief does not tell when he means to come, and the approach of death is sudden and unexpected. And if a man knew for certain that the thief would come at such an hour of the night, he would watch. And if a man would know that he was to die at such a time, he would be very circumspect a little before that time. But this is wisely concealed, that we may be continually on our guard and lead such a holy life as that we need not have cause to fear the approach of death.

Now, the Christian that would truly prepare for death must watch over the motions of his own heart, that he may know how he stands affected to the gospel. He must watch over his corruptions and over his graces, that he may weaken the one and strengthen the other. He is to watch over his senses—his eyes, his ears, and his tongue—and he is also to watch over his prayers, and look after them. He is like a wise merchant, to watch over his gain or his loss in his heavenly trade. He is to watch over the different opportunities that may occur of bettering and improving his spiritual condition. In a word, he is to watch over his life and conversation, so that it may be agreeable to the gospel, and when this is the case, we can easily see that the life is kept from many faults and blemishes into which the unguarded Christian may fall.

A watchful Christian is like a man in full armour watching his house. He is not afraid of a thief in the night, for he is awake and in armour. He is not afraid of an attack, and his house is safe. He is prepared for what may happen. Death cannot hurt him, for he is in full armour, and may sing, 'O death, where is thy sting?' He has gone with his conscience to get it cleansed in the blood of sprinkling, and he has avoided thousands of sins that might otherwise meet him at death. And as death comes unawares, whenever he hears the knock, he takes up his arms. He lifts up his soul to God through Christ, and his sins are not a clog to his faith. He pleads the sacrifice and the intercession of Christ, and is happy. And though his own works are not the ground of his hope, yet it affords pleasure to his soul that his works now meet him. His sobriety, his self-denial, his prayers, and his alms, like a refreshing gale, meet and cheer his conscience. He now rejoices how he spent the Sabbath, and how he improved the means of grace.

But, on the other hand, we may see the unwatchful Christian when arrested by the messenger of death. No sooner does he knock like a thief in the night than he starts out of the sleep of sin, disturbed by the unwelcome and unexpected guest. He thinks of his armour, but his armour has been long ago laid aside. He attempts to pray, but his laziness, his worldliness, his intemperance, and his unchristian conversation stare him in the face and are a burden upon his faith. The Sabbath Day and the means of grace which he trifled away as small things, and which he thought he could overtake at his leisure, he now sees to be matters of great importance, and therefore his terror increases.

The messenger continues to knock. Will now his drunken companions, his worldly schemes, or his great profit help him in the day of wrath? He threw away his armour, prayer, and a holy life, and therefore the enemy will find him naked when he makes his attack. And should not these thoughts give us concern in time, make us improve our talents, and fear lest we be beaten with many stripes? For we cannot deny but we knew our Master's will, though we did it not.

The good and evil steward

Verses 45–47. *Who then is a faithful and wise servant, whom his lord hath made ruler over his household, to give them meat in due season? Blessed is that servant, whom his lord when he cometh shall find so doing. Verily I say unto you, That he shall make him ruler over all his goods.*

This portion of Scripture, in a particular manner, applies to the faithful ministers of the gospel. Luke informs us, in chapter 12 at verse 35, that our Lord exhorted all his followers to have their loins girded about and their lamps burning, so as to be prepared for the coming of their Lord. When Peter asked him whether this command was general to all Christians, or directed in particular to the apostles, our Lord directs his answer in such a way as that we may see that, though it belongs in a certain sense to all, it particularly belongs to the ministers of the gospel. They are set over the house of God, to give his people their portion of food in due season. Now, some require some kind of food, some another; some require terror, and others stand in need of comfort; some are weak, some are strong. Their states, their circumstances, and their needs are various. To do duty carefully requires prudence, skill, and address [expertise], and who is sufficient for these things? And in case the servant should prove unfaithful, lazy, and wicked, his danger is pathetically [movingly] described in the following verses: 48, 49, 50, and 51.

> Verses 48–51. *But and if that evil servant shall say in his heart, My lord delayeth his coming; and shall begin to smite his fellowservants, and to eat and drink with the drunken; the lord of that servant shall come in a day when he looketh not for him, and in an hour that he is not aware of, and shall cut him asunder, and appoint him his portion with the hypocrites: there shall be weeping and gnashing of teeth.*

If he takes encouragement from his Lord's delay to indulge his lusts and associate with drunkards, and, instead of feeding them, to use his people ill, his Lord will come when he least expects it, and assign him his portion with hypocrites and unbelievers. Luke observes further here that our Lord informs us that the servants who knew their Lord's will shall be beaten with many stripes, and those who knew it not shall be punished with few.

We see, then, the danger of bad Christians and bad ministers, for we see the Word speaks to all ranks of people, good and bad. And it concerns each of us to know how far we are interested in the doctrine.

Practical inferences

It remains now that we conclude this prophecy with some practical inferences for regulation and conversation [orderliness and behaviour].

1. First, if the apostles and primitive Christians had need of the caution and exhortations in this chapter, how much more have we? We find that the greatest saints in Scripture are as cautious, as guarded, and as circumspect as the meanest Christian can be. Job speaks of making a covenant with his eyes, and the Psalmist prays to turn away his eyes, that they may not behold vanity. Great grace does not put

people beyond the reach of such advice. Solomon got them, and the Word shows that he had need of them. Paul keeps under his body, and advises the Christian to work out their salvation with fear and trembling. The danger to which we are exposed should double our diligence, and make us stand upon the watch, and not sleep in security.

2. Second, the great reward promised to the watchful Christians should make us constantly watch and pray (Luke 12:35). The destruction of Jerusalem is an event already past, but death and judgment are before us. And this consideration should make us holy in heart and life, and the more holy, the more happy. The pleasures of another life are inexpressible. For these heavenly pleasures we should surely forsake the pleasures of sin. Let us despise earthly pleasures, for the joys of heaven are promised to the watchful Christian.

3. Lastly, if the clergy have their large share of the difficulties of the Christian life, it is surely the great duty of the people of God to pray for them. You have heard that, if they neglect their duty and associate with drunkards, the Lord Jesus Christ will cut them in pieces, and assign them their portion with hypocrites and unbelievers. Brethren, pray for us, that God would make us faithful to our trust, and go before you in the way to heaven. Next to our own souls, we should care for you. If you thrive, we shall be happy. Be faithful to God, and your prayers shall be heard, for the effectual, fervent prayer of a righteous man availeth much. You have heard that Aaron and Hur supported the hands of Moses in the war against Amalek. You should do the same if you expect the victory. What cause of comfort when ministers and people do their duty! This will prepare them to meet with joy and gladness in the realms of light above.

May God bless his Word through Christ. AMEN.

Matthew chapter 25: verses 1 to 13

I N the preceding chapter, our Lord has given us a prophecy of the destruction of Jerusalem, and now he comes to speak in this chapter, both in parables and in plain language, of the great events that will happen at the time of the general judgment.

In the words just now read, we have a description of those who profess the Christian religion and their fate hereafter, and this is given us in a strong and beautiful parable, which I shall endeavour to explain, and conclude the doctrine with some practical inferences. And may you and I, my friends, have an eye to heaven for the influences of the divine and Holy Spirit, to make the Word of salvation and grace effectual to our souls.

The parable of the ten virgins

Verse 1. *Then shall the kingdom of heaven be likened unto ten virgins, which took their lamps and went forth to meet the bridegroom.*

Our Lord, like a wise teacher, adopted his parables to local customs, practices, and phrases which were prevalent in these days in Judaea. If we were fully acquainted with these, the explanation of Scripture and of parables would be still more easy to us. Inattention to this has made some commentators in Europe fall into blunders in explaining Scripture, and perfect ignorance of Eastern usages has made infidels to dash themselves in pieces against the rock of salvation.

In this verse, our Lord gives us a general character of all professors. They are called virgins because all are called to be saints. They are said to be ten, because there were seldom fewer than ten at a Jewish marriage, and it was an ordinary observation with them that less than ten did not constitute a congregation.

We find they took their lamps to be in readiness to meet the bridegroom. Among the Jews, the bride was carried in the night to the house of the bridegroom by lamps; torchlight was used by other nations. The lamp of profession is necessary, for there must be a form as well as the power of religion. It is true, there might be form without power, but if the power comes, religion will show itself in a form.

> Verses 2–3. *And five of them were wise, and five were foolish. They that were foolish took their lamps, and took no oil with them.*

Professors, we see here, are only divided into two sorts: wise and foolish. There are varieties of opinion among Christians, and no doubt everyone thinks his own opinion and his own form the best. But, in fact, there are only two sorts: good and bad, righteous and wicked. And our Lord here gives us one great characteristic of false professors. They had no oil in their lamps.

Some were wise, some were foolish. We know the manner in which folly and wisdom show themselves in the affairs of this life, and it is so in spiritual concerns. A foolish person neglects his true interest and would part with his most valuable effects for mere trifles. If a man spends his fortune upon his lusts or in the prosecution of idle or imaginary schemes, he is justly called a fool.

Now Scripture, that infallible judge of men and things, gives the epithet of 'fool' to the sinner. And as to his everlasting concerns, he may be a fool, though he makes a profession of religion. Like a natural fool that would give gold for gewgaws [worthless decorations], the fool in religion forfeits the joys of heaven for the joys of sense. He has the lamp of a profession, but he sees, it seems, no difference between an empty lamp and a lamp that has oil. He contents himself with a form, but makes no preparation for eternity. If the world thrives with him, or if he can gratify his lusts, he does not ask at his conscience whether the grace of God is in his soul or not. Content with a religion that is neighbour-like, he hopes to go to heaven, of course. He does not enquire what opinion God has of his state, speaking to him in his Word, but what is the opinion of the multitude. If they pronounce him good, he is happy; but they may be wrong.

Who could distinguish in the daytime by looking at the outside between an empty lamp and a lamp full of oil? It is one great property of folly to be wise in its own conceit. The foolish virgins did not see the folly and absurdity of going to meet the bridegroom in the night without oil in their lamps, till the night itself convinced them. At this time, and in this world, the folly of empty profession does not appear to them. Any profession may serve before men, as an empty lamp may do well enough in the daytime.

Verse 4. *But the wise took oil in their vessels with their lamps.*

The true Christian makes a profession, but is not satisfied with a profession without the life and power of religion. He takes care to provide the holy anointing, the oil of grace in his soul. The holy oil, which burned continually in the sanctuary (Exodus 27:20), was an emblem of the oil of grace. It was to burn continually, and the holy lamp of divine faith and love should always burn in the heart of a Christian. The apostle exhorts Christians not to quench the Spirit (1 Thessalonians 5:19), and King David, after his great fall, prays to God not to take his Holy Spirit from him. True Christians know that the flame of heavenly grace is what will qualify them to meet the heavenly bridegroom with joy at his coming.

But if holy souls are the bride, who are the virgins in the parable? Let it be observed that the parables are not to be cut up and made to answer in everything. We are particularly to observe the sense and substance of the parable. Wise virgins certainly represent the bride, but we know this is a parable, and the intention of it is to show the necessity of holy qualifications and continual watchfulness. The virgins were to meet the bridegroom in the night, and as they could not know at what hour he might come, they must watch, in order to be in readiness when they heard the call. Grace in the soul and holy watchfulness in the life will fit us for his presence.

The Church is sometimes compared to the bride: at other times, as in the parable, to the virgins that accompany her. The wise virgins are not satisfied without a principle of faith in the heart, and a life and conversation suitable to the gospel.

If a wise man has a title, he wishes to increase his fortune, that he may live in a style suitable to his rank. He knows that a title without a fortune would only expose him to contempt. An actor upon the stage that represents a king, prince, or great man, may think himself happy if he acts his part well. Not so, the good Christian. He is unhappy if he is not what he appears to be. The approbation of God and the gratulation [rejoicing] of his conscience are the source of his joy, and not the praise of men. He knows that faith is what purifies the heart, and a good life is what keeps conscience clean. This, then, is his great aim. Without feeling the love of God in his soul and faith in the Messiah, the praise of men would only hurt his feelings. When the holy Psalmist complained of an absent God that hid his face, would it give him pleasure on these occasions if some Israelite began to praise him for his valour in killing Goliath, his great skill at the harp, his happy talent in poetry, and the beautiful Psalms he composed? Surely not! His pleasure would arise from a renewed view of the Messiah in whom he trusted, and from the breathings and influences of the Holy Spirit upon his soul. When he enjoyed these, there was peace and happiness within, and his obedience would be prompt and cheerful, and this is the character of all the people of God. Nothing but himself can make them happy. If he smiles, there is joy within, but if the mind is dark with unbelief, nothing can please them. One thing is needful, and when they secure this, everything else is comparatively little in their sight.

When the men of the world say, 'What shall we eat and drink, and how shall we procure the perishing commodities of time?' the language and the prayer of their soul is for the light of God's reconciled countenance. This will put joy in their hearts, to which other people are strangers. They love the bridegroom and prepare for his coming.

Verse 5. *While the bridegroom tarried, they all slumbered and slept.*

There is a great distance of time between the first and second coming of Christ. The delay is so long that it has furnished pretexts for the infidel to deny Scripture and sink himself into the pleasures of sense. Because sentence is not speedily executed, sinners are emboldened to prosecute their lusts, and the empty professor, by associating with such companions, learns by degrees to imbibe their sentiments. Notwithstanding their profession, they find their humours and spirits to be congenial to that of the infidel world around them. The natural effect is spiritual sloth, and the transition is quick from sloth to sleep in sin. They first slumbered, and then slept. And this, in part, might and did happen to the wise virgins. Even the holy apostles slept in Tabor and Gethsemane.[17] All have need of watchfulness, and the apostle, in Romans 13:11, exhorts the Christian to awake out of sleep—a proof that even good men may fall into security and be off their guard. The different warnings and exhortations of Scripture set this doctrine in a clear point of view.

Verse 6. *And at midnight there was a cry made, Behold, the bride-groom cometh; go ye out to meet him.*

When people generally least expect it, they may be summoned by death to judgment. The great day of the Lord will come as a thief in the night. It comes unexpectedly on the wicked world. It comes even at midnight: they are alarmed by the sound of the archangel and the trump of God. How dreadful, then, will the alarm to judgment be to a guilty world! It is the time many of them set apart for the prosecution of their lusts. Some are arrested with the gains of injustice in their hands, some at their cups, and others in the very act of lewdness. In the midst of their wickedness, they hear this sound, 'Arise, ye dead, and come to judgment.' The trembling of the earth and the burning of the elements make their hearts terribly afraid. Professing Christians are summoned to meet the King of

---

[17] Mount Tabor is one of the suggested sites of the Mount of Transfiguration. [RJD]

saints. All the virgins slept the sleep of death, and when the judgment comes, and they are called to meet the Lord, they must obey the summons. May God prepare us for the event.

A great cry is heard in the night—much more awful than that heard in Egypt, when they were alarmed by the death of their firstborn. Night is a still and solemn season: the least noise is heard, and the least cause is often ready to breed terror. At such a season, then, when men least expect it, people may hear the sound of death, and afterwards of judgment.

Verse 7. *Then all these virgins arose, and trimmed their lamps.*

It is true the wise virgins fell asleep as well as the foolish. Good and bad sleep the sleep of death, and though it be true that sometimes the sleep of security might seize the wise as well as the foolish virgin, great after all is the difference between them. The one had provided oil; the other had neglected the great work of their salvation. When the cry is made and the alarm given, and they began to dress their lamps, the one find they had oil, and were ready to go and meet the bridegroom. The others have only empty lamps. They were not therefore in a condition to go and meet the bridegroom.

Verse 8. *And the foolish said unto the wise, Give us of your oil; for our lamps are gone out.*

Ashamed and alarmed at their condition, we are told, 'And the foolish said unto the wise, Give us of your oil; for our lamps are gone out.' When death and judgment come, professors of a profane, worldly spirit will find to their cost that religion was more valuable than they thought. At death, they see their lamps are gone out. At that awful period, they wish to have what they once despised. But they rebelled against the Spirit that would anoint them, and therefore their candle is put out (Job 18:6), and now they see their loss to be great.

They ask oil from the wise virgins, but they have none to give. Every man must stand for himself. Their lamps are gone out. They ask oil from the wise virgins. It seems they thought they had oil. What has thus extinguished the lamps? Let the question be asked at a dying professor, and they will answer with trembling lips. In one, it was extinguished by filthy lusts; in another, by the social glass; and in another, by the carking [distressing] cares of this life. Some extinguished it by a foolish conversation and idle talk—and, alas, all of them, by inattention to things that belonged to their peace. They are now upon the bed of death, and trouble and anguish is come upon them. They misspent their day, and now the night is come, and they have nothing.

In this darkness and anxiety of soul, they apply to the wise virgins for some of their oil. Even wicked Balaam wished his latter end might be like that of the righteous. They despised them in their life-time, and looked upon them as fools. They believed that people might go to heaven with much less religion than they had. They thought they spent too much of their time in the duties of holiness and in preparation for eternity. And though they ridiculed them for their preciseness and singularity, they now wished to be like them. They ask of their oil.

Verse 9. *But the wise answered, saying, Not so; lest there be not enough for us and you: but go ye rather to them that sell, and buy for yourselves.*

If we were to suppose a good man standing at the bedside of a poor, foolish professor, in his distress, he asks the prayers of the righteous, but the righteous has not enough and to spare of grace. The only advice he can suggest is to go to the heavenly market, where people may buy without money and without price. But, alas, there is no time for this, for the sinner is hurried by death to judgment. Or should we even suppose, as in the parable of the rich man speaking to Abra-ham, that they ask the assistance of the saints, even at judgment. We find that the holiness of the saints is only sufficient for themselves. They cannot help their friends or acquaintances. They upbraid them, it seems, for not making a proper use of their day of grace. As the language of despair will make them call upon the hills and mountains to cover them, the very same language may make them call for the assistance of the saints when it will be too late.

The meaning of their answer seems to be this: that if the Saviour, whom they despised, will not pity them, what can they do? Saints, it seems, cannot pray for those who die enemies to the King of saints. Let us pray in time.

> Verses 10–12. *And while they went to buy, the bridegroom came; and they that were ready went in with him to the marriage: and the door was shut. Afterward came also the other virgins, saying, Lord, Lord, open to us. But he answered and said, Verily I say unto you, I know you not.*

What thoughts foolish professors had at death, and whatever presumptuous hopes they might entertain, we cannot say, but one thing is certain, that the good Christians who were watchful and in readiness are received into the joy of their Lord.

We find from the parable that some people may die with a lie in their right hand. They entertain presumptuous hopes of heaven, though they live in sin. We read in the 7th chapter of this same gospel, as well as in the text and in the last part of this chapter, that reprobates and wicked people plead their profession, and even several things they did. But we find that their plea will be in vain, for our Lord tells them he did not know them. It seems, then, notwithstanding their profession, they were workers of iniquity, and therefore were never in the love and favour of the Saviour. The apostle tells us that all that name the name of Christ should depart from iniquity, and it seems those whom he rejects were workers of iniquity. They profess to call the Lord 'Lord' (Luke 6:46), but did not obey his law. They pretended to believe and trust in him and expected salvation from him, but their faith was not of the genuine kind, else it would have taught them obedience. The most splendid profession of the lips, without obedience in the life, will not save. So faith, if genuine and true, will first purify the heart, and then make the life holy, and where this is wanting, though we should speak with the tongues of men and angels, it avails us nothing. How vain, then, are the pretensions of hypocrites! They plead their empty profession, and yet the true saints cannot plead their works as the ground of their justification in the sight of God—and yet good works are rewarded as the genuine fruits of the Spirit. Let us cultivate faith, and faith will produce works.

Verse 13. *Watch therefore, for ye know neither the day nor the hour wherein the Son of man cometh.*

This is the general inference which our Lord makes from the parable. If we watch continually over our hearts and lives, this will show us the necessity of asking and cultivating the grace of God. When we look within, we may find something similar to the original chaos. We shall find emptiness and confusion, and this will excite us to pray for light, and that the Spirit of God would move upon the waters. And when he comes, we will be careful to cherish his motions, and beg of him to keep his hand to his new creation. Adam was to keep and dress the first garden, and when the heart of man becomes the garden of God, man is to cultivate it and watch over the precious plantation. If he allows it to be overgrown with thorns, himself may be saved as by fire. Solomon, the King of the Church, was to have a thousand pieces of silver for the garden, and those who kept the fruit, two hundred. Let us therefore watch and pray, and await the coming of our Lord.

Practical inferences

We conclude with a few practical inferences.

1. First, have we the oil of grace in our lamps? Let us deal honestly with our consciences. If we say we hope so, is this a sure foundation? Would we reckon him a wise man that said he hoped he had a right to such a town [farm or estate], and yet after all could produce no evidence of his right? But some, perhaps, will say they do such and such things, they attend means and ordinances. Alas, we read of many that had these very claims and yet were cast out. Even some

concern for the soul is not enough (Luke 13:24). Cain and others had terror, but if we come weary and heavy laden to Christ, we are safe. But is it so that we are afraid we may be yet destitute? If so, let us go to the fountain. Let us come empty, and throw ourselves at his feet. Let us forsake all our sins, and come honestly to our Saviour, and he that cometh shall not be cast out.

2. We may here see the advantages of self-examination and watchfulness. The one will prevent self-deception and the other begets security. They will show the best their weaknesses, and will show to all the necessity of betaking themselves in time to Christ for salvation and happiness.

3. Lastly, we may see the great mercy of God in that we may yet have an opportunity of procuring the oil of grace for our souls.

Permit me, then, to address myself to two sorts of persons who now hear me. First, the openly wicked, and next, those who content themselves with a mere form. Will you then, my friends, go on in a state of indifference to true religion? You have the offer, and the work of the Spirit will make you effectually happy. But if you despise it—or, which is nearly as bad, if you deceive yourselves, and refuse to become open to conviction—you are undone.

I conclude with a few short advices:

1. Call to remembrance your sins—confess and forsake them.
2. Be not satisfied with being half-religious.
3. Make peace with God and with conscience.
4. Pray earnestly for the influences of the Spirit.
5. Improve time, and especially the Sabbath.

Matthew chapter 25: verses 14 to 30

MANKIND were not sent into the world like the brute creation or the birds of the air, to play, to eat, drink and sleep. They were created for a nobler end—namely, to glorify God and to enjoy him for ever. Inferior creatures, when they come to die, lie down in the dust, and have no fear for what is to come; nor have they cause. Man is an accountable creature, as we learn from the words just now read. Though people now live as they list, they must die, and after death are to be called to account for the use they made of all the opportunities God has put in their power to promote his glory, their own salvation, and the salvation of those around them.

Parable of the talents

In speaking further on the parable of the talents, I shall:

1. Explain the parable in a short paraphrase.
2. Show you some of the reasons which the faithful servants might have to improve their Lord's money.
3. Mention the arguments that might induce the wicked and slothful servant to hide his Lord's money in the earth.
4. Point out to you the danger of such characters.
5. Lastly, make a practical improvement of the doctrine.

1. I shall explain the parable in a short paraphrase.

In general, the man travelling into a far country is our Lord Jesus Christ, who is gone into heaven, and is hereafter to return to judge the quick and the dead. The servants are professing Christians. The faithful servants are those Christians who improved their time, secured their own salvation, and did all they could to procure the salvation of those around. They lived to God, they dedicated their hearts and their lives to his service, in order to promote his glory.

The slothful servants are those who did not truly believe the gospel, had enmity to the peculiar doctrines and leading duties of Scripture, and who endeavoured to persuade themselves that God is not what his Word represents him to be. More particularly, we shall find their character by looking over the different verses.

> Verses 14–15. *For the kingdom of heaven is as a man travelling into a far country, who called his own servants, and delivered unto them his goods. And unto one he gave five talents, to another two, and to another one; to every man according to his several ability; and straightway took his journey.*

In these words, we have a description of the state of Christians in all ages of the Church. Our Lord bestowed upon his servants his goods. To some, he gave more; to others, he gave less; but he gave some to all. The means of instruction and the ordinances of religion are the talents bestowed upon Christians.

> Verses 16–18. *Then he that had received the five talents went and traded with the same, and made them other five talents. And likewise he that had received two, he also gained other two. But he that had received one went and digged in the earth, and hid his lord's money.*

We see here the different use these servants made of their Lord's money. Some received five talents. These were the apostles and men who had eminent gifts and graces in the Church. They got great grace, and improved it to the highest degree. Others got two talents, and these are ordinary pastors and Christians, and they improved them likewise. Those who got the one talent may represent the bulk of those who hear the gospel.

We find the slothful servant hid his Lord's money in the earth, and this points out the character of worldly Christians, whether clergy or laymen. They bury their talents in the earth. Instead of improving their advantages to the glory of God, they seek their happiness in worldly pleasures. Whatever mental abilities, learning or knowledge of the gospel they may possess, these are hid like money buried in the earth. Though you were in their company or in their houses, you cannot discern religion more than you could see money hid under the ground. Their religion is buried in the cares and bustle to acquire riches and pomp, honour or pleasure. As money hid in the earth can be of no service to the possessor or to any other, so likewise their knowledge of religion they never reduce to practice. The things of this world take up their time and attention, and exclude all thoughts of hereafter.

Verses 19–23. *After a long time the lord of those servants cometh, and reckoneth with them. And so he that had received five talents came and brought other five talents, saying, Lord, thou deliveredst unto me five talents: behold, I have gained beside them five talents more. His lord said unto him, Well done, thou good and faithful servant: thou hast been faithful over a few things, I will make thee ruler over many things: enter thou into the joy of thy lord. He also that had received two talents came and said, Lord, thou deliveredst unto me two talents: behold, I have gained two other talents beside them. His lord said unto him, Well done, good and faithful servant; thou hast been faithful over a few things, I will make thee ruler over many things: enter thou into the joy of thy lord.*

When the Lord of the servants made his appearance and called them to account, we see by these words that he bestows a rich and liberal reward upon those who faithfully improved their advantages. Happy are those who make a good use of the time and talents bestowed upon them. Those who got the two talents are rewarded as well as those who received the five. There are different degrees in glory as there are men of different abilities in the Church, but we find they are all happy that enter into the joy of their Lord. Blest is the state of faithful servants.

Verses 24–30. *Then he which had received the one talent came and said, Lord, I knew thee that thou art an hard man, reaping where thou hast not sown, and gathering where thou hast not strawed: and I was*

307

afraid, and went and hid thy talent in the earth: lo, there thou hast that is thine. His lord answered and said unto him, Thou wicked and slothful servant, thou knewest that I reap where I sowed not, and gather where I have not strawed: thou oughtest therefore to have put my money to the exchangers, and then at my coming I should have received mine own with usury. Take therefore the talent from him, and give it unto him which hath ten talents. For unto every one that hath shall be given, and he shall have abundance: but from him that hath not shall be taken away even that which he hath. And cast ye the unprofitable servant into outer darkness: there shall be weeping and gnashing of teeth.

In these awful words, we find the fate of wicked, slothful and worldly Christians. The man with one talent hid his Lord's money in the earth. He formed hard and awful opinions of God, as requiring from his creatures what they are not able to perform. Instead of trading with his Lord's money or putting it in the bank, he hid it in the earth.

Now, this represents the fate of those who find pretexts for their own slothfulness, enmity, and indifference to religion. If people neglect prayer to God, if they despise the duties of religion and the care of the soul, they have an excuse at hand. They have temporal concerns to look after, and they look upon God as either very severe or absolutely merciful. Either extreme is injurious to the Creator, and he resents such opinions and practices severely, as the text informs us. However easy it may be for people to excuse themselves to men for their neglect of the one thing needful, we find that this will not answer before the judgment seat. All the pleas and excuses of the slothful servant go for nothing. The reward he might get was bestowed upon the man that improved his talents, and for hiding his Lord's money, he is hurried into utter darkness, to a place of unavailing sorrow and misery. And this method of proceeding sets the mercy and justice of God in the clearest light, vindicates the divine attributes before surrounding and applauding multitudes, stops the mouths of sinners, and excites the gratitude of saints.

2. I shall show you some of the reasons which the faithful servants might have to improve their Lord's money.

In things belonging to this same life, men of commonsense are actuated by some motive or other for what they do, and though some of their actions might appear to those around them foolish and absurd, if they knew their reasons, they would justify their conduct. It is so in the important concerns of eternity. If the eyes of mankind were opened, they would see the propriety of everything the people of God do to secure their own salvation, and if salvation is a great word, they will not be surprised to find them willing also to promote the salvation of others. They can produce solid and substantial reasons, and if people were open to conviction, they would soon see the force of them.

(1) The faithful servants saw the value of the talents. People are reckoned wise men who love and improve their money. It was the advice of a prudent, worldly man to take care of the pence, and then a man will naturally take care of the pounds. If we see a young person very careful of small sums, we are ready to prognosticate his future success in the world. And this often happens, for God rewards honest industry in this same life.

Now, the Christian sees the value of the soul, the value of grace, the value of time, and its connection with eternity, and this makes him improve his opportunities, because he sees they are precious. A sensible worldly man will improve a good harvest day, and will avail himself of wind and tide to promote his interests, but as he knows that there are but few days that bring him great profit, he does not neglect small profit. If there are days in which he may gain pounds, he does not reckon the day lost in which he can gain shillings. The good Christian is in the same way: there are some days which, in his own experience, enrich his soul, but he does not neglect any day in which he can get improvement. Like the men going to Emmaus, when he cannot enjoy the presence of his Lord and Master, he goes where he can find two or three of his gathered together, and there he meets his Saviour in the comforts and promises of his Word.

(2) They saw that it was their Lord's money, and that they must account for it. A Christian is like the overseer of a great man who is gone from home and left his concerns in his hands. Now, in a stew-

ard it is required that a man be found faithful. He must not use freedom with what belongs to his master, or handle his money as if it were his own. Now, everything we possess belongs to God, and we must not say with some wicked characters, 'Our tongues are our own: who is Lord over us?' Whatever rank a Christian is in, he considers God as the possessor and Lord of heaven and earth, and himself only as his servant. Impressed with this thought, he does not use the world as if he himself was lord of what he possesses. Whatever advantage he enjoys, whether in a temporal or spiritual view, he improves as a person that must give account. Has he riches? He does not squander them on his lusts or increase them at the expense of his fellow creatures. If he has an opportunity of the gospel, he is wise in his day, and lays hold on eternal life. Whether he is poor or rich, his great aim is to act his part properly, and have clear accounts when his Lord calls him.

(3) He was actuated by love to his Lord and to his interests. The faithful servants, whether they obtain five or two talents, each are equally faithful to their Lord. They found that their Lord had bestowed his money upon them. They feel gratitude and love, and this excites them to improve their advantages. Whatever they enjoy, they know the way to obtain more is to make a good use of what they have. Has God bestowed his grace upon them? Due improvement has doubled their talents. Do searching thoughts occasionally possess them that they have not grace? By waiting on the means and crying earnestly to heaven for that precious gift, they knew that thousands have obtained grace. They wait likewise, and God, in his mercy, meets their souls. They are grateful for the day of small things, and feel the promptings of love and gratitude for the smallest thing they enjoy. This increases their stock and turns their water into wine. The least thing that proceeds from this divine principle is accepted by the gracious King of heaven, and turns to their account. It is like the philosopher's stone, that is said to convert everything into gold. Good Christians love their Saviour, and when they feel this, it makes every duty delightsome to their souls.

(4) The prospect of reward might excite the diligence of the faithful servants. In the Old as well as in the New Testaments, we find the people of God are animated with the cheerful hope of a happy immortality. If the Israelites were happy at the thought of possessing the earthly Canaan, the people of God in all ages were looking for a heavenly country, and for a city that hath foundations, whose maker and builder is God. The hope of this made them follow their Lord and Master through every trial and difficulty. It was the 'joy that was set before him' that made the great Head of the Church, the King of Zion, despise the shame of his cross, and go with alacrity to meet his sufferings. Though they do not work for heaven as if they were under the first covenant, they work from a principle of love, and they know their labour shall not be in vain in the Lord. He has procured grace for them, and shall have the glory of all their works. And their labours of love shall be rewarded, though eternal life is the gift of God. Heaven was purchased by the Saviour, and yet his people are rewarded by free grace.

3. I shall mention the arguments that might induce the wicked and slothful servant to hide his Lord's money in the earth.

However degenerate human nature is become, men have now and then some thoughts of the hereafter. Instead of encouraging thoughts that would lead them home to God, however, they rather stifle them. They content themselves with a superficial reformation, and are not willing to go further. Unbelief is at the bottom of all our disobedience, and false opinions are the food and nourishment of unbelief. They mutually strengthen each other and keep sinners from God. Some of these follow.

(1) Some believe that God is a hard Master, calling us to duties we have no strength to perform. And why should we make the attempt?

If we yield to this cruel thought, it will breed enmity to the God that made us. It is true that God calls us to believe and repent, and that of ourselves we cannot do either. But does this excuse us for unbelief and impenitence? It surely does not. At the same time that our Lord and his disciples show the weakness and corruption of our nature, they show also the malignant poison and danger of unbelief. Our Lord tells the Jews, as he also tells us, that no man can believe except the Father draw him. But does not our Lord also inform us that, if we are convinced of our weakness and call for his assistance, that he will give his Holy Spirit? God offers strength, and he never yet refused any that came to him.

Did God do any injury to his people, Israel, at the shore of the Red Sea when he desired them to proceed forward? Was there anything cruel in the command? They could not proceed, and yet it was their duty to obey. By attempting, however, to proceed, a glorious miracle is wrought in their behalf. It is the same in spiritual concerns. God commands us to believe, to repent, to obey, to fight against the world, flesh and devil. It is certain we cannot perform these duties, but is there any cruelty in the precious command, and what would induce us to believe that God is a hard Master? When we see our weakness, and when unbelief, enmity, and hardness of heart are our burden and we apply to almighty power, it is exerted in our behalf. The withered hand receives strength, and the bloody issue of sin is stopped, and we are assisted in our conflict against our inveterate companions and the snares of our spiritual enemies.

(2) Others, again, have dark views of the doctrine of election. If God has not chosen them, they say all their endeavours are useless.

The plain answer to this is: Secret things belong to God; our business is not with the doctrine of election, but with the calls and invitations of the gospel. There are general calls both in the Old and New Testaments to believe. If we cast ourselves honestly upon the faithfulness of God, we shall find him true to his promises. I have no business to know whom God hath chosen, but it becomes my duty to believe in Christ. It was the duty of an Israelite to follow Moses through the Red Sea, and not to stand on the shore enquiring whether God meant to save or drown him. By following the pillar of cloud, he lands safe on the other side.

(3) Others, again, think that God will not be so severe as to destroy the work of his own hands.

It is very true that man is the handiwork of God, and he was origi-
nally a beautiful piece of workmanship indeed, but we know that
creatures of superior rank fell from God, and are now 'reserved in
chains of darkness till the judgment of the great day'. This thought
should be stifled, for it is dangerous to the soul, and proceeds from
our natural enmity and unbelief. Several sinners were persuading
themselves that God would not destroy them for taking some pleasure and neglecting the affairs of their souls, but, alas, the delusion
of their opinion appeared to them in the near views of death and
eternity. Such sinners have been often spectacles of terror and
objects of pity to such as have been witnesses of their dying agonies.

But to speak more particularly to this point, it is not God that
destroys: it is the sinner himself. Salvation is the work of God, but
destruction is the work of the sinner, and if the sinner obstinately
refuses to forsake sin, the cause of his misery, and lives and dies in
sin, it is just of God to forsake him and leave him to perish in his
rebellion.

(4) Lastly, others take refuge in an absolute unscriptural view of
divine mercy. They do no harm, or if they are sinners, they hope
God is merciful, and then they set up an absolutely merciful God
without justice, without holiness, and without truth.

But to show the absurdity of this unscriptural view of mercy, let us
take another of the divine attributes, and reason about it without
book [in an unlearned way]. God has almighty power. Let us then
suppose that some poor, foolish man argues in this manner: 'God
has infinite power, and I hope he will either create another world,
or at least cause a new island to emerge out of the sea, and make me
lord and master thereof.' We may now ask, 'What authority hath this
poor man from commonsense or from Scripture that almighty
power will form such an island?' Such, then, is the sandy foundation
of that man who forms unscriptural views of divine mercy. Infinite
wisdom is the best judge how mercy is to be extended, as it is the
best judge also how far the power is to be exerted. God has revealed
his mercy in the gospel, and if we are wise, we will receive it through
the hands of a Mediator. Otherwise, God is a consuming fire.

4. I shall point out the dangers of such characters.

(1) It often happens that gross sinners take concern for their souls: these take none.

In all ages of the Church, we could mention several great sinners that have been converted to God, but it is very difficult—and in cases, I had almost said, impossible—to strike conviction into the hearts of slothful sinners that think well of their own state. 'What ails them?' they say.

In our Saviour's time, the Pharisees could boast that they fasted and prayed. These people, however, notwithstanding their duties, were covetous worldlings, and hid their Lord's money in the earth. They resisted the grace of God, at the same time that publicans and great sinners repented and believed the gospel. The gross sinners of Corinth are converted. The polite philosophers of Athens ridiculed the apostle and his doctrine. And as the pride of learning made these reject the gospel, the pride of duties and great spiritual riches make such persons hide their Lord's money in the earth.

(2) Doing nothing for the soul is the road to perdition.

Scripture informs us that if the tree does not produce good fruit, it is cut down and cast into the fire, and the doctrine of the parable informs us that the unprofitable servant is cast into outer darkness to the place of misery and woe. And this proves to us the great danger of such persons. These people will easily see the awful situation of gross sinners that live in open rebellion to the revealed will of heaven—and, alas, their own situation is equally dangerous, and their sin and their punishment may be equally great. There is a stigma set upon the young man in the gospel, the Church of Laodicea, and the proud Pharisee, as well as there is upon Jezebel and Simon Magus.

It seems, then, that people may be unprofitable servants though they perform some unavailing duties in religion. A heap of chaff may have a great bulk, but a landlord will not receive it from his tenant for rent instead of wholesome grain. Can duties without the love of

God, proceeding from hearts full of enmity, corruption, and unbelief merit the reward of heaven? If we do nothing at all, or rest in duties without a Saviour, we are unprofitable servants. The garden will be overgrown with thorns: that is the property of the slothful servant. It is in spiritual, as it is in natural, things: if a garden is not kept in cultivation, it will produce useless and noxious weeds, and spiritual sloth will have the same effect upon the inner man.

Persons professing religion are often slaves to unsanctified and irregular passions. They attempt to reconcile the gratification of their lusts with attendance upon religious duties. The harlot paid her vows (Proverbs 7:14). The Pharisee that devoured widows' houses made long prayers, and paid by these. But such characters take no pains with the heart, and do not seek to eradicate and destroy their evil propensities. Accordingly, they are as ready to cheat, to lie, to curse and swear, to scold, to give bad language, to get drunk, and indulge their appetites after leaving church as they were before. They take no pains with the improvement of their minds and the government of their minds. So their lives are disgraced with several ugly lusts, and their devotions are preceded and followed by their unbridled and furious passions and unruly appetites.

Practical inferences

Let us now apply the doctrine to our consciences.

1. Are we slothful or faithful servants? Is the general course of our actions, in spite of human weaknesses, such as may encourage us to hope that the God of truth will say to us, 'Well done, good and faithful servant: enter into the joy of your Lord.'

Are we honest in our dealings with God and man? Do we impose upon the ignorance of our fellow men, by asking three times the value of what we give them? Would we take upon ourselves to ask such a price if the Saviour himself was standing by? Do we frame our actions as if he were present?

315

2. If the man that hid his talent is as lost, what will become of those who abuse their talents by drink, by uncleanness, by tricks and villainy? What will come of the covetous wretch that is conscious he imposes upon his neighbour, that sells his conscience to increase his gain, and buries his talent in a heap of lying tricks and excuses?

3. Lastly, we see that such characters are cast into outer darkness. This is the emphasis of their misery—they do not see the face of God, or the cheering light of the gospel. There is no promise of mercy in the regions of despair. They no longer impose by false appearances.

Let us repent and be wise in time, and God bless his Word.

Matthew chapter 25: verses 31 to 46

W E are informed by the apostle that life and immortality are brought to light by the gospel. The doctrine of a future state of rewards and punishments is more clearly revealed than it was under the Old Testament. Though the pagan philosophers have many beautiful sentiments about it, they often speak with doubt and uncertainty about this great point. Our Lord, therefore, in the latter part of this chapter, tells us in plain language of a future judgment. I shall therefore offer some few thoughts upon this portion of Scripture, and conclude with practical inferences.

The Day of Judgment

Verse 31. *When the Son of man shall come in his glory, and all the holy angels with him, then shall he sit upon the throne of his glory.*

Nothing is more august than the description which the Scripture gives of the Day of Judgment. The great King of saints, the incarnate God, shall descend from heaven, attended by his holy angels. His chariots are said to be twenty thousand, even thousands of angels. It is not a few legions that will come upon that illustrious occasion, but the whole angelic host. They shall descend so far as to be in sight of some particular spot of this earth, and when this happens, he shall sit upon a great white throne. In comparison to this, what are the thrones of earthly sovereigns and short-lived kings but idle sport and pageantry?

Verse 32. *And before him shall be gathered all nations: and he shall separate them one from another, as a shepherd divideth his sheep from the goats.*

317

The great white throne shall be visible to the whole human race, for all nations shall be gathered before him, and when this happens, a division shall be made, for the righteous shall be separated from the wicked. Though they lived together in this life, the righteous, discerning Judge shall put them asunder. Though vile hypocrites and slippery sin-exercising professors meet here with his people, in that day they must appear in their proper colours, and have their portions accordingly.

They are divided only into two sorts—the sheep and the goats. The righteous are compared to sheep—a harmless, innocent, useful animal. Christians are remarkable for their innocent simplicity, integrity, and usefulness of their lives. In the East, sheep were taught to follow the shepherd. They knew his voice and followed him, and he led them into green pastures, cooling shades, and refreshing streams; and the people of God thus follow the Saviour. The goat is a lascivious, quarrelsome, and stinking animal, and therefore a semblance of the wicked. They gratify their lusts, live in malice and envy, and their ill savour is felt in their conversation and dealings. Their conversation is idle and useless at best. It has often a sting in it, and is calculated to do hurt, and to sow spiritual poison. They are the friends of sin at heart, and if they find the smallest shadow, they are ready to extenuate guilt and excuse the sinner. If a goat, a fox, a wolf, or a tiger could speak, each of them would excuse what himself is guilty and fond of. And this is the true character of the wicked. From the grossest tyrant that fills a throne to the meanest beggar in rags, every one of them, without exception, will defend sin. The goat has a rotten smell, and the sinner has a rotten breath, and you will discover it in the nauseous manner in which he supports sin.

Verse 33. *And he shall set the sheep on his right hand, but the goats on the left.*

A distinction shall then be made between the righteous and the wicked. In this world, we may observe very often virtue in misery and want, and impudent, bare-faced evil triumphant. The good man may pine in prison or sink under contempt, while the ungodly race flourish like the palm tree. Truth, freedom, and religion may be trampled underfoot, and wickedness ride in state and triumph. But the Saviour, who is no respecter of persons, shall give to each their due. The righteous shall sing and shine, and the wicked be sent to the regions of despair.

> Verse 34. *Then shall the King say unto them on his right hand, Come, ye blessed of my Father, inherit the kingdom prepared for you from the foundation of the world.*

In this address of our Lord to his people, we see that they are indebted for their happiness to the distinguishing, everlasting love of God. They are blessed of the Father, and the kingdom is prepared for them from the foundation of the world. As the earthly Canaan was promised and prepared for the seed of Abraham, Isaac and Jacob, the heavenly Canaan was prepared for the spiritual seed of Christ. It is not given in consequence of their own merits. They are indebted to the love and grace of God for the kingdom they possess.

> Verses 35–36. *For I was an hungred, and ye gave me meat: I was thirsty, and ye gave me drink: I was a stranger, and ye took me in: naked, and ye clothed me: I was sick, and ye visited me: I was in prison, and ye came unto me.*

In these words, we find the true character of the people of God. Though good works are not the procuring cause of their salvation, they are their distinguishing marks.

Love to the Lord Jesus animates all the chosen people of God, and the manner in which they show this is by love to his people and to his cause. The Psalmist (Psalm 16) acknowledges that his goodness could not reach to God, but that he would show love to the excellent of the earth, in whom were all his delight. And what is done to these, our Lord takes as if it were done to himself. 'I was hungry,' says he, 'and ye gave me meat: I was thirsty, and ye gave me drink,' etc.

They also love his cause, and this he also considers as done to himself. 'I was in prison, and ye came unto me.' They not only support his people in low circumstances, but they also countenance them when suffering for righteousness' sake. They support the good cause, and do not forsake his people, even in prison. They love virtue and religion in the meanest garb, and when they see grace shining, even in poverty and rags, they can love and esteem the saint.

> Verses 37–39. *Then shall the righteous answer him, saying, Lord, when saw we thee an hungred, and fed thee? or thirsty, and gave thee drink? When saw we thee a stranger, and took thee in? or naked, and clothed thee? Or when saw we thee sick, or in prison, and came unto thee?*

In these words, the modesty, humility, and self-denial of the saints is very conspicuous. Conscious of their own unworthiness and the great disproportion between their poor services and such a glorious reward, they seem to blush with holy confusion at the thought. A sense of coldness in their love to the best of friends and benefactors makes them ask, 'When saw we thee an hungred?' etc. Let it be remarked that these are 'parabolical' expressions—not that these very words will pass between Christ and his people, for they surely knew that they performed these good works. But this shows their wonder and astonishment at the goodness of their Saviour.

> Verse 40. *And the King shall answer and say unto them, Verily I say unto you, Inasmuch as ye have done it unto one of the least of these my brethren, ye have done it unto me.*

The connection between Christ and his people is such that he considers the injuries done them, and the benefits bestowed upon them, as done to himself. When Saul persecuted the Church, he considers it as done to himself. And he accepts even the cup of cold water given to one of his people as if he got a refreshing drink. And in the words of the text, he informs that the love shown to his people in acts of kindness and mercy is the best proof we can give of our love to Christ himself. If we love a little grace in one of his people, it may be naturally concluded that we love the great fountain from whence this grace proceeds, and that is Christ our Lord.

Verse 41. *Then shall he say also unto them on the left hand, Depart from me, ye cursed, into everlasting fire, prepared for the devil and his angels.*

After pronouncing the sentence of absolution to his people, he now turns to the wicked and pronounces their awful doom. They had heard the gospel and rejected all the offers of mercy proposed to them. Instead of embracing the blessed news, they gratified their cursed lusts, and preferred the service of the devil to the glorious freedom and privileges of the children of God. And as they associated with wicked spirits, they now share their punishment. The fire was prepared for reprobate angels, and if they rushed into it with their eyes open, the blame is at their own door. The justice of God is clear: they got many warnings, and held a deaf ear to the calls of the gospel.

Verses 42–43. *For I was an hungred, and ye gave me no meat: I was thirsty, and ye gave me no drink: I was a stranger, and ye took me not in: naked, and ye clothed me not: sick, and in prison, and ye visited me not.*

It is necessary once more to observe that these are parabolical expressions. We are not to suppose that there will be no other process but what we have in these words. There are many thousands of crimes for which the wicked shall be condemned, but there is none mentioned here except one—that is, want of love to Christ and his cause, showing itself in their indifference to his people. The want of love to Christ shows itself in many ways. Some persecuted and murdered his followers; others mocked and ridiculed them. A third set despise the message they bring from God, break his holy day, and set light by his gospel. And the persons mentioned in the text are only said to neglect his people, and do them no good. But this we find is enough to condemn, though nothing else was against them. Mere indifference to the cause and people of God is proof of want of love to Christ. Now, as eternal life is the free gift of God through our Lord Jesus Christ, want of love to the great donor is cause sufficient and just to exclude people from the benefit.

Verses 44–45. *Then shall they also answer him, saying, Lord, when saw we thee an hungred, or athirst, or a stranger, or naked, or sick, or in prison, and did not minister unto thee? Then shall he answer them, saying, Verily I say unto you, Inasmuch as ye did it not to one of the least of these, ye did it not to me.*

We find these persons attempting to justify themselves, and attempting, as it were, to deny the charge. They ask when they saw him in such circumstances. We cannot suppose that none of this great multitude gave nothing to the poor: many—perhaps a great part of them—did. But it seems they did not give it to Christ, and this stops their mouth.

It also confutes [refutes] that senseless opinion of the common people that alms procure heaven, and that people are happy who give away a great deal of their substance. But, it may be asked, 'Have they given it to Christ?' Several causes may make people very liberal of their means. Some do it from a natural kind of generosity, as some people are constitutionally sober and chaste; others are bountiful to procure to themselves a great name. Many part with their gear [possessions] to flatterers, and others do it, hoping it will be a compensation for their sins, and open to them the portals of paradise. These have their reward: they have a name in the world; some gentlewomen have dressed the present of a self-designing person for himself, and made him carry it home in his belly. In this way providence uses those that would purchase heaven with their works.

People may say at the Day of Judgment that they gave meat and drink and clothes to flatterers, to travellers, and to the poor. But what have they given to the Saviour? Alas! this question spoils all their works.

But here it is necessary to make one remark. Some persons may ask, 'Are we then to give nothing to the poor but when we find the love of Christ in our souls?' You surely are! It is the duty of people to pray to God when they do not find faith and repentance in their souls. If persons were not to pray but when they are sure they find the workings of the Spirit of God upon their souls, they would effectually hurt their own spiritual interest, and this would serve as a pillow for their sloth. In like manner, there is a danger that covetousness may suggest such thoughts to the covetous heart. Let us do what we know to be duty, and at the same time pray to God to put a true principle of grace within us, and let us not rest satisfied without that. There are many things we can do, and if we leave them undone, we sin. But, on the other hand, if we do them not from a right principle, we lose our reward. Let self-righteous Pharisees look to this. Let them examine their works and tremble.

Verse 46. *And these shall go away into everlasting punishment: but the righteous into life eternal.*

In these words, we have the strongest proof of a future state. There is everlasting punishment; there is life eternal.

Divines speak of the punishment of sense and the punishment of loss. The punishment of sense is the pain which their souls and bodies suffer for ever. Scripture uses very strong expressions, such as fire and brimstone, a worm, and a bottomless pit: awful images indeed! May God give us grace to turn from the road that leads to that place of woe. There is also the punishment of loss, and some blind sinners seem to see little in that. The loss of God—alas, how great, how unutterable, how terrifying the idea! Certain enormous sinners, in the near view of death, would have reckoned it a relief if they could hide themselves from God in the thick flames of hell. Sinners, will you sell his favour for a trifle?

And now an objection is to be answered. God is merciful, and therefore some may ask, 'How is it consistent with his goodness to punish his creatures with everlasting destruction?' To this it may be answered that there is no foundation in Scripture or reason for supposing that God will annihilate any soul which he has created, and if he continues them in being—which we have every cause to believe he will—reason as well as Scripture will tell us that if they continue sinners for ever, they must be punished for ever: sin in its very nature will bring misery. If unsanctified passions and unruly affections tear the soul, that soul must be miserable.

And if it be asked, 'Why does not an infinitely gracious God pour down from heaven a flood of his love and grace to quench the flames of hell, and make them good in spite of them?' let it be observed, then, once for all, that the Judge of all the earth will do right. When God is pleased to reveal to us the reasons of his conduct, we shall be satisfied with what he does.

We find in Scripture that the inhabitants of heaven praise him in the highest strains for punishing the wicked. God has already opened the windows of heaven and poured down a flood of love and grace upon the sons of men. They refused the offer of his grace and preferred their lusts. And though the pains of hell were suspended, and that they came out of the pit and got a second offer, God foresees that they would abuse his grace as formerly.

'Why God does not make them good and holy, whether they would or not?' or, 'Why he does not annihilate them?' are questions we cannot answer in our present state. At any rate, it seems this is not for the glory of God. And as punishment frightens from sinning, it may be a means of keeping millions of rational beings in a state of purity and perfection. It is our duty rather to believe than to doubt or dispute against the words of God.

Let us now turn to the bright side of the cloud. It is said here that the righteous go to life eternal, and to this doctrine we surely can have no objection. There is a future state of happiness, and we may now enquire what it is that makes people happy even in this life. And the chief ingredients in earthly happiness are health, competence, contentment, friendship, and the gratification of our lawful wishes.

Now, the happiness of the next life is:

1. Holiness, which is the health of the soul.
2. Satisfaction and contentment with its own happy state.
3. The friendship and society of God, angels, and good men.

4. A boundless prospect of never-ending felicity, and new scenes of pure and permanent pleasures, and nothing wanting to complete our happiness.

1. First, holiness, which is the health of the soul!

When people meet, they generally enquire about one another's health. It is the balm of life, and what enables us to enjoy and relish all its pleasures. Without health, riches and honour and pleasures are things without taste. We cannot enjoy them without this greatest of all temporal blessings, and holiness is what enables us to relish the pleasures of eternity. Without holiness, we cannot enjoy the presence of God, the society of the blessed, the songs of angels, and the refined pleasures of the higher house.

An incaverned mole,[18] if suddenly brought to the light of day, would start back again to the dark, thick element from whence she came. Holiness is vital to the happiness of heaven. The pleasures there are of a pure and sublime nature. A hog from the sty or a dog from his kennel are as fit companions for the King's Court as unclean sinners for the joys of heaven. They incapacitate their own minds for those pure enjoyments: holiness is what enables them who are admitted there to relish their delights. The more pure and virtuous our minds are, the more we feel and anticipate the pleasures of the blessed. If we are holy, we will be happy.

2. Second, satisfaction and contentment with its own happy state.

I have heard of a gentleman that enjoyed so much domestic happiness that he said he would take an eternity of such bliss. People may sometimes enjoy a half-hour of such happiness, but alas! it lasts but short, and it is seldom without a sting. The people of God, it is true, sometimes enjoy pleasures to which the world are strangers. They do occasionally go up to the mount, and sometimes are made to say, 'It is good to be here.' But even these seldom enjoy these moments of delight. While they partake of them, they naturally wish them to continue longer. Their devotion, however, is often interrupted by

---

[18] A mole in darkness underground, as if in a cavern. [RJD]

the weakness of nature, the hurry of the world, the temptation of their spiritual adversary, or the corruption of their hearts. But in that happy place, they never meet with any internal or external impediments to interrupt their happiness.

3. The friendship and society of God, angels, and good men.

Friendship is one of the strongest and purest pleasures of life. Men of the highest rank and talents saw a blank in their happiness without this cordial. Aeneas had a friend, Achates; Augustus, the Roman emperor, had Maecenas; and even David, the man after God's heart, was happy in the friendship of Jonathan and Hushai. The more virtuous our friends are, the more happy the cement. How happy, then, beyond imagination, is the man who has God for his friend, and that for ever. He enjoys his company and is happy in his presence. He also enjoys the company of an innumerable company of happy beings.

In this life, we sometimes enjoy happiness in some select companions. A union of sentiments and congeniality of soul may occasion such pure pleasures as taste strong of heaven. But even good men have their defects, and we cannot be entirely and completely happy in their company. That happiness, however, is reserved for the 'general assembly and church of the firstborn'. There is none in that great and happy society but perfect characters, men of complete virtue and grace. There is not a fault nor a foible, a weakness or imperfection, to be found among them. They are complete in spiritual beauty, and adorned with every perfection that can endear them to one another, and attract their mutual love and esteem. Exalted above all the rest is seen the great Immanuel, the Head of the Church, and he is the life and soul of the whole company. He is the sun that enlightens that spiritual world, and the river that makes glad the city of God. The company never part, and their enjoyments are always new.

4. A boundless prospect of never-ending felicity, and new scenes of pure and permanent pleasures, and nothing wanting to complete our happiness.

The pleasures of eternity are always before us, and the pleasures are always various and new. If, even in this transitory scene of things, there is such a variety of pure and innocent pleasures arising from the investigation of different kinds of truth and from a contemplation of the works of creation, how great is the source of pleasure in the next!

We see here but a small part of creation, and our pleasures are but stinted in comparison with what they shall be hereafter. People in the higher department of life, whose rank and fortune enable them to arrive at the highest pitch of knowledge, reckon their education complete when they have made the tour of Europe.[19] To a man of virtue and an inquisitive turn of mind, such travel will open up a source of new and various delights, and after all, how small is his knowledge in comparison to the lowest saint in the kingdom of God?

Only a few of mankind can make such a tour on this earth, but there all his people, we have cause to believe, will make a tour of creation—and what source of new pleasures and wonders! The Psalmist gets a humbling view of himself by contemplating the nocturnal heavens, and he calls upon the whole heavenly host to praise and bless the Lord. And if the contemplation of God's works affords a part of our happiness in this life, it will surely afford a great part in the next. In this state of distance and ignorance, we can know but little, and even that little is known by the help of glasses [telescopes] and other instruments. But then, the body shall be spiritual and can wing its way to the most distant parts of material creation, and there gratify its holy curiosity by taking a satisfactory view of the works of God. The bodies of the saints will rise above the earth and meet

---

[19] The 'Grand Tour' was a journey through Europe, especially Italy, undertaken by upper-class young men—mainly British—for education and cultural refinement, often marking their coming of age. Beginning in the second half of the 17th century and dying out two centuries later, the tour followed a standard itinerary and formed an established part of aristocratic education. [RJD]

their Lord in the air, and if so, they can go to other parts with equal ease and freedom.

The best glasses cannot afford the acutest philosophers as much knowledge in a course of years as a single saint can acquire in one half-hour by travelling to the place and seeing things with his eyes. Creation then will open new scenes constantly of ever-various delight, and enable them to offer so many more acts of rational worship. And no doubt the providence of God, which is over all his works of creation, will afford never-ceasing sources of pleasure and praise.

But there is a subject which will afford them higher joy and delight. There is a Man in heaven exalted above all the cherubim and seraphim of glory. Principalities and powers are subject to him. This is the most astonishing sight in heaven. Incarnate love is the wonder and the delightful theme of eternity. Man in union with Deity—God manifest in the flesh—will be the song of angels, the admiration of the redeemed for ever and ever. To worship a mere man would be idolatry: to worship the incarnate Divinity is the highest act of worship in heaven. They worship him that is upon the throne, and the Lamb for ever and ever. They worship the sacred Three, and the Lord who shed his blood to redeem their souls. And this their happiness is to continue through all the ages of eternity, and this is what crowns their bliss. It is a happiness without end, and may God prepare us for it by his grace.

Practical inferences

I conclude with some practical inferences.

1. First, we should examine whether we have cause to fear that the righteous Judge will say to us, 'Depart, ye cursed,' or to hope that he will invite and welcome us as the blessed of his Father.

For this purpose, let us examine our hearts, our duties, and our motives of action. Are our hearts changed from the love of sin, and do we believe, obey, and love our Lord Jesus Christ? Do we perform not only the easier duties of our common Christianity, but the duties also which are more difficult? Are our motives carnal or spiritual? And here we should seriously deal with ourselves, and if we have some cause to doubt our state, let us earnestly cry to God to make his own work, and let us not put anything in the way to hinder the work of his Holy Spirit.

2. Second, if the punishment of the wicked is everlasting, this should strongly induce us to turn and avoid all sin. This disease will rage in their souls through all eternity.

How awful, then, are disorderly passions! When they become riveted to the soul, they become a second nature, and they naturally bring misery along with them. The slaves of sin are miserable, even in this same world where they have something to gratify their unruly appetites, but in the world of spirits, their hungry passions will rage, and nothing to feed them. Our wisdom, therefore, is to bridle them and, by the grace of God, get them under the power of religion. And if a person is willing to submit to Christ, iniquity will not prove his ruin. His grace and Spirit can conquer sin, and make us run the way of God's commandments. The way to be happy here, as well as hereafter, is the due government of the passions. Let us ask the Spirit of Christ for this purpose.

3. Third (lastly), if heaven is a place of such consummate happiness, we should go and get our souls washed in the Redeemer's blood, to qualify us for being admitted to that holy place. Nothing unclean shall enter.

Sinners should take advice, and flee immediately to the place of safety and city of refuge. And let us take notice that, as our souls are polluted with guilt, nothing can wash away our sins but this fountain. The sacrifice and merits of the Son of God are—and should be—our only plea. This opens the gate of heaven. Peace of conscience flows from faith in his blood, and obedience is the fruit of both. And this will sanctify and spiritualise our thoughts and affections. The people of God have their 'fruit unto holiness, and the end everlasting life'.

May God bring us to this life through the merits of our Lord and Saviour Jesus Christ. AMEN.

Matthew chapter 26: verses 1 to 25

WHEN the time drew nigh that the Redeemer should finish the great work he had to do, he concluded his work as a teacher and prophet, and now prepares himself to act his part as the high priest for his people by offering up a sacrifice for their sins. He was the Lamb slain from the foundation of the world, and the evangelical prophet informs us he made his soul an offering for sin, and made intercession for transgressors. Accordingly, the providence of God ordered all circumstances so that he should at the very time of the passover show himself to be the Lamb of God that taketh away the sin of the world. The Jews were now convened from all quarters to celebrate the great feast of the passover, and little thought when they were putting the Saviour to death that they were fulfilling an ancient prophecy concerning their own great Messiah.

I shall endeavour to explain this portion of Scripture, and conclude with some practical inferences by way of improvement.

The plot of the chief priests

Verses 1–2. *And it came to pass, when Jesus had finished all these sayings, he said unto his disciples, Ye know that after two days is the feast of the passover, and the Son of man is betrayed to be crucified.*

'Ye know', says our Lord, when he had finished his doctrine, 'that after two days is the feast of the passover, and the Son of man is to be betrayed to be crucified.' We have the history of the passover in the 12th of Exodus. When God had destroyed the firstborn of the Egyptians, he ordered his own people to slay a lamb for every family, and to sprinkle the blood of the lamb upon the upper post and two side posts of the door, and to roast and eat the flesh of the paschal lamb. Accordingly, the destroying angel passed over every door where he saw the blood. In memory of this wonderful deliverance, the feast of the passover was kept every year by the Jews. Our Lord, who came to fulfil the law, observed this feast very regularly, and as he was the true Paschal Lamb, it was necessary that he should suffer at this very time.

> Verses 3–5. *Then assembled together the chief priests, and the scribes, and the elders of the people, unto the palace of the high priest, who was called Caiaphas, and consulted that they might take Jesus by subtilty, and kill him. But they said, Not on the feast day, lest there be an uproar among the people.*

In this deepest of tragedies, we see the wonderful wisdom of God overruling the blackest actions of men, and from the greatest evil producing the greatest good. Though the high priest and the other members of their great council are willing to put our Lord to death, they chose rather to employ villainy and deceit to accomplish their purpose than open force, and though they thirsted for his blood, they did not wish to put him to death at the time of the feast. But the providence of God overruled their deliberations, so that he must suffer at this very time, and no other. And this was wisely done to accomplish the prophecies of Scripture and to strengthen the faith of his people. His enemies are afraid of an uproar among the people if he suffered at this particular time. Though few believed him to be the Messiah in the Scripture sense of the word, yet many thousands among the Jews believed him to be an extraordinary personage, and if they had not conducted their plot with all the privacy of fear, they could not get the people deliberately to crucify the Lord of glory.

Christ anointed at Bethany

> Verses 6–13. *Now when Jesus was in Bethany, in the house of Simon the leper, there came unto him a woman having an alabaster box of very precious ointment, and poured it on his head, as he sat at meat. But when his disciples saw it, they had indignation, saying, To what purpose*

is this waste? For this ointment might have been sold for much, and given to the poor. When Jesus understood it, he said unto them, Why trouble ye the woman? for she hath wrought a good work upon me. For ye have the poor always with you; but me ye have not always. For in that she hath poured this ointment on my body, she did it for my burial. Verily I say unto you, Wheresoever this gospel shall be preached in the whole world, there shall also this, that this woman hath done, be told for a memorial of her.

In this extraordinary story, there are several things worth our particular attention. Our Lord foresaw his own death and sufferings, and as the circumstances of his death were such as that his pious and affectionate friends could not bestow that honour upon his precious body which they would otherwise incline, the Spirit of God stirred up Mary, the sister of Lazarus, to anoint his body beforehand.

This action, though an illustrious proof of her faith and love, gave offence, as if there was needless waste and expense. It was even surmised that she did a wrong thing, and that it might have been much better to give the money that bought it to the poor. The disciples were offended, and this shows us that the poison which lurks in the heart of one man, when it breaks out in words, may hurt and contaminate others unknown to themselves.

The apostle John explains this story of Matthew. He informs us it was Judas who found fault with the woman, and made a pretence of zeal for the interest of the poor, not that he cared for the poor, but that he was a thief, had the bag, and carried the money. Now, what he said through mere malice and covetousness affected the upright, honest minds of the rest, and raised their indignation against an action which they ought to approve. And this circumstance should make us examine what spirit we are of, and how far we are competent judges of the motives and actions of others. The apostles supported the opinion of Judas, but our Lord, who knew the heart, supported Mary and approved of her action.

Some things are dark to us because we do not know the motives which people may have. We should therefore ask direction from

God before we hastily condemn or approve the action of others. In things that are dark and dubious, our safest way is to judge upon the side of charity, and to put the most favourable construction upon the words and actions of other people. But though we are to judge favourably of the actions of others, we should search to the bottom the sentiments of our own hearts. We may think that we are actuated by a view to the glory of God, when in fact we are swayed by the covetous motives of our own hearts, or fired by a false zeal. Though we ought to be tender in our opinions of others, we ought to be jealous of our own hearts. Jehu thought he was promoting the glory of God when he was promoting his own temporal interest, and the enemies of the gospel thought they were serving God when they murdered the followers of God. And if people may really commit great sins when they think they are performing great duties, how awful is the sin and hypocrisy of such as pretend the purest principles, the glory of God and the good of men, when they must be conscious that they are actuated by motives the very reverse. Let us beg of God to make our motives honest, that we may be enabled to promote his glory.

In this history we likewise learn how beautiful everything is in its season, and when this happens, our duty will not interfere with another. What may be duty at one time ceases to be duty when that occasion is over. Mary performed a very essential duty here, and from the character which we have of her in the gospel, it would be cruel to suppose that she was deficient in her duty to the poor. But there is a time for everything, and our Lord informs us that we may always help the poor when we see their need.

When two duties are to be performed, the most essential for the time is to be performed first. If a man has called to see a sick friend at the point of death, and at the same time was called to perform another very essential duty which he might afterwards perform at his leisure, common sense and a well-informed conscience will tell him what he ought to do.

A covetous worldling may say, like Judas, if he is called upon to attend some religious duty occasionally, 'Why call upon us when we are busy? Why such haste of time?' But we may tell them in the words of the text, 'Ye have the world always, but this opportunity ye have not always.' You hear the language of Judas and his followers as they show how little they care for Christ.

The treachery of Judas

Verses 14–16. *Then one of the twelve, called Judas Iscariot, went unto the chief priests, and said unto them, What will ye give me, and I will deliver him unto you? And they covenanted with him for thirty pieces of silver. And from that time he sought opportunity to betray him.*

In these awful words, we see the final end of the religion of the covetous. Judas followed Christ while he believed he could make anything of him. No doubt he looked for some profit under him if he was to be promoted to be a temporal king. But when our Lord began to thwart his avaricious views, he meditates a scheme of revenge. Stung at his disappointment in following a man who always spoke of a spiritual kingdom, he at last becomes weary of his service. While there is any prospect of his being a great man, he follows him.

There are many in these days who have the religion of Judas. If the landlord or rich tenant of whom they hold [*i.e.* of whom they hold land by feudal tenure] is a religious character and attends religious duty, they attend because they see this is for their interest. But if things take a contrary course, they go to the world and ask, 'What wilt thou give me, and I shall change and sell my religion?' Judas sold his religion and his soul for thirty pieces of silver, and many would sell their religion for a creel of seaware,[20] for a stoup [cask] of whisky, or for a small pendicle of land.[21] The man that takes money for the hire of his boat upon the Lord's Day sells his religion and Saviour for a few shillings.

---

[20] Seaweed, of a type used as fertiliser. [rjd]
[21] A small piece of land rented to a sub-tenant. [RJD]

Judas sought an opportunity to betray him, and how small is the excuse that will make many turn their back upon him! How trifling is the thing that will keep them from the precious means of grace! And we may take notice that all these deviations from our duty to our Saviour are so many lesser species of the sin of Judas. As far as we are kept back by a covetous heart, we follow that unhappy traitor. When people give up the means of grace, the language of their conduct is, 'What will I get, and I shall desert my religion?' And whatever profit or pleasure may promise them, they have but Judas's pennyworth at last.

> Verses 17–19. *Now the first day of the feast of unleavened bread the disciples came to Jesus, saying unto him, Where wilt thou that we prepare for thee to eat the passover? And he said, Go into the city to such a man, and say unto him, The Master saith, My time is at hand; I will keep the passover at thy house with my disciples. And the disciples did as Jesus had appointed them; and they made ready the passover.*

According to the law of Moses, we read that at the time of passover, they abstained from leavened bread for seven days, and upon the first of these days, the disciples came and enquired of him where did he wish to prepare the passover.

And in performing the great and solemn duties of religion, it is incumbent upon his disciples to consult his Word and call upon his name by prayer. It is incumbent upon us, in things that are dark to us, always to consult him and ask direction from his Word, providence, and Spirit. There was a great throng of people at Jerusalem at this time, and had they consulted the motions of their own minds or the mere dictates of common sense, without applying to the Saviour, there was every likelihood they would have gone wrong. We stand in need of direction in small things as well as in great concerns, and small things may have connection with things of great importance.

Our Lord then gave the proper direction to such a man, and informed them that a man carrying a pitcher of water would lead

them to the man's house. Small things in the cause of divine providence lead the people of God in the right way. He did not tell the
man's name, and though this circumstance was small, it showed the
wisdom of the Saviour. Had he told his name, this would have given
Judas an opportunity of disturbing the Lord's Supper. Our Lord
knew what was preparing in his heart, and therefore concealed the
man's name, and this should be an example to us. When we suspect
people from unfavourable circumstances in their conduct to be ill-
inclined to religion, we ought to beware of them. And though we
cannot exclude them, we ought not to admit them to the intimacy
that belongs to the people of God. Though our Lord knew that
Judas was a hypocrite and a thief, yet, like a wise man who has a
dishonest servant, of whom himself and others are suspicious, he
does not dismiss him till he proves by his conduct that he is a villain.
But he takes good care that such a servant should not be trusted
with anything of consequence.

Had Judas known where the passover was to be kept, he might have
brought the band of soldiers to the house and prevented the cele-
bration of the Lord's Supper. The Lord therefore wisely concealed
that from him, so that he could not execute his purpose till the work
of God was over.

> Verses 20–21. *Now when the even was come, he sat down with the
> twelve. And as they did eat, he said, Verily I say unto you, that one of
> you shall betray me.*

And in this, the wisdom and patience of our Lord discover themselves. He permits Judas to sit down, though he knew what was in
his heart. He did not exclude Judas till Judas excluded himself. And
this shows us what is the rule proper for churchmen to follow. Sealing ordinances are not to be refused to people, though we suspected
they lived in sin, if we cannot prove our suspicion. We may show
their danger, and give them our best advice agreeably to Scripture.
Even Judas is permitted to sit down with the rest (verse 21), and as
they did eat, he said, 'Verily, I say unto you, that one of you shall
betray me.' The meek and lowly Saviour, we see, had an enemy and

traitor among his domestics [intimate friends]. But the perfidy of the apostate disciple is not unknown to our Lord. He informs them all that he knew this awful fact. He gives the general notice to render Judas inexcusable, or give him time to repent. He does not mention one in particular, for the deed was so base, and the calling of an apostle so honourable, that he spared mentioning names till the thing discovered itself. Had he mentioned Judas by name, such is the boldness of villainy that he might deny the fact. A thief is not clever at his business unless he can boldly deny the theft. We might all have seen such instances. Our Lord does not, therefore, tax him more than one of the rest when he informs them of what would happen. We are by our doctrine to reprove sinners, and hypocrites must be conscious when they are touched. If they do not retrieve [repent], they may see what they have cause to expect.

Verse 22. *And they were exceeding sorrowful, and began every one of them to say unto him, Lord, is it I?*

The information struck them with sorrow and surprise. They did not doubt their Lord and Master; they were too well acquainted with him to suppose that he would say anything but truth. Conscious, however, as they were of the innocence of their own thoughts with respect to this horrid crime, they paid more regard to the declaration of their Lord than to their own hearts. Being some years in his company, they could not be ignorant of the doctrines of Scripture. They had heard of the corruption of human nature and the deceitfulness of the human heart. They did not reply in the language of Hazael of old, 'Is thy servant a dog, that he should do such a thing?'

Though they were strangers to this crime, they could not be ignorant of the evil propensities of sin. Penetrated with humility and sorrow, each of them asks with fear and trembling, is himself to be the person? Now, this may show us the nature of true humility. Their pride does not rise at the idea of such a thought. No, they are rather afraid of themselves. Would any man venture to tell Lot, David, Solomon, or Peter beforehand that they would fall into such sins? Lord, lead us not into temptation, but deliver us from evil and sin.

The knowledge the people of God have of the corruption of the heart makes them walk humbly with their God. Even the holy apostles, who were so eminent in grace, believe the possibility of falling into such a sin as betraying the Saviour of the world, and if the apostles were afraid, who dare be off their guard? Had their fear been of the wrong kind, the Saviour, who often rebuked them for weakness of faith and slavish fear, and guarded them against both, would have now rebuked them also. But he saw that their guarded caution was wholesome for their souls.

Let us not be high-minded, but fear. Holy David fell into uncleanness, wise Solomon committed folly, and the strongest man upon earth was weak as a child when exposed to temptation. They are fools who trust to their own hearts. Great is our need, each and all of us, to keep near the Shepherd of our souls, and depend upon his strength and grace alone for our safety. We have another lesson likewise from the words. The apostles were honest, and wished to be kept from sin, and God took care of them notwithstanding their fears.

Verse 23. *And he answered and said, He that dippeth his hand with me in the dish, the same shall betray me.*

To prevent the anxious and distressing fears of his true disciples, he gives them a sign by which they might be relieved. The apostle John informs us that our Lord gave the bit [morsel] or sop to Judas, and this shows that he sat very near him at table, and therefore that his perfidy and ingratitude were great.

Verse 24. *The Son of man goeth as it is written of him: but woe unto that man by whom the Son of man is betrayed! it had been good for that man if he had not been born.*

He informs us that the Saviour was to suffer for the sins of his people, but that the person who was to deliver him up to death was miserable past expression. He had been happier to be without existence than to exist in misery and pain.

Sinners, we see, can have no excuse for their sins, though they are instrumental in bringing forward the decrees of God. They had no such intention. Nebuchadnezzar gratified his ambition, Judas his covetousness, and the Jewish rulers and teachers their envy and malice, and yet they promoted the decree of God and the salvation of men in the death of Christ.

> Verse 25. *Then Judas, which betrayed him, answered and said, Master, is it I? He said unto him, Thou hast said.*

In these words, we find the true characteristic of hypocrisy. Judas, lest he should be suspected, asked the question likewise, and gives our Lord a title of higher respect (as learned men observe) than any of the rest.

Sycophants give sweeter words than true and genuine friends, and from weak people, who are still more open to flattery, obtain more of their favour. But our Lord knew what was in the heart. He did not trust to profession. He saw the most secret hypocrisy and detected it. He told Judas that his treason was not hid from him. Such, however, was the infatuation and blindness of this unhappy man that, instead of relenting and giving up his wicked design, he hardens himself in his iniquity and persists in his desperate crime. He gives himself up to be ruled by the enemy of his soul in following the corrupt motions of his own covetous heart: such is the motion of sin downward. Behold the fearful end of covetousness.

Practical inferences

1. If there was a traitor and a thief in the family of Christ himself, this should calm the spirits of such of the people of God as meet with such an awful dispensation, and make them submit with patience to their lot. The thought that they have such a domestic may hurt their feelings, and even spoil their freedom. But we see the meek Lamb of God suffer Judas to be in his family, and even admits him to his table.

Our spirits are in danger of being ruffled when we see instances of villainy and boldness in our servants. But let us not lose our self-command, or hurt ourselves for them. Shall we lose our patience because they lost their virtue, honesty and shame? Notwithstanding the impudence and villainy of Judas, we see the calm serenity of Christ. Let us then in such cases imitate his precious example. The presence of Judas at the passover did not spoil the work of God, and why should the like spoil our family worship or our attendance upon duties, public or private? Such things are permitted for our good. The villainy of Judas only hurt himself, but did not affect the other apostles. Let us look up to God.

2. If the apostles were wrong in supporting the opinion of Judas, this should make us very cautious and suspend our judgment in such cases till providence gives further light. If the apostles had some little patience, Judas had showed himself in his proper colours. Let us beg of God to give us patience to wait for light to direct us. Time will bring many things to pass, and will show us whether we are right or wrong in some of our opinions.

3. Lastly, the apostles were afraid of falling into sin, and this is a strong argument for prayer and watchfulness. There are some sins so very enormous that perhaps we think ourselves secure from them. But our security may deceive us, and nothing can effectually secure us but the grace and protection of our great Shepherd. We have need of prayer, and to prayer let us join our own honest endeavours, else we but mock God and hurt our souls. If we are honest in our petitions, God can and will keep us. We know not how far the evil principle within can go, and the dangerous and malignant nature of sin. And however strong our corruptions may be, if we put ourselves under the protection of our Saviour, he will keep us from sin and preserve us to his everlasting kingdom. Let us get our consciences sprinkled with his blood and our souls strengthened with his grace.

May God bless his Word to our souls. AMEN.

Matthew chapter 26: verses 26 to 50

SCRIPTURE informs us that our Lord Jesus Christ came into the world to save lost sinners, and the love which made him undertake this mission never left his heart for one moment. He did not neglect the dearest interests of his people at the time that himself suffered the deepest distress. It was the very night that he was betrayed that he instituted the sacrament of the Supper to be a token of his love.

In the words just now read, there are several things, of which we shall speak a little, and conclude with practical inferences.

Institution of the Lord's Supper

Verses 26–28. And as they were eating, Jesus took bread, and blessed it, and brake it, and gave it to the disciples, and said, Take, eat; this is my body. And he took the cup, and gave thanks, and gave it to them, saying, Drink ye all of it; for this is my blood of the new testament, which is shed for many for the remission of sins.

After the passover, our Lord appointed the sacrament of the Supper to succeed it in the Church. He took bread and brake and blessed it, and gave it to his disciples as a symbol of his broken body. He also took the cup of salvation and ordered all his disciples to drink of it. It was a symbol of his blood, which was shed for many for the remission of sins, and in order to partake properly of this sacred feast, the apostle Paul advises every man to examine himself.

We are to examine ourselves as to our knowledge of this divine mystery, that we may discern the Lord's body. This is not ordinary bread, nor is it an ordinary feast. We are to examine ourselves if we have the marks of true communicants. We ought to have true sorrow

342

towards God, and faith and trust in the Lord Jesus Christ as our Saviour and King.

In primitive times, the deacon, or servant of the Church, cried before the holy communion, 'Holy things to holy persons,' and the presbyter, 'Lift up your hearts.' Instead of giving our Lord the kiss of Judas, we should worship him with the humility of the penitent thief. Judas still continued a thief and went on in a course of sin, and if we do the same, the sacrament will be of no service to us. And though the blood is shed for the remission of sins of many, we cannot expect any benefit if we continue in sin.

Our Lord told that the hand of the person who would betray him was with him on the table. The thief, the heart murderer, the liar, the swearer, the Sabbath-breaker, and the unclean person should think upon this awful scripture and tremble. If such characters approach in their sins, without reformation and without repentance, awful is their condition and fearful will be their end. But if we approach with the full resolution of forsaking all sin in the strength of grace, though our hearts are not as we would wish them, let us put them in our Lord's hands to wash and soften them.

The blood was shed for the remission of sins. Let us look to the blood of Christ in the sacrament. As it was shed for our sins, let us get it applied to our consciences. We are to put the hand of faith upon the head of our sacrifice. As he shed his blood for sinners, let us believe, so as to get the comfort of this truth to our souls. It was shed for many.

Christ is a sufficient sacrifice and a healing fountain, and all are invited to come and be clean. If we only come to the sacrament without coming to Christ, we remain foul. Our great duty, then, is to receive Christ, to receive the atonement. Let us then repent, forsake sin, and believe the gospel. Whether then pride, self-righteousness, or some darling lust impede our faith, let us turn from them, let us look to Christ, that we may obtain the pardon of sin. There is pardon here for the greatest of sins. If we have faith to believe and resolution to forsake them, we may here get their pardon sealed in the blood of Christ.

Verse 29. *But I say unto you, I will not drink henceforth of this fruit of the vine, until that day when I drink it new with you in my Father's kingdom.*

After our Lord's resurrection, he continued with his disciples forty days, and during that time it is very likely that he gave the sacrament of the Supper to them. As he ate and drank with them, and instructed them in things pertaining to the kingdom of God, we may naturally think that he gave the symbols of the bread of life and the cup of salvation to his followers. Other divines, however, are of opinion that he speaks of the joys of the kingdom of heaven under this similitude. The kingdom of heaven, or paradise of God, is truly a feast, and brings his people to the house of wine.

I can see no harm though we understand the words in both these views, or if we choose to follow one of the two opinions, we cannot be wrong in either. We have the natural meaning of the fruit of the vine if we understand it of the sacrament given on earth as the beginning of his kingdom. If we understand it as the spiritual meaning, it signifies the joyful meeting our Lord had with his disciples in his heavenly kingdom. And he had a taste of these joys when he gave them the first sacrament of the Supper upon earth.

Jesus foretells Peter's denial

Verse 30. *And when they had sung an hymn, they went out into the mount of Olives.*

It seems, then, the work of God was concluded by a psalm or hymn. The Jews used to sing the great hymn or Hallelujah at the feast of passover, and it is very likely that our Lord sang these Psalms from 113 to 118 upon this occasion. But though our Lord and his disciples were now in the joys and triumphs of faith, yet trouble is near. The Christian life is but a warfare at best. We must follow the example of our Lord. Though it was now long of the night, he went to the Mount of Olives. He knew well the things that were going on, and prepares himself for suffering. He did not wish to give disturbance to the house in which he lodged, and therefore removed first to the Mount of Olives, and then to Gethsemane. He did not wish to be apprehended in the house, and therefore retired to the garden.

Verse 31. *Then saith Jesus unto them, All ye shall be offended because of me this night: for it is written, I will smite the shepherd, and the sheep of the flock shall be scattered abroad.*

After joy, people may prepare for some temptation, and the temptation may be sore. The disciples of Christ were now happy with their Lord and Master, and were under no apprehension that danger was so very near. Our Lord knew, and therefore forewarned them. If we have faith, it will be tried, and sometimes the trial will be great. And though God's people will come off conquerors at last, it often happens that they get wounds in the day of battle.

All the disciples lose their courage this night, forsake their Lord and flee, and then Peter, the most courageous of them all, is overcome by a servant girl. And this shows what the best would come to if not supported by grace. Well may we all pray, 'Lead us not into temptation.' The cause of their fall or offence was the smiting of the shepherd. There was a temporary suspension of their faith, hope, and courage when they saw the approaching sufferings of their Lord.

Verse 32. *But after I am risen again, I will go before you into Galilee.*

Though the sheep were scattered, yet, like a true shepherd, he gathered them again to the fold. He promises here that after his resurrection he would meet them in Galilee, where a number of his followers were. And we are expressly told that he met them in a mountain in Galilee, and it is very likely it was Mount Tabor, which is supposed to be the Mountain of Transfiguration. Though he met some of them first in Judaea to settle their wavering faith, it was in

Galilee that he gave the most conspicuous view of himself, and continued longer with them.

Galilee, it seems, had more Christians in proportion than other parts of Palestine, and it was here he promised to meet and comfort them. He had, it would appear, more friends and fewer enemies in Galilee than in Judaea. His followers might have more leisure and be in less danger here from persecution and disturbance. And when we expect to meet the Lord in the mount, we ought to consult himself. If we consult flesh and blood in things belonging to God, we are in danger of going wrong. The more we seek his own glory, the more we are sure of comfort.

> Verses 33–35. *Peter answered and said unto him, Though all men shall be offended because of thee, yet will I never be offended. Jesus said unto him, Verily I say unto thee, That this night, before the cock crow, thou shalt deny me thrice. Peter said unto him, Though I should die with thee, yet will I not deny thee. Likewise also said all the disciples.*

In these remarkable words, we see the firm and honest resolution of the disciples of Christ. They were at this time warm with his love, and had been lately partakers of his table. But however sincere their intentions were, they were yet strangers to their own hearts and to the power of inward corruption and outward temptation. Peter, in particular, professes his resolution: than deny him, rather to suffer death. The rest, equally honest and sincere, make the same profession. Our Lord, however, knew what he said, for he foresaw their weakness in the hour of trial. To Peter, who was more sanguine than the rest, he prophesies a fall.

The design of all God's dispensations is to cure his people of their particular corruptions. The good apostle had pride, and he was permitted to fall, in order to humble him all his days. The rest forsook him, and this showed them their own weakness and the need they all had to trust more in Christ than in their own resolutions, however true and honest they were. And this history may teach us the useful lesson of humility, self-denial and watchfulness. Lord, guide us by thy grace and keep us near thyself.

Jesus prays in Gethsemane

Verse 36. *Then cometh Jesus with them unto a place called Gethsemane, and saith unto the disciples, Sit ye here, while I go and pray yonder.*

After continuing with his disciples some little time on the Mount of Olives, he led them to the garden of Gethsemane, which lay at the foot of the hill. He knew what was approaching, and to prepare himself for his sufferings, he ordered them to sit where they were while he retired to pray.

The apostle to the Hebrews and Luke inform us what kind of prayer this was. It was strong crying and tears, attended with a bloody sweat and inexpressible agony. His distress was so great that an angel from heaven was sent to strengthen his human nature, which was now like to faint under his sufferings. And when his sufferings came such a length that his holy human nature stood in need even of comfort from others, he took some of his disciples to be witnesses of his agony.

Verses 37–38. *And he took with him Peter and the two sons of Zebedee, and began to be sorrowful and very heavy. Then saith he unto them, My soul is exceeding sorrowful, even unto death: tarry ye here, and watch with me.*

He chose three to be witnesses of his agony, and no doubt he knew which of the apostles were the fittest for this purpose. His soul was now in deep distress, and he concealed from the other apostles the situation he was in. Likely it is that their minds were not strong enough to bear such a weight. He was true God, and now he shows himself to be true man, with all the infirmities of sinless human nature. Though he was the Son of God, he must have a human nature to suffer in for his people. And when the most awful crisis of his sufferings begins, he says, 'My soul is exceeding sorrowful, even unto death.'

And now, it may be asked, what ailed the Saviour? It surely could not be the prospect of his bodily sufferings and death. Many of the martyrs rejoiced when they embraced the stake. It was undoubtedly the sufferings of his soul, when he made it an offering for sin. Justice arrested him, and he had to wrestle with and endure the wrath of God. His soul was exceeding sorrowful, even unto death. And no wonder! He bore the weight of all the sins of his people. And if the sins of one man will make him miserable for ever, is it a wonder that the sins of many ten thousands make our Saviour to complain.

There was no visible cause to bring such a confession from his sacred lips. He was not yet delivered into the hands of sinners. His sufferings oftener than once brought him to his knees, and the agony of his soul brought a bloody sweat upon his body. And the conflict was so strong that, when he first tasted the bitter cup, he felt a reluctance to drink the whole. We read that he was delivered up by the Holy Ghost for forty days to be tempted of the devil. He does not demur or stagger at the prospect of the trial, for he knew he would come off conqueror. And we may well believe that all that men and devils could do to him would not make him utter such a complaint. He stood in our room, and therefore had to bear the wrath of incensed omnipotence.

Verse 39. *And he went a little further, and fell on his face, and prayed, saying, O my Father, if it be possible, let this cup pass from me: nevertheless not as I will, but as thou wilt.*

The great Redeemer knew the business that brought him to the world, and that God had provided him a soul and body in which he was to suffer. In the 17th chapter of John, he prays the Father to glorify him with the glory he had with him before the world was. He speaks there as the Word that was with him from all eternity, but in the words just read, he speaks in his sinless human nature. He took our nature, free from sin, but though free from sin, he had an aversion from pain and punishment. And surely it was not ordinary pain or punishment that would make him talk in this emphatic strain.

We have, then, cause to believe it was not what he suffered in the body he deprecates. He prays, if it were possible to save the human race some other way, that God would do so, but corrects his holy human will that flees from pain and submits to the divine will. These may convince us how great were his sufferings. We cannot doubt but he dreaded something more than his bodily passion.

Verses 40–41. *And he cometh unto the disciples, and findeth them asleep, and saith unto Peter, What, could ye not watch with me one hour? Watch and pray, that ye enter not into temptation: the spirit indeed is willing, but the flesh is weak.*

In every view, it is a truth that he trod the winepress alone, and of the people there was none with him. Notwithstanding the professions of his apostles a little ago, he finds them now asleep. He desired them to watch with him, and as the language of Peter was stronger than that of any of the rest, he speaks to him in particular. He renews his advice: 'Watch and pray, that ye enter not into temptation.' But as he knew human nature, he excuses them by acknowledging that, though the spirit is willing, the flesh is weak. Our Lord saw danger near, and therefore desired them to watch and pray, and if they had followed the advice and example of their Master, there is cause to believe they would be kept from sin.

It is the opinion of some divines that the sleep that fell upon the apostles at this time proceeded from the agency of the spirits of darkness. Small as the comfort was of seeing the apostles awake and speaking to him, our Lord did not enjoy it in this hour of darkness.

Verses 42–44. *He went away again the second time, and prayed, saying, O my Father, if this cup may not pass away from me, except I drink it, thy will be done. And he came and found them asleep again: for their eyes were heavy. And he left them, and went away again, and prayed the third time, saying the same words.*

Though his apostles were asleep, our Lord was awake and suffering. We cannot account for these strong petitions in any other way than by supposing he speaks of the suffering of his soul. And is this the prayer of the head of the Church, the prayer of him who came to seek and save lost sinners? It is, and this shows that he was truly man. He proved himself to be more than man, and will do so soon by his resurrection. But he must be like his people, and feel like a faithful High Priest, as they do.

And this shows us in what manner God answers the prayers of his people. He gives what is best for them. He gave Christ's human nature strength to bear his sufferings, but did not remove the cup. He strengthened Paul to bear, but did not remove the thorn. And in this way, all the prayers of his people will be heard.

> Verses 45–46. *Then cometh he to his disciples, and saith unto them, Sleep on now, and take your rest: behold, the hour is at hand, and the Son of man is betrayed into the hands of sinners. Rise, let us be going: behold, he is at hand that doth betray me.*

He had desired them to watch on their own account. He knew the danger to which they were exposed. He now informs them that the danger is near, and tells them what it was, so that after hearing it, they might make their choice, either to sleep, or arise and go and meet their and his enemies.

The betrayal and arrest of Jesus

> Verses 47–50. *And while he yet spake, lo, Judas, one of the twelve, came, and with him a great multitude with swords and staves, from the chief priests and elders of the people. Now he that betrayed him gave them a sign, saying, Whomsoever I shall kiss, that same is he: hold him fast. And forthwith he came to Jesus, and said, Hail, master; and kissed him. And Jesus said unto him, Friend, wherefore art thou come? Then came they, and laid hands on Jesus, and took him.*

While the disciples were sleeping securely, our Lord was praying. In consequence of his prayers, his human nature is strengthened to bear his sufferings, which were now very near. An apostate disciple betrays him to his enemies, and betrays him by a sign of love. He kissed him, and the Lord bore it with his usual meekness, but at the same time upbraids his perfidy and hypocrisy.

Practical inferences

We shall now conclude with some practical inferences.

1. First, here we may perceive the wonderful love of Christ to his people. He did not forget them when his own state was lowest. He remembered them when his sufferings were at their greatest height, and if he loved us, we ought also to love him. Our love to him will show itself if we forsake sin and follow his holy footsteps. If we come to him, we need not doubt his love. Let us forsake our lusts and idols, and this will prove to our own hearts that our faith is sincere. And if we wish to repent, he is exalted a Prince to give this grace to those who sincerely ask. He waited to be gracious, and our scarlet and crimson sins he is willing to forgive upon our repentance. And though sin is riveted to our nature, his blood can cleanse and his Spirit can work a radical cure. Let us taste his love, and this will cast out the love of sin, slavish fear, and every inordinate lust and passion.

2. If Christ suffered, we may hence conclude what they have cause to expect who continue in sin. It is the doctrine of Christ himself: if these things are done to the green tree, what has the dry and barren tree to expect? Vengeance will pursue sin. We have our share of it, and spiritual wisdom will direct us to flee to the city of refuge. If people slight the remedy, they must die in their sins.

3. Lastly, we see the awful end of the religion of the covetous. Judas sells and betrays Christ for money. Let every man examine whether there is a Judas in his own heart. You say you would not betray or sell Christ. Take care, then, that you do not harbour his enemy. If

you indulge sin and lust of any kind, it will eat out the life of your profession. Come, then, with your sins to Christ to get them crucified.

May God bless his Word. AMEN.

Matthew chapter 26: verses 51 to 75

THE blessed Saviour is now delivered up to the hands of his enemies, and the meek Lamb of God is taken, that he might be offered up as a sacrifice for the sins of his people. And now we may stand a moment and behold with amazement the calm dignity with which he meets his fate.

His behaviour upon this trying occasion is marked with his usual humility and resignation. But he has now a different part to act, and he never before appeared so great. Formerly he appeared as a prophet and teacher in Israel; he is now to enter upon his office as High Priest, and assert his right as a king and conqueror. But as his kingdom was not of this world, the weapons of his warfare were not carnal, but spiritual. He appears alone upon the field. Men and devils and the justice of God stand in battle array against him. Without dismay in his countenance, without an ill-natured or angry sentiment in his heart, the great conqueror stands alone in the fight. But we shall have a more clear view of the great hero by following him through all the parts of his sufferings, and explaining the words as they stand in order.

The high priest's servant smitten by Peter

Verse 51. *And, behold, one of them which were with Jesus stretched out his hand, and drew his sword, and struck a servant of the high priest's, and smote off his ear.*

The wisdom of God saw meet that four men should write the history of the gospel, and what is wanting in one is made up in another. John informs us it was Peter who cut off the ear of the high priest's servant. He had promised fervently to his Lord and Master that he would follow him to death. Actuated therefore by love and zeal for his cause, he draws his sword and is determined to fight. But though attached to his Master, he did not take the proper way to show his love. Instead of consulting his Lord, he consulted the impulse of his own temper, and suddenly draws his sword, and this may furnish us a lesson. Though Peter loved his Lord and Master, it does not therefore follow that he acted right. There are many pious people, of whose sincerity and grace we cannot entertain a doubt, and yet some part of their conduct, arising from wrong views of religion, certainly merits blame. But let us not censure their conduct harshly. The great apostle fell, and so may others.

> Verses 52–54. *Then said Jesus unto him, Put up again thy sword into his place: for all they that take the sword shall perish with the sword. Thinkest thou that I cannot now pray to my Father, and he shall presently give me more than twelve legions of angels? But how then shall the scriptures be fulfilled, that thus it must be?*

Though our Lord knew that Peter loved him, yet he rebukes him for the method he took to show his love. Peter was but a private character, and therefore revenge does not belong to him.

Self-defence is not here forbidden, but when a man is arrested by those having authority, however ill they may employ it, we are not to rebel. The soldiers had authority from the high priests and the Roman governor, and though they abused this authority to the worst of purposes by destroying the life of an innocent person, yet he gave Peter to understand that he must not resist. His drawing of the sword could be of no service. In such cases, those who have recourse to force generally perish with the sword. But he informs him that he could easily defend himself if that had been for the glory of God, for he could command presently more than twelve legions of angels to rescue him. And this was a force more than sufficient to destroy all the powers of the Jews and Romans. If one angel in one night destroyed 185,000 of the Assyrians, what would upward of 80,000 angels do if they got permission? They would in a moment destroy all the enemies of Christ, root and branch.

But if this had happened, the end of his coming into the world had been defeated, and all the ancient prophecies had proved delusion. And however precious the life of Christ was, the truth and the glory of God are still more precious, and these required that his soul must be an offering for sin. The Scriptures foretell that he must suffer, and therefore every circumstance in his life and death must infallibly happen. The end of his coming into the world was that he might lay down his life for the sins of his people. The glory of God in the display of his attributes, as well as the salvation of men, required that he should suffer.

To check the impetuosity of Peter's temper and reconcile him to this event, he shows him the necessity of accomplishing the prophecies of Scripture, to which it seems hitherto he had been a stranger. Peter, like the rest of his nation, had been dreaming of the temporal kingdom of Messiah. But his kingdom was not of this world, and he must suffer before he can reign. Peter is an emblem of all the people of God. They are often seeking happiness in this life, and even dreaming of a heaven beneath the skies. To undeceive them in this respect, therefore, they meet with dispensations as unexpected and as contrary to their inclinations as the death and sufferings of Christ were to the holy apostle. The death of Christ was a grievous dispensation to him, and yet it was the beginning of his hope and the foundation of his happiness.

We seek happiness, and we often expect that God would give us it in our own way. There is death brought upon our expectations, and we find that at last our disappointments are the gracious appointments of heaven. We look for temporal and spiritual happiness to flow to us agreeably to our own wishes. It is our mercy that we are disappointed.

The Israelites wished to go by a shorter way through the wilderness to Canaan, and the apostles looked for grandeur and riches under the reign of Messiah. But God in mercy disappointed their hopes. Not so their prayers, for the one came in God's good time to the promised land, and the others got spiritual riches and the highest seats in the kingdom of heaven. Let it then be our business to seek the glory of God, our own salvation, and the accomplishment of Scripture.

Luke informs us that our Lord touched the ear of the high priest's servant, and instantly healed him, and he did this that the good cause might not suffer reproach, and to defend his poor servant. Now, this circumstance may show us that when people have truly the glory of God in view, and are actuated by love to Christ, that himself will appear for them at last. It does happen, and it often did happen, that people went beyond the line of duty in the cause of Christ. In such cases, God will pity and pardon the errors of his people, and always defend his own cause. And though men may punish and blame them, the Saviour, who searches the heart, will approve their motives and pardon what is amiss. Our duty is to consult the Word, and follow the saints only as far as they follow Christ.

Christ deserted by his disciples

Verses 55–56. *In that same hour said Jesus to the multitudes, Are ye come out as against a thief with swords and staves for to take me? I sat daily with you teaching in the temple, and ye laid no hold on me. But all this was done, that the scriptures of the prophets might be fulfilled. Then all the disciples forsook him, and fled.*

But though our Lord is the meek Lamb of God, he is sensible of [he felt] the injury, of the great indignity they offered him. Though he was a public teacher in Israel, he always appeared as a poor man, without pomp or parade, without arms, and without earthly power.

There was no necessity to bring such a company of men in order to apprehend him. He appeals to the consciences of his enemies and tells them he often taught in the temple. They heard his doctrine and witnessed his miracles, and they even recently witnessed a most astonishing miracle in curing the servant of the high priest. This must convince them that the person they had to deal with was more than man, and it is really astonishing how far prejudice, malice, and hardness of heart had blinded their eyes. They saw so much innocence, so much sweetness, so much heavenliness, so much power and dignity in this man, that it is surprising they apprehended him. The way to account for it is that the Scriptures must be fulfilled. They were hardened in their sins, and this rendered them fit instruments for bringing about the deepest tragedies. God foresaw and foretold this, and it infallibly must happen.

But if the death of Christ must happen, will not this excuse the persons who brought about that event? By no means. They were free agents, and were agitated by their lusts and passions. Nebuchadnezzar, Alexander and Caesar were free agents, and fit instruments in the hand of God in punishing wicked nations. But God had no hand in their sins. In like manner, the Jews are instrumental in the death of Christ, though it is decreed and predetermined by God. But how God decrees and overrules the sinful actions of men without having any hand in their sins is a question too deep for any finite intellect till God is pleased to make the doctrine plain. And this will happen in the land of light and vision.

And when the disciples saw their Lord and Master apprehended, instead of standing by their resolutions and promise, they all forsook him and fled. This shows us the weakness of human nature at best. We may well exclaim, with the Psalmist upon another occasion, 'Lord, what is man?' The slavish fear of man which bringeth a snare, and their own fear, made them desert the friend whom they loved as their own souls.

We may behold this sight with admiration [wonder], with love, and with pity. Let us not, however, be severe in our animadversions [criticisms] upon their conduct. What would ourselves do in similar circumstances? It was, however, but a temporary suspension of the acting of that divine principle of love in their souls. Afterwards we find that they acted a bold and intrepid part, and that no threats or terrors could tempt them to deviate from their duty or desert their crucified Master's cause.

We see here, as in a glass [mirror], our own weakness and our need of constant supplies from the fulness of our Redeemer. He promises grace, and that our strength shall be adequate to our day. He will not forsake us.

Christ in the high priest's palace

Verse 57. And they that had laid hold on Jesus led him away to Caiaphas the high priest, where the scribes and the elders were assembled.

Conscious as the high priest and Jewish rulers were of the iniquity of the wicked scheme they had in hand, they wished to give the colour of law to their proceedings. Accordingly, they form a court and cite witnesses. But however regular their proceedings were, they knew they were going to put an innocent person to death.

Wickedness armed with power can do a great deal to establish iniquity and crush the innocent. An unjust judge is never at a loss, because the instruments he employs are equally base with himself. He promotes his own cause, and not the cause of virtue and religion. Jezebel is determined to have the life of Naboth. For this purpose, she procured a worthless court and wicked witnesses. The Jewish rulers are determined to put Christ to death. They stick at nothing to carry their point. They accuse him of blasphemy against God and treason against the emperor. And though they can prove none of their charges, they extort sentence of death from the terrified mind of Pilate.

Verse 58. But Peter followed him afar off unto the high priest's palace, and went in, and sat with the servants, to see the end.

Some may have blamed Peter for venturing into the palace, and thus exposing himself to his enemies. And true it is that the company of the wicked has been often a snare to the souls of good men. Bad company has often robbed good Christians of their comforts and exposed them to temptation and sin. And this was the case with the apostle. But though he was permitted to fall into sin, to humble him all his days, we have cause to believe it was not idle curiosity that brought him to the palace at this time. He loved his Lord and Master, and wished to know his fate. He did not even suspect that there was any danger or that he would be taken notice of. He was introduced by the apostle John, and thought himself safe in his company. But there is danger often when we least expect it. The girl who opened the door, by the question she asked and the words she spoke, seemed to recognise his features, and betrayed him into sin. How weak and frail are the resolutions of the best!

> Verses 59–61. *Now the chief priests, and elders, and all the council, sought false witness against Jesus, to put him to death; but found none: yea, though many false witnesses came, yet found they none. At the last came two false witnesses, and said, This fellow said, I am able to destroy the temple of God, and to build it in three days.*

Our Lord was a man of consummate holiness and purity. His character was so unsullied that he could ask the Jews, who were ready to catch and calumniate, 'Which of you can convince me of sin?' And if there had been any blemish in his life, they were ready to detect and spread the same. It was impossible that they could hurt him by truth.

The high priest and the council knew this, and therefore have recourse to lies. They were well aware that honest men would never accuse Jesus of Nazareth of any crime. Such persons were not fit for their purpose, and they would not employ them. They sought for false witnesses, but could not find any fit for this purpose. Not but they found characters base and worthless enough to enter into their views. But though they were willing, they were not able to fabricate anything that could hurt him. Their lies and falsehood were so full of absurdity and contradiction that they could not agree together. In telling their stories, the one contradicted the evidence of the other. And this is always the character of liars.

Truth is uniform and consistent. But the liar is confused in his mind, and still varying in his answers. Conscious that he has told lies when he is cross-examined, and examined over again and asked new questions, he must have recourse to a new set of lies to keep the former in countenance, and the end generally is that the fabric he has been thus building tumbles down about his ears and buries him in confusion and shame. Such was the fate of the enemies of Christ. Their employers were ashamed of the instruments they used, and as they could not set up a lie to the purpose, they were obliged to lay them aside as useless.

At last, there came two false witnesses, alleging that they heard him declare he could destroy the temple of God and build it in three days. But it was well known that our Lord taught by parables. The priests, the scribes, and elders, and the nation in general knew his manner of teaching. It is well known that the Eastern authors delight in this figurative mode of speaking and writing. He said many things in his doctrine which they knew could not be understood literally. He taught them that he was the Son of God, and as the presence of God was in the temple of Jerusalem, it now tabernacled in his person. He did not say that he would destroy the temple of Jerusalem, but he told the Jews that though they would destroy the temple of his body, he would build it in three days, and he did so accordingly. But even the manner in which they told this story overthrew their testimony, for they did not agree together: all they could have to say against him was by mentioning his parabolical expression, which they either misunderstood or grossly misapplied. They might likewise accuse him for saying he was the manna that descended from heaven, and that his flesh and blood were meat and drink, which people must eat and drink that they might have life.

These and many such expressions were fresh in everyone's memory, and could never be cause of condemnation and death. In every country where regard is had to justice and truth, to humanity and candour, a teacher, if accused of erroneous doctrine, is allowed to justify and defend his opinions if they are agreeable to the Word of God. If he is accused of a capital crime, he is permitted to defend himself either personally or by counsel, as he thinks best for his purpose. But Christ had to do with unjust judges and a partial [biased] jury. He knew that their minds were steeled with prejudice and malice, and therefore did not think it worth his while to make any defence before them. He knew they would not give him a candid hearing, or acquit him and let him go.

Verse 62. *And the high priest arose, and said unto him, Answerest thou nothing? What is it which these witness against thee?*

The high priest, to conceal the malice and wickedness that lurk in his heart, puts on the appearance of candour and impartiality. He pretends to feel for the state of the prisoner, and gives him, in appearance, an opportunity to defend himself. Hypocrisy is never so odious as when it puts on the semblance of friendship, virtue, or religion.

Verse 63. *But Jesus held his peace. And the high priest answered and said unto him, I adjure thee by the living God, that thou tell us whether thou be the Christ, the Son of God.*

The Saviour still continues silent, and this answers to an old prophecy concerning him: 'He is brought as a lamb to the slaughter, and as a sheep before her shearers is dumb, so he openeth not his mouth.'

There were two causes of our Lord's silence at this time. Luke informs us that he would not plead his innocence or make any defence, because they were determined not to believe or let him go. Now, when a prisoner is in such a predicament, a formal defence would be vain. His judges and accusers were as much convinced of his innocence as any speech could convince them. He did not therefore speak, where speaking could answer no end. But there was another cause of his silence. Though he could clear himself before men of any positive crime and could plead innocence, yet he considered himself as before a higher tribunal. He was innocent in himself, but he stood charged with the guilt of all his people, and therefore was dumb before his accusers.

The high priest was very conscious of the purity of his spotless life, and therefore reserves his great charge for the last, and asks a question, by which he would give sentence against himself by the confession of his own mouth. He bids him declare solemnly upon oath whether he was Christ, the Son of God. The Jews did not believe he was the Messiah, and therefore the question is a snare for his life.

Verse 64. *Jesus saith unto him, Thou hast said: nevertheless I say unto you, Hereafter shall ye see the Son of man sitting on the right hand of power, and coming in the clouds of heaven.*

As our Lord was solemnly charged, in name of the living God, to tell the truth and nothing but the truth, he declares before witnesses that he was the Messiah, and that he was the Son of God, who would hereafter appear in the clouds and judge the world.

Verses 65–66. *Then the high priest rent his clothes, saying, He hath spoken blasphemy; what further need have we of witnesses? behold, now ye have heard his blasphemy. What think ye? They answered and said, He is guilty of death.*

A declaration so solemn as that made by our Lord deserved a serious hearing. This, however, he does not obtain, for they all accuse him of blasphemy and adjudge him to death all at once. But if he who was the true man deserved death for blasphemy in calling himself the Son of God, what did the man who spoke to Abraham deserve, for we find that the father of the faithful calls him Lord, and the man who spoke to him in the original language is denominated Jehovah? And how did the good man know that the person who spoke to him was God Almighty in a human form? He must have known it either by his telling him so, or by some miracle wrought to convince him. Now, Abraham believed all at once, for he saw by faith God in the man. He did not, like the high priest, rend his clothes and accuse him of blasphemy.

Now, the miracles our Lord wrought to convince the Jewish nation that God appeared in a human form as he did to Abraham were greater than anything done to convince the Old Testament saints. In spite of all that they saw and heard, they sentence him to death, and are determined to reject every evidence. This truth that God did appear in a human form was not more incomprehensible to them than it was to Abraham, and yet when it was declared to them upon oath by a man that never told a lie, they refuse his witness, and condemn him to death besides.

Verses 67–68. Then did they spit in his face, and buffeted him; and others smote him with the palms of their hands, saying, Prophesy unto us, thou Christ, Who is he that smote thee?

Their treatment of Christ from first to last is not only unjust, but also inhuman. Even sympathy and humanity are due to the greatest criminals. But what belongs to such is refused to the Prince of Peace and Lord of glory. As if the punishment of the cross had not been sufficient, they abuse him with spittle and insult him with cruel mocking. They ridicule his prophetic office, and with cruel insult ask him who smote him. If they looked upon him as a person of weak intellect, who assumed to himself divine honour, they ought to pity and dismiss him. Such persons, if let alone, generally fall into oblivion, if not contempt. If they suspect him of deeper designs, they ought at least to lead a proof and convict him of treason. This, however, they could not do, for he told them that he had a spiritual kingdom, and consequently did not say he was an earthly king.

It is true he called himself Messiah and the Son of God. But this is the unanimous language of the prophets. And whether the epithets they bestow upon the person who was to come apply to Jesus of Nazareth or not, they apply to some man. If our Lord was guilty of blasphemy, the Messiah, whatever time he appears, must be guilty of the same, for the child mentioned in Micah and Isaiah is the Mighty God, and had his existence from the days of eternity.

That God and man should meet in one person is a truth too deep for the greatest effort of human reason to fathom or comprehend. But though we cannot comprehend, we are required to believe. And our belief is not a blind assent: it is a natural conviction. We believe an incomprehensible truth because God has revealed it and proved it by the most astonishing miracles. They were convinced of the purity of his life; they saw and heard his work. And when a man of such character and such credentials appeared before them, they were utterly inexcusable that did not give him a candid hearing. Instead of this, they use him with inhuman barbarity.

The fall and repentance of Peter

Verses 69–75. *Now Peter sat without in the palace: and a damsel came unto him, saying, Thou also wast with Jesus of Galilee. But he denied before them all, saying, I know not what thou sayest. And when he was gone out into the porch, another maid saw him, and said unto them that were there, This fellow was also with Jesus of Nazareth. And again he denied with an oath, I do not know the man. And after a while came unto him they that stood by, and said to Peter, Surely thou also art one of them; for thy speech bewrayeth thee. Then began he to curse and to swear, saying, I know not the man. And immediately the cock crew. And Peter remembered the word of Jesus, which said unto him, Before the cock crow, thou shalt deny me thrice. And he went out, and wept bitterly*

In these words, we have a history of the fall and repentance of the apostle Peter. We may see here as in a glass the weakness of human nature, and the frailty of the strongest vows unless assisted by divine grace.

Peter is allowed to fall for several wise reasons. He is permitted to fall, to show himself and succeeding generations the folly of trusting to our own strength. He is permitted to fall, to show the faithfulness of God's promises, notwithstanding the sins of his people; to show also the certainty of perseverance in those who have honest hearts. He is permitted to fall, to show God's readiness to pity and pardon all true penitents, and make them taste of his love. Come, see and believe.

Lastly, among other causes, he is permitted to fall, to expose the pretence to infallibility in those who call themselves his successors. There was none of the holy apostles could lay less claim to infallibility than Peter, and surely there never were clergymen fell into greater errors and sins than his pretended successors: in anything we cannot call them his successors, except in his falls.

Practical inferences

I conclude with some practical inferences.

1. First, in the profession and conduct of Peter, from first to last, we read a lesson of humility. 'Let him who thinketh he standeth take heed lest he fall.' If Peter fell, we have cause to pray, 'Lord, lead us not into temptation.' This is a loud call to us to put ourselves under the protection of the great Shepherd of Israel. And if we do so, though our grace is much weaker than that of the apostle, God is able to keep us from falling, and he will do so if we trust in him and keep in the path of duty. His everlasting arms can protect us from inward and outward temptation to sin.

2. Second, in these words, we see the awful character of liars. A liar never spares any character, whether sacred or profane. Even Christ himself cannot escape their malignant tongues. False witnesses traduce his character in order to put him to death, and to this day, liars oppose his cause and calumniate his people. And what will be given to the false tongue? Burning coals of juniper, and their portion in the lake that burneth with fire and brimstone, which is the second death.

3. Third, are we offended with those who abused our Lord's face with spitting? We look with horror on them who spat in his face and mocked him, saying unto him, 'Prophesy unto us, thou Christ, Who smote thee?' Have you a curiosity to see people guilty of this very sin under the clear light of the gospel? Wait, then, some minutes after sermon, in the kirkyard of this parish, and you will see that awful sight.

4. Lastly, we all know that an oath determines every controversy. Jesus Christ has declared upon oath before witnesses that he was

the Son of God. And if he was, how awful is the condition of all those who despise and reject his gospel! What proof do you want of this truth? You have prophecy and miracles, and a succession of faithful witnesses preaching the gospel since the days of the apostles. You have also a constant return of the day in which he rose from the dead once in seven days. And if you reject these evidences, how can you escape the wrath of the Lamb? You must rank with his friends or enemies. This is the accepted time. Oh then, believe his gospel and obey his laws.

Matthew chapter 27: verses 1 to 10

I N the former chapter we find that the high priests and elders had condemned Christ to death by an unjust sentence, and now they lead him to Pontius Pilate, the Roman governor.

Christ delivered to Pilate

Verses 1–2. When the morning was come, all the chief priests and elders of the people took counsel against Jesus to put him to death: and when they had bound him, they led him away, and delivered him to Pontius Pilate the governor.

Some time before this, the sceptre departed from Judah, and all the power of life and death was taken from the Sanhedrin. They were willing, but were not able by any judicial act of their own to put him to death. It seems they took counsel about their bloody resolution. But what counsel was necessary? If he was guilty, the thing would speak for itself. One would think there was no necessity for deliberation in the case. When a criminal is convicted, the consciences of mankind are satisfied about the justice of the sentence. But it seems they were afraid of something. They therefore bind him and bring him to Pontius Pilate, the governor. They wish to give their malice and wickedness the appearance of law and justice. They trump up a story of sedition and blasphemy, and terrify Pilate to give sentence, though convinced of his innocence.

The suicide of Judas

Verses 3–5. Then Judas, which had betrayed him, when he saw that he was condemned, repented himself, and brought again the thirty pieces of silver to the chief priests and elders, saying, I have sinned in that I have betrayed the innocent blood. And they said, What is that to us? see thou to that. And he cast down the pieces of silver in the temple, and departed, and went and hanged himself.

In these awful words we have one testimony, and though it comes from the mouth of an enemy, it is equal to a thousand witnesses to prove the innocence of the precious Saviour. The unhappy man who betrayed him, stung by the reproaches of his own conscience and lashed by the tumult of his angry thoughts, comes before the Sanhedrin to make his confession. He now saw the horrid crime of which he was guilty, and in this distracted state of mind throws the money at their feet. It is said that he repented—that is, he had the first part of repentance, a sense of guilt. But, alas, he did not proceed further. He is abandoned by God to commit a still greater crime.

Why, poor, unhappy Judas, did you not throw yourself at the feet of your much-injured Master, and implore his pardon? Instead of this, he goes and becomes his own executioner. Had he waited four or five days with patience under his terrors till the Lord rose from the dead, who knows what would have happened? But we see in this awful example the end of the sin of covetousness.

Judas is a beacon and a pillar of salt to sinners. We may see the danger that people are in who get repeated warnings. He is called a devil long before now, and this is a proof he was indulging sin unknown to others, though it was visible to the divine Saviour. And you may see by the terrible story what may possibly be your fate if you continue in sin. You have got warning much oftener than Judas did of the danger of Sabbath-breaking, covetousness, uncleanness, lying, and other sins. Your consciences are dead, but they must awake sooner or later, and if you continue to rebel against the Word of God and your own consciences, we cannot promise but your latter end may be like Judas. And when your consciences awaken after a long course of sin, the devil may be permitted to tempt you to despair, so that you may either hang or drown yourselves. Remember, you got warning.

Now, if the young and old sinners that frequent this house are not in some sense even worse than Judas himself, they ought to take warning. Indeed, we read in the 109th Psalm that Judas had children, and it is probable that Balaam had children also (Psalm 109:10). And from the conduct of some of my hearers, a person would be led to suspect that the blood of Judas and Balaam was running in their veins. They were incorrigible sinners: they got warning, they sinned against the light, and they died before their time. Oh, ye sinners of Lochcarron and Kishorn, do ye mean to follow their example? Whether these men were your predecessors according to the flesh, we cannot say, but we can prove that some of you are their true and genuine spiritual offspring.

We see also by the story that some sinners must be made examples. The justice, the truth, and the goodness of God require this. This example was necessary at the time to clear the character of Christ. The Sanhedrin and the Jews in general, in spite of them, had two witnesses that bore witness to the innocence of our Lord, whom they unjustly put to death. The witnesses are Judas and Pilate. And as they were enemies, their united testimony must sound loud in the ears of the Jewish rulers. The very argument they brought against Christ before Pilate, that he was the Son of God, terrified him still more than he was before. His miracles prove that he could not be an impostor or have intercourse with impure spirits. The holiness of his life refuted the calumny. His saying, therefore, that he was the Son of God, when they saw the works of God, should procure the more credit to his doctrine. And if the Sanhedrin and Jewish nation are spared for many years, it is to render them at last signal examples of divine vengeance.

We see likewise here the perverseness of the Jewish Sanhedrin. Instead of taking warning from the example of Judas and giving up their intended sin, they harden themselves in their wickedness. And this is the case with sinners to this day. The dying agonies of their companions in iniquity do not frighten them from sin.

Again, we have another lesson from these words. If people are under terror of conscience, it shows them where they ought to go. Judas went to the wicked, and they laughed him to scorn. This shows us that if we would wish for comfort, we must go to the Word, and the Word directs us to Christ. Now, this shows us the folly of sinners who rest in their duties. We see that Judas repented—nay, he went further—he restored the money and left it in the temple. But as he did not go further with his repentance, he died in despair. Let us not therefore stick where Judas did: let us go further, and have recourse to the blood of sprinkling.

But, in the last place, if the repentance of Judas was incomplete, even though he restored the silver, what shall we say to the repentance and religion of those who retain the wages of iniquity and the sinful penny in their houses? If people steal or defraud their neighbours in any way and retain this cursed penny, you can easily see that they have not gone as far as Judas himself. Now, if conscience can tell people that they have what does not belong to them, they are a step behind Judas in their religion.

How awful is the condition of those whom even Judas will condemn in the Day of Judgment! Have you your master's or neighbour's goods or lands or money? You hear that Judas made restitution— and does your conscience remain quiet and asleep when you know you have not? Awful is your condition, and terrible will be the bed of death! And know this, that the warning Judas got by the doctrine of Christ made him still the greater sinner. Your delusion, then, must be great if you hope to get to heaven when the conduct of Judas must condemn you. Restore the money, or whatever else it is you possess unjustly. And after you have done so, rest not in this till your conscience is cleansed in the Redeemer's blood. And be sure that you never can get true rest when sin unrepented of lies upon your conscience. Be wise in time, and hasten to the Saviour.

Verse 6. *And the chief priests took the silver pieces, and said, It is not lawful for to put them into the treasury, because it is the price of blood.*

In these words, we have the true picture of hypocrisy. Though these monsters of iniquity are acting a very deep tragedy, they feel no remorse at committing murder and taking away the life of an innocent person, and yet they show great squeamishness at putting the money into the treasury. We read of some that strain at a gnat and swallow a camel. Several bloody butchers, who have stained their consciences with the murder of the saints, might feel uneasy at eating flesh during the time of Lent. And there are many who feel no remorse at turning poor families adrift, who would think they did a wrong thing if they kept their half-penny from the poor upon the Sabbath. Some people would feel uneasy if they did not pay debts contracted by gaming and wickedness, who sit very easy under the reflections that they hurt honest tradesmen's families by not paying their debts.

Verses 7–8. *And they took counsel, and bought with them the potter's field, to bury strangers in. Wherefore that field was called, The field of blood, unto this day.*

It was the intention of these wicked men to bury the memory of Jesus Christ and the memory of their own wickedness at the same time. Instead of this, the character of our Lord shone more conspicuously after death than it did before. The man whom they crucified with every public mark of ignominy and contempt is worshipped upon earth and exalted above the angels of heaven. Angels worship him above, and his saints worship him here. And instead of concealing the crime of his murderers, this very circumstance of purchasing the potter's field served to perpetuate the baseness and infamy of the whole transaction by which he was betrayed, condemned and crucified.

It often happens that all the methods which sinners take to conceal their own crimes, or to oppress the righteous, turn to their own confusion and the glory of the people of God. The very means which sinners take to conceal their infamy serve to make their crimes the more publicly known. This happens particularly to the unclean and the covetous, as Scripture and other histories abundantly testify. The righteous will be in everlasting remembrance, and the memory of the wicked will rot.

> Verses 9–10. *Then was fulfilled that which was spoken by Jeremy the prophet, saying, And they took the thirty pieces of silver, the price of him that was valued, whom they of the children of Israel did value; and gave them for the potter's field, as the Lord appointed me.*

Although this was but a trivial circumstance, it was the subject of ancient prophecy. They were fulfilling the Scripture, not only unknown to themselves, but even in spite of themselves.

Commentators, however, have taken more pains than were necessary in clearing Matthew of what they reckon a mistake, whereas there was no mistake in the case. Mark, in the beginning of his Gospel, citing two ancient prophecies, says that they were written, whereas Matthew only says that this prophecy was said by Jeremiah. Now, Jeremiah might have said things that are not written in his book, and there was a tradition among the Jews it is very likely to this purpose. We know that several good men had prophecies which are not in Scripture. Thus we read in Jude of the prophecies of Enoch, and Paul mentions a saying of the Lord Jesus Christ which is not in one of the four Gospels. We have no doubt but Enoch made such a prophecy, and we need not doubt but our Lord made such an expression as Paul mentions in the 20th chapter of Acts, verse 35. And why should we doubt but Jeremiah said the very words of this prophecy, as well as Zechariah, though it is not written in his book? Matthew had the Spirit of God, and modesty should make us acknowledge rather our own ignorance than an error in any part of holy writ.

The Evangelist here adds that this happens by the express appointment of God. And if such a small prophecy as this must be literally accomplished, we need not doubt but the great prophecies respecting the great body of the Jewish nation must be accomplished also.

Practical inferences

I conclude this lecture with some practical inferences.

1. First, from the unhappy fate of this wicked man, we see how awful and dangerous it is to indulge sin or lust of any kind. Sin of any kind is a worm at the root of our profession. You see the love of money is the root of all evil. It was the ruin of Achan, Gehazi and Judas, and it is still the ruin of thousands. And wherefore are such instances recorded in Scripture? It is no doubt that we might beware of such dangerous rocks. We blame Judas for selling the Saviour of the world for thirty pieces of silver. And what shall we say to those who sell his love and favour for less? But whatever profit people get by selling the soul, they make but a bad bargain at best.

2. Second, we see here the danger of those who take some concern for their souls if they do not apply to Christ. Some people, when they get convictions, labour to suppress them. They go to the bottle or to the card table, or to some other idle or sinful amusement. They thus take poison instead of medicine, as has sometimes happened to persons who get things from an unskilful apprentice in an apothecary's shop. And should even people go to their duties instead of their Saviour, they have but miserable comforters to a sin-sick conscience at best. Judas restored the money, but as he did not go to Christ, his duty left him under the power of despair. Duties will not cure the soul unless it receives the atonement.

3. Third, if the most wicked characters have so far a veneration for sacred things as not to bring the price of blood to the treasury, what shall we say to those who would even get drunk in the house of God if they got liberty?

4. Fourth (lastly), we see here how shocking is the memory of the wicked. Is not this an awful thought? If the saints and holy angels

will say of any one of you, 'There is a poor lost soul who had pleasure in wickedness while on earth.' People mention his Sabbath-breaking, his covetousness, and his lies, after his death. He did not relish holy things or holy conversation. He is now with devils. Repent, then, give up your sin, come to Christ.

God bless his Word. AMEN.

Matthew chapter 27: verses 11 to 32

WE proceed to make further observations upon the words read in your hearing, and conclude with a few practical inferences.

Christ at Pilate's judgment hall

Verses 11–14. *And Jesus stood before the governor: and the governor asked him, saying, Art thou the King of the Jews? And Jesus said unto him, Thou sayest. And when he was accused of the chief priests and elders, he answered nothing. Then said Pilate unto him, Hearest thou not how many things they witness against thee? And he answered him to never a word; insomuch that the governor marvelled greatly.*

Scripture is the best interpreter of Scripture, and if we find it dark to us in one part, we always find light thrown upon that part in another. The Evangelist John (18th chapter, 13th to 37th verses) will explain to us more fully this part of Matthew. There we understand that he was examined by the high priest and Roman governor, and gave satisfactory answers as far as was necessary to clear his innocence. He does not deny but he was King of the Jews. He was of the royal family of David, his lineal descendant, and his heir according to the flesh. He acknowledges that he is the person pointed at by the ancient prophets. But at the same time, he informs us that his kingdom was not of this world, and therefore Pilate and Caesar had nothing to fear from him as a temporal king. And it is very likely that this was the enmity which his countrymen, from the highest to the lowest, had at him. For if he had exerted the power he showed in working miracles and doing good to the souls and bodies of men, in raising armies and expelling the Romans, they would joyfully receive such a Messiah with open arms. But when they find they had nothing to expect from him, and that their hopes from him as a temporal Messiah are at an end, they conspire against him, and resolve upon his death.

He made a full and a candid confession of the truth before Pontius Pilate all at once, as he had done before the high priest formerly. And after he had done so, he did not think himself obliged to answer every idle, captious or ensnaring question that might be asked at him. To what I have observed upon the 63rd verse of the former chapter, I here add that our Lord was silent for two reasons:

First, his great wisdom must have known what was the proper line of conduct for him to follow. He knew the will of God—when he ought to speak, and when he should be silent. It appears, then, that his silence was more for the glory of God than if he should speak. His silence might gall the consciences of his accusers more than a formal defence. He showed them by his conduct that he was perfectly sensible [aware] of their injustice and wickedness, for he knew well they were all convinced of his innocence. When he knew that his accusers and his judge were conscious of his innocence, why should he tell them by a formal speech what they knew already?

Second, he was silent, to show his people that he went willingly to death. If he had made a formal defence, we need have no doubt but his oratory would have exceeded all the Greek and Roman eloquence. Had he exerted his powers this way, he might have defeated the end of his coming into the world. Now, the end of his coming was to die for our sins. It was necessary he should show us the greatness of his love in being willing to die for us. And if he foresaw that even such a speech would have no effect upon the obdurate hearts of his enemies, he also foresaw that if such a speech had been extant in the gospels, unbelievers in all ages would make a handle against him. They would say that such a flood of oratory indeed showed the talents of the man, but that it showed also too great fondness for life, and an unwillingness to suffer death; that though his followers boasted of the intenseness of his love to them in suffering death for their sakes, and laying down his life as a ransom for their sins, his enemies would very readily answer that the speech which he made showed clearly that he went not willingly to death.

Now, our Lord showed by his conduct that he was above the love of life and the fear of death. He cleared his innocence sufficiently, and if he had gone further, people might say that he died with reluctance. It is true that he prayed that the cup might pass by him, but it was not the death of his body but the agonies of his soul that he prays against. This prayer showed that he was true man, but it showed also that he was a perfectly holy man, and that he submitted without a murmuring thought to the will of God in suffering death for the sins of his people. The Roman governor marvelled greatly when he saw his courage and constancy, and the cheerfulness with which he was willing to meet death in one of its most terrible forms.

> Verses 15–18. *Now at that feast the governor was wont to release unto the people a prisoner, whom they would. And they had then a notable prisoner, called Barabbas. Therefore when they were gathered together, Pilate said unto them, Whom will ye that I release unto you? Barabbas, or Jesus which is called Christ? For he knew that for envy they had delivered him.*

We have here a remarkable portion of Scripture, and a piece of history that displays the corruption of human nature to its fullest extent.

It seems it was customary among the Jews for the governor to release a prisoner at the feast of the passover. And they had at this time a very notable prisoner called Barabbas, who, it seems, had been guilty of murder some time before. Pilate, it is likely, with no bad intention, proposed the two prisoners to them, and bade them name their choice.

Now, one would imagine that by contrasting their characters, they would be at no loss what choice to make. The bare mention of their names would direct them what choice they ought to make. But the infatuated multitude, instigated by their wicked rulers, demand a murderer instead of the righteous One. Pilate knew that it was for envy they had delivered up Jesus Christ, and Pilate might naturally think that they would choose a good man, whose life was holy and whose miracles had benefitted the nation at large. But in this he was deceived. The malice that made the rulers imprison Christ made them urge the people to ruin him.

The Jews are a picture of human nature to this very day. Not only upon Sabbath, but upon every day, Pilate's question may be asked at every man, 'Whom will he choose? *Sin,* the murderer of his soul, or the Lord Jesus Christ, the chiefest among ten thousand, and altogether lovely?'

Whatever their mouth may say, ask the questions at their conduct and you will then infallibly discover their choice. Ask at the bold, impudent transgressor, who not only has committed sin, but also shamelessly defends it, and says he is not ashamed of what he has done. And though he has been convicted of wickedness, he gives you the worst language in his head. Such wretches clearly prefer Barabbas to Christ. In a word, all persons who have the gospel clearly preached to them, and yet go on in the way of their heart, show evidently that they prefer the enemy of their peace to the Friend of their souls.

> Verse 19. *When he was set down on the judgment seat, his wife sent unto him, saying, Have thou nothing to do with that just man: for I have suffered many things this day in a dream because of him.*

Some suppose this dream was sent by the enemy, who now began to suspect that the death of Christ was to be the salvation of his people. Others that it was sent by God to bear witness of the innocence of our Lord. Scripture does not say which. The woman seems to have had good sentiments, and as she heard of this man's character and the fame of his miracles, her conscience seems to have been extremely agitated. And what troubled her in the day might naturally follow her in the night. And if the enemy now at last discovered that he was the Messiah, there is no absurdity in supposing that the enemy, from a bad design, might wish to prevent his death, and that a good angel might concur in stirring her conscience to send word to her husband, because she believed his innocence. At any rate, the dream evidently showed the general opinion entertained of the sanctity of Christ. And in this view the wisdom of God saw meet that it should have place in the gospel.

Verses 20–21. But the chief priests and elders persuaded the multitude that they should ask Barabbas, and destroy Jesus. The governor answered and said unto them, Whether of the twain will ye that I release unto you? They said, Barabbas.

But the chief priests and elders persuaded the multitude that they should ask Barabbas and destroy Jesus. 'The Governor answered and said unto them, Whether of the twain will ye that I release unto you? They said, Barabbas.'

Pilate, though a bad man in other respects, did not wish to put Christ to death. He therefore asks the question, which of the prisoners they wished to release. And it is likely that the people, if left to their own free choice, might be induced by reason and conscience to ask the release of Christ. But their rulers were wicked, and the capricious, fickle mob, who were crying 'Hosanna to the Son of David' the other day, now gave their vote against him.

We may see here what unsanctified nature will do in every temptation. The most ignorant person in the mob knew that Jesus Christ was a holy and a good man, and that he was cruelly injured though innocent. Though conscience and his innocence will plead for Christ, base servility and the fear of man plead against him, and this prevailed. And some evil principle in human nature always prevails against his cause to this day. But for pleasure, ambition, or riches, all that hear the gospel would be Christians. But some lust blinds their eyes, and they prefer Barabbas to the cause of God.

Verses 22–23. Pilate saith unto them, What shall I do then with Jesus which is called Christ? They all say unto him, Let him be crucified. And

*the governor said, Why, what evil hath he done? But they cried out the
more, saying, Let him be crucified.*

There is no alternative—if the one is released, the other, it seems,
must be crucified. Pilate now appeals to their consciences, and asks,
'What has he done?'

To this they would give no answer, and having resolved to stifle
conscience, they cry out the more, 'Let him be crucified.'

And this is the natural progress of sin. When the sinner's conscience
is whipped by the Word, and the doctrine entirely condemns him,
he must either forsake sin or harden himself in wickedness. We condemn the Jews, and very justly, for taking away the life of an innocent person. But if we trample upon the law of God, are we not in
this respect equally guilty? Is not the thief or the robber who hurts
a poor man who cannot defend himself, guilty of a similar crime?
Any man that oppresses the cause of God and does violence to his
own conscience must smart for it unless he repents and forsakes his
sin.

We may ask at sinners to this day, 'What evil hath the gospel done?
What evil is in the Sabbath? What is the harm of telling the truth
and dealing honestly? What evils are there in living soberly, righteously, and godly?' When the conscience is pressed with such questions as these, there can be no answer. And as such questions must
naturally condemn sinners, they drown them in the cares and pleasures of this life. The more they hear their duty, the more they sin, as
the Jews cried the more, 'Crucify him, crucify him,' when an appeal
is made to their consciences. And this is the most hopeless stage of
obstinacy in sin. Woeful is the condition of sinners when this is the
case. They are open to all kinds of judgments.

Verses 24–25. *When Pilate saw that he could prevail nothing, but
that rather a tumult was made, he took water, and washed his hands
before the multitude, saying, I am innocent of the blood of this just person:*

*see ye to it. Then answered all the people, and said, His blood be on us,
and on our children.*

If any man of thought and reflection considers the history of the
Jews from the time of Abraham to this day, he will naturally be led
to see the wonderful providence of God to that nation. They were
always under the protection of his providence while they did their
duty and lived in his fear. But when they rebelled against the law,
they were always chastised and punished till they returned to their
duty again. They were often delivered by their judges, and even
brought back from the captivity of Babylon.

They are now fugitives and vagabonds through the earth for these
1800 years nearly, and it may be asked, 'What was their particular
crime?' They were cured of their favourite sin, idolatry, since the
captivity, and as to other gross crimes, they were guilty of them formerly, as well as at the destruction of the city by Titus. What crime
then, is yet unrepented of? We cannot think of any but the murder
of Christ. That was a crime so heinous that a pagan and idolater, a
gross sinner, and even a murderer, is afraid to imbrue his hands in
the blood of such an innocent and holy person. He takes water and
washes his hands. And though fear makes him yield to the mob, he
acknowledges the innocence of the victim of their fury.

Frantic with rage, they cry out, 'His blood be on us, and on our
children.' Their prayer is answered, and the curse they imprecate still
hangs over their ill-fated seed. If the question is asked at the Jews,
'What is the cause of their long rejection and captivity?' they may
mention this and that and the other sin. But we learn from the
prophets, more especially Jeremiah and Ezekiel, that they had very
heinous crimes among them in their days. And Isaiah calls Jerusalem
Sodom, a proof that the very same sins were predominant in the one
as in the other. And how comes it that these sins are punished, not
only so very signally, but that the punishment is protracted so long?
The truth is the nation has not yet returned to God. One of their
own prophets can inform them that if the wicked forsake his way,
that God will abundantly pardon.

God has been visiting the iniquity of the fathers upon the children for many generations. And this is the answer to the prayer of their guilty ancestors. His blood is still required at the hands of their children, and they will continue fugitives and vagabonds among the nations for signs and wonders till they acknowledge this great crime, and repent and turn to God. By persisting in their infidelity, they make the sin of their ancestors their own sin, and are punished accordingly.

The Jews, then, remain monuments of God's vengeance, and they never will return to Palestine or experience the favour of the God of their fathers till they confess the heinous crime of murdering Christ and rejecting the promised Messiah. When they returned formerly to the favour of God, they always acknowledged the sin they were guilty of. As therefore they are not yet restored to the favour of God and to the land of their fathers, it appears clearly that they have not yet confessed or deplored the sin that excludes them.

The perverse prayer of the ancient Jews hinders the efficacy of the blood of sprinkling from doing good to their children. His blood must plead for or against every nation or country where his gospel is preached. And though no nation has suffered so much temporal calamity as the Jews in consequence of rejecting the gospel, no nation or country can reject it without temporal and spiritual danger.

Verse 26. *Then released he Barabbas unto them: and when he had scourged Jesus, he delivered him to be crucified.*

Barabbas, the murderer, is released to the Jews at their desire, but not before Pilate had remonstrated against their enormous wickedness. The providence of God made use of Pilate—a blind pagan, a heathen—to deter a people who had the oracles of God in their hands from committing so black a crime. But when God saw that they were bent on their ruin, they got their desire.

It is said of their forefathers that he granted their request and sent leanness into their souls. When Israel rejected the counsel of God, he gave them up to the counsel and lust of their own depraved hearts. And a greater curse a man cannot get than his own sinful will. The Jews got a curse with a vengeance when they got Barabbas instead of Christ. And sinners that enjoy the light of the gospel and hear wholesome doctrine for their souls cannot get a greater judgment than that the providence of God would lock them up from these benefits, and give them up to their own ways. The providence of God might raise up something to keep from a man a bad wife, a large farm, or a dangerous post. If, after all, he pursues his own plans, he may succeed, but it is at the expense of his happiness and peace of mind. An ungodly wife will embitter all his days, a large farm will distract his mind with carking [distressing] cares, and a dangerous post will expose him to many sins. And by preferring Barabbas to Christ, he may please himself for a minute, but he offends his Creator and loses his soul. These are alarming thoughts, but they are searching and wholesome truths.

We are deceived if we suppose that no man can prefer Barabbas to Christ but the ancient Jews. The unlucky exchange is still going on. The apostle assures us that these things are writ for our example, either to avoid or follow, as we learn in the 10th of 1st Corinthians, and if we prefer Barabbas, we are always sure to crucify the cause of Christ. So did the Jews, and so must we in like manner.

Pilate scourged him, and then gave him up to be crucified. In poor Pilate we have an emblem of sinners to this day. Every man that does wrong contrary to his better judgment is acting such another part as Pilate did upon a smaller scale.

Christ scourged and derided

Verses 27–28. *Then the soldiers of the governor took Jesus into the common hall, and gathered unto him the whole band of soldiers. And they stripped him, and put on him a scarlet robe.*

The sufferings of the Saviour now began to thicken and come upon him sevenfold. He stood in our room, and our sins took hold upon him. Sin brings shame, and as he stood our sponsor, has suffered shame for our sakes. In the Saviour just now we may see what we had deserved. Sin robbed us of our innocence, and took away the image of God. The Saviour is stripped of his clothes, and covered with a scarlet robe. This was done by way of derision, to mock him in his kingly office.

And the sinner may see by this what he has cause to expect, unless he repents and forsakes his sins. The sinner expects happiness in the gratification of his vicious [evil] desires. Instead of enjoying happiness, he meets with misery. Our Lord is here treated as a sinner by the just judgments of God, for he was our surety. He is therefor mocked, and they add insult to cruelty, as if they had said, 'You called yourself the King of the Jews, and kings should wear scarlet or purple and fine linen.'

And thus devils will hereafter insult the misery of the poor wretches whom they have deceived to their ruin. You expected to be as gods upon earth by having your own will and rejecting the will of your Maker. You now see your fatal mistake. You are robbed of the garment of your innocence, and you will now be clothed with the robes of fire and brimstone, and this is what you get by gratifying your passions and seeking your happiness in the perishing pleasures of sense. And as our Lord is made a spectacle of derision to cruel soldiers, sinners will be objects of scorn to cruel devils. And as they cannot carry it as the Saviour did, they must sink under their sorrows. This is the wages of sin.

Christ mocked by the soldiers

Verses 29–31. *And when they had platted a crown of thorns, they put it upon his head, and a reed in his right hand: and they bowed the knee before him, and mocked him, saying, Hail, King of the Jews! And they spit upon him, and took the reed, and smote him on the head. And after that they had mocked him, they took the robe off from him, and put his own raiment on him, and led him away to crucify him.*

In the Roman soldiers we see what our sin can do. We are surprised and even shocked at such injustice, cruelty and barbarity. But if we examine our hearts, there is in every child of Adam a principle that would crucify and insult Christ. Our sins were the instruments in the hands of these wicked men.

Let us calmly consider this. Sin still insults and crucifies him. Perhaps we think that if we witnessed the scene upon Calvary hill, we would have no hand in such a wicked tragedy. A young person, a stranger to his own heart, before he has tasted the pleasures of sin, is shocked at the character of the libertine and prostitute, the thief, the villain, the robber and the murderer. But in a few years he becomes as bad himself, and if we had lived then, we do not know what we would do.

But let us ask a question. The people that mocked and murdered Christ were his professed enemies. We are his professed friends. They bowed the knee and mocked him. We worship in his house as his friends and people. These people, after bowing their knees, spat on him, abused and crucified him. And if we break his laws, profane his Sabbaths, and mock his people, are we not much worse than the Jews and Romans? They were enemies, and we call ourselves his friends. Now, the question we may naturally ask is this, 'Which act the most consistent part?' We leave your consciences to answer. And the answer you must give will condemn you if you are guilty of these or worse sins.

Verse 32. *And as they came out, they found a man of Cyrene, Simon by name: him they compelled to bear his cross.*

The Evangelists Luke and John inform us that our Lord himself carried his cross. It seems the loss of blood and the anguish of his sufferings by scourging were such that they compel another man that met them to carry the cross after him.

We are called upon now to witness a wonderful and a moving scene. Behold the meek Lamb of God carrying his cross. You have heard the other day of deep and unsearchable providences. What would one of the glorious spirits that surround the throne, a being of a most comprehensive mind, think of this astonishing sight? He saw the Son of God led to carry the instrument of his suffering, like a criminal, to the place of execution. What would he say of such a dark providence till it was explained?

The man that carried the cross after him is a picture of us. He was compelled to carry the cross. Perhaps you say, had you been there, that you would carry the cross altogether, to free him of the heavy burden. But alas! are you not always almost compelled to carry the cross after him? Are you willing to take trouble, for this is to drink of his cup, and to carry his cross? Alas! we are not, and it takes us some time before we cheerfully submit to carry our burden—the cross, whatever it is, is a burden—and we are desired to carry our burden to the Lord and cast it upon him. And though the cross be bitter, the fruits of this tree are wholesome and sweet.

Every Christian must have less or more of it, and we ought to leave this to the man who has the management of the wheels of providence. And though the flesh may rebel at first, let us yield to carrying it meekly after Christ. If we commit our cause to God as Christ did, he will manage it for us. The cross will prepare us for the Christian's heavenly crown.

Practical inferences

And now, having mixed so many practical observations in the body of the lecture, I conclude it with the following useful, practical remarks that we ought to view the history—and especially the sufferings—of Christ with an eye of faith. This is not a dry, speculative observation. It is the life and marrow of the gospel. Christ's suffering for our sins is the strongest argument to hate and forsake sin.

When we consider the gospel in this view, it becomes a precious and a consolatory doctrine. It is the foundation of all our hopes and the source of all our joys. And this throws light upon the darkest providence that ever mankind witnessed. We see a precious, poor man ill-used, bought and sold, spat upon, scourged, crucified and slain. But he rises again, ascends to heaven, assumes all power, gives efficacy to his gospel, rules as King, and will reign through all eternity.

AMEN.

Matthew chapter 27: verses 33 to 54

THE providence of God is a great depth, and his ways are wonderful. He brings to pass his decrees and the counsel of his will by methods that to us appear unlikely and dark. The Jews and Romans agreed to oppress a poor man. He comes to his death without a murmuring word or a repining thought against the mysterious providence that permitted such wickedness. Our Lord knew that his enemies were bringing about the salvation of his people, unknown to themselves, and even contrary to their intention. They had not the glory of God in view, but the gratification of their own malevolent passions. But God overrules the most wicked actions to the purposes of his own glory and the good of mankind. And though the permission of gross, unjust, and heaven-daring actions may offend blind mortals that see not far before them, God has just, holy and righteous reasons for what he does and for what he permits. He is always carrying on some future designs, and we shall understand his dealing here. And the things that are acted this day upon the theatre of Europe are to carry on some great design of providence. But I proceed to explain the words just now read.

The crucifixion

Verses 33–34. *And when they were come unto a place called Golgotha, that is to say, a place of a skull, they gave him vinegar to drink mingled with gall: and when he had tasted thereof, he would not drink.*

The apostle to the Hebrews and the book of Leviticus inform us that the bodies of the beasts which were offered for sin, and whose blood was brought into the sanctuary, were burnt without the camp. And our Lord, that he might sanctify the people with his own blood, suffered without the gate. Golgotha or Calvary hill was on the outside of the city of Jerusalem, and to the north or north-west of the hill of Zion. The signification of these two words is 'the place of a skull'. It seems to have been the place where criminals were executed. There is a tradition among the Orientals that the first man, Adam, was buried here. It was believed by some of the ancients that when the blood of the Redeemer fell upon the place where Adam was buried, that in consequence of this, he recovered life and was one of those saints who rose after his resurrection, entered the city, and appeared to many. Whatever be in this, we know that the death of our Lord procures spiritual and eternal life for millions.

When they came to this place, his enemies gave him to drink vinegar mixed with gall. It was customary with the ancients to give persons led forth to execution some kind of strong drink to alleviate their misery, and it is likely his friends might prepare such a drink for the Saviour. But the soldiers, with barbarous cruelty, gave vinegar mixed with gall, which he would not drink. King David, an eminent type of our Lord, complains that his enemies gave him vinegar and gall. In the smallest things, the Scripture must be fulfilled. Though our Lord was thirsty after tasting the drink, he would not drink the bitter potion. The vinegar was mixed with some ingredient bitter as gall, but as it had an intoxicating quality, calculated to make one forget his pain, he would not drink, lest any would suspect that he stood in need of such drink, or that he did not go cheerfully to death.

Verses 35–36. *And they crucified him, and parted his garments, casting lots: that it might be fulfilled which was spoken by the prophet, They parted my garments among them, and upon my vesture did they cast lots. And sitting down they watched him there.*

They fixed his precious body to the cross, naked, between two thieves, and divided his garments among them, casting lots. Small as this circumstance is, it was prophesied by the Psalmist, and it was exactly fulfilled in his great antitype. We see that all the ceremonies and sacrifices are typical of some great future event. The Roman soldiers fulfil Scripture unknown to themselves, and so do we. They expose our Lord to shame. Adam made himself naked before God. That monster, the human heart, is as open to God as the light of the sun can make things open to our view. And our shameful thoughts or spiritual nakedness is more nauseous to him than the spectacle of a naked person can be to our eyes. To cast a veil over our spiritual nakedness, our Lord suffers naked before the multitude.

Is there any among us who has of spiritual pride what will deny that he is naked before God to his shame? If there is, let his conscience answer the following question. Can any man or woman in this congregation take upon them to say that his or her thoughts for one day are such as that they could be read or published to the world as the thoughts of such a person? Where is the person that is so hardy, so bare-faced and so impudent as to bear this? Unless it be a madman or a fury from hell, no human being could bear the thought. And if we could not endure such an idea, how awful is the spiritual nakedness of the human soul!

How much then are we indebted to him that procured a garment of righteousness to cover our nakedness! Such as accept of this righteousness will be clothed before the judgment seat, and such as do not, will appear naked, and their own thoughts will confound them before the Judge. How mad are sinners that continue in their sins, for they will appear naked hereafter! And if our Lord and Saviour suffered shame for the sins of others, what shame and confusion of face will seize guilty criminals when their own sins will appear before them!

The caution and care of his enemies made them sit down and watch him on the cross. Likely it was usual to watch criminals, but it is more than probable that the Jewish rulers were doubly apprehensive of something. They had heard of his miracles, and they might suspect that he would do something to effect his escape from the cross. Though the malignity of their hearts made them insult him, the terror of their consciences made them still afraid of him. And what they did upon this occasion is a great prop to our faith. We know it was the person who suffered upon the cross that was buried in the Garden of Gethsemane and that rose again from the dead. His enemies watched him on the cross and watched him in his grave. We are obliged to them for their malignant offence, because we have here an additional argument to strengthen our faith.

Verse 37. *And set up over his head his accusation written, THIS IS JESUS THE KING OF THE JEWS.*

No doubt Pilate did this as an insult to Jesus Christ and to the whole nation at large. His question before now was very emphatical: 'Shall I crucify your King?' In this circumstance we see the malignity and unmanliness of the Jews in general, the accomplishment of Scripture, and a strong foundation for our faith as Christians.

The malignity and unmanliness of the Jews is conspicuous, and their disgrace deserves to be writ in large characters. No other nation but themselves ever were guilty of such action. To the honour of our nation, it can be said that though a reward of several thousand pounds was offered to any that would apprehend the unlucky descendant of their ancient kings, no man in Scotland was found base enough to apprehend him or receive such a reward. How much less would the nation at large bear the insult of seeing him publicly executed. And though his religion lost him his right to the crown, the nation in general did not lose their feelings as men and as countrymen. And as to the Jews, even allowing that their accusation of Christ was as true as it was false, their conduct was base. He was the descendant of King David, and if he had set up for a temporal King, no man had a better title.

We have here also the accomplishment of Scripture and a strong foundation for our faith as Christians. The genealogy of our Lord is laid down by two of the evangelists, and he is considered as the son of David by his nation in general. Now, though there was nothing in the conduct of our Lord that could justify the idea of his setting up as a temporal sovereign, there was something about him that showed him to be an extraordinary personage. The sanctity of his life and the fame of his miracles drew the attention of mankind. Add to this that he was descended of the race of their ancient kings, and if the people had not known this, they could not entertain an idea of his being the Messiah. The Messiah was to be of the tribe of Judah, to descend from Jesse, and to be born in Bethlehem. He was to work wonderful works and to be a spiritual king. The nation saw works of wonder performed by this man, and the reward they bestow on his holy life and his heavenly miracles was to crucify him between two malefactors.

The character of Messiah and the accomplishment of prophecy meet in Jesus of Nazareth, so that wicked Pilate and the ungrateful Jews are helpers of our faith. He is more than the King of the Jews: he is the King of saints. Let us lift up our eyes to the cross, and seek our salvation in Jesus Christ.

> Verse 38. *Then were there two thieves crucified with him, one on the right hand, and another on the left.*

Are we offended at this insult more than the rest of his sufferings? What! Will the innocent, the holy Jesus, be put on a level with the most execrable malefactors? Yes, it must be so, for Scripture assures us that he was to be numbered with transgressors. Whoever reads the fifty-third chapter of Isaiah about the suffering Messiah need not be surprised or offended at the scandal of the cross. Our iniquities were laid upon him, and even God himself bruised him and put him to grief. Every part of ancient prophecy must be fulfilled. Are we offended at anything that will strengthen our faith? Had this part of our Lord's story been concealed, and that an infidel had asked us how we could apply that part of the fifty-third chapter of Isaiah to Jesus Christ—'And he was numbered with transgressors'—we would be at a loss what answer to make. But as we find this in the Gospel, our answer is clear. Many of his people deserved the death of the cross, and therefore our Lord was crucified between two thieves.

> Verses 39–44. *And they that passed by reviled him, wagging their heads, and saying, Thou that destroyest the temple, and buildest it in three days, save thyself. If thou be the Son of God, come down from the*

cross. Likewise also the chief priests mocking him, with the scribes and elders, said, He saved others; himself he cannot save. If he be the King of Israel, let him now come down from the cross, and we will believe him. He trusted in God; let him deliver him now, if he will have him: for he said, I am the Son of God. The thieves also, which were crucified with him, cast the same in his teeth.

To complete the baseness of their character, they add the most cowardly insult to the greatest cruelty. King David, a type of our Lord, foreseeing by the spirit of prophecy the fate of Messiah, has given us the very words of his enemies when they insulted him. Whoever reads the 22nd and 69th Psalms and compares them with the history of the Gospel will see the literal accomplishment of prophecy in the sufferings of Christ. The things that are mentioned in these Psalms never happened literally to King David, even when persecuted by Saul and by his rebellious son Absalom. And what incontestably proves that this is a prophecy concerning Jesus Christ, let us advert to the 25th verse of the last-mentioned Psalm. There the Psalmist prays against the enemies of Christ in the following strong and energetic expressions: 'Let their habitation be desolate; and let none dwell in their tents.'

Their usage of Christ is the cause of the prayer against them. And the prayer of the Psalmist has been answered in its utmost latitude. The palaces of Jerusalem and the habitations of the common people have been desolate for several centuries. The country of Palestine, though once one of the most fertile spots or countries in Asia, and in the highest state of cultivation, is now so much altered for the worse, that some who travelled there have been led almost to doubt the authority of Scripture. But this very portion of Scripture may show us that the nation deserved their fate. When a whole nation, from the highest to the lowest, agreed to put an innocent person to death, we have in few words a complete description of their character. They were arrived at the utmost pitch of wickedness. And as their descendants are not yet ashamed of the baseness of their ancestors' conduct, the curse hangs over them still.

The very thieves insult him, perhaps with some view to curry favour to themselves and obtain a release. And here we see the sovereignty of God. One of these miscreants is touched by grace, takes concern for his soul, and turns to God. He rebukes his brother in wickedness, acknowledges the justice of his own sentence, and applies for mercy and pardon to the suffering Saviour. He obtains mercy, and is that very day admitted to paradise.

Verse 45. *Now from the sixth hour there was darkness over all the land unto the ninth hour.*

In this wonderful phenomenon we see the hand of God in an eminent degree. We know the cause of ordinary eclipses according to the rules of astronomy. But there could be no eclipse of the sun in the ordinary course of things at this time, as the passover was celebrated at the full moon. It was therefore an extraordinary darkness. But what natural cause God employed to occasion it, we cannot take upon us to say, as the Scripture does not inform us. And we are not obliged to follow the speculations of philosophers. In matters of mere conjecture, they may be as far out as other people. But whatever be the cause, it was a terrible darkness, and no doubt it was calculated to strike terror into the spectators, and more especially into the consciences of the perpetrators of this deepest of tragedies.

It was over the whole land. Some think it was confined to Judaea only, but it is probable it was more extensive, for the heathens mention it. The darkness was so great that the stars were seen at noonday. It was so remarkable that a heathen is reported to have said, 'Either that God himself suffered, or sympathised with one that did suffer.'

Some of the first Christians mention this darkness in the discourses they address to the heathens. And they might well do so, for it could not be accounted for by the ordinary laws of nature. It was the immediate hand of God. To the Jews, it was a dreadful presage [sign] of their future darkness and rejection. To mankind in general, it was an emblem that the sun of righteousness was under an eclipse. Our

Lord at this time felt a suspension of comfort and spiritual darkness upon his holy and sinless soul. This was the time of his deepest suffering, for God did hide his face from a soul that never sinned. He stood in our stead and drank the cup of wrath. No wonder though there should be darkness upon his soul.

At this time, all the claims of a broken law were lodged in court, and the great Surety was obliged to pay our debt and obtain a full discharge at once. And it seems it took some time to settle the account and pay the great sum. He did not do it all at once, for the darkness continued from the sixth to the ninth hour—that is, from our twelve o'clock to three in the afternoon. Although almighty power could create a universe in a lifetime, yet we are told it took him six days to finish the creation. In like manner, it took our Lord three long hours upon the cross to satisfy divine justice for his people. Though every part of our Lord's holy life and sufferings was on our account, this was the finishing out of his obedience. And by his complete obedience unto death, there was a complete garment of needlework of wrought gold prepared to cover the naked souls of his people.

Verse 46. *And about the ninth hour Jesus cried with a loud voice, saying, Eli, Eli, lama sabachthani? that is to say, My God, my God, why hast thou forsaken me?*

Men of great learning and abilities, when speaking of this scene, have made use of strong language indeed. They made use of such expressions as gave others room to insinuate that they thought he spoke the language of despair. We shall not take upon us to defend the unguarded expressions of good men. But surely they could have no such thoughts, whatever their expressions might be. When our Lord prayed that the cup might pass by him, a person might be led to suspect that he wished to decline suffering for his people. But surely our Lord knew his business in the world. But this shows that though his human nature was without sin, it recoiled from suffering if that had been consistent with the divine will. In like manner, at this time he complains of dereliction, but without any tincture [trace] of despair. The words he uses are very strong, and they show us the intensity of his sufferings.

It is natural for good men to talk about this portion of Scripture agreeably to their own spiritual feelings. The comforts of grace are very refreshing to the soul of a Christian. And when he experiences the terrors of the law, and spiritual darkness soon after, no wonder though his language should be abundantly strong. If a person were to feel the cold blast of December after the pleasant warmth of June, it is natural for him to complain severely of the change. People experience something of this in warmer climates than even ours. If a person peruses the devotional exercises of some of the people of God, he finds how strongly they complain when there is a suspension of spiritual comfort.

Our Lord partook of our human nature and therefore complains upon the cross. We have cause to believe that the enemy who was always ready to tempt him would try his strength upon him, even in his distress, as he did formerly when he was hungry in the wilderness. He felt the malice of wicked men, his own instruments, and it is likely Satan himself and the spirits of darkness would make their last furious attack at this time of suffering and distress. But till God his Father left his soul and hid his face, we do not hear him complain. His sufferings were inexpressible, and the language of the Greek Church in her liturgy is the language of strict propriety. Addressing the Saviour, she implores him by his unknown sufferings. They made him complain upon the cross, 'My God, my God! why hast thou forsaken me?' Our Lord suffered for the sins of his people.

The most terrible effect of sin is being forsaken of God. He abandons the sinner to his confidence and to the fury of his lusts for ever. Now, though our Lord was free from sin and from an evil conscience in the sense in which criminals feel them, it is a truth that sin was imputed to him. And if so, he understood, by what he suffered, the terrors that take hold of an abandoned sinner. He stood our Surety, and felt our sufferings. And the worst part of suffering is a sense of the anger of God and hiding his FACE from the soul.

If good men, therefore, have made use of expressions which cannot be entirely defended when speaking of this portion of Scripture, we ought freely to excuse them. Every man of thought and reflection will find a difficulty here. How can an innocent person complain that God did forsake him unless he stood in the place of others? But still there is a difficulty, for his conscience was clear and his heart and life holy. But SIN was imputed to him, for he was our sacrifice, and as an unholy thing lay upon him, he must suffer before he can get rid of the burden. And this part of his suffering in particular made him bitterly to complain. Nor would he have made use of such strong language if he did not feel deeply what he said. But that his complaint was perfectly free from despair we learn from the evangelist Luke, for he tells us that he delivered his pure and holy soul into the hands of God his Father, and thus delivered up his spirit.

Verses 47–49. *Some of them that stood there, when they heard that, said, This man calleth for Elias. And straightway one of them ran, and took a spunge, and filled it with vinegar, and put it on a reed, and gave him to drink. The rest said, Let be, let us see whether Elias will come to save him.*

In these people we have an emblem of two classes of sinners. Some of them are so cruel and hard-hearted that, instead of sympathising with his bitter complaint (for they knew his distress), only offer him vinegar to drink. And this is often all the comfort the people of God can expect from the wicked. All the alleviation they give their misery is the vinegar of bitter reproach and insult. And they should not complain of tasting a little of what their Lord and Master was made to taste before them.

Others again mistake his meaning entirely. From their ignorance of the Hebrew and Syrian dialects, they thought he implored the assistance of the prophet Elijah. And this is the fate of many sinners in our day. They neither understand the language of Scripture nor the language of providence. And by their criminal ignorance of both, they stumble like blind men in the noonday, and fall into everlasting perdition.

Ignorance of Scripture and providence is the cause of many sins. Some of them might say this through mere insult and mockery. And others, perhaps, might really think Elijah would come and relieve him. But what happened was more for the glory of God and the honour of the Saviour than if Elijah was sent from heaven to bring him down from the cross. It was necessary that he should die and be buried and then rise again. And surely it showed more of the power of God to raise a dead man from the grave than to save a living man from death. It is not in the way that our fond and foolish idea might suggest that God comes with his answer and help to his people. God the Father heard the prayer of his Son, our Lord Jesus Christ, in a way that will be the joy and astonishment of eternity. And though we may think that something may happen, as if we got an extraordinary answer like Elijah coming to help us, it is more for our good that our hopes were dead and buried, and then God will come right early to our assistance.

Verse 50. *Jesus, when he had cried again with a loud voice, yielded up the ghost.*

The evangelist Luke tells us that he recommended his soul into the hands of his Father, and John says that he said, a little before his death, that the great work was finished. And Matthew here informs us that it was with a loud voice he yielded up his spirit. Notwithstanding all his sufferings, he was still strong, and he could live much longer. But he now died of his own accord, for the work was finished, and this put an end to his sufferings. And it is worthy of our notice that he died at the time of the evening sacrifice, and then his soul ascended into paradise to plead the efficacy of his blood. All the types in the Old Testament meet in our Lord, and we see the wisdom of God directing every circumstance in his life and death. The time of his death is mentioned, that we might see that he is the great sacrifice offered for our sins.

Verses 51–53. *And, behold, the veil of the temple was rent in twain from the top to the bottom; and the earth did quake, and the rocks rent;*

and the graves were opened; and many bodies of the saints which slept arose, and came out of the graves after his resurrection, and went into the holy city, and appeared unto many.

In these words, we have a group of the most astonishing miracles and wonderful events, and they tend evidently to prove the divinity of the glorious person who now did suffer. The veil of the temple was rent, and this must have struck the priests in waiting, and given them some searching thoughts. The way to the holiest of all was now laid open. When the veil of Christ's flesh was broken, the veil of our sins was rent also, and access was opened to the highest heavens. The veil was very thick: it was a valuable piece of cloth, and nothing but divine power could thus rend it from top to bottom.

The earth did quake and the rocks rent. It is well known that earthquakes in the Scripture are reckoned signs of the anger of God and tokens of his awful presence, and this we learn from the 18th and 104th Psalms, and his appearance to the prophet Elijah when he fled from Jezebel. The wonderful appearances, therefore, at the death of Christ made all the spectators to fear, and they could not but acknowledge the hand of God in them.

Verse 54. *Now when the centurion, and they that were with him, watching Jesus, saw the earthquake, and those things that were done, they feared greatly, saying, Truly this was the Son of God.*

We find in these words that the miracles which happened at this time made a pagan and idolater to acknowledge not only the innocence but the greatness of the person who now suffered. The Roman centurion confesses that this was the Son of God. And however much the Jewish nation and their rulers were judicially blinded and hardened, the sight they saw might have astonished and terrified them. Even wicked Pharaoh might have acknowledged the finger of God in the miracles of Moses. How much more must then the Jews and their priests and rabbis have seen the hand of God in the miracles of Christ, and in the events that happened at his death and resurrection! But they have no impression upon them, further than to render them inexcusable. And though the people that were always spectators of his works continue hardened, the pagan centurion only acknowledges the truth, and does not suffer the convictions of his own mind, and honestly confesses his faith before the multitude.

Practical inferences

From the miracles thus explained, we make the following remarks.

1. First, the sacred historian takes notice of some circumstances in the sufferings of our Lord, which are of small account in themselves but tend greatly to strengthen our faith. And these are his being offered vinegar upon the cross, and the soldiers dividing and casting lots for his clothes. We see in the Book of Psalms that these things are prophesied of Messiah, and we see them fulfilled in Christ, and his enemies, without their own knowledge, fulfilling the Word of God. And this serves to convince us that Christ is the person spoken of. Nothing is small that concerns the Lord Jesus Christ, and the things that happen to his people are the result of infinite wisdom and the answer of prayer.

2. Secondly, in the awful and astonishing miracles that happened at this time, we have a proof of the anger of God against the Jewish nation. He would not work such great works without a cause. He gives tokens of his presence, but they are angry tokens. God was at this time punishing sin in the person of his Son, but as the instruments were acting a base and sinful part, he is resolved to punish them, and he gives them here presages [forewarnings] of their future darkness and rejection. The present state of the Jews and their fate since the destruction of Jerusalem is a proof of this truth and a comment upon this doctrine.

3. Lastly, we may see here that the greatest miracles are insufficient of themselves to change the hearts of those who are determined to prosecute their lusts and follow their own opinion and ways in direct opposition to the light. Our Lord preached holy and heavenly doctrines, and confirmed them by the most illustrious miracles. They

had no effect upon the majority: instead of doing them good, owing to their own wickedness, they did them great evil. They hardened themselves past cure, and their leaders are foremost in this great sin. They insult Christ upon the cross, notwithstanding what they saw and heard. And to the shame of the Jewish nation, a Roman centurion and his soldiers relent at the sight, though they continue obdurate in wickedness. The centurion relents at first, and his soldiers followed his example, but the Jews blind and harden themselves, and are proof against every means. The most powerful means and doctrines are lost upon the wicked. And the cause is, they are determined to continue in sin. The sermons of Christ against covetousness made no impression upon Judas or upon the worldly Pharisees. They crucified Christ, and so do their followers to this day.

May God keep us from sinning against the light, and bless his Word. AMEN.

Matthew chapter 27: verses 55 to 66

I N the words we heard just now, we have an account of the burial of our Lord and the different things attending that solemn work. We shall speak a little about these events, and conclude with some practical remarks.

The women at the cross

Verses 55–56. *And many women were there beholding afar off, which followed Jesus from Galilee, ministering unto him: among which was Mary Magdalene, and Mary the mother of James and Joses, and the mother of Zebedee's children.*

In these words, we have an account of some of the sorrowful spectators of this awful transaction. Among those who followed Christ during his ministry, there were not only a number of valuable men, but some respectable and pious women. And they accompanied him not only to his cross, but also to his grave.

Some of their names are also handed down, and will be had in everlasting remembrance, *viz.* the two Marys and the mother of Zebedee's children. They were at some distance, but they could see the sight, and no doubt the sight was cutting to their souls. They trusted in him as their God and the Redeemer of Israel. It is not likely that they knew anything of his resurrection more than the apostles did, and when they saw him hanging on the cross, what a dreadful trial to their faith! They saw him dead upon the cross, and saw that he was buried in the grave, and their hopes for a moment seemed to be buried with him. Unbelief might now suggest, 'Is this the man to whom you trusted your soul and your everlasting interests? If he was

God, how could he die? And if he was a good man, how could he deceive?'

These, no doubt, are searching thoughts, and it is more than probable they had some such reflections, for unbelief, upon much less trying occasions, is very busy with the people of God. But faith has the happy art of answering every question. The holy virgin was among the pious women that at this time surrounded the cross. It was at this time the prophecy of old Simeon was accomplished. A sword did pierce her soul, and her thoughts did bleed inwardly. And here we see what almighty and invincible grace can do. Women are the weaker sex, but grace made them strong, and notwithstanding the perilous situation in which they stood, they followed their Lord and Master to his cross.

We have, likewise, an instance of what sincerity in profession will do. A few days before this, the multitude followed Christ with hosannas and the voice of triumph. When things took a contrary turn, they change their tune and cry out, 'Crucify him.' But these precious women are as true and constant in their profession under all the circumstances of disgrace attending his sufferings as they were when the tide of popularity ran in his favour. If people can be religious when they have few followers, and more especially if they are so when exposed to ridicule and contempt for their profession, they have the witness in themselves, and the Lord whom they confess thus before men will confess and reward them before men and angels.

Joseph of Arimathaea

Verses 57–60. *When the even was come, there came a rich man of Arimathaea, named Joseph, who also himself was Jesus' disciple: he went to Pilate, and begged the body of Jesus. Then Pilate commanded the body to be delivered. And when Joseph had taken the body, he wrapped it in a clean linen cloth, and laid it in his own new tomb, which he had hewn*

out in the rock: and he rolled a great stone to the door of the sepulchre,
and departed.

In this remarkable short story there are some things well worth our
attention and study. Our Lord, during his lifetime, though the most
precious gift of heaven, was a man of sorrows and acquainted with
grief. Though the brightness of his Father's glory, and the most
beautiful of the sons of men, yet he was despised and rejected by
them, for they saw no form or comeliness in his person. Instead of
receiving him with the highest mark of respect, they insulted his person, ridiculed his doctrine, and despised his miracles. They pursued
him with hatred, traduced his character, and put the worst construction upon all his words and actions. Not satisfied with all this, they
plot against his life and succeed in putting him to an ignominious
death. But when even his sufferings are at an end, and the great debt
of human guilt paid, there is respect paid to his person and memory
afterwards. Nicodemus and Joseph of Arimathaea, who are both
respectable personages—and the last in particular is here called a
rich man—went to Pilate and begged the body of Jesus.

It was customary with great men in the East to hew for themselves
sepulchres in rocks, to distinguish their graves from those of the
common people. It was prophesied of Messiah (Isaiah, chapter 53)
that he would make his grave with the rich. Accordingly, though it
was intended no doubt by his enemies to bury him with the wicked,
and the intention is called an act in Scripture, yet it is otherwise overruled by the good providence of God. This great and good man,
from a principle of love to his Saviour, procured from Pilate the
liberty of burying him in his own sepulchre, and this is the accomplishment of prophecy and support to our faith. Had he been buried
among other bodies, this had given his enemies a pretext to say that
it was not his body that rose, but some other. But he was buried in
a new sepulchre, and we are sure it was his body that rose again from
the death. We are sure that he who was buried for our offences rose
again for our justification.

In the history of Joseph of Arimathaea, we have a specimen of the
progress of divine faith. He was a disciple of Jesus, but privately, for

fear of the Jews. But though his faith was at first opposed by slavish fear, he now rises superior to every such consideration. Notwithstanding the critical situation in which he stood, the fear of ridicule, and the danger to which he might be exposed by confessing Christ, he went boldly to Pilate, asked the body, bestowed upon it the highest honours, and laid it in his own grave.

In Joseph we have a picture of some great men and gentlemen. They have a warm side to the gospel, but are afraid and ashamed to make a public profession and boldly to avow the religion of Christ and keep up family worship. The sneer of their companions and the contempt of the proud make them afraid. But if the good work is begun, however weak and unpromising the appearance, it will surely thrive and prosper and come to a happy conclusion. Like wholesome grain in the earth, though its growth may be retarded by a stone or some other body, bere [a hardy type of barley] rises, and will produce crop.

Gentlemen should imitate the courage and magnanimity of Joseph of Arimathaea. And in truth, we ought all to follow his example. We ought to use the Word of Christ as he used his body. Wicked people despise and crucify the Word of God, but the good man will take it down from the cross and bury it in the sepulchre of his heart. And he will take care to have this sepulchre hewn in the rock. God promises a new heart, and he will plead the promises. And as Joseph secured the body from wild beasts and other enemies by laying a great stone at the mouth of the sepulchre, the Christian will defend the Word which he hid in his heart by the grace of watchfulness and prayer. And though the powers of hell are combined to prevent the growth of the Word, as his enemies watched the sepulchre of Christ to prevent his rising, yet as sure as the one rose, the other will grow. If Christ is found in the heart, though to our apprehension dead and buried, he will rise again. His Word, notwithstanding the load of corruption and unbelief that lies above it, will rise again and triumph over all the lusts and corruptions of the heart.

The women at the sepulchre

Verse 61. *And there was Mary Magdalene, and the other Mary, sitting over against the sepulchre.*

By this they showed indeed their love and regard for the dead body of the Lord, but at the same time, they seem to have doubts about his resurrection. While Joseph and Nicodemus were busy within the sepulchre performing the last offices to the body of their Master, they sat over against the sepulchre and observed where he was laid, that they might come after the Sabbath was over in order to anoint him. And if we have Christ within us, we will imitate them in this respect. They prepare sweet spices to anoint him. Christ is, as it were, sometimes lying dead in the means, but as we know it is there he is to be found, we will show respect to the place where his honour dwelleth, and prepare our sweet spices. We will endeavour to exercise faith, prayer and patience, and be found in the practice of every Christian duty till he rise again in the means.

The burial of Christ

Verses 62–66. *Now the next day, that followed the day of the preparation, the chief priests and Pharisees came together unto Pilate, saying, Sir, we remember that that deceiver said, while he was yet alive, After three days I will rise again. Command therefore that the sepulchre be made sure until the third day, lest his disciples come by night, and steal him away, and say unto the people, He is risen from the dead: so the last error shall be worse than the first. Pilate said unto them, Ye have a watch: go your way, make it as sure as ye can. So they went, and made the sepulchre sure, sealing the stone, and setting a watch.*

Little did the enemies of Christ think that the malignity of their hearts and their malicious insinuations served more illustriously to set forth the glory of Christ and prove without controversy that he was the true Messiah by his resurrection from the dead. And yet, so it was. They call him a deceiver, and their descendants are not afraid and ashamed to do so to this day. Their malice and wickedness blind their hearts, and they stick at nothing to compass their wicked designs. They must have been conscious that they told a gross falsehood, and that this was a good man, and no impostor and deceiver.

But the truth is, they were afraid of his resurrection, for our Lord said that he would rise the third day. And if we examine the conduct of the chief priests and Pharisees, nothing can be more wicked and absurd. Our Lord called himself the Son of God. If he was so, how foolish was their attempt to seal the stone and set a watch! If he was a deceiver, how absurd was their labour! For what purpose would his followers steal his dead body? If he had continued dead, it would be an easy task to convince them that he was not the Messiah and that their hopes were vain. They would soon return to their old habits and ways of thinking, and the high priests had nothing to fear.

The apostles themselves had not the finishing proof of his being the Messiah till he rose from the dead. And how could they convince others that he rose by being in possession of his dead body? By fabricating such a falsehood, they would forfeit the happiness here and hereafter. They could expect nothing in this life but disgrace, persecution, poverty, and death in its most dismal form. And to suppose that a number of rational creatures would concur in publishing a falsehood that would make them miserable here and expose them to the wrath of God in the world to come, is an absurdity too big for any man but a Jewish high priest and a hypocritical Pharisee.

In examining the history of his resurrection in the next chapter, I shall point out to you the folly of supposing that a number of poor, unarmed men could possibly steal the dead body of our Saviour. And if the body of the Jewish nation had not been judicially blinded, they would not believe such a lie. Pilate therefore gave them permission to seal the stone and set a watch. And if any man can believe that a few unarmed fishermen could steal him from the Roman soldiers, he is prepared to swallow any absurdity. But of this we shall speak, God willing, in the next chapter.

Practical inferences

Meantime, we shall conclude with some practical inferences.

1. Here we may observe that, though our Lord pronounced woes against some of the cities of Galilee, he had some faithful followers from that place. However few will believe, yet where the gospel is faithfully preached, some will believe and be saved. Our Lord had some in Galilee, and he has a remnant in the worst places and in the worst of times. And these few will be dreadful witnesses against sinners and unbelievers.

2. We find here an accomplishment of prophecy. It was said that Christ was to make his grave with the wicked, and with the rich at his death. Now this came literally to pass. He was numbered with transgressors, and was crucified between two thieves. And the wicked who had such power over him might have buried him in the graves of the common people. But the wisdom of God prevented this. Joseph of Arimathaea procured liberty from the Roman governor to bury him in his own grave. There is respect paid to him at his death, and this is a prelude to his exaltation. All the prophecies to a hairbreadth are accomplished in the person of Jesus Christ.

3. Lastly, we see that everything that is done against Christ and the interest of his religion will only serve the more illustriously to promote his cause and glorify his name. Jesus Christ, the true Joseph, is sold as a slave by his brethren, the Jews. He is falsely accused and put to death as a sinner. And as the sufferings of Joseph are the cause of his exaltation, the sufferings of Christ and the plans of his enemies to hurt his cause and ruin his character are the very things that promote the one and exalt the other. And this will be the fate of all his followers. The stone will be removed, and all their enemies will be conquered.

May God bless his Word. AMEN.

Matthew chapter 28: verses 1 to 20

WE are come now to the most conspicuous part of the history of our Lord: his resurrection from the dead. And as this is the foundation of our holy religion, it is necessary we should be acquainted with the arguments that prove the divine truth.

Now, the arguments that prove this truth are the testimony of several honest, unexceptionable characters that saw him after his resurrection and sealed the testimony with their blood. Several hundred persons saw him and conversed with him, and then his testimony is found in the four evangelists. And as the story was difficult to gain belief, the divine power that raised him from the dead was exerted to work the most astonishing miracles to gain credit to the doctrine. And the hand of God was so visible in the conversion of many thousands in primitive times, and these converts were so much convinced of the divinity and resurrection of our Lord, that death in all its most terrible forms could not frighten them to renounce these cheering and animating truths. But there is an argument of a very different complexion that gains my assent to the truth. I mean the perverse obstinacy of adversaries and the pains they took, contrary to their own conviction, to obscure the glory of the Redeemer by propagating the most palpable and glaring falsehoods. I shall speak a little to the words as they be in order.

The resurrection

Verse 1. *In the end of the sabbath, as it began to dawn toward the first day of the week, came Mary Magdalene and the other Mary to see the sepulchre.*

Inferences:

1. Resurrection; a proof; work finished; debt paid, discharged and procured.
2. We should rise from the grave of sin.

The history of our Lord was writ by the four evangelists, and they all agree in the testimony they give. It is true they vary a little in the account they give, but this is only an argument in their favour, and a proof they did not by collusion, but by the inspiration of the Holy Spirit.

The first Christians, who had access to know the truth and who saw nothing discordant in the different accounts, they kept their history as a precious deposition and have handed it down to us pure and clear. If there are some seeming inconsistencies to be found in their accounts, this is entirely owing to our ignorance and not to any inaccuracy in them. If there had been any such, the primitive church and the other apostles had too much honesty and good sense not to see such glaring defects. Had this been the case, they knew they were open to a stroke from their enemies. And when they saw nothing dark or discordant in their different accounts of this great event, we only show our ignorance and folly if we pretend to correct them. How many things have happened even in the last century which were clear enough to the writers and to the readers of these times, which may now be enveloped in darkness to us? And yet these events may be strictly conformable to truth.

We learn from the four evangelists that our Lord rose very early upon the first day of the week, and that his resurrection was first made known to the women that came to the sepulchre. The apostle John mentions Mary Magdalene; the other evangelists mention other women. One speaks of young men, another of angels; one, of one angel, and then of two. But if a person finds inconsistencies here, he is very fond of finding them. If four honest men give an account of the same story, they would tell it very differently and yet very truly—and yet to a person who knew all the circumstances, their accounts were very consistent and very plain, and this is the case with regard to the gospels.

The blessed women came early to the sepulchre, even before the apostles themselves. But early as they appeared, the Lord rose before they came. They had no intention to fabricate such a story as his resurrection: they had no idea of such an event, for they came to anoint the body. When such was their design, nothing but ocular demonstration could convince them of the truth. And as a woman introduced death and misery into the world, a woman had the honour to be the mother of the great Messiah, and women were the first that brought the glad tidings of his resurrection. But it is an astonishing fact that in the list of blessed women mentioned by the evangelists, there is not a word of the blessed virgin. None of them mention her appearance at the sepulchre or her being one of the witnesses of his resurrection. It is, however, more than probable that she was present with the other women, though infinite wisdom saw proper to conceal her name. One thing is certain, that she was neither worshipped by the apostles nor by the other women, nor by the primitive Christians. It was long after this period that idolatry got footing in the Church.

Verses 2–3. *And, behold, there was a great earthquake: for the angel of the Lord descended from heaven, and came and rolled back the stone from the door, and sat upon it. His countenance was like lightning, and his raiment white as snow.*

To show that God was well pleased with the undertaking and finished work of his Son, the great Messiah, an angel was sent from heaven in human form to remove the stone from his sepulchre and proclaim the news of his resurrection. There was a great deal of grandeur and majesty in his appearance. His face shone like lightning, and his garments were white like snow. And to prove that he was a messenger from God, there was a great earthquake.

Verse 4 *And for fear of him the keepers did shake, and became as dead men.*

(N.B. An angel being sent hindered the Jewish rulers from putting another dead body in place of Christ.)

An earthquake is one of the most terrible things in nature, and a proof of the power and presence of God. It is so awful a phenomenon that the stoutest heart trembles, and men who are familiar to danger stand appalled with terror. The Roman soldiers were struck with awe, fell to the ground, and became like dead men, and thus are forced, in spite of the Jews, to give witness of the resurrection of Christ. And though they suffered themselves afterwards to be corrupted with a bribe, they could not but give testimony to the truth, and are the unwilling witnesses of his resurrection, and are obliged to proclaim the rising glory of the Saviour. Terror extracts an unwilling tribute to the prisoner whom they were watching, and whom neither they nor the power of death could hold any longer.

Vain is the power of man when God is determined to work. The Jewish rulers, assisted by Pilate and his soldiers, endeavour to keep Christ a prisoner in the grave. Heaven despises his impotent attempt. When the morning of the third day begins to dawn, a strong angel from heaven shakes the earth and removes the stone from the cave. And after doing so, with calm composure he sits upon the stone. From the terror with which the guards were struck, it would appear that he looked upon them with a stern countenance. The angel cared little for their arms or military defence, and notwithstanding the boldness and intrepidity for which Roman soldiers were remarkable, they are thunderstruck with fear and become like dead men. The terror of these men appears in their faces. In the meantime, the prisoner whom they guarded comes out of his grave with silent dignity, and they have not the courage to hinder or pursue him.

> Verses 5–7. *And the angel answered and said unto the women, Fear not ye: for I know that ye seek Jesus, which was crucified. He is not here: for he is risen, as he said. Come, see the place where the Lord lay. And go quickly, and tell his disciples that he is risen from the dead; and,*

behold, he goeth before you into Galilee; there shall ye see him: lo, I have
told you.

But though the angel was a source of terror to the soldiers, he spoke
in kind and comfortable language to the women. In hearing the terrors of the Lord, the people of God to whom the promises do
belong are often afraid, as the women were here. The royal Psalmist
and Heman were afraid of the terrors of the Lord, and the Israelites
at Mount Sinai trembled at his voice. But though the people of God
are afraid, the Word speaks comfort to them. The language of the
angel to the women is, 'Fear not ye: for I know that ye seek Jesus,
which was crucified.' And though the Word speaks awful terror to
the wicked that hear without concern, we are empowered by the
gospel to speak comfort to those who came here to seek Jesus who
was crucified.

After dissipating their fears, he assures them that he was risen from
the dead, as himself had told before his death. And to give them
ocular demonstration of what he said, he invites them to come and
see the place where the Lord lay. After doing so, he bids them depart
with speed and inform his disciples of the joyful news, and tell them
that he would go before them into Galilee, and that they would see
him there. And to remove all doubt, he informs them that he gave
them the word and authority of an angel for their faith.

In the meantime, we may observe that our Lord was better than his
word to them. It is very true that he met them in Galilee as he promised, but it is equally true that he met them even before then. He
saw their anxiety, their doubts, fears, and unbeliefs, and this might
retard their journey to Galilee. He therefore made himself known to
some of his disciples, before that he met them all in Galilee, and this
encouraged them to prosecute their journey to that place with cheerfulness. They were now convinced that they were not deceived by
the illusions of fancy—that what they saw was a reality. They were
perfectly conscious that they saw a heavenly messenger and an
empty grave.

Verse 8. *And they departed quickly from the sepulchre with fear and great joy; and did run to bring his disciples word.*

Satisfied, therefore, that their Lord and Master was risen from the dead, we find that 'they departed quickly from the sepulchre with fear and great joy; and did run to bring his disciples word'. There was something so awful in the superior sanctity of a heavenly messenger, though in human shape, that they were struck with fear. They could not appear before him, though a creature, with such humble confidence as they could do to their incarnate God, but as his words were so kind and his news so cheerful, they departed with great joy, and even ran to give the joyful tidings to his mourning followers.

It is, indeed, somewhat remarkable that the women were afraid of the angel, but we do not read that they were so much afraid of a person greater than all angels, than all the heavenly hosts. The angel could not have such a feeling for our case as the glorious One who assumed our nature and was like us in all things, except sin. But though they had fear, it was a fear mixed with joy. They rejoiced for the resurrection of Christ. And this is the great cause of joy to all the people of God. The language of worldly people is, 'Who will show us any good?' The language of a Christian is, 'Lift upon us the light of thy countenance.' And it is in Christ we can see the face of a reconciled God.

We see here what made these blessed people happy. It was the revival of their hopes by the resurrection of Christ from the dead. If we rejoice in other things, in worldly objects, our hopes may soon fail. The poor man upon the bed of death cannot rejoice, though he may call the cattle on a thousand hills his own. But if we rejoice in God, our hopes are well-founded. And we see the nature of true spiritual joy—it wishes to communicate happiness.

The women hasten to communicate the news to the disciples. When people rejoice in worldly happiness, their views are mean and terminate in the dead sea of self. They pursue their self-interest at the expense of others. Not so the Christian. His views are not bounded by the things of time. And as his chief happiness is in the things of eternity, his heart expands, and he wishes to embrace the whole human race. He will, therefore, like these holy women, show people what he rejoices in and wherein he places his chief happiness. His language, like the Psalmist, is, 'O taste and see that God is good;' like the woman of Samaria, 'Come, and see a man that told me all things that ever I did. Is not this the Christ?' In a word, the Christian wishes to make others happy like himself.

> Verses 9–10. *And as they went to tell his disciples, behold, Jesus met them, saying, All hail. And they came and held him by the feet, and worshipped him. Then said Jesus unto them, Be not afraid: go tell my brethren that they go into Galilee, and there shall they see me.*

By comparing the different evangelists, it would appear that Mary Magdalene came twice to the sepulchre, and at the last time saw the Lord. Although the evangelists are perfectly true in their relation to the resurrection, they are not careful as to every minute circumstance and the precise time in which it happened.

The sepulchre was near the city, and from the anxiety of the apostles and the women, it is more than probable that they might have gone to the sepulchre oftener than once that morning. Our Lord might have spoken a few words to Mary Magdalene and ordered her to go in haste and acquaint his disciples. And as the other women were ordered by the angel to go and acquaint his disciples with the joyful news, they might retire a few minutes before Mary Magdalene, who might soon follow them, and meet or overtake the Lord with the rest. The circumstances are true enough, though the evangelists have not told them in the exact order and time in which they happened.

When he met the women, he saluted them with 'All hail!' He spoke peace to their hearts and convinced them it was himself. He permitted them to lay hold of his feet, and they worshipped him. This he did not allow Mary Magdalene to do, because she was to enjoy this privilege in company with the other women, and as he wished to give the news immediately to the apostles. And though Mary

Magdalene had the honour to see the Lord first of all, to reward her uncommon attention and love, any further answer to her is reserved till he met the other women—a proof that he gives more of his presence to two or three gathered together in his name than to one, however remarkable for piety and grace. If this was not the case, where were the advantages of the peculiar privileges of public worship?

And this may show us the duty of those who have tasted of heavenly grace: they are to give the news to others. Samson gave the honey he found in the lion to his father and mother, and we should give the consolations of the gospel—as far as in us lies—to others also.

The women are ordered a second time to go and tell the news to the apostles. He promised to meet them in a mountain in Galilee. He knew that he had many enemies in Judaea, and though many of the people of Galilee made a bad use of his gospel, he had many true friends in that place. It was far safer for his followers to meet and see him in Galilee than anywhere. It was in a mountain that he made the appointment, and it is likely it was Mount Tabor. It was in the midst of a great plain and opposite to Mount Hermon, which lay to the south. The words of the Psalmist (Psalm 89:12) seem to confirm the opinion that it was here he was transfigured, and that it was here he met his disciples.

He told them not to be afraid: it seems he saw their unbelief and fears, notwithstanding the proof that he had given that he rose from the dead. And as they might rest satisfied that it was himself and not another that spoke to them, he bade them give the proof they saw and heard to his disciples.

The report of the watch

Verses 11–15. *Now when they were going, behold, some of the watch came into the city, and shewed unto the chief priests all the things that were done. And when they were assembled with the elders, and had taken counsel, they gave large money unto the soldiers, saying, Say ye, His disciples came by night, and stole him away while we slept. And if this come to the governor's ears, we will persuade him, and secure you. So they took the money, and did as they were taught: and this saying is commonly reported among the Jews until this day.*

In this malignant [baleful] story, we have an additional support to our faith as Christians. As the women had retired from the grave and gone to bring his disciples word of the news, some of the watch came and informed the priests of all the things that happened. After a meeting of their Sanhedrin, they had a consultation, and in imitation of the master they served, they forged a tremendous lie. But it has so much the appearance of falsehood in the front of it that it is surprising how any person of common sense could be imposed upon by such a shocking story. But as one crime naturally makes room for another, the Jews and their rulers were judicially blinded and hardened.

But let us examine the facts. The watch informed them of what they saw and heard. They heard an artless story from men who had no interest to deceive. The soldiers experienced an earthquake and saw a glorious vision of angels, and were therefore convinced that the prisoner they watched in the grave rose from the dead and escaped. Instead of being convinced by such a proof of his heavenly mission, the priests and rulers resolve to fight against God and their own consciences by contriving a falsehood. But it was necessary to get the soldiers to act a part in the villainy, and therefore tried what money could do. Such as can do a base thing for money themselves think that others can easily be corrupted, and they often succeed. Contrary to the light of their consciences, the priests offer and the soldiers receive a bribe. As the crime was enormous, the money must be large.

They fabricate and spread a story that his disciples stole his body in the night while the guard were asleep. One can scarcely say whether the story is more base than stupid. If the disciples believed that their Master was an impostor, what temptation had they to steal his body and tell a falsehood? That would make God and men their enemies.

Common sense cannot swallow the idea. Let a Jew, let a Deist, believe nonsense if they choose.

But again, is it a profitable case that a whole guard of Roman soldiers, men remarkable for their military discipline, would fall asleep when so much depended upon their continuing awake? Curiosity, fear, shame, and sense of honour and glory would at this critical season operate with their fullest influence upon their minds. And if they were asleep, will ingenuity, will common sense, and common honesty receive their testimony? How could they know who stole him if themselves were asleep? Besides, if this was the case, why did not the high priests and Pilate, who were no friends to Christ or his apostles, search Jerusalem to find the dead body, and then punish the authors of such an enormous feat? His disciples loved him too much to be in a hurry to bury him. To this we may add that it was impossible for the disciples to break the seal, remove the stone, and carry away the dead body without considerable noise. And if they discovered, or even suspected, that this was done by his disciples, why had they not the courage to pursue them and bring back the body?

These things could not happen without a miracle, and the Jews are not willing to believe such. Though they deny the miracles of the gospel, they cannot establish this story without a miracle equal to them. But the fabrication is so big with absurdity, contradiction, and weakness that it confutes [disproves] itself. Christianity, therefore, is founded upon a rock, and all the waves of infidelity will dash themselves against it in vain. Christ rose from the dead, and all the nonsensical arguments of his enemies will fall with confusion upon themselves. They dash themselves to pieces against the Rock of salvation, and Christianity will always triumph in spite of them.

The great commission

Verses 16–17. *Then the eleven disciples went away into Galilee, into a mountain where Jesus had appointed them. And when they saw him, they worshipped him: but some doubted.*

Our Lord continued forty days upon earth after his resurrection, and during that time, he could show himself alive often to his followers. He informed his apostles before his death that, after his resurrection, he would go before them into Galilee, and he sent them word after his resurrection that he would meet them in a mountain there. He chose a mountain as a more retired and private place, and therefore safer for them to meet him. It is very likely that it was here he showed himself to five hundred at once, as the apostle Paul informs us in the First Epistle to the Corinthians.

We are informed in the Acts that he spoke to them the things belonging to the kingdom of God. His doctrine before and after his resurrection was the same. He met his disciples several times and gave them the most infallible proofs of his resurrection. But though he did so, it seems the unbelief of some of them was very strong. Accordingly, we find that he upbraided them with this inexorable [stubborn] sin. It was the enemy of their own peace and quiet, and dishonourable to their Lord and Master.

But before he ascended into heaven, he gave such proof to every one of them in particular as he could require. He bids them handle him and satisfy themselves that it was a real body they saw, and that it was his own gracious mouth that spoke to them. As the apostle Thomas was full of unbelief and doubted the truth of his resurrection, he bids him put his finger in the print of the nails and thrust his hand into his side, and this removed his doubts and unbelief.

During the forty days he abode on earth, after giving them the most infallible proof of his divinity and resurrection, he explained the truths of the kingdom of heaven to them, and no doubt gave them a glimpse of the joys of immortality by a sight of the heavenly Canaan.

Verses 18–20. And Jesus came and spake unto them, saying, All power is given unto me in heaven and in earth. Go ye therefore, and teach all nations, baptizing them in the name of the Father, and of the Son, and of the Holy Ghost: teaching them to observe all things whatsoever I have commanded you: and, lo, I am with you alway, even unto the end of the world. Amen.

It appears from these words that Matthew gave the substance of all the conversations and appearances of Christ during the forty days he remained upon earth after his resurrection. We learn from the other evangelists that he met the disciples several times before his ascension, and instructed them in the truths of the kingdom of heaven.

He here informs them all power in heaven and earth was given him as Mediator, and that he would exert this power for the good of his people. And in consequence of this power, he gave his apostles a commission to go and teach all nations, baptizing them in the name of the Father, Son, and Holy Ghost. The gospel was to be offered to all mankind, for the kingdom of God was not to be confined any longer to the territory of Judaea. And baptism was to be the seal of the covenant. We learn from the apostle Paul that it was to succeed circumcision, and as we know that children had the benefit of this rite under the Old Testament, we may conclude they will not fare worse under the New. Will the Saviour who took little children in his arms and blessed them, and desired to suffer little children to come to him, make the door of grace narrower or curtail their privileges more than they were before he came in the flesh? We think not. He ordered to baptize in the name of the Father, Son, and Holy Ghost. This is the doctrine of Scripture. There is one God and three persons, and this is the faith of the true Catholic Church—the people of God in all ages.

He commanded his apostles also to instruct the disciples in all the holy precepts which he had given them. The doctrine of Christ is a doctrine of godliness—a pure system of holiness—and he concludes with a gracious promise: 'Lo, I am with you alway, even unto the end of the world.'

As the apostles were not always to continue upon earth, it is clear that this promise belongs to the teachers who, actuated by the Spirit, follow the example and preach the doctrines of the apostles. The religion of Christ is not a religion of names, and we know that men of this description have been found among several sects or names of Christians. The promise, therefore, belongs to the faithful followers of the Lamb who preach the doctrines of the apostles. If Christ finds any to preach the gospel, he furnishes them with the learning, gifts, and graces that qualify them for the work. And if any other sect of Christians deny the ordination of such men, they betray themselves and show unto the world the narrowness of their views and the illiberality of their sentiments. In fact, we find valuable Christians and valuable teachers among all sects of Christians. And if they are followers of Christ, can any other pretend to unchurch them with impunity?

Practical inferences

Having now explained the words, I conclude with some practical inferences.

1. The resurrection of Christ is a proof that the work he undertook was finished, the debt paid, and the discharge procured. God the Father declared different times that he was his beloved Son, in whom he was well pleased. And by raising him from the dead, he showed that he was satisfied with the great sacrifice he offered for our sins, and when the debt was paid, the Surety should get a discharge. And our great Surety received his discharge in the most public manner. His resurrection from the dead provides everything that the prophets and the gospel have said concerning him. The natural inference is, we may trust our souls to such a Saviour.

2. If we have a share in his resurrection, we should rise from the grave of sin. Some sleep in the grave of sensuality, some in the grave of covetousness, and others in the grave of malice and envy. But if we live in sin, we cannot be said to rise with Christ. As sure as Christ rose from the dead, those who belong to him rise from the grave of

sin. And if we rose with Christ, we set our affections on the things which are above. His people seek not their happiness in the things of time or any species of worldly enjoyment. Their happiness is in God and in the joys of eternity. If we then seek our happiness in the heavenly Canaan, that good country that flows with milk and honey, we need not regret the fleshpots of Egypt. We should be satisfied with manna, though we should not get flesh in the wilderness. We know where Christ sought happiness. Let us follow his example.

3. Lastly, though he did not remain long on earth after his resurrection, he is still with his people to the end of time. He is now in heaven, the mountain of myrrh and the hill of frankincense, but he is present by his Spirit in the Church, and while his people enjoy his presence, they are in the suburbs of heaven. He liveth for ever to make intercession for them, and we have proof of this by hearing the joyful sound. The interests of his Church are continually upon his heart, and if any person trusts himself to the Saviour, he is always secure. He is with his people in time as well as in eternity. He is the same yesterday, today, and for ever.

The promise that he will be with his servants in the ministry to the end of time is a proof he will always have a Church. He will have so while sun and moon endure. And if we are true members of his Church, we may plead his promise. He will guide his people even unto death. And as sure as he will be with them in time, he will be their portion through all eternity. Happy, then, are his sheep, for he will lead them into green pastures. Happy are those who follow the Lamb. He will lead them into living fountains of water and wipe away all tears from their eyes. Go to the Garden of Gethsemane. See his grace. Believe and be happy.

AMEN.

The Lord's Prayer

THIS is the prayer which our Lord taught his disciples, because he gave it to them as a rule by which to regulate their prayers. Though it is commonly called the Lord's Prayer, it is not so called because he used it himself—this he could not do, as he had no sin to pray for the forgiveness of—but as it was our Lord that taught it to his followers.

As we are taught this precious form of sound words from our earliest infancy, we do not see so much in it as it really contains. I compare the Lord's Prayer to a purse of gold, which a rich man puts in the hand of his friend. He knows it is money he got, but he does not see the value of it till he opens it, and then he sees that all the coin it contains is of the most precious metal. And when we begin to examine and explain these precious petitions and desires that are expressed here, we may say with truth that if any man can repeat this prayer with a true spirit of devotion, happy is it for him. The words are easily repeated, but to repeat them from the heart requires the assistance of grace. We shall therefore explain the words, and conclude with some practical inferences.

Our Father which art in heaven

Matthew chapter 6, verse 9. *After this manner therefore pray ye: Our Father which art in heaven, Hallowed be thy name.*

Ye shall therefore pray in this manner. This shall serve as a form to direct you in your addresses to the great Majesty of heaven. As a child repeateth after his master, we are to take special care that all our prayers be agreeable to this rule. If our prayers, and the spirit of our prayers, is contrary to the spirit and doctrine of this prayer, we do not pray agreeably to the will of God. We are then to approach the throne of grace with humility, with reverence, and with love. God is a Spirit, and we ought to worship him in spirit and in truth.

'Our Father who art in heaven.' In these words, we have the doctrine of the Father and the Son. If we believe in the Son, God is our Father in covenant. Though we by nature are enemies, yet in Christ we ought to look upon God as our Father and Friend. He hath reconciled us by the blood of his cross, and we ought to pray for his Spirit, who will enable us effectually to cry, 'Abba, Father.'

There is a great deal of divinity in these two words, 'Our Father,' and oh that we could repeat them with true filial confidence! It is our duty thus to look upon God in Christ; for he made him to be sin, who knew no sin, that we might be made the righteousness of God in him. And he entreats us to be reconciled to God and receive our pardon through Christ. And if God is our Father, we are brethren, and we ought, therefore, to love one another as such. The Spirit of the gospel is a spirit of love, and if we love God, we will naturally love our brethren, and love will naturally teach us to do them good, and to promote their temporal and spiritual interest.

He is our Father in heaven, and this teaches us our great and glorious privileges. Scripture informs us that he is everywhere present, but his peculiar habitation is heaven. This is the habitation of his holiness, the high and holy place where he hath erected his throne, and where he meets his people. Here an innumerable host of angels worship him. It is here the glorified body of our Saviour is, angels, principalities and powers being subject to him.

The heavens are higher than the earth, and we may believe that the extent of them is great in proportion. The extent of this inferior creation is very great, and if God built such a large habitation for beings that are confined to bodies, how extensive are the spaces prepared for unembodied spirits, and for the pure and spiritual bodies of the saints after the resurrection. What we can see with our bodily eyes is but a small part of creation. A man of great learning observes that if all the places upon which the sun shines were extinguished, they would not be missed in the creation any more than a grain of sand from the seashore.

We only see the outskirts of creation; we live in the suburbs. The city of the great King and the ivory palaces are hidden from our view. Our gross sight could not bear the vision of the heavenly Canaan. And as Scripture points to us the glory of this happy place by several beautiful images, the design of all these images is to raise our thoughts and affections to the things that are above. Our thoughts are called away from this dark and dreary wilderness to a place large as our wishes, lasting as our immortal souls, and beautiful beyond the utmost stretch of imagination and thought. In this place God sits enthroned on high, and on his right hand the great Mediator, to whom and through whom we may address our prayers, and by whose prevailing intercession we may humbly look for an answer. The glorious Intercessor receives the prayers of his people, mixing them with the incense of his precious merits. As many of their petitions may not be strictly agreeable to the will of God, he sends them down again by the hands of the Holy Spirit, and when he brings them entirely to the will of God, and when his good time arrives, he gives them an answer. As their prayers, as proceeding from them, are mixed with sin, he purifies them and presents them to his Father, and in this way they find acceptance in the Beloved.

Hallowed be thy name

'Hallowed be thy name.' We sanctify the name of God when we pray that veneration to his name which is due to him. His Word reveals his name, and when we worship him in heart and in life, we sanctify his great name. He requires worship from all his rational creatures. We therefore glorify God and sanctify his name when we confess our sins to him, and lead a holy and a regular life. Those who disgrace their profession by immoral lives are said in Scripture to profane his holy name, and our Saviour informs us that we glorify our

Father who is in heaven by the light of our good life, and by such works as adorn our profession.

Thy kingdom come

Verse 10. *Thy kingdom come. Thy will be done in earth, as it is in heaven.*

The kingdom of God upon earth is the reign of Messiah. And this kingdom consists in righteousness, and peace, and joy in the Holy Ghost. Messiah is the Prince of Peace, and his kingdom in the latter days is to extend far and wide. He is to rule from sea to sea, and from the rivers to the ends of the earth. He is to rule the nations, for God has promised him the heathen for his inheritance, and the uttermost parts of the earth for his possession. By the nature of the promise, we may understand that this is not to happen all at once. It is the work of time. Though the kingdom is promised him, he is desired to ask it, and he is said to sit at the right hand of God till his enemies are made his footstool.

Our Lord, then, it would appear, is pleading for this promise, and he has made it our duty to plead for it also. His kingdom has made its appearance, and these promises have been partly fulfilled, for the gospel has made conquest in the most distant corners of the globe. Christ is worshipped from the rising to the setting sun. But if we are to believe the writers of the Old and New Testaments, his kingdom has not yet made that glorious appearance which is to be made upon earth. Nation still lifts up sword against nation, and they still learn the art of war. If nations and individuals who profess the name of Christ were influenced by the principles which they profess to believe, they would beat their swords into ploughshares and their spears into pruning hooks. When the kingdom of God appears with glory in the general conversion of mankind, this change will literally take place, and we are taught to pray for this, and believe the promise about its accomplishment. A thousand years is short in God's sight, though the time appears long to us. The doctrine that is to accomplish this is revealed to us in the gospel, and when the Spirit of God will make the belief of the gospel general, these glorious effects will soon take place.

Though the Scriptures assure us of the glory of Messiah's kingdom in the latter days, it does not say that this kingdom would make this glorious appearance all at once. It was to be set up during the fourth monarchy, according to the prophecy of Daniel, and this clearly refers to the Roman Empire. It was to appear like a stone cut without hands, and afterwards the stone was to become a great mountain and to fill the whole earth. It was first to be very small, like the grain of mustard seed, and afterwards become great and powerful. So that the argument of the Jews against Christianity, from the wars and bloodshed among the Christians, falls to the ground. We learn from one of their own prophets that it was to destroy the fourth monarchy or Roman Empire, that its first appearance would be like a stone cut without hands, but that it would afterwards become a great mountain and fill the whole earth. Christianity thus has hitherto triumphed over all opposition, like a stone cut without hands, for nothing but the power of God could establish it in the world. Jews and pagans, philosophers and rhetoricians, sensualists and worldlings, the learning and the power of the world appeared against it; still, it stood its ground in the midst of all the commotions of the kingdoms of the earth.

It will hereafter appear with great outward lustre and inward spiritual beauty, which it has not done hitherto, for the nominal Christianity is the established religion of several kingdoms and countries in the world: they are far from being ruled by the genuine spirit of the gospel. When societies or individuals among them breathe the true spirit of the gospel, and appear against sin and the works of darkness among professing Christians, they meet with all the hard names that malice and falsehood can invent. Such, then, as have the glory of the kingdom at heart are taught to pray for its prosperity in the world.

The establishing of Christianity as a national religion is not what is here meant, but the saving influences of the Holy Spirit working repentance and bringing people from darkness to light, and from the power of Satan and their own lusts to the kingdom of the Prince of Peace. Though the bulk of professing Christians are as bad as infidels, their false profession is an acknowledgement of Christianity, and if every individual among them believed it, we would soon see the kingdom of God. When a genuine Christian prays for the advancement of the kingdom of God, he means something more, surely, than a bare profession of Christian religion. This he sees already in the country wherein he lives, but he cannot say that the kingdom of God is among them of a truth. He sees many of them sunk in ignorance, and multitudes sunk in vice. Among those who preserve a regard for decency of character, he observes a form instead of the power of godliness, the means substituted in place of the Saviour, and a partial kind of morality, instead of that universal obedience and true holiness which is the genuine fruit of true faith.

We are then to pray for the kingdom of God till such time as it appears upon earth, and nations as well as individuals imbibe the true spirit of the gospel. When this event takes place, there shall be no use for warlike instruments, for mankind in general shall cultivate the art of peace. There shall be nothing to hurt or destroy in God's holy mountain, for the earth shall be full of the knowledge of the Lord, as the waters cover the sea.

Whatever appearances may be now against it, this happy period is fast approaching. Two arguments put this beyond the reach of doubt: the truth of Scripture, and the many prayers of the Church of God for this happy and glorious event.

Thy will be done in earth, as it is in heaven

'Thy will be done in earth, as it is in heaven.' This is a rational and a pious wish, but unholy and carnal reason may suggest that, however desirable such a wish may be, the state of the world in general renders the accomplishment of it improbable, if not impracticable. But, that the time is coming when the will of God will be generally obeyed in earth as it is in heaven, appears to me from the following reasons.

1. Our Saviour desires us to pray for such an event, and several parts of Scripture give us room to believe and hope for it. But without citing texts, let us only examine this pious wish in our Lord's Prayer, which almost every child can repeat. Would the great Teacher sent from God encourage us to pray for a thing that God never meant to do? We can never believe this. Is there any part of Scripture where people are encouraged to pray for a thing, but that thing is accomplished? The return of the Jews from Egypt and Babylon is the subject of many prayers, and they would not be encouraged to pray if God did not mean to answer.

Common sense may tell us that it is not our duty to pray for what God does not intend to perform. If my friend was newly dead, I have no ground from Scripture to put up such a prayer for him as Martha did for her brother Lazarus. God encouraged the prayers of Hezekiah and Jehoshaphat against their enemies. And we know the consequence.

He taught his people by the prophet Hosea what form of prayer to use, and there is a gracious answer, as we read in the last chapter of his prophecies. And would this petition or wish be put in the mouth of the Church for several centuries without any prospect of an answer? Would God Almighty tantalise the hopes of his people? Is it not said in Scripture that he is gracious to the gracious, and upright to the upright? We can say with truth that his people have been very upright in praying that the will of God might be done upon earth, and his kingdom come in the conversion of Jews and Gentiles to the Christian faith. Himself has taught us to pray for this, and may we not conclude that he means 'sooner or later' to answer all those prayers of his people?

He teaches us to pray for our daily bread, and is it not our duty to believe that we shall obtain this? We surely may look for it when he desires us to pray for it, and this is our duty. And if it be our duty to look for the daily bread when God encourages us to pray for it, shall unbelief or carnal reason make me doubt but God will answer a prayer of unspeakably greater consequence—the general spread of true religion through the world?

2. The united wishes and prayers of the people of God encourage me to look for the event. There is no desire, natural or spiritual, among people but has some correspondent object. The philosophers make use of the argument to prove the immortality of the soul and a future state. They tell us there is a strong desire implanted in the soul after such a state, and they thought it rational to suppose that God would grant that desire. The general desire in people after immortality is one of the proofs of a future state.

Now, this wish for a general spread of the gospel through the earth is not merely the desire of one here and there, but the general wish of all true Christians: it is natural to them. And will this strong and general wish be frustrated? It is not such a wish as Moses had for going to Canaan, or Abraham for Ishmael?—it is a common and general wish. I could believe that, upon occasions, a few of the people of God might be wrong in their opinion, or form a wrong wish or desire, but is it agreeable to reason or Scripture to suppose that the whole of the world continues in all ages to have a wish not agreeable to the will of God? Religion is the most precious thing upon earth, and such as experience the power of it upon their own souls wish that it may become a general blessing to mankind. I conclude, then, that their prayers will be answered in the latter days, when all nations shall be converted.

3. Lastly, it appears to me that the glory of God requires that this should be the case. Satan has got his will over mankind in general, and he ruleth powerfully and effectually in the children of disobedience. They do his will and obey his motions [promptings]. And though there has been a revelation of the will of God given to mankind, the greater part of them are ignorant of it, and such as have it and hear it refuse to obey. May not the enemy brag that he divideth the earth with the Son of God, and that the greater part of mankind are obedient to his will? But the day will come when the earth will be full of the knowledge of the Lord, as the waters cover the sea.

Satan is a usurper, and will be dispossessed. Hitherto the cause of vice seemed to triumph. Hereafter the cause of God and religion will triumph and prosper. We read of a new heaven and a new earth. That God will cleanse this earth for the use and service of his people seems to be the doctrine of Scripture, and from the strong language of the prophets and apostles, this earth will be the very image of heaven. The will of God will then be done on earth as it is in heaven.

Give us this day our daily bread

Verse 11. *Give us this day our daily bread.*

The generality of the people of God in all ages have been but in ordinary circumstances, and many of them in straitened circumstances. They are then taught to depend upon their heavenly Father for their bodily food. As the Israelites in the wilderness had a daily portion of manna for their food, that they might constantly depend upon God, we are here desired to ask our daily bread. The Israelites had a livelihood of the manna, for it lasted forty years, but they were allowed but little for every day. Good people often wish to lay by money. This—it would appear in many cases—is not good for them. When the Israelites gathered manna to lay by, it bred worms and stank. What was kept for Sabbath and what was laid up in the golden pot did not. If godly people that should depend upon God, and are taught their duty by the leadings of Providence, are not satisfied if they do not lay by money, they may obtain their wish, but it may breed worms, and give them vexation. We are sometimes surprised that the substance of good creatures that was laid by in an honest way should melt away as the snow before the rain.

Whatever comes of the substance of the wicked? To this I answer that God is a jealous God, and though their souls are saved as by fire, yet the instrument of their idolatry must be destroyed. If we seek the kingdom of God, we shall obtain all other things that are necessary for us, and this should satisfy us, for he will never forsake us.

Forgive us our debts, as we forgive our debtors

Verse 12. And forgive us our debts, as we forgive our debtors.

The great design of the grace of God is to break the power of sin in our hearts and bring down the pride of our nature. The work of grace is to bring our will to the will of God, and he will require us to deny our own wills and seek the divine glory in everything. Pride and anger have taken strong hold of our nature, and when we receive an injury or insult, whether real or imaginary, we are very ready to resent it, and return injury for injury.

The reverse of this spirit and conduct is the doctrine of the gospel. We are to forgive injuries, and pray for our enemies, and till we do this, we are not to expect forgiveness. In the nature of things, we are not in a fit frame of soul for obtaining mercy while we retain sentiments of anger and revenge against our brother. Our complaint may be just and the injury we receive may be great, but still we are to bring our injuries to the foot of the cross. God promises to throw our sins in the sea, and we are to throw our injuries in the sea likewise. If in injuring us they have discovered a spirit of enmity and ill-will against the cause of God and religion, they are still greater objects of pity. By praying for our rancorous and bitter enemies, we show ourselves to be actuated by the spirit of the meek and compassionate Saviour, who said upon the cross, 'Father, forgive them; for they know not what they do.' It will prove us to be the children of God, as the contrary spirit of revenge will prove that we remain yet strangers to the grace of God, of a truth.

Lead us not into temptation, but deliver us from evil

Verse 13. And lead us not into temptation, but deliver us from evil.

Sin is the greatest of all evils, and the cause of every evil, and every other evil that meets us. With regard to temporal things, we are to be resigned to the will of God, whether we pray for or against them, but in praying against sin and temptation to sin, we are to pray absolutely and with all our heart and soul. We are to pray against temptation to sin, and if the temptation is permitted, we are at all events to pray against our yielding to temptations. We are to pray earnestly that God would not give us up to the lust of our own hearts, and that he would keep us from those sins which are agreeable to the bent of our corrupt nature. And if God answers us in the petition, it is a great mercy, and we should humbly thank him.

Let not our sullen pride refuse to do this by saying that this is no more than restraining grace. Be it so. Let his name be praised for restraining grace, and let us wait and look for sanctifying and saving grace. Neither let us yield to unbelief, who whispers to us that we shall one day fall into the hands of Saul. The God who hitherto hath taken care of us will never leave nor forsake us, and he will be our guide, even unto death.

The conclusion of the Lord's Prayer

Verse 14. For thine is the kingdom, and the power, and the glory, for ever. Amen.

Let us trust in his grace. And we are to conclude our prayers by ascribing kingdom, power, and glory to God. His kingdom is an everlasting kingdom, and he will reign for ever and ever—and to express our faith and hope, let us say, 'Amen'.

Inferences

1. If this is a rule by which to direct our prayers, let us examine our prayers, whether we live according to our prayers, and whether we can honestly repeat our own petitions. If we live in malice or envy, can we pray for pardon of our own offences? If our lives are contrary to the gospel, can we say, 'Thy kingdom come'? And if our will is in direct opposition to the will of heaven, can we consistently say, 'Thy will be done'? And if we live in sin, are we sincere when we say, 'And lead us not into temptation'?

2. If we are sincere, our own endeavours will cooperate with our prayers. For instance, we pray for the kingdom of God, and that his will may be done on earth, as well as in heaven. If a physician was praying for the life and health of his patient, will he not give him the medicines that will be of service to him? And if we pray for the salvation of people's souls, will not our advices and endeavours do something to rescue their souls from sin?

3. Scripture says that the kingdom of God will appear gloriously upon earth. Though this is not accomplished, let not infidelity shake our confidence in divine promises. His time is not yet come, but is drawing near. Let us then wait with faith and patience.

www.ingramcontent.com/pod-product-compliance
Lightning Source LLC
Chambersburg PA
CBHW060322100426
42812CB00003B/857